Handbook of
Dermatology and Venereology

Handbook of Dermatology and Venereology

Hossain

M.D.(Bern), D.Sc. (Medicine) (Warsaw), M.Phil. (London), D.T.M. & H. (Edinburgh), D.V. (Liverpool), D.I.H. (St. Andrews), D.P.H. (Edinburgh)

A. I. T. B. S.

AITBS PUBLISHERS, INDIA

MEDICAL PUBLISHERS

J-5/6, Krishan Nagar, Delhi-110051 (INDIA)
Phone: 011-40167052, 49067602
E-mail: aitbsindia@gmail.com & aitbsindia@hotmail.com

This Edition Edited by AITBS.

First Edition: 1999
Second Edition: 2006
Third Edition: 2028

ISBN: 978-81-85386-90-4

Published by:
Virender Kumar Arya for
AITBS Publishers, India
MEDICAL PUBLISHERS
J-5/6, Krishan Nagar, Delhi - 110051 (INDIA)
Phone: 011-40167052, 49067602
E-mail: aitbsindia@gmail.com & aitbsindia@hotmail.com

Printed by AITBS, Delhi

Preface to the Third Edition

The First and Second Edition of the book would be so quickly exhausted was beyond my anticipation. I am grateful that the readers popularly consumed my work and I express my sincere gratitude to all concerned.

I am however sorry and apologise as the Third Edition of the volume could not be published earlier. The overwhelming pressure from the publisher was persistent but I failed to comply with the same for my chronic illness.

However, after a great labour the Third Edition of the volume has now come out and I would highly appreciate valuable suggestions from the reader.

The dosage of the drugs used in this volume unless and otherwise stated is given for the adults.

Hossain

Preface to the First Edition

It is not essential that every book must include a preface but this is the only opportunity an author avails of to express his/her sincerity and ambition and apologise for any pitfalls or shortcomings.

Hence, this preface.

Several standard textbooks of dermatology and venereology, either independently or conjointly, are available. All these books are no doubt technically very rich in both contents and lucid descriptions, for which they are also voluminous.

Yet this volume,
HANDBOOK OF DERMATOLOGY AND VENEREOLOGY,
has been presented with a humble ambition of making the specialties more easy and brief which may consume least time in going through. The volume therefore excludes detailed description and includes the essential facts of the disease processes in a concise form.

Hossain

Contents

Part I
Dermatology

CHAPTER 1

About the Skin

With delicate structure skin is a complex, elastic, fibrous sheath, with rich supply of blood vessels, nerves and lymphatic. The external surface of it is covered by greasy mixture of exfoliated epidermal cells, sebum, sweat and varieties of additives from external source

It is the vital structure that encases the whole body surface and serves several functions of the body. Being an external cover it protects all living tissues and organs of the body, acting as a barrier shield against everything of exogenous origin. It is also responsible for maintaining the body heat regulation, while due to the presence of various types of glands in it, skin is capable to maintain various secretion and excretion. In addition, it has the ability to absorb and store certain elements required for the body maintenance. The skin has a rich network of nerves and various types of specialised secretory end-organs for which it is extremely sensitive against every kind of sensation and stimuli and hence, it works as a sensory organ of the body.

The skin (Fig. 1.1) is divided into two layers: the most superficial or epidermis and the deep or dermis. Beneath this there is a specialised layer of subcutaneous tissue or ***hypoderm*** that not only act as nutritional storage reserve, but also protects the internal tissues against trauma and also acts as an insulator. Appendages of the skin is the third layer of skin, which include sebaceous glands, hair follicles and nails, are the outgrowths of the epidermis.

As emphasised epidermis is the external portion of skin. The cells in this layer do continuously multiply without causing any increase in its thickness, because the cells die regularly and continuously blown away by the wind, and are continuously replaced by the newly formed cells. The protection mechanism of the barrier is therefore continuously maintained with new cells protecting the tissues and organs of the body. However, the layer is composed entirely of cells that are keratinocytes and melanocytes. Keratinocytes (squamous epithelial cells) are derived from the Malpighian layer and are responsible for biosynthesis of soluble molecules for functional regulation of the epidermal cells. Melanocytes are derived from the neural crest and assume dendritic form, and are responsible for the productions of melanin pigments, which form a screen ro, protect the skin from the harmful ultraviolet in the sunlight. Following formation melanin pigment is deposited on the intracytoplasmic structures, and is delivered to the surrounding keratinocytes through the dendritic processes of the melanocytes. The production of melanin can however be exaggerated from a variety of stimuli, such as sunlight. In addition, the middle of the epidermis contains Langerhan's cells, which are histiolytic cells responsible for the transmitting antigenic signals to the lymphoid cells.

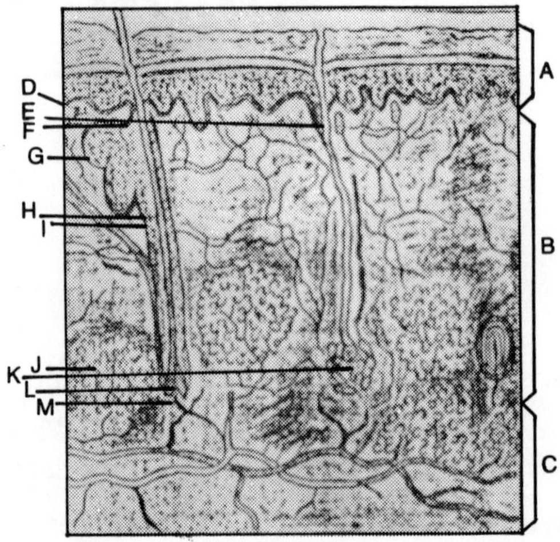

Figure 1.1: Diagrammatic illustration of skin. A. Epidermis; B. Dermis; C. Subcutaneous tissue; D. Papillae; E. Duct of sweat gland; F. Capillary loop in dermal papilla; G. Sebaceous gland; H. Hair shaft; I Hair follicle; J. Adipose tissue; K. Eccrine sweat gland; L. Hair matrix; M. Capillary loop in hair papilla.

The **epidermis** (Fig. 1.2) develops from squamous epithelium and is composed of five layers, beginning with the most exterior; the stratum corneum, the stratum lucidium, the stratum granulosum, the stratum Malpighii and the stratum germinativum.

The ***Stratum corneum*** (*horny layer*) is the outer or surface layer of the epidermis, composed of dead epithelial cells lying in layers of flattened, non-nucleated, cornified cells, usually showing vacuoles. The periphery of it shows loss of cellular outline and is replaced by the keratin. Its thickness varies greatly being thinnest in the eyelids, forehead and prepuce of the penis, and thickest in the palms of the hand and soles of the foot.

The ***stratum lucidium*** (clear layer) lies between the stratum corneum and stratum granulosum, and is a pale, waxy-looking layer. It is composed of several layers of flattened, distended irregular cells, with shrunken nuclei, which eventually disappeared. The layer contains deposits of eleidin, a refractable substance related to keratin.

Following this there is a thin ***stratum granulosum*** (*granular layer*), composed of several layers of flattened, coarsely granular cells. The granules are elongated, irregular shaped, and contain keratohyalin. The thickness of this layer varies greatly but most prominent at the soles and palms.

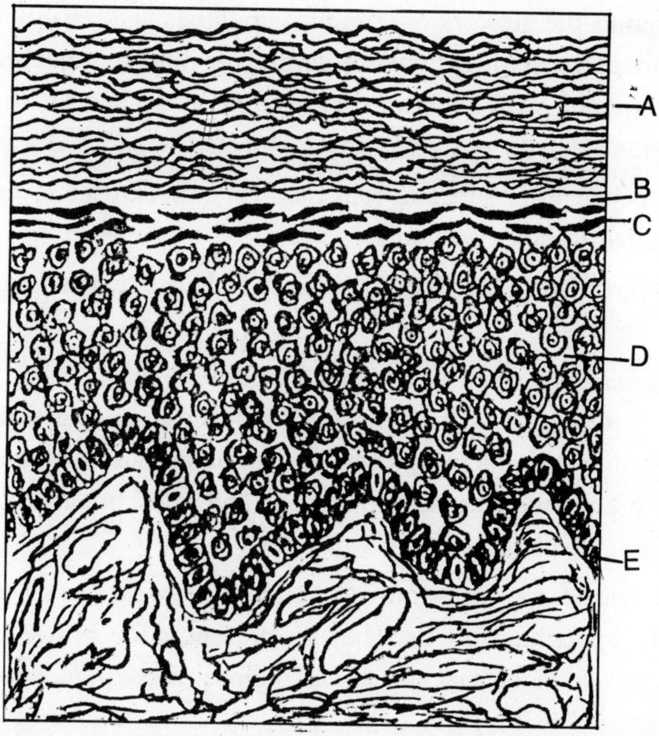

Figure 1.2: Diagrammatic illustration of epidermis. A. Stratum corneum; B. Stratum lucidium; C. Stratum granulosum; D. Stratum Malpighii; E. Stratum germinativum.

Beneath stratum granulosum there is thick ***stratum Malpighii*** (*basal cell layer*) and contains varying number of prickly cells, rete Malphigiii. This layer is therefore also known as *prickly-cell layer*. It is actually composed of several layers of polygonal keratinocytes, looking like mosaic, connected to each other by intercellular bridges. The polygonal cells appear flattened in the higher layers and consist spongy protoplasm and often-large nuclei, usually oval-shaped.

Then there is ***stratum germinativum***, the innermost portion of epidermis, and is composed of a single row of columnar cells. The epidermis as a whole originates from this layer. It is composed of single row of columnar cells, arranged perpendicularly to the skin surface on a wavy baseline line. The cells undergo mitosis, resulting reproduction of more and more cells, which are pushed off to the superficial layers. Some of the cells contain melanin pigment.

The cells of the epidermis multiply continuously. The epidermis is however never thickened from such a multiplication because as the surface cells die, they are blown away by the environmental wind and are replaced by the new living cells.

Beneath the epidermis there is **dermis** or **corium** (Fig. 1.1), which is separated by a specialised membrane, known as basal lamina, which contains a few scattered collagen fibres on the dermal aspect. Dermis consists of bundles of collagen and elastic fibres. Ir is responsible for giving strength and elasticity to the skin, and is profoundly supplied with the blood vessels.

Beneath the basal lamina the network of terminal capillaries and sensory nerve endings cause finger-like projections of the dermis, known as dermal papillae. It projects into the epidermis as dermal papillae, alternating with downward projections of epidermis, the rete pegs. It is the deepest part of the skin

Epidermal appendages or subcutaneous tissue is a specialised layer and contains sweat and salivary glands, hair follicles and nails.

Sweat glands are distributed all over the body and have two varieties: eccrine gland and apocrine glands.

The ***eccrine glands*** are small-sized sweat glands with long tubular, folded like irregular coils that lie with reticular layer of the dermis or in the subcutaneous tissue and open into the ducts which pass through the epidermis. They are very numerous in number and are distributed all over the body, most abundant being in the palms and soles, but absent in the nail beds, the margins of the lips and the glans penis.

The ***apocrine glands*** are comparatively large-sized sweat glands, and develop from the epithelial cells of the upper hair follicle. They are present in the axillae, nipples and areola of the breasts, umbilicus, and in the anal and genital regions. These glands produce a watery fluid, called apocrine sweat.

The **sebaceous glands** are the derivatives of the pilosebaceous apparatus, and develop as small saccular glands. They are widely distributed all over the body. They grow in the dermis but occur more superficially in the eyelids, external auditory meatus, and margins of the lips, nipples, penis, and inner surface of the prepuce, labia minora and anal region. They are more numerous and larger on the scalp, forehead, ears, face, sternal and interscapular regions but absent in the palms and soles. Their ducts open into the hair follicles but in the non-hairy areas, they open directly on the surface of the skin.

Hair is present in most parts of the body, and contains a shaft or stem, which at the lower end forms a bulbous swelling (bulb) which embraces the hair papilla. Hair follicle is a pouch-like depression, which contains the bulb and part of the shaft. The intrafollicular portion of the hair is known as root.

Nails are convex-shaped translucent horny plates that develop on the dorsal aspect of distal phalanges of the fingers and toes. The exposed part of it is called the body that has a free edge while the other end, called the root, is embedded in the skin. The specific portion of the dermis, which lies under surface of the body, is called nail bed.

Alike all other tissues and systems of the body skin is also apt to show varieties of pathological lesions due to functional abnormalities, genetic aberrations, trauma, irritation and allergy. Environmental influence may also play some part in it, while infection and infestation may at times gain entry into it and thus produce various skin disorders. In addition, several dermatological manifestations are often appearing associated with a large number of internal diseases. The prevalence of skin disorders is therefore often very common for one reason or another.

Characteristically some cases of dermatological lesions may not give rise to any specific subjective symptoms while others do. Of those, which present with the subjective symptoms may give rise to itching, burning, stinging, tingling, prickling, sensation of heat or cold, or pain. In other cases there may be a change in sensation.

The clinical picture of most skin diseases however varies widely. The symptoms, on the other hand, may be modified or be obscured by extraneous influences. Yet, the characteristic lesions which are often encounter with may include:

Atrophy represents thinning and wrinkling of skin.

Crust (scab) is a dried mass of serum, pus or blood, and epidermal debris. Depending upon the cause its size, shape, colour and thickness vary.

Erosion represents loss or part or whole of the epidermis.

Eruption is, in fact, a small, usually linear lesion, caused by scratching rubbing or picking.

Excoriation (scratch mark) is superficial abrasion of skin causes due to excessive scratching in itching.

Fissure is a linear crack into the epidermis or to the dermis, usually caused by injury or disease.

Hypertrophy simply means skin overgrowth that occurs due to an increase in the number or size of the cells in one or more layers of skin, commonly affecting the epidermal layer. It may be generalised, as that is evident in acromegaly, or localised as seen in keratosis in old age.

Keratosis indicates presence of circumscribed overgrowths of horny layer of the epidermis. When there is hypertrophy of the horny layer (stratum corneum) it is known as **hyperkeratosis**. When the thickening of horny layer of the epidermis is generalised, i.e. superficial overgrowth of horny layer, it is then called **keratoderma**. Sometimes when the nuclei in the cells of stratum corneum are retained, it is then designated as **parakeratosis** and is seen in eczema, psoriasis, and seborrhoeic dermatitis. **Dyskeratosis** indicates imperfect keratinisation in which some cells of the epidermis undergo premature or atypical keratinisation as it is seen in carcinoma, Paget's disease of the nipple and Darier's disease.

Lichenification represents a leathery induration and thickening of skin.

Macule is non-elevated spot-like flat lesion of small size. Its margin may be circumscribed and distinct but may also be indistinct and fades into the surrounding area. It may cause alterations in the colour of the skin, and may appear as an erythematous lesion, or as a pigmented lesion. When it develops occupying a large area, it is then known as **patch**.

Papule is a solid tumour-like elevation of varying size ranging from a pint-point to that of a pea or larger, and is well circumscribed. The tops of the papule may be round, conical, flat or umbilicated, and may appear as white, red, black, brown or of skin colour. When the papules grow further so as to assume other characteristics they are then described as ***papulo-vesicle*** or ***papulo-pustule***, accordingly. When large number of papules confluent together it is then called **plaque**. On the other hand, **nodules** are called when they are palpable as solid mass but may or may not be elevated.

Pigmentation is chiefly cause by melanin and influences the colour of skin. When there is excessive deposition of pigmentation in the tissue, causing darkening of the skin as compared to the surrounding skin colour, it is called **hyperpigmentation**, but **hypopigmentation** or **depigmentation** when there is loss of pigmentation, indicating lightening of the skin as compared to the surrounding skin colour. **Leucoderma** is however called when there is localised but total absence of pigment. When this absence of pigment occurs as a generalised feature, it is then known as **albinism**.

Pustule is a small superficial elevation of the skin that contains pus. These lesions may develop as such due to infection or may develop from seropurulent evolution of the papules, vesicles or bullae.

Scale is dry or greasy heaped up laminated mass of the epidermis. It may be thick or thin, and may be closely or loosely adherent. Its size, shape and colour vary widely. Scaling is common in many inflammatory disorders of skin, usually associated with epidermal oedema and parakeratosis.

Scar is the new formation of connective tissue that develops on a healed destructive lesion.

Telangiectasia is called when there is localised dilatation of the cutaneous vessels.

Ulcer represents a circumscribed break in the skin. Its size and shape may vary widely.

Wheal or **hive** is an evanescent, oedematous, elevated, flat swelling, surrounded by red areola. The wheals may be discrete or may coalesce together to form a plaque.

Vesicle is circumscribed blister-like epidermal elevation of varying size and shape, and contains serum or plasma. When pierced or ruptured, the contents of the vesicle ooze out. It is of small size that varies between pinpoint and small pea. When however the vesicle develops in larger size, it is then known called **bulla (blister)**.

CHAPTER 2

Disorders due to Naevus and Pigmentation

NAEVUS

Naevus (pleural: **naevi**) or **mole** is a most common form of congenital pigmentation, occurring at birth or at any time during puberty. It may be hard or soft in consistency, and assume variable sizes. The naevus may grow slowly or may remain static but never disappears spontaneously.

The soft naevus is classified into pigmented flat macule and cellular naevus.

In *pigmented flat macule and patch* (*lentigo*) there is hyperplasia of melanocytes and a great increase in the melanin, resulting linear type hyperpigmentation of the basal cell layer in the epidermis. The epidermis is thickened and shows few naevus cells. In senile lentigines (lentigines pleural of lentigo) there is however downgrowth of the epidermis, hyperkeratosis and a disruption in the epidermal ridge pattern due to elongation, tortuosity and budding of the rete ridges.

Cellular naevus characteristically shows the presence of naevus cells. When it develops with nests or clusters of melanocytes at the epidermo-dermal junction, it is then called *junctional naevus*. In *intradermal naevus* however there are both melanocytes and naevus cells in the dermis. The overlying epidermis may be slightly atrophic or slightly hyperkeratotic. Naevus cells are large and oval, and are found in the nests, cords or sheets in the upper corium and sometimes in the dermal papillae. *Compound naevus* is a combination of both junctional naevus and intradermal naevus, and shows retention of melanocytes at the epidermo-dermal junction, and within the dermis.

Clinical Manifestations

Pigmented flat macule and patch, also known as **lentigo** (pleural: **lentigines**), has two types: juvenile and senile. Juvenile type usually develops during the infancy, by the first two years of life. The patient presents with symmetrically distributed, flat, smooth, noninfiltrated, dark brown or black, macule or patch of varying size anywhere on the body, including the covered parts of the body. The lesion may be single or multiple, and may increase in size but becomes static during adulthood. The lesion may also involve mucous membrane. It however does not give rise to any symptom but when it assumes large size, and develops on the uncovered surface of the body, it may cause embarrassment and cosmetic problem. Lentigo however does not show any influence on exposure to, or protection from, sunlight, and may rarely cause malignancy.

Senile lentigo develops in elderly persons. It presents with symmetrically distributed, discrete, hyperpigmented macules on the exposed parts of the body and shows no relation to the exposure to, or protection against, sunlight. The lesions may accompany depigmented spots and chronic actinic degenerative changes.

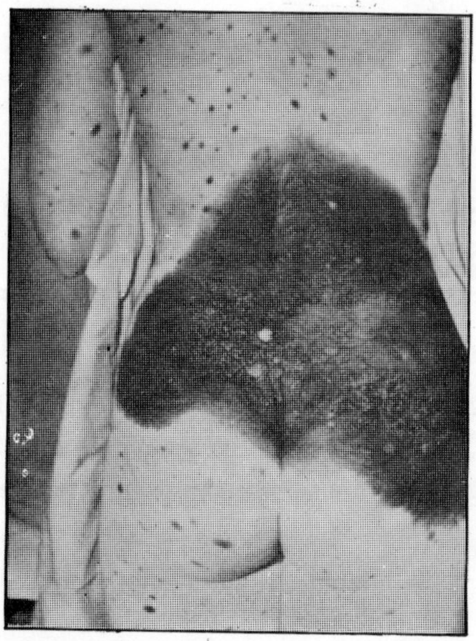

Figure 2.1. Hairy naevus on the back.

Cellular naevus presents with flat, slightly raised, soft, circumscribed papule, nodule or plaque, of varying size anywhere on the body. The naevus may be single or multiple, and be pigmented or of skin-coloured. When it assumes quite a large size, it is then frequently referred as **giant naevus**. The surface of the naevus may be smooth, hairy (**hairy naevus, hairy moles**) or verrucous (**verrucous moles**). The naevus may assume enormous size and may well be hairy in hairy naevus (Fig. 2.1). Sometimes a pigmented naevus may show a halo of depigmented area around the naevus (**halo naevus**). The pigmented naevus may usually appear singly as slate blue or bluish-black (**blue naevus**) occurring on the back or buttocks, in infancy or in early childhood. The naevus is well-circumscribed, round or oval macule, and is characterised by highly pigmented dendritic naevus cells within the middle of the deep dermis.

Junctional naevus gives rise to flat but may also be lentigo-like elevated, brown or black, pigmented macule anywhere on the body (Fig. 2.2). The naevus is more common in children but in adults its number is less numerous. Junctional naevus however shows a great tendency to malignancy when it generally gives rise to an appearance of a drop of brown paint with a spreading margin.

Intradermal naevus or **common mole** presents with elevated, light brown or even black soft papule (Fig. 2.3 and 2.4). The surface of the naevus may be smooth, hairy, or even verrucous. The naevus generally remain benign all through the life.

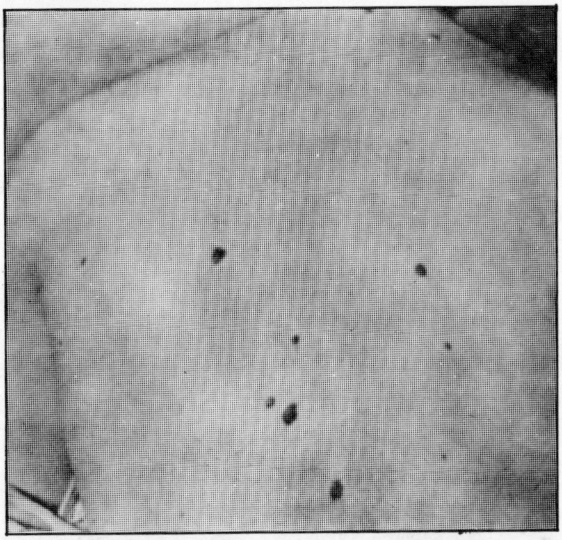

Figure 2.2. Pigmented junctional naevi on the back.

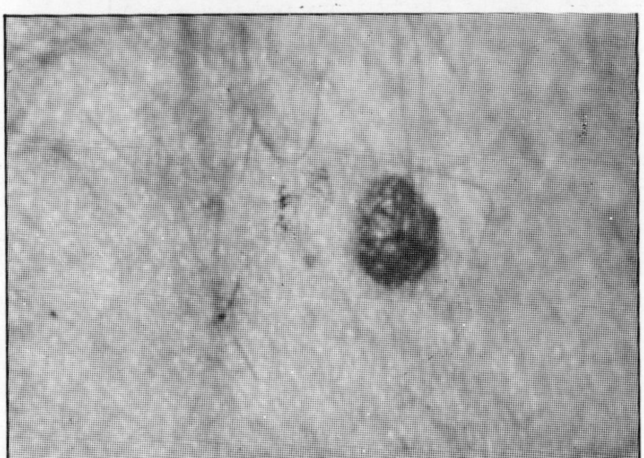

Figure 2.3. Intradermal naevus on the neck.

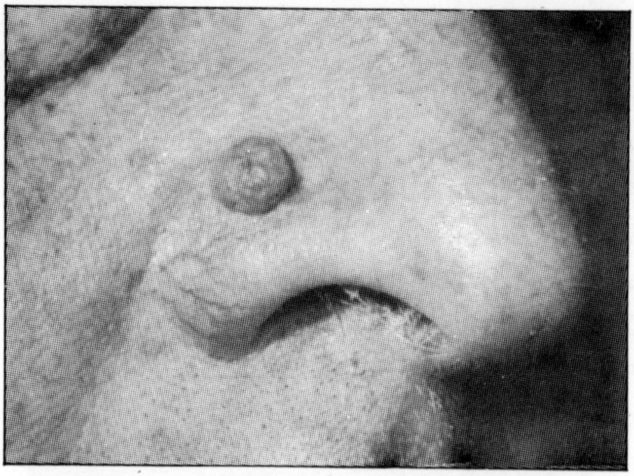

Figure 2.4. Intradermal naevus on the nose.

Compound naevus is a naevus of mixed variety of junctional naevus and intradermal naevus. It presents with soft, slightly elevated light brown to black, pigmented papules. It predominantly occurs in childhood. Development of it in the adults is less frequent but when it does, it may lead to malignancy.

Dysplastic naevus (Fig. 2.5) appears histopathologically perhaps as to be a variant of compound naevus. It however assumes much larger size than that of acquired form and occurs in a large number, perhaps in hundreds. It gives rise to flat macules to slightly elevated patches anywhere on the body, both exposed or unexposed to sunlight. The margins of the lesion show irregular contour. Development of this naevus also shows a familial tendency. The lesions usually appear clinically static but generally reckoned as precursor of malignant melanoma.

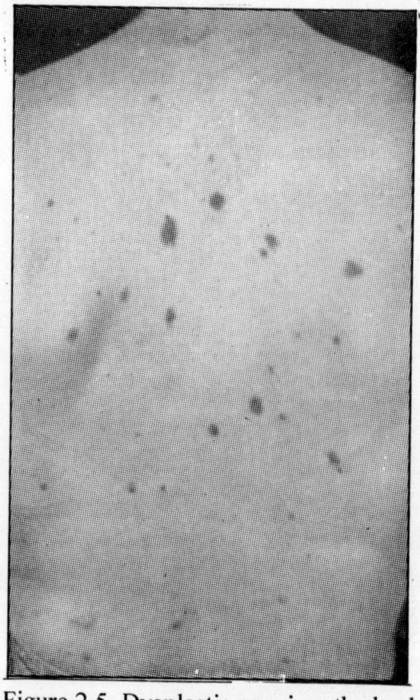

Figure 2.5. Dysplastic naevi on the back.

Occasionally a naevus may cause pressure or friction. Repeated trauma can however cause easy bleeding and may even lead to a benign naevus to malignancy.

Diagnosis

Diagnosis pf naevus is easy on clinical grounds.

Yet, a few naevus may at times however pose certain confusion. Lentigines, for example, may need to be differentiated from junctional naevus and seborrhoeic keratosis.

Treatment

Most naevi are, in fact, benign and hence they do not require any form of treatment. The prospect of treatment appears occasionally only when a naevus causes any amount of irritation or pose as a cosmetic problem.

Small naevi may however be concealed through local application of a covering agent may be given for cosmetic purposes. In other cases, removal of the lesions may be considered even though in cases of lentigines, removal of the lesion is extremely difficult and usually leads to scarring.

Naevus that may later cause malignancy is removed through surgical excision.

EPIDERMAL NAEVUS

Epidermal naevus is also known as **verrucous naevus and hard naevus**. It usually develops during birth but some may also develop later during the first year of life.

Pathological changes the condition show are hyperplasia of the epidermis, particularly in the stratum corneum, with thickening of glandular or perigalndular structures. The lesions however do not usually show any presence of naevus cells.

Clinical Manifestations

The condition presents with elevated, sharply demarcated, hard, roughly surfaced, papules or nodules. The lesions are localised and generally distributed unilaterally. The lesions however vary greatly in size, distribution and clinical appearances. They are usually hairless. Some cases may show extension of the lesions during the early years of life but later become static. They can occur on any part of the body, and give rise to no symptom.

Sometimes the lesions may develop in linear configuration as continuous or broken streaks, bands or patches (**linear naevus, naevus unius lateris**), usually affecting the extremities and the trunk.

Sometimes the lesion may develop resembling acne when it is known as **acneform naevus** (Fig. 2.6).

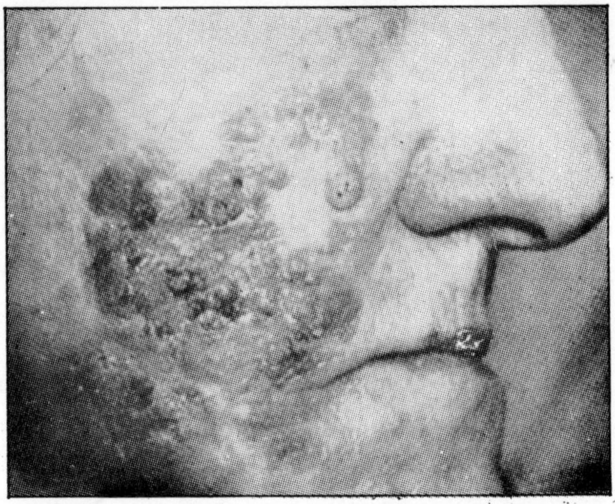

Figure 2.6. Acneform verrucous naevi.

When the lesions develop exaggeratedly with localised horny dysplasia on the trunk and extremities. It is then known as **Ichthyosis hystrix**. The lesions usually occupy extensive area, and are distributed asymmetrically.

Epidermal naevi do not give rise to any subjective symptom. They are in general benign growth and only very rarely may lead to malignancy.

Diagnosis

The condition is diagnosed on clinic al grounds.

It is however differentiated from psoriasis, which develops with symmetrically distributed scaly lesions and when the scales are removed on pressure, it leave multiple bleeding points on the surface. Lichen planus linearis may however remain indistinguishable with linear naevus and only skin biopsy can differentiate to conditions.

FRECKLES

It is a benign disorder of abnormal pigmentation resulted from exposure to sunlight or ultraviolet light. The lesions disappear largely during the winter or when exposure to sunlight or ultraviolet light is prevented. The condition is quite common on fair skin but rare on dark skin. The condition is also known as **ephelis**.

The lesions usually develop during childhood, particularly between the ages of 3 and 4 years, and tend to persist throughout the life.

Pathological changes show increased melanin pigment in the basal keratinocytes, produce in response to sunlight. Melanocytes are however normal or may show slight enlargement.

Clinical Manifestations

It presents with multiple, small, discrete, circular, grouped or confluent, tan-red or light brownish or blackish, evenly pigmented macules. The lesions are distributed symmetrically and usually develop on the exposed parts of the body, such as face, neck, shoulders, dorsum of the hands, and extensor surface of the forearms. The lesions can also develop on the unexposed parts of the body but only when they are exposed to the sunlight or ultraviolet light. The lesions tend to fade in winter and reappear in summer in a cyclic pattern. The condition however does not give rise to any symptom.

Continued exposure to sunlight or to ultraviolet light makes the lesions of freckles to increase in number and to become darker, and the surrounding skin may become red and sore, but the lesions fade on protection from further exposure.

Diagnosis

It is diagnosed on clinical gourds.

It is however differentiated from lentigo that occurs in infancy and gives rise to darker lesion and shows no influence on exposure to, or protection from, sunlight or ultraviolet light. Senile lentigines, on the other hand, develop in elderly people, often accompanied by depigmented spots, senile purpura and chronic actinic degenerative changes in the skin. Xeroderma pigmentosa is differentiated for having atrophic patches and telangiectasia, and a familial history is available.

Treatment

The susceptible persons are given protection through local use of sunscreen and by covering the exposed parts of the body with clothe. Localised lesions may be removed by careful application of solution of phenol or by hydrogen peroxide. Topical corticosteroids in combination of a bleaching agent, such as hydroquinone, 2%-5%, appear to be quite beneficial, and require long-term continuation. Local application of keratolytic agent is also effective.

As the condition is dependable on the exposure to light, the principle of management and control aim to the prevention against further exposure to sunlight and ultraviolet light.

CHLOASMA

It is a disorder of hyperpigmentation of skin of unknown origin. It is also known as **melasma**. Sometimes it may develop due to some internal disorders. Use of certain cosmetics can also produce the condition. In women it may however occur due to the effect of oestrogen and, also, from taking oral contraceptives. Exposure to sunlight may accentuate the pigmentation.

It commonly affects middle-aged persons, and is more common in women than in men.

Pathologically the condition has two types: epidermal and dermal. Epidermal type shows localised deposits of melanin in the stratum Malpighii (basal layer). In dermal type there are macrophages in the superficial dermis that have pigmented melanin from the epidermal layer.

Clinical Manifestations

It presents with superficial, non-elevated, smooth, often poorly defined, brownish or blackish patchy pigmentation. The lesions are often distributed symmetrically, and generally develop on the face, particularly on the bridge of the nose, upper lip and forehead. In addition, the lesions appear on the nipple and areola, axillae, groins and external genitalia. The condition however does not give rise to any symptom.

In women, the condition often produces mask-like darkening of the face during pregnancy (**chloasma gravidarum**), involving the cheeks, temples and forehead. The lesions often disappear spontaneously following termination of pregnancy.

Diagnosis

It is diagnosed on clinical grounds. Examination by the Wood's light can however confirm whether the hyperpigmentation is due to epidermal type or to dermal type of lesion.

It is differentiated from other causes of hyperpigmentation.

Treatment

Appropriate measure is taken in cases where the causative factor is known. This includes avoidance of offending cosmetics and oral contraceptive, and identification and appropriate management of the internal disorder.

Topical application of hydrogen peroxide may be beneficial. Keratolytic agents, such as salicylic acid, 3-5%, or urea, 10-20%, is also effective but with variable effect. Epidermal types however respond well with topical application of bleaching agent, such as hydroquinone, 2-4%, perhaps in combination with corticosteroids. Oral administration of vitamin C, 500 mg daily, has also sometimes shown to have good therapeutic effect. If needed topical sunscreen may be for protection against the exposure to sunlight. The treatment usually needs to be continued for sometime.

Resistant cases may need 10% aqueous solution of trichloroacetic acid for superficial cauterisation.

XERODERMA PIGMENTOSUM

Xeroderma pigmentosum is a rare familial disorder, inherited as an autosomal recessive trait, and develops due to defect in repair of ultraviolet light-damaged DNA. The condition is characterised by hyperpigmentation, depigmentation and telangiectasia due to hypersensitivity to sunlight.

The condition usually starts in the infancy, often within the first year of life, but may be delayed, to the extent it may develop in adult life.

Pathological changes in the condition show hyperkeratosis and marked acanthosis of the rete Malpighii. There are increased deposition of melanin in the stratum germinavitum of the epidermis and plenty melanocytes in the superficial layer of the dermis. Destruction of both collagen and elastic fibres is evident.

Clinical Manifestations

It presents with mild erythema and gross freckle-like macules, usually worse on the face and other exposed parts of the body, such as neck, hands and arms, but can also involve other parts of the body as well. The freckles generally coalesce together. At a later stage the condition give rise to pigmented macular lesions with atrophic patches and telangiectasia. Exposure to sunlight aggravates the condition. Sometimes it may also affect the eye, producing lacrimation and photophobia, and may finally lead to conjunctivitis, keratitis or even ocular neoplasms. The condition frequently shows an association with neurological defects, such as impaired speech and hearing, convulsions, and mental deficiency.

Much later, depigmented macules appear between the hyperpigmented lesions, and the skin becomes atrophic and hypertrophic. Finally, continued exposure to sunlight may lead to the development of epidermal scarring and frequently epidermal malignancies, such as squamous-cell carcinoma and basal-cell carcinoma, and malignant melanoma.

The course of the condition is very variable. It may develop aggressively and may cause fatality even in the childhood. Conversely, the condition may not cause much harm in others, and the patient may lead an almost normal life span. The severity of the condition does, in fact, depend upon the amount of ultraviolet radiation to the body.

Diagnosis

Diagnosis of the condition is made on clinical grounds, aided by skin biopsy. A family history of the condition is also available.

The condition is differentiated from freckles in which there is no family history while the condition does not give raises to any depigmentation and telangiectasia. Lentigines are differentiated from the condition for having the lesions on the covered parts of the body as well and the lesions do not show any influence on exposure to sunlight. Radio-dermatitis may however cause certain amount of con fusion but there is always a history available on the exposure to radiation.

Treatment

No specific treatment of the condition is available. The patient is only given absolute protection against the exposure to sunlight. The patient is therefore advised to cover up the exposed parts of the body with clothing and to use heavy topical sunscreen, especially containing titanium dioxide. Other topical sunscreens are often useless, as they cannot confer a heavy protection.

In cases of malignancy, appropriate measures such as surgical excision, need to be taken as they develop and as soon as possible.

ACANTHOSIS NIGRICANS

It is a rare condition of hyperpigmentation of skin. It occurs in young people (***juvenile*** or ***benign type***) perhaps due to increased hormonal output during puberty, and also from metabolic and digestive disorders. In adults (***adult*** or ***malignant type***) it may however occur in association with internal malignant disease, though there may not be any such history of malignancy in many. There may also be an association with obesity and endocrine tumours.

The condition produces acanthosis with atrophy of the prickle cell layer, and hyperkeratosis. Both basal layer and upper part of the dermis show dense melanin pigment, with slight perivascular lymphocytic infiltration.

Clinical Manifestations

It gives rise to symmetrically distributed hyperpigmented streaks or patches, with thin warty growth of papillary hypertrophy, commonly occurring on the axillae (Fig. 2.7), groins, flexures of elbows and knees, inner aspects of thighs, submammary region, genitalia, neck, face, umbilicus and anus. The lesions are soft and velvety on touch, and only rarely may involve large area of the body. When the lesions develop on the palms and soles, they produce hyperkeratosis. Occasionally pigmented spot and minute warty growth may be seen on the oral mucosa and vagina.

In **pseudo-acanthosis**, a variant of the condition, areas of pigmented papules develop on the body folds, neck and intermammary areas in the obese persons.

Diagnosis

The condition is diagnosed on skin biopsy.

Treatment

In the treatment of the condition appropriate measurement is aimed for the correction of the underlying cause. Surgical excision of the lesions is considered for the cosmetic problem. Bleaching of the area may be tried with hydroquinone, thiouracil, glutathione or sodium molybdate, but the result is frequently unsatisfactory. Ointment or paste of salicylic acid may also be tried for the purpose. Vitamin C is a potential reducing agent for melanin formation and hence, it is worthwhile to try with it.

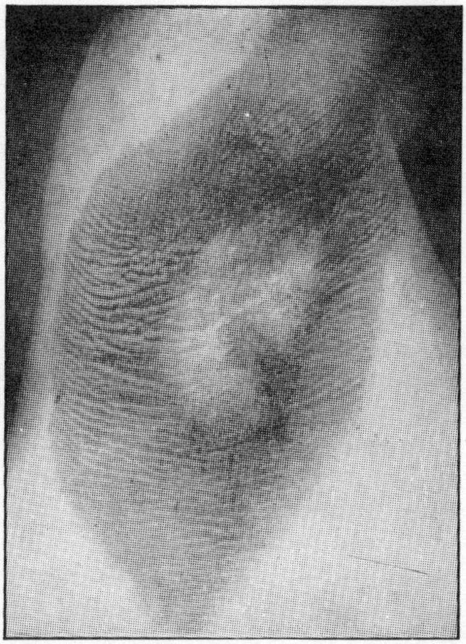

Figure 2.7. Acanthosis nigricans on axillary area.

INCONTINENTIA PIGMENTI

It is a rare disorder or an autosomal dominant trait, causing patchy hyperpigmentation. It develops within the first few weeks of life and predominantly affects the girls.

The lesion shows heavy deposition of melanin.

Clinical Manifestations

It presents with crops of inflammatory papules, vesicles or bullae, occurring on any part of the body, mostly on the trunk and less frequently on the extremities. The lesions may cluster together to form patches or may run a linear course, with no distinctive pattern. Later, the lesions become wart-like papules. In addition, hyperpigmented patches of irregular shape and size often develop along with the skin lesions (Fig. 2.8). The pigmentation of skin does not cause any symptom but persists for long even after the disappearance of the skin lesions, and eventually fades away leaving no sequel but there may be slightly atrophic depigmented spots.

Diagnosis

The condition is diagnosed on the basis of family history and skin biopsy.

Treatment

Depigmentation of skin is often unsatisfactory. Use of bleaching agent, such as B.A.L., thiouracil or hydroquinone, may however give variable success.

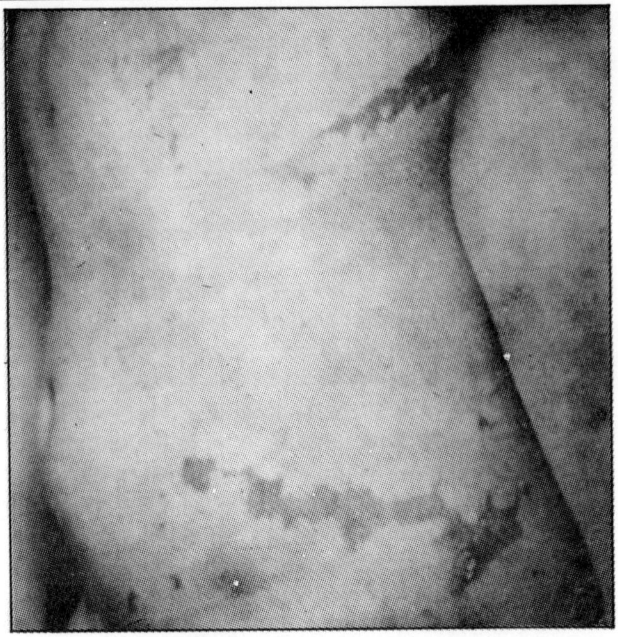

Figure 2.8. Incontinentia pigmenti.

PITYRIASIS SIMPLEX

The condition is also known as **pityriasis alba**. It is a benign skin disorder of unknown origin. Development of the condition is however frequently found attributable to low-grade streptococcal infection, while it may follow gastroenteritis, dysentery, and use of broad-spectrum antibiotics. Lack of exposure to sunlight and avitaminosis may also play some part in its causation.

It principally affects the children and adults very rarely.

Clinical Manifestations

The condition presents with hypopigmented macules of various size and shape, usually on the face, mostly forehead, chicks and chin, but may also involve the neck, arms and shoulders. The patches are poorly demarcated, and are covered with adherent furfuraceous scales. Sometimes the margins of the patches may show erythema

The condition does not usually give rise to any symptom except perhaps mild pruritus in occasional cases. The lesions persist for some time and disappear spontaneously without any scarring.

Diagnosis

It is diagnosed clinically.

The condition is differentiated from vitiligo, which has no scales, and the lesions do not resolve spontaneously. Tinea versicolor is differentiated for having gradually increasing hypopigmented patches, covered with fine or brawny scales.

Treatment

The condition does not require any form of treatment. The patients may however be given improved nutrition, supplemented by ample vitamins, and are encouraged for exposure to fresh air and sunlight.

If any medical therapy is needed, the patient may be given mild antiseptic for topical use.

VITILIGO

It is a common acquired condition of primary pigmentary disturbance of unknown origin, but causes a stoppage of melanin formation by the melanocytes. Strong suggestions however support for autoimmunity, and the condition is often seen to be determined genetically. Some cases therefore give a family history. It is also produced due to trauma and prolonged pressure (for example, tight binding of petticoat), and following healing of the wounds.

The condition shows certain association with thyroid diseases, Addison's disease, pernicious anaemia, diabetes mellitus, morphea, and malignant melanoma. Nutritional imbalances to a few elements, and use of certain drugs or chemicals can also produce the condition.

Although it may develop at any age, in general circumstances a considerable proportion of the cases occur before the age of 20 years.

Leucoderma is a loosely applied terminology used to express depigmented skin lesions. In fact, until and unless a diagnosis of a depigmented area is confirmed and, also, in the early stage of development of vitiligo, leucoderma is used frequently, instead.

Histologically vitiligo shows no abnormality except partial or complete loss of pigment-producing melanocytes within the epidermis.

Clinical Manifestations

It presents with flat, irregular shaped and sized, circumscribed, completely depigmented macules or patches, surrounded by normal or hyperpigmented skin (Figs. 2.9 and 2,10). The lesions may develop on any part of the body but usually on the face, hands, feet, axillae, groins, and genitalia. The lesions may also coalesce together to form large patches, or though rarely, may involve the whole skin surface, including the eyes and hairs. On the other hand, sometimes the lesions may appear as hypopigmented rather than depigmented. The lesions become more obvious in summer because of the increased pigmentation in the surrounding skin. In some cases, however, the lesions may be seen developing on extensor surfaces only.

There is however no symptom and no structural change, nor is there any loss of sensation. In the dark-skinned persons however the condition causes great frustration and social embarrassment.

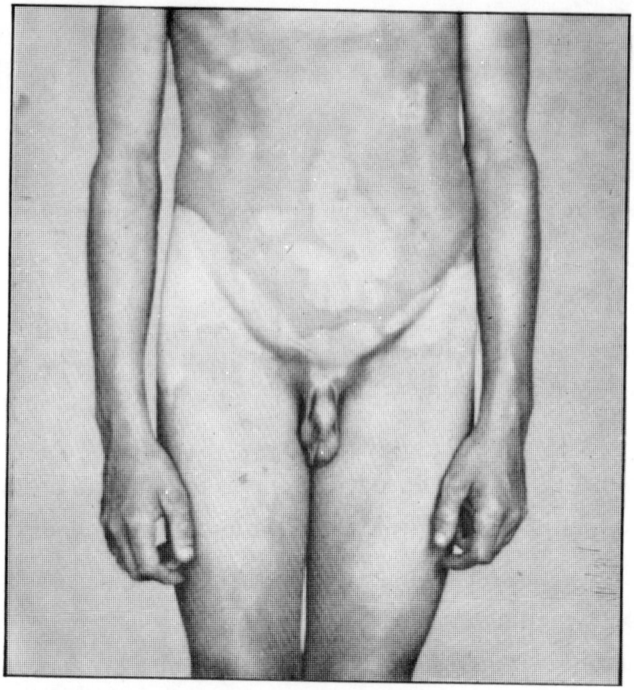

Figure 2.9. Vitiligo

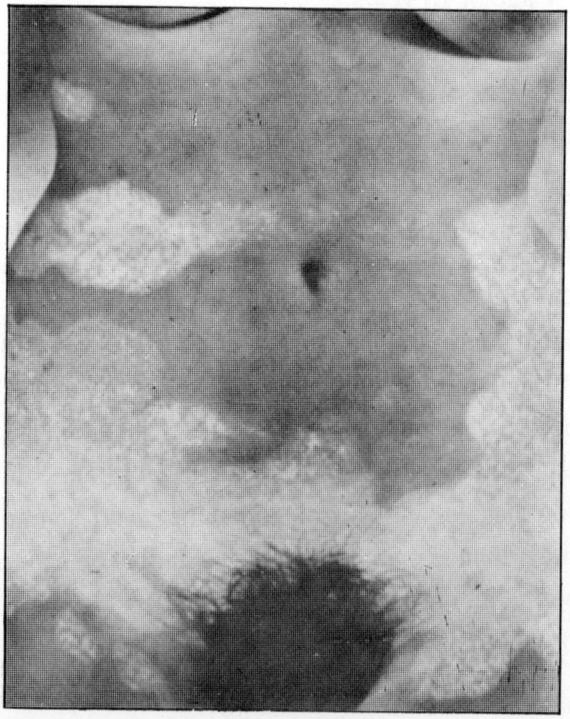

Figure 2.10. Vitiligo.

Diagnosis

Diagnosis is easy clinical grounds. It light coloured skin, however, the lesions may not be apparent until the skin is tanned or exposed to Wood's ultraviolet long-wave light.

It is differentiated from albinism which shows complete absence of melanin on skin biopsy; from pityriasis simplex which presents with poorly demarcated hypopigmented areas covered with adherent furfuraceous scales; and tinea versicolor for having slightly hypopigmented macules covered with fine or brawny scales while the causative organism can be identified from the lesions. Leprosy is differentiated from the condition for having anaesthetic lesions. Sometimes morphea can also cause confusion but presents with discrete atrophic smooth lesions, surrounded by violaceous zone or by telangiectasia.

Treatment

In the treatment of the condition the causative factors, if known, must receive immediate attention and management.

Small lesions on the exposed part of the body may be concealed with a covering agent, if required, for cosmetic purposes.

Otherwise, the treatment is given with psoralen or its derivatives, of which ammoidine appears to be the most potent drug. Depending upon the extension of involvement of the lesions the treatment may be given locally or systemic or both. Whatever the mode of medication may be, the treatment needs exposure of the affected parts to the sunlight or ultraviolet light. In cases of topical administration, the affected area is painted with ammoidine, 0.7% solution. The treatment is instituted initially in a dilute form, for example 1:10 dilution with alcohol, and the concentration is increased gradually to the tolerance of the patient to the effective level without causing any reaction, such as photosensitivity and blister formation, and if not otherwise, the target is being to apply the solution as it is and naturally without any dilution. If any reaction develops with any particular concentration, the medication is discontinued for a few days till the reactions subside and then the treatment is again given and continued with the next dilution which had been tolerated by the patient. Following topical application the affected part of the body and after half-an-hour to two house, is exposed to sunlight or ultraviolet light initially for 2 to 5 minutes, and the time of exposure is increased gradually to 15 to 30 minutes once daily.

In cases of systemic medication the patient is given ammodine, 10-40 mg daily orally in the morning, on empty stomach and before breakfast. If the lesions are too extensive, the oral medication may be given twice daily, once on empty stomach in the morning, and the second dose at any time before noon. After half-an-hour to two hours since taking the oral medication, the patient is advised to expose the affected parts of the body to sunlight or ultraviolet light for not less than 30 minutes.

In cases of photosensitivity reaction with psoralen, repigmentation may be induced by selective use to ultraviolet light of A wavelength.

In rapidly developing vitiligo, topical corticosteroids, perhaps supplemented by systemic corticosteroids, may be given. In cases of failure, surgical treatment is given with melanocyte grafting.

Vitiligo is however extremely difficult to treat in fair-skinned individuals. Treatment with psoralen also appears unsatisfactory in them. The cases then treated along with cosmetic line.

ALBINISM

It is an autosomal recessive disorder and is characterised by complete absence of melanin in the skin, hair and eye. The condition may be total or complete, and partial or incomplete.

In total or complete albinism, though the melanocytes are preset but they cannot form melanin due to lack of, or absence of, enzyme tyrosinase. In incomplete or partial albinism, melanocytes can however produce melanin but the quantity is scarce.

It occurs at birth and persists throughout life.

Clinical Manifestations

The condition typically presents with white skin, pale yellow or white hair, and red, pink or blue eyes. In addition, there is increasing hypersensitivity to sunlight, and the person eventually develops photophobia, nystagmus, and defective vision.

In partial albinism, however, the eyes may maintain their colour, or only one eye may be affected.

Diagnosis

Diagnosis is quite easy in cases of total albinism but may sometimes cause certain confusion in cases of partial albinism. Otherwise, the diagnosis is made on clinical grounds, perhaps aided by skin biopsy, if needed.

The condition may b differentiated from vitiligo in which it produces white patches surrounded by normal or hyperpigmented skin. In addition, there is no hypersensitivity to sunlight. Leprosy can produce white patches that occur not due to any defect in melanin formation but due to interference with the nerve supply. In addition, it gives rise to the development of anaesthetic lesions.

Treatment

No effective therapy of the condition is available. The patient can however be given protection through the use of clothing and wearing dark glasses. In addition, topical use of sunscreen may also appear beneficial.

CHAPTER 3

Disorders due to Inflammation and Allergy

ATOPIC DERMATITIS

Atopic dermatitis or **eczema** or **atopic eczema** is one of the most common dermatological disorders. It is a condition of superficial inflammation of the skin. The aetiology of the condition is not precisely known but it may be a result of allergic phenomenon or of hypersensitivity. However, there may usually be a personal or family history of atopic disease (hay fever, asthma, **atopic dermatitis**), with a tendency of IgE mediated disorders. Dry, hyperirritable skin, and increased susceptibility to bacterial, viral or fungal skin diseases, and food allergens may act as predisposing factors. Greasy skin and hyperhidrosis are other predisposing factors. General physical debility, psychological stress, extreme environmental influence, all can contribute significantly to the development of the condition.

The condition runs a chronic course or there is a chronically relapsing dermatitis with acute exacerbations.

Pathological changes the condition presents with show hyperkeratosis, parakeratosis, and intercellular and intracellular oedema of the epidermis (spongiosis), consisting few leucocytes, in the early stage, and formation of intraepidermal vessels in more severe reaction. In chronic and subacute cases there are marked acanthosis with elongation of rete pegs and inflammatory exudate, containing eosinophils and histiocytes.

Clinical Manifestations

In infants, generally well nourished, the condition develops during the second or third month **(infantile eczema)** but otherwise it develops before the age of 6 months. It usually presents with bilateral erythematous patches on the cheeks. The erythematous patches show minute epidermal vesicles, which rupture of the skin surface, causing oozing of fluid and thus, produce weeping and crusted lesions (Fig. 3.1). The lesions may rapidly spread to the folds of the neck and eyelids, frequently involving the extensor surfaces of the body. The buttocks are however frequently become affected. Sometimes the lesions may even become a generalised erythroderma with considerable desquamation. Soon the vesicles are replaced by the papules, and the lesions appear to be erythematous papular or papulovesicular. The skin becomes very irritable and the infant scratches the lesions violently. Exudation may sometimes be most marked. Scratching and rubbing of the lesions, and perhaps addition of secondary infection, results crusts, pustules and infiltrated areas, and the skin take the characteristic lichenified appearance.

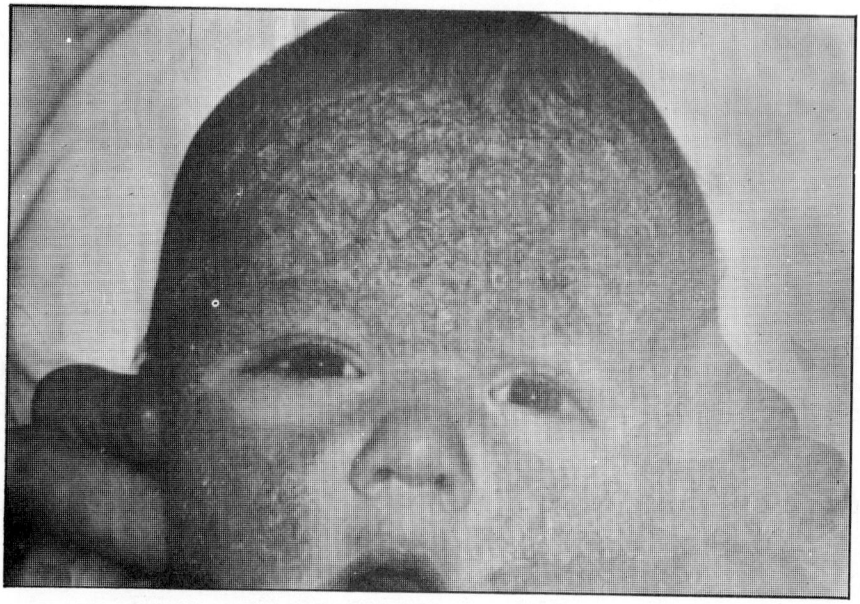

Figure 3.1. Infantile eczema.

Progression of the condition is variable. Some cases may resolve while in others, it may progress to childhood type or even to adult life.

The lesions may therefore develop in some older children as a direct progression of infantile eczema, and show remission and relapses. Generally there is however a relative or complete remission of the condition for some varying period of years. The lesions may be localised and the dry papules appear as excoriated, lichenified, poorly demarcated plaques, and usually involve the flexural creases, particularly the antecubital (Fig. 3.2) and popliteal (Fig. 3.3) fossae and behind the neck. The lesions may also involve other parts of the body, including wrists, fingers, ankles and toes. The lesions are generally less exudative but more dry.

Pruritus is the constant presenting feature of the condition, and the skin appears thickened. The affected area may therefore show scratch marks, erythema, pigmentation, vesiculation, and secondary infection. In addition, the patients may have other allergic manifestations.

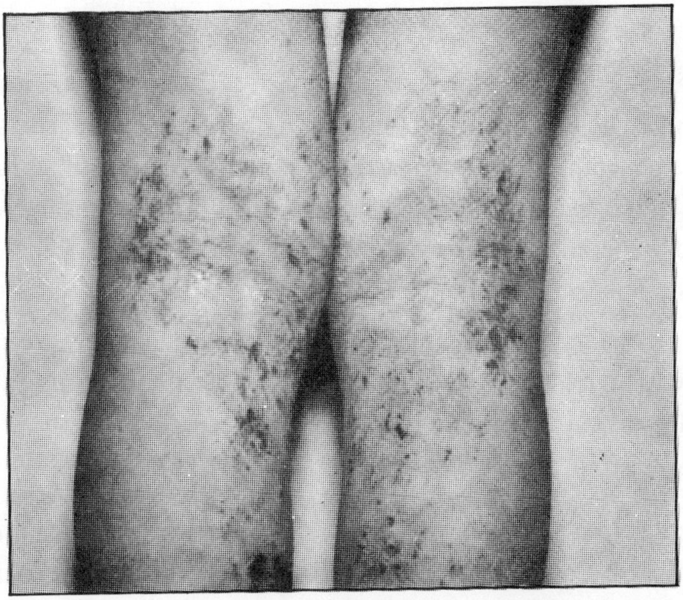

Figure 3.2. Atopic dermatitis on flexure surfaces of elbows.

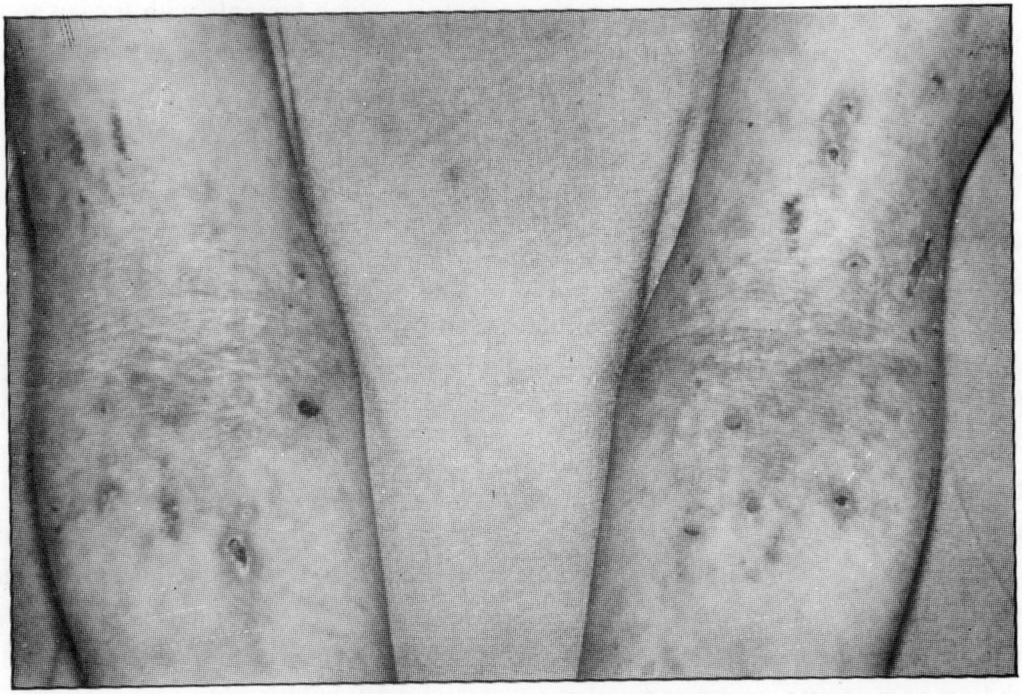

Figure 3.3. Atopic dermatitis on popliteal fossae.

As the age advances the lesions may show remissions and relapses, and become more dry and lichenified, or the condition may resolve.

A proportion of cases may however continue to adult life with variable severity of symptoms. The patients may therefore present with localised, erythematous, scaly, papular or vesicular, or lichenified itchy lesions, involving particularly the flexural areas of skin. Sometimes the lesions may be generalised and the flexures show more lesions than the other parts of the body. The patches of the lesions tend to coalesce together. The lesions may be hyperpigmented or hypopigmented, generalised, and are always excoriated. Skin appears dry and thickened. Sometimes the lesion may also become exudative and crusted or infected.

In all cases secondary bacterial infection and lymphadenopathy are common. There may also be intolerance to high temperature and humidity. The condition may also lead to Kaposi's varcelliform eruption as complication.

Diagnosis

Diagnosis is made on clinical grounds, aided by the characteristic distribution of the lesions. A history of atopic disease may be available. Patch test may also be done to detect the epidermal sensitivity. Blood characteristically shows high level of IgE.

It is differentiated from seborrhoeic dermatitis, which presents with greasy and scaly lesions, usually involving the scalp and face. Contact dermatitis gives a history of exposure to the offending agents and the lesions occur on the exposed parts of the body. Lichen simplex chronicus presents with thickly arranged flat papules with no exudation, occurring frequently on the back of the neck.

Treatment

Cleanliness of the affected area is an essential component of the management of the condition. The patient is given emollients, such as soft paraffin, 14.5%, with hypoallergenic anhydrous lanolin, 1%, and liquid paraffin, 12.6%, cream to be applied two or three times daily, or white soft paraffin 10% with liquid paraffin and coconut oil, to spray after bathing over clean dry skin from approximately 8 inches. Otherwise, the patient may be given bath emollient, such as colloidal oatmeal, 5% bath oil, 20-30 ml in bath or apply direct to skin when showering, or light liquid paraffin, 91%, with cetyl dimethicone, 5%, add 15 ml (children, 5-10 ml) to bath and soak for 10 minutes. A soothing compression with normal saline pr potassium permanganate, but with hypertonic saline solution in cases of lichenified lesions, two or three times a day, followed by, if needed, topical corticosteroids, and the treatment frequently appears satisfactory. Lesions with light or moderate exudation may however be given dressings with polyurethane.

Otherwise, the patient is given soothing compressions with normal saline or potassium permanganate in acute cases, and hypertonic saline in lichenified lesions, followed by topical corticosteroid application may be frequently satisfactory. Topical application of ointment containing 6% benzoic acid and 3% salicylic acid, applied three to four times daily, may also be beneficial. Gamolenic acid, 160-240 mg (children aged over 1 year, 80-160 mg), twice daily orally, squeezing contents of the capsule onto food or into a drink, or swallows directly, is also beneficial.

Topical corticosteroids have a special value in the treatment, and the cases may be treated with hydrocortisone cream, 0.5%, apply thinly 1-2 times daily, or alcometasone dipropionate, 0.05% cream or ointment, applied thinly 1-2 times daily. Cases unresponsive to less potent corticosteroids may be given hydrocortisone butyrate, 0.1%, applied thinly 1-2 times daily, beclometasone dipropionate, 0.026% cream or ointment, applied thinly 1-2 times daily, or fluocortolone, 0.25% cream or ointment, applied thinly 1-2 times daily.

The patient is also given oral anti-allergic drugs, such as chlorpheniramine, 4 mg every four to six hours (children: 1-2 years, 1 mg twice daily; 2-5 years, 1 mg four to six hourly; 6-12 years, 2 mg four to six hourly), promethazine, 10-25 mg two or three times daily (children: 2-5 years, 5-15 mg; over 5 years, 10-25 mg daily), or trimeperazine, 10 mg two or three times daily (children over 2 years, 2.5-5 mg three or four times daily), is extremely beneficial.

Some patients may however need systemic corticosteroids, such as prednisolone, 20-40 mg (children: 1-7 years, 5-20 mg; 7-12 years, 10-30 mg) daily in divided doses orally.

Chronic cases may however need a treatment with radiotherapy.

Severe refractory eczema is best managed under specialist supervision, and may require phototherapy, systemic corticosteroids, or other drugs acting on the immune system.

Skin dryness and consequent irritant eczema may require application of emollients such as aqueous cream and emulsifying ointment.

In addition, oral administration of vitamin A, 50,000-100,000 u daily orally, and parenteral or oral administration of calcium gluconate, may be also of some benefit.

In cases of secondary bacterial infection, the patient is given appropriate antibiotic.

During acute stage of the condition, however, every precaution is taken so that no children can come in contact with herpes simplex infection, or vaccinated for smallpox.

NUMMULAR ECZEMA

Aetiology of nummular eczema, also known as **discoid eczema**, is still not known precisely but it may be a variant of atopic dermatitis (eczema). The condition may develop due to allergic manifestations, psychological stresses, focal sepsis, and debility. Sometimes it may be a manifestation of lichen simplex chronicus (neurodermatitis). It is often found associated with dry skin, and is commonly seen during the winter.

Clinical Manifestations

The condition generally begins with itchy, scaling or vesicular patches developed on the dorsum of the hands, extensor surface of the arms, legs, thighs, shoulders, buttocks, breasts and nipples.

Later, they form discrete, coin-shaped, erythematous, oedematous, vesicular and crusted patches. The plaques may enlarge in size with a tendency of clearing of the centres. The lesions appear symmetrically. In extensive cases, the lesions may appears as papules or papulovesicles, and show exudation, and become thickened and scaly. The patient may complain of varying degree of pruritus but that seldom lead to excoriation and lichenification.

The condition runs a chronic and recurrent course.

Diagnosis

The condition is diagnosed on clinical grounds.

The condition may however need to be differentiated from infected eczema, which is characteristically featured by pruritus, excoriation and lichenification, and complicated by secondary bacterial infection. Dermatophytosis, particularly tines corporis, may however cause certain amount of confusion but the tinea lesions characteristically show well-defined, raised, active margins of papulovesicles and healing scaly centres, while the lesions are not distributed symmetrically.

Treatment

Management of the condition is aimed for elimination or correction of the underlying conditions responsible for producing the condition.

The affected areas are treated with soothing compression of normal saline or potassium permanganate, followed by topical; administration of corticosteroids. The patient may also be given massage with oil for the dryness of the skin.

Oral administration of anti-allergic agents, such as chlorpheniramine, 4 mg four to six hours daily (children, 1-2 years, 1 mg twice daily; 2-5 years, 1 mg four to six hours daily; and 6-12 years, 2 mg four to six hours daily) may be quite beneficial.

SEBORRHOEIC DERMATITIS

Seborrhoeic dermatitis or **seborrhoeic eczema** is a chronic inflammatory disorder of skin that results from inflammation of the sebaceous gland. Although the aetiology of its causation is still not known but genetic factors, involvement of infection, inflammation, or environmental factors may be responsible for the development of the condition. On the other hand, perhaps there may be an association of the condition with the presence of increasing number of commensal and lipophilic yeast, *Pityrosporum ovale*. Susceptibility to the condition appears to be due to constitutional factors. Severity of the condition however shows a seasonal variation, while psychological stresses make the condition worse.

The condition is associated with species of the yeast Malassezia and affects the scalp, paranasal areas, and eyebrows.

It affects all ages equally.

Pathological changes of the lesions show low-grade inflammatory process. There are spotty parakeratosis, acanthosis, spongiosis, and vesicle formation in the epidermis, and dilatation of subpapillary vessels in the corium with perivascular infiltration with lymphocytes.

Clinical Manifestations

The condition presents with erythematous plaques with fine, loosely adherent, greasy, yellowish or brownish-yellow scales and crusts usually on the scalp, which spread to the face, ears, axillae, chest, submammary folds, umbilicus, groins, and gluteal creases. The lesions may be of any shape and size, and show recurrences and exacerbation. There may be little or no oozing, with or without troublesome itching, and may seldom become generalised. There may be fissuring, loss of hair, and secondary bacterial infection.

In acute exacerbations, there may be swelling of the face or of the cheeks and ears, with rawness, exudation and scaling, giving a moist, yellow, crusted appearance. In fair persons, skin appears orange-red coloured.

Chronic cases are however less severe. and may present with dusky red patches and plaques with overlying fine-scales on the eyebrows, ears, nasolabial folds and eyelid margins.

The condition may also give rise to fissuring, loss of hair, and secondary bacterial infection. Pruritus is usually mild in the absence of psychological stress or superimposed contact dermatitis.

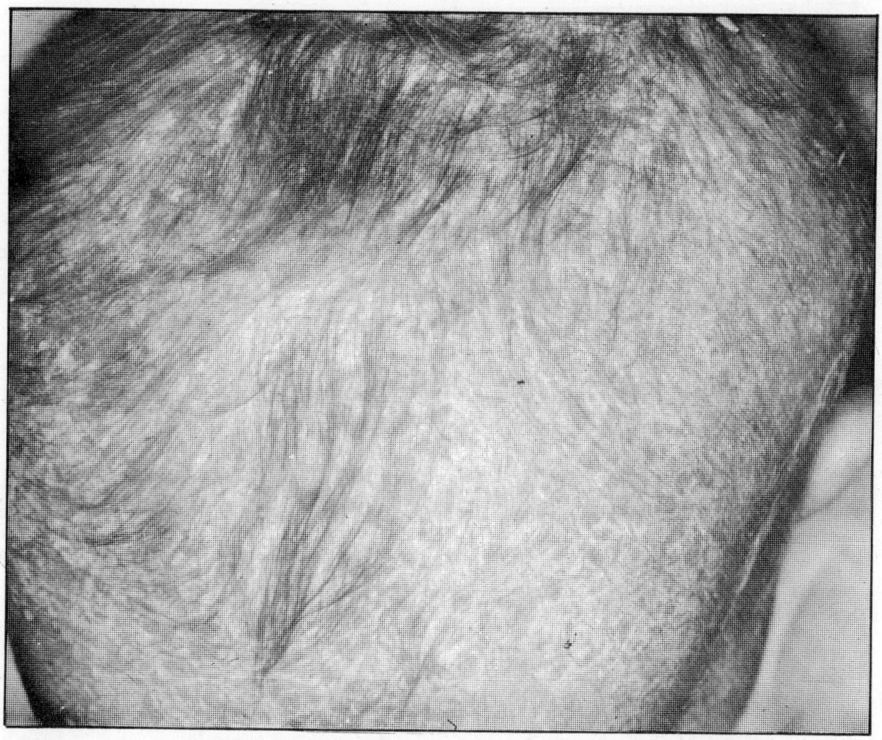

Figure 3.4. Seborrhoeic dermatitis on the scalp.

On the scalp it produces **dandruff (pityriasis capitis)** and has two forms of presentation: dry and oily. The dry form (**pityriasis sicca**) presents with fine, thin, powdery, whitish or greyish, dry or slightly greasy scales, which may become loose and fall on the shoulders. The lesions however do not cause erythema. Hair appears dry and lustreless but they do not fall. There may be mild to moderate itching.

The oily form (**pityriasis steatoides**) may accompany erythema, and produces well-defined, circumscribed patches, or diffuse distribution of waxy, greasy, yellowish, thick scales and crusts. It causes slight itching. The hair may be matted, and show a tendency to fall. This may therefore lead to the development of premature boldness. The lesions however frequently spread to the forehead, ears, neck, and on other flexures and hairy areas.

It may affect the infants during their first few weeks of life, and gives rise to dirty, thin or thick, whitish or brownish crusted lesions on the vertex of the scalp, known as **cradle cap** (Fig. 3.4). It does not cause inflammation or oozing but causes slight itching. Frequently the condition is found associated with a widespread or flexural erythematous skin rash.

Also, in the infants the condition may give rise to extreme erythema with the formation of scales on the buttock (Fig. 3.5). The infant may show similar reddening lesions on the truck and legs.

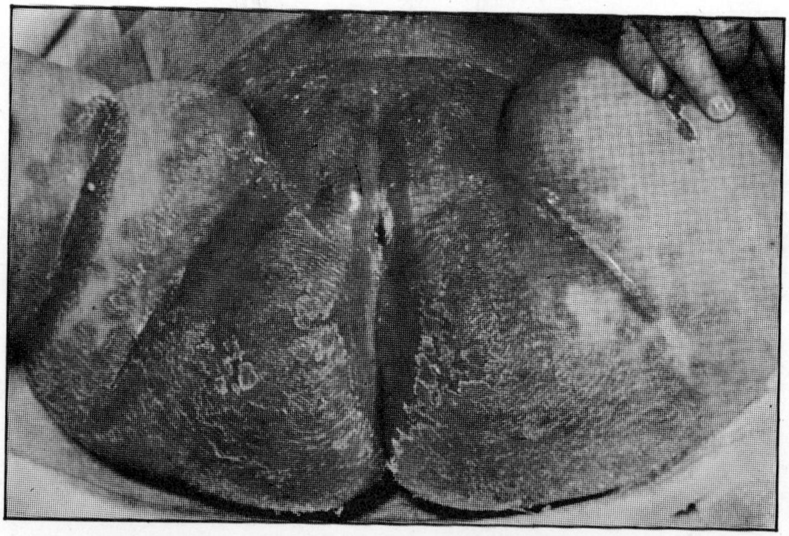

Figure 3.5. Seborrhoeic dermatitis on the buttocks.

It produces yellowish scaly patches or erythematous rash on the supraorbital region. The lesions are pruritic. Involvement of the eyelids produces erythematous, marginal blepharitis. It produces yellowish or reddish-yellow scaling, perhaps with fissures on the nasolabial creases and nasal alae. Involvement of the ears and retroauricular fold produces scaly pruritic patches.

Involvement of cheeks, nose and forehead produces eruptions covered with greasy, yellowish or yellowish-red scales. In axillae, the lesions develop on the skin fold at the apex and then spread to the neighbouring skin. Similar lesions are also seen on the breasts, under the breasts, and on the umbilicus.

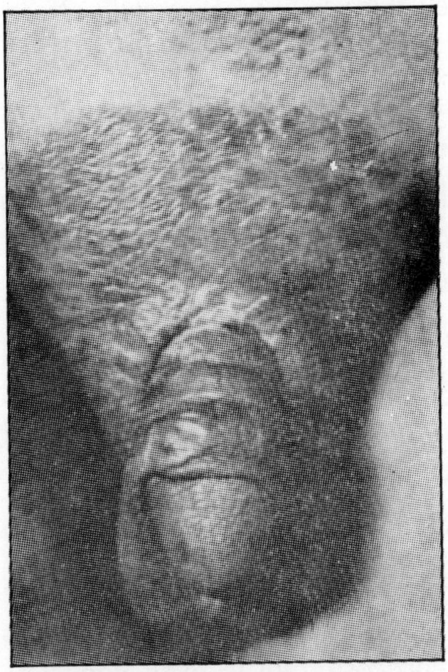

Figure 3.6. Seborrhoeic dermatitis.

Involvement of the groin and gluteal region is common, and the lesions appear symmetrically, with fine scales. The margins of the patches are poorly defined. In severe cases it may give rise to psoriasiform lesions (Fig 3.6).

On the extremities however the lesions peculiarly resemble to the eczematoid form and do lack the characteristic colour and fineness of the scales. There may be vesicular eruptions or the lesions may appear diffusely thickened and scaly when it involves the palms and soles.

Diagnosis

Diagnosis is made on clinical grounds alone.

It is differentiated from atopic dermatitis, which presents with extremely itchy lesions with no scales but perhaps little exudation. Psoriasis gives raise o well-demarcated lesions covered with greyish-white or silvery-white crusts which when removed on pressure leave bleeding bases. Intertrigo is differentiated for having localised erythematous lesions on the flexures. Lichen simplex chronicus is differentiated for having flat papules arranged thickly with no exudation or scaling.

Treatment

No specific treatment is available. Exposure of the affected area to fresh air and improvement of nutrition are important for palliative treatment.

Local application of corticosteroid is however often rewarding. Ointment containing lithium and zinc sulphate, applied twice daily, is also equally effective. In addition, or alternatively, the patient may be given ketaconazole, 2% cream, to be applied topically once or twice daily.

Involvement of scalp and dandruff require shampoo or other suitable preparations containing povidone-iodine, benzalkonium, cetrimide, selenium, or a combination of them in coal tar and salicylic acid or allantoin. Severe cases may need systemic corticosteroids, such as triamcinolone, 4-12 mg daily in divided doses orally, or betamethasone, 2-3 mg daily in divided doses orally. Chronic cases are better treated with topical sulphur and ichthammol.

The patient is also given oral antihistamine, such as chlorpheniramine, 4-8 mg four to six hourly daily (children aged 1-2 year, 1 mg twice daily; 2-5 years, 1 mg four to six hourly; 6-12 years, 2 mg four or six hourly), or promethazine, 10-25 mg two or three times daily (children 2-5 years, 5-15 mg; 5-10 years, 10-25 mg twice daily).

Intractable cases are treated with itraconazole, 100 mg daily orally for 2 weeks.

Acute cases may require appropriate antibiotics, such as tetracycline or fluocloxacillin. Local application of corticosteroids is often beneficial but in cases of bacterial involvement or a suspicion on thereof, topical corticosteroids is given along with antibiotic.

Cradle cap in infants may be treated with olive oil or arachis oil applications followed by shampooing.

For dandruff shampoos containing antimicrobial agents, for example, pyrithione zinc and selenium sulphide may be given with benefit. Shampoos with coal tar, as used in psoriasis, can also be beneficial. For more persistent or severe dandruff or for seborrhoeic dermatitis of the scalp the patient should be given shampoo, containing ketaconazole. Alternatively, the treatment is given with corticosteroid gels and lotions.

Severe cases may need systemic corticosteroids as well as given orally.

Chronic cases better treated with topical sulphur and ichthammol.

Intractable cases may however respond well itraconazole, 100 mg twice daily orally, for 2 weeks.

CONTACT DERMATITIS

The condition is also known as **occupational dermatitis, industrial dermatitis, eczematoid dermatitis** and **dermatitis venenata**. It is an acute or chronic inflammatory process that develops from direct contact on the skin surface with certain chemicals and other irritants, including varieties of substances of animal, vegetable and mineral origin. In this condition though the sensitisation of skin is generalised, the lesions are generally strictly localised, and chiefly involve the exposed parts of the body coming in direct contact with offending agent. The condition however does not affect to all exposed but some of them may acquire the condition. This makes it clear that perhaps there is delayed hypersensitivity reaction involved in its development.

It produces intracellular oedema and intra-epithelial vesicle formation, with mononuclear cells in the vesicles, and oedema and perivascular infiltration with mononuclear cells in the dermis.

The condition produces intracellular oedema and intraepithelial vesicle formation with mononuclear cells in the vesicles, and perivascular infiltration with mononuclear cells in the dermis.

Clinical Manifestations

The onset is often abrupt. It presents with erythematous macular, papular or papulovesicular eruptions, chiefly involving the exposed parts of the body. It usually affects the eyelids, cheeks, or neck with extremely pruritic red scaly patches. The lesions may be acute, subacute, or chronic, and may vary from transient redness to severe scaling with bullae formation, distributed asymmetrically. Pruritus is a common feature.

There may also be hotness and swelling of the areas with exudation and crusting, and excoriation.

Secondary bacterial infection may follow.

Diagnosis

History of exposure to the offending agent and the distribution of the lesions are often sufficient for the diagnosis. Patch test may be helpful diagnostic aid for identifying the specific allergens.

It is differentiated from atopic dermatitis and other form of eczema but they have different distribution pattern of the lesions and have no history of exposure to any chemicals or irritants.

Treatment

The patient is immediately removed from further exposure of the offending agents. Soothing local compressions with normal saline or potassium permanganate, followed by topical application of corticosteroids may be sufficient in many cases. In severe or extensive cases, however, systemic corticosteroids, such as prednisolone, 40 mg daily for 7 days followed by gradual withdrawal in the subsequent week, or betamethasone, 1.5-5 mg for a week and then tapered off gradually in the subsequent week, may be given in divided doses.

The patient is also given antihistamine, such as chlorpheniramine, 4 mg every four to six hours orally, cyproheptadine, 4 mg three or four times daily orally, or promethazine, 10-20 mg two to three times daily orally, for the relief of itching.

In cases of secondary bacterial infection, appropriate antibiotic is given.

Avoidance of exposure to the offending agents is the best way of prevention of the condition. It also needs appropriate preventive measures, including of provision of protective clothing, at work.

LICHEN PLANUS

It is a recurrent, non-infectious, pruritic, inflammatory disorder of the skin and mucous membrane. The aetiology of the condition is not however known. Reaction to certain drugs, such as β-blockers, antimalarials, thiazides and gold, and, also, of chemicals can, however, produce the condition. It may also have an association with emotional tension and stress. The condition appears to involve immunologically mediated attack by T-lymphocytes on the lower epidermis.

The condition occurs at any age but peak incidence occurs in the middle-aged persons. It is however rare in children.

Pathological changes show follicular hyperkeratosis, perifollicular acanthosis with elongation of rete pegs, granulosis, liquefaction necrosis of basal cell layer, and infiltration with lymphocytes, histiocytes and occasional plasma cells, separated by bundle of collagen.

The condition shows a tendency of spontaneous remission but otherwise may persist for years together. Rarely a few cases may change to exfoliative dermatitis.

Although no aetiology is known **Graham Little syndrome** may be a rare form of lichen planus.

Clinical Manifestations

The condition develops gradually or abruptly, and gives rise to small, multiple, purplish or violaceous, flat-topped or umbilicated, smooth, glistening, slightly raised, polygonal papules, distributed symmetrically, commonly on the flexor surfaces of the forearms (Fig. 3.7), wrists, around the ankles, and on the hips, shins, trunk, mouth, glans penis and vaginal mucosa. The papules are pinhead sized, usually clustered in groups, with whitish puncta or streaks (**Wickham's striae** are white streaks on the surface of the papules, which are the characteristic feature of lichen planus). The papules show a tendency of scaling, and may well be generalised. There may be no symptom or the patient may complain of mild to severe itching. Skin my show hyperpigmentation or hypopigmentation. Scarring alopecia may develop due to the lesions on the scalp. Nails may also show longitudinal ridges and severe dystrophy.

In its acute form it gives rise to widespread lesions, which start from the inner aspects of the arms and spread rapidly. The affected parts may become diffusely erythematous and oedematous from ulceration of the papules. The eruption, in addition, may include papulovesicles ort bullae. The lesions however heal spontaneously after a few months. Otherwise, the condition appears with localised lesions and shows periodic exacerbations in the chronic stage.

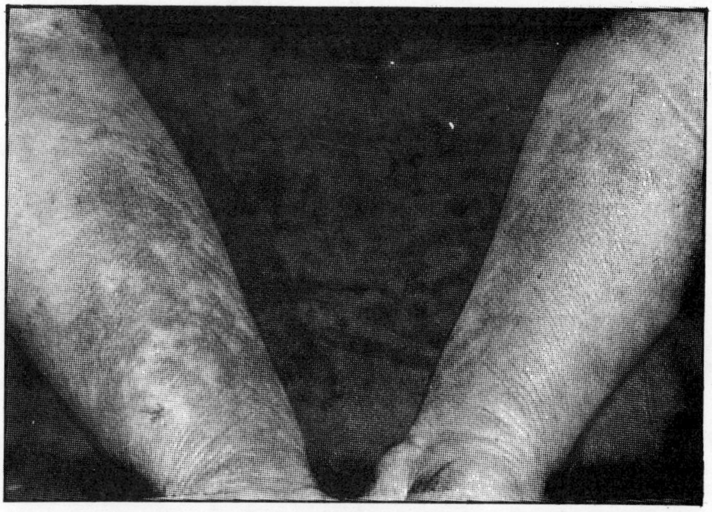

Figure 3.7. Lichen planus on forearms.

When the condition involves mucous membrane the lesions occur as angular or linear, milky-white papules or plaques or as reticulate pattern appear on the inner side of the cheeks (Fig. 3.8), and on the palate, lips and tongue. White, flat, angular papules, arranged in rings, appear on the glans penis, labia, vaginal mucosa, and anus. The mucosal lesions may also show ulcerations. On the shaft and glans penis, labia and anus, the condition persists with white, flat, angular papules, arranged in rings. The lesions, however, tend to be more persistent than the cutaneous lesions.

Involvement of the nails may lead to severe dystrophy.

The condition shows chronic exacerbation and remissions, and has several clinical variants with certain distinctive features.

Lichen planus linearis presents with extremely itchy, band-like patches along the extremity, more commonly posterior aspect of lower extremities, and about the trunk. The distribution of the lesions resembles herpes zoster infection.

When the lesions of lichen planus develop on the parts of the body exposed to sunlight, and the lesions become aggravated due to exposure to sunlight, the condition is then known as **lichen planus actinic**.

Lichen planus annularis presents with single or multiple, ivory coloured nodular lesions that feel firm and doughy on palpation. The lesions appear in the ring-form with raised margins and violaceous halo, and the centres are often violaceous and may sometimes be atrophic (Fig. 3. 9). Although the lesions may appear anywhere but show a predilection doe the hands and fingers. Occasionally small, pinhead-sized papules may also be seen within the ringed lesions or elsewhere on the body.

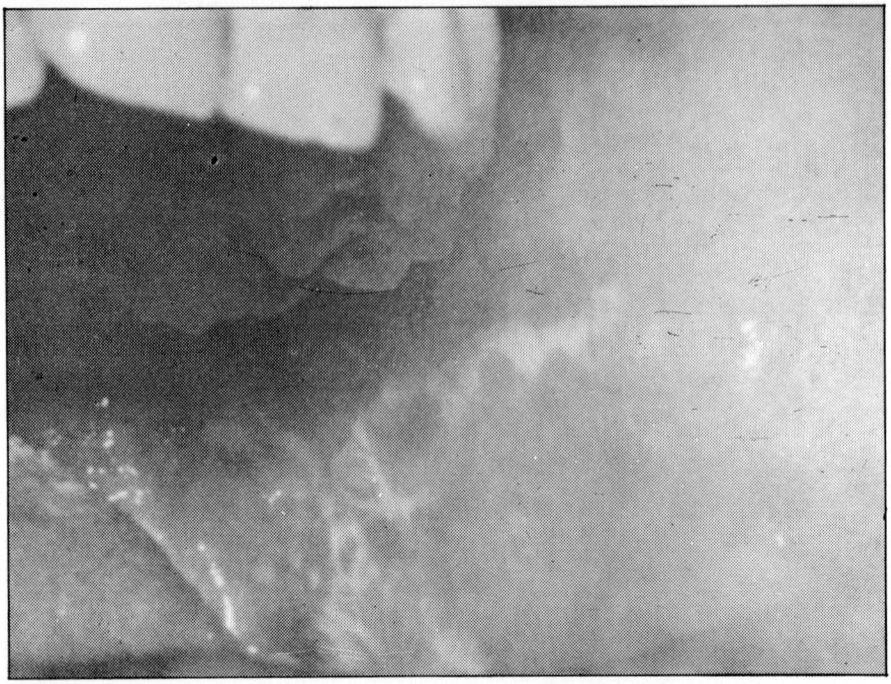

Figure 3.8. Lichen planus on buccal surface.

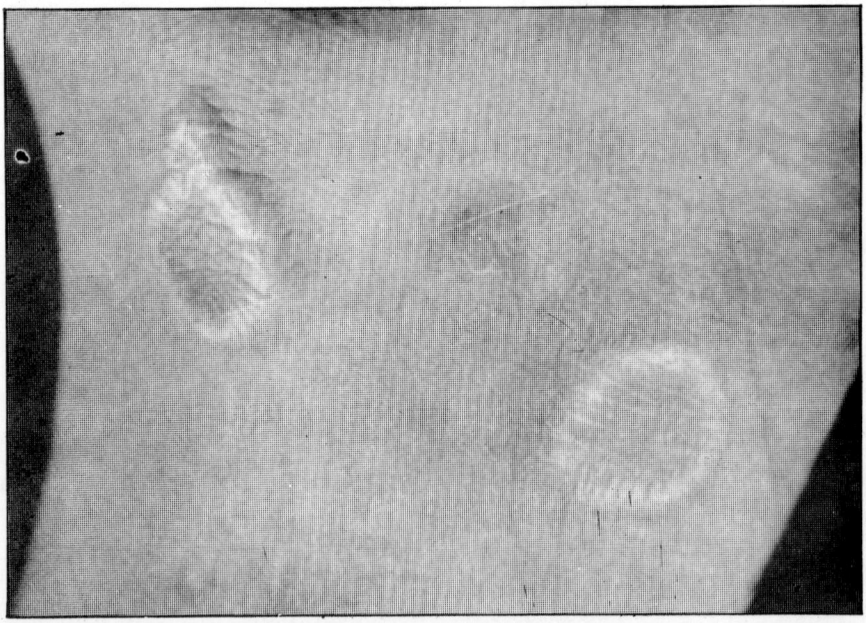

Figure 3.9. Lichen planus annularis.

In **lichen planus hypertrophicus** or **lichen planus verrucosus**, the lesions are severely itchy, dry, nummular or palm-sized, violaceous papules or plaques, covered with thick, hyperkeratotic scales, and mimic psoriasis. The lesions are distributed symmetrically, and mostly located on the shins.

Asymmetric annular lesions with a central hyperpigmented and atrophic white area, surrounded by an active erythematous raised border, manifest lichen planus atrophicus. The lesions are generally seen on the dorsal aspects of the hands and, rarely, on the face. In rare cases, the atrophy may be extensive. Ulcerations may also develop.

Lichen planus bullosus presents with pemphigus-like tense vesicles and bullae that form a part of the characteristic violaceous skin eruptions. The lesions however heal with atrophy.

In **lichen planopilaris** or **lichen planus follicularis** there is itchy, violaceous, patchy eruptions of spiny follicular papules, occurring at the hair follicles of the forearms and legs. On the scalp it causes permanent loss of hair (**cicatricial alopecia**) with atrophic scarring and pigmentation. Chest, back and upper arms also show flat, lichenoid lesions.

In other rare clinical varieties of the condition, the lesions may be congested and soft with diffuse and uniform erythema (**lichen planus erythematosus**), or haemorrhagic (**lichen planus haemorrhagica**).

Lichen planus resolves over a period of months, and most cases clear up within 2 years. The condition can, however, cause recurrences and malignancy as complications.

Graham Little syndrome presents with follicular lichen planus, giving rise to patchy eruption of spiny follicular papules. The lesions frequently occur upon the scalp with loss of hair and thus, presents with irregularly shaped bald patches that usually persists permanently. The skin lesions are not usually pruritic.

Diagnosis

Diagnosis of the condition is made on skin biopsy. If the subject is exposed to an injury, the lesions of lichen planus can be reproduced at the site of injury (**Köbner's phenomenon** represents a reaction in which any injury can produce a typical lesion at the site of trauma as it is seen in conditions like lichen planus, psoriasis, infected eczematoid dermatitis and verruca plana).

It is differentiated from atopic dermatitis which presents with dry, thick, patches, or plaques, or localised erythematous, scaly, papular or vesicular lesions, with absence of Wickham's striae; from pityriasis rosea which presents with fawn-coloured, erythematous, scaly, papules or nodules and the condition shows remission in a few weeks and the recurrences are rare; from herpes zoster which presents with crops of lesions, usually unilateral that appear along the distribution of the nerve and the condition begins with constitutional symptoms; from pemphigus in which the crops of diffusely scattered flaccid or tense bullae develop, showing a predilection for the areas of pressure or friction, and positive **Nikolsky's sign** (is a clinical test and is called positive when rubbing off an area causes easily detached epidermis from the underlying skin as it is seen in pemphigus); and dermatitis herpetiformis in which lesions have pigmented spots on healing. The condition is also differentiated from erythema multiforme bullosum in which the lesions are more localised and inflammatory and tend to spread peripherally to fuse together; from psoriasis that presents with well-demarcated lesions covered with greyish-white or silvery-white scales, and when the covering scales are removed on pressure they leave multiple tiny bleeding points on the base; and from syphilis in which a history of suspected sexual exposure may be available and the patient presents with other symptoms and signs of syphilis, including positive serological tests for syphilis. Discoid lupus erythematosus is differentiated for having localised erythematous plaque, usually single, or large patches from coalescence, and show telangiectasia, while involvement of the scalp causes scarring alopecia. Pityriasis rubra pilaris, on the other hand, presents with follicular, conical, pinhead-sized papules covered with scales or horny plugs, and skin shows increasing sensitivity to any change of weather. In addition, lichen planus may need to be differentiated from candidiasis, aphthous ulcer, leucoplakia, scabies, pediculosis, and carcinoma.

Treatment

There is no satisfactory treatment available of the condition. Withdrawal of the drug or chemical, if reckoned to have any aetiological influence, is highly desirable.

Asymptomatic treatment may not require any form of treatment. Mild cases are treated with topical corticosteroids. Rarely severe form with erosive lesions and widespread severely pruritic skin lesions may occur and this sort of cases will require systemic corticosteroids. The patient may therefore be given prednisolone, 20-40 mg daily in divided doses orally and continued till clinical improvement is achieved, following which the dose is reduced gradually to an effective minimum maintenance dose. If administration of systemic corticosteroids poses any difficulty, the patient may then be given dapsone, 100 mg twice daily orally, even though the action of dapsone is quite slow. Much better result can however be achieved if both systemic corticosteroids and dapsone are given concurrently, and once the condition is controlled, treatment with dapsone is continued alone.

Localised lesions can be treated with coal tar lotion, X-ray or Granz ray.

The patient may also be given antihistamine, such as hydroxyzine, 25 mg at night orally increasing as necessary to 25 mg three or four times daily (children 6 months-6 years, 5-15 mg daily increased if necessary to 50 mg daily in divided doses; over 6 years, 15-25 mg daily increased if necessary to 50-100 mg daily in divided doses), or cyproheptadine, 4 mg three or four times daily orally (children 2-6 years, 2 mg; 7-14 years, 4 mg; both three times daily).

Actinic variety of the condition is however given through protection against sunlight exposure, covering the area with clothes. In addition, or alternatively, the patient is given topical application of sunscreen.

PITYRIASIS ROSEA

It is a mild inflammatory but self-limiting disorder of unknown origin.

It affects all ages but occurs more commonly in children and young adults.

Pathologically the condition shows nonspecific dermatitis. It produces epidermal oedema, moderate vascular dilatation, and infiltration with polymorphonuclear and round cells in the upper part of the corium. Epidermis shows acanthosis and parakeratosis, with intercellular and intracellular oedema.

Clinical Manifestations

The condition begins abruptly with no or little constitutional symptoms, such as malaise, headache, mild fever and lymphadenopathy. Generally a single, well-defined, red, patchy lesion (herald patch), covered with scaling develops. Following this the characteristic generalised lesions develop as nonconfluent, oval or circular, erythematous, macules or papules on the trunk (Fig. 3.10). The lesions show depression at the centres, surrounded by more prominent and pink borders. The lesions show a characteristic distribution with the long axes of the ovals lying parallel to each other along the rib lines. The lesions may also occur on the proximal extremities, sides of the neck and, occasionally, on the face. Sometimes however the lesions may develop with papular variety only (Fig. 3.11).

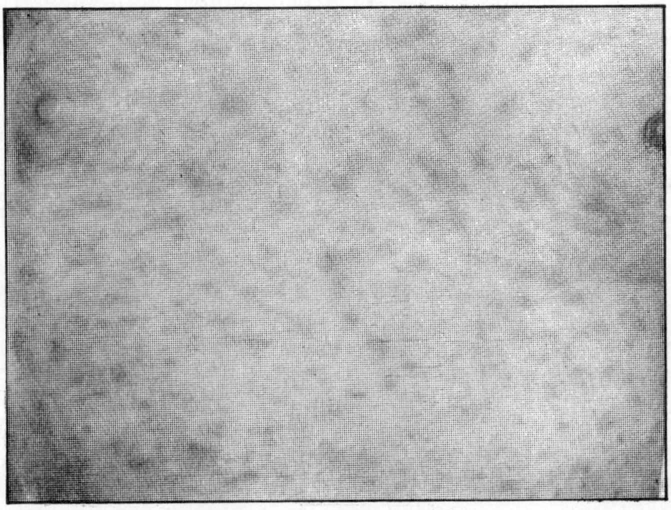

Figure 3.10. Pityriasis rosea.

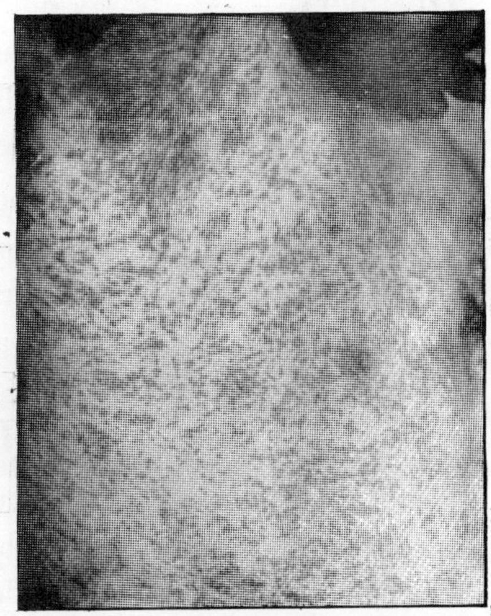

Figure 3.11. Papular type of pityriasis rosea.

The condition does not give rise top any subjective symptom except pruritus which is usually mild but may occasionally also be troublesome.

The condition is self-limiting, and the lesions begin to peel within a few days. Spontaneous remission of the condition is therefore common after a few weeks, usually within 1 to 6 weeks. Recurrence of the condition is quite rare.

Diagnosis

The condition is diagnosed on clinical grounds. The characteristic lesions and their sudden onset with herald patch ease the diagnosis with confidence.

The condition is differentiated from seborrhoeic dermatitis in which there is no onset with herald patch, nor is the condition self-limiting, while the lesions show greasy scales; from drug eruptions or allergy where there is a history of exposure to the offending drug; and from pityriasis versicolor in which the thick-walled budding spores and short bent hyphae can be demonstrated from the lesions. Tinea corporis is differentiated for having lesions with acute vesiculated margins and healing scaly centres can be identified in the scrapings of the lesions. The condition may also need to be differentiated from syphilis which gives rise to symptoms and signs of syphilis and a suspected history of sexual contact with positive serological tests for syphilis. At times psoriasis may also cause certain amount of confusion but the condition presents with well-demarcated lesions covered with greyish-white or silvery-white scales, which when removed on pressure leave tiny bleeding points on the base.

Treatment

The condition does not require any form of treatment except psychological assurance. The patient needs to appreciate the self-limiting nature of the condition. Exposure of the lesions to sunlight or ultraviolet light is beneficial.

Yet, if any form of treatment is required, the inflamed and itching lesions are given topical application of a soothing lotion or coal tar lotion. In cases of troublesome itching, the patient may also be given antihistamine orally. Medication with corticosteroids, particularly its systemic use, is avoided unless situation warrants.

ERYTHEMA MULTIFORME

Aetiology of this condition with acute inflammatory eruption of skin and, occasionally, of mucous membrane is unknown. In some instances, it may however occur due to use of certain drugs (for example, sulphonamides and salicylates) or due to systemic infection, malignant and chronic disease of internal organs, vaccination, and X-ray and from the use of certain drugs. The condition is usually benign and self-limiting, but the acute form may be fatal. When the lesions appear as vesicles or bullae, it is then known as **erythema multiforme bullosum** but **erythema multiforme exudativum** when there is exudation.

It commonly develops in the temperate climate, with seasonal variation in the spring and autumn and usually affects the young adults. It is more common in men than in women.

Although the pathological changes of the condition depend upon the severity of the clinical features, in general, it show oedema of dermal papillae, swelling of collagen fibres, dilatation of vessels, and perivascular infiltration with lymphocytes and, also, a few polymorphonuclear leucocytes and eosinophils. In addition, there may be spongiosis and intraepidermal oedema, or vesicle and bullae formation.

Stevens-Johnson syndrome is an acute but rare form of the condition. In some cases the condition may develop due to certain diseases and malignancy, systemic infection, drug reaction and vaccination, and perhaps results as a hypersensitivity reaction.

Clinical Manifestations

The condition begins suddenly with generalised, symmetrical eruptions, often arranged in concentric rings. The lesions are slightly raised; erythematous, flat-topped papules or oedematous macules, wheals, vesicles, or bullae, and the latter are surrounded by erythematous halo. The lesions appear on any part of the body, but usually on the distal part of the extremities, the face, and the neck (Fig. 312). Sometimes the lesions are urticarial, pustular or haemorrhagic. The lesions are multiple and polymorphic, and tend to spread to the periphery and to fuse together. The lesions may involve the entire body but when they develop on the hands and feet, they present with characteristic feature of dusky red coloured centres, which may be slightly depressed, and the lesions are surrounded by elevated erythematous rings (Fig. 3.13).

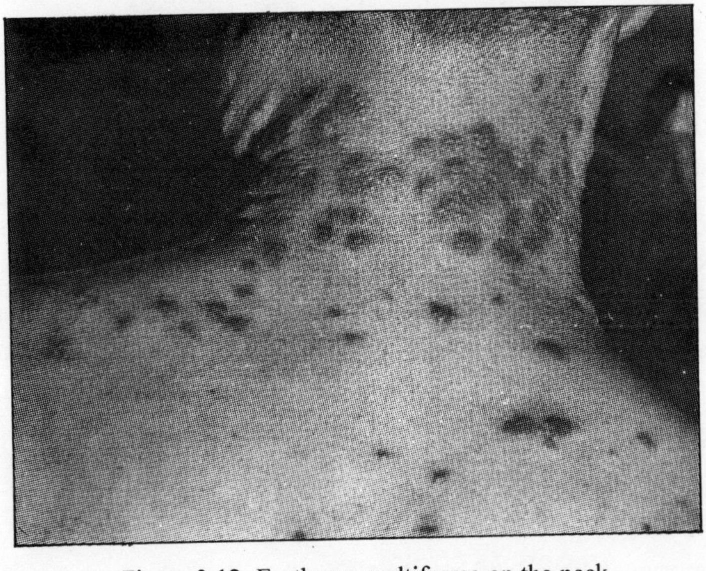

Figure 3.12. Erythema multiforme on the neck.

The lesions may be itching, burning sensations, soreness due to erosions of the mucous membrane lesions in the mouth, genitalia and eye, aches and pins, fever and malaise.

The condition may give rise to erosions, usually haemorrhagic, of the mucous membrane of the mouth, eye, and genitalia. These lesions may develop either independently or along with skin manifestations.

Otherwise, malaise, fever, joint pains, and occasionally, other constitutional symptoms manifest the condition. The lesions may cause itching and burning, and soreness of the oral and genital lesions.

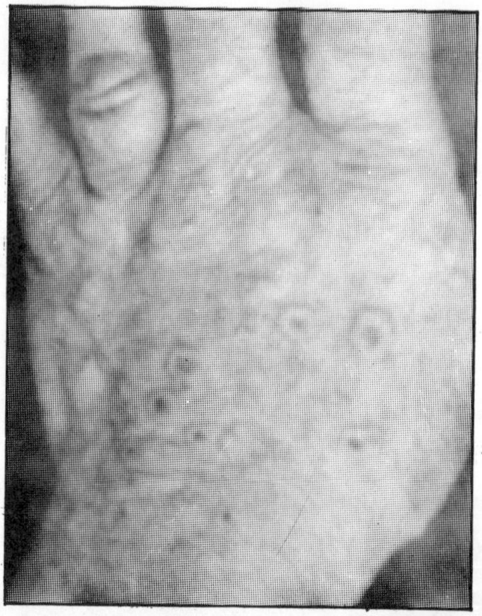

Figure 3.13. Erythema multiforme on the hand.

Generally the lesions develop within a few days and subside within a few weeks, usually 2 to 4 weeks. In others, the condition may however run a protracted course.

Sometimes however the condition may present with discrete or grouped vesicles or tense bullae, surrounded by erythematous rings. This variety is the condition is known as **erythema multiforme bullosum** (Fig. 3.14). **Bullous pemphigoid** is a variant of chronic erythema multiforme bullosum and generally affects the elderly people. This variety is characterised by the formation of large, tense bullae, usually on the groins, lower abdomen, thighs, flexure surfaces of the upper extremity and axillae. The lesions generally remain localised for some time and then may become widespread. Buccal involvement is however rare. The bulla finally ruptures and heals quickly leaving no scarring.

The acute and severe form of the condition is known as ***Stevens-Johnson syndrome***. It is however an extremely case nowadays. Yet, when it develops, it begins suddenly with extensive bullae formation, high fever and prostration, and may occasionally be even fatal. There are bullae on the skin and ulceration on the anogenital region. It also produces blisters and erosions in the oral cavity, causing stomatitis and difficulties in swallowing, chewing or eating. It frequently affects the conjunctivae, giving rise to conjunctivitis with swelling and pus. The eruptions also produce ulcerations in the urethra and respiratory tract.

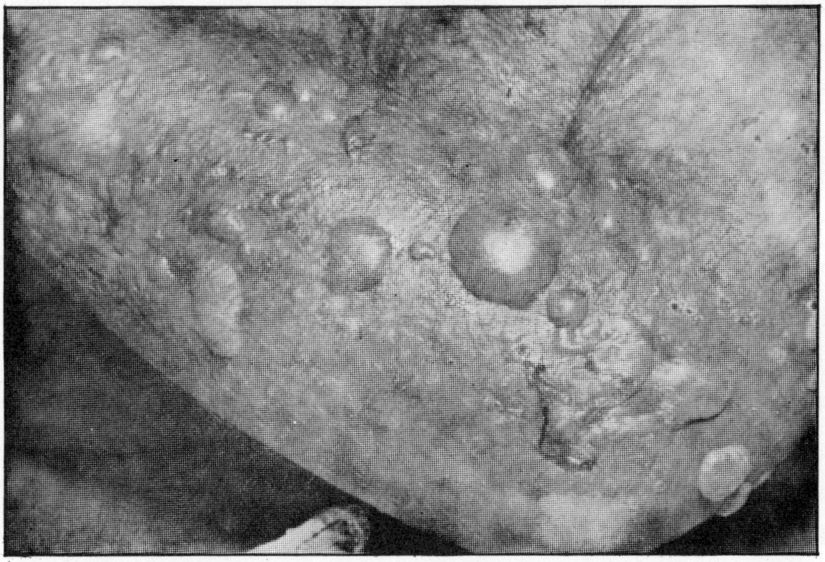

Figure 3.14. Erythema multiforme bullosum.

The condition can cause systemic involvement of the internal organs as complication.

Diagnosis

It is diagnosed on clinical grounds.

Skin lesions of the condition is differentiated from systemic lupus erythematosus which presents with 'butterfly' eruptions on the face and frequently involves multisystem of the body; from discoid lupus erythematosus which presents with localised erythematous plaques covered with adherent scales and produces horny follicular plugging and scarring; from pemphigus which gives rise to positive Nikolsky's sign (is called positive when rubbing off causes easily detached epidermis from the underlying skin) and Tzanck test (altered epithelial cells disruption of intercellular connections in the smear from the base of a bulla or of vesicle scraping); and from pemphigoid which does not give rise to any symptom and shows recurrences. Dermatitis herpetiformis is however differentiated for having clusters of polymorphic rash with marked itching, which may even cause insomnia and nervousness.

The mucosal lesions are differentiated from secondary syphilis, allergic stomatitis, herpetic stomatitis and pemphigus.

Treatment

In the management of the condition removal or adequate control or appropriate treatment of the causative factor, where known, requires prompt attention.

There is however no known therapy of the condition. The patient is therefore given supportive treatment as required. Mild cases may not require any medical support but otherwise the patients are given relief with application of soothing agent. Oral antihistamine, such as chlorpheniramine, 4 mg every four to six hours, promethazine, 10-25 mg two or three times daily, or cyproheptadine, 4 mg three or four times daily.

Other cases are treated with corticosteroids, such as prednisolone. In severe cases it is given at 60-80 mg daily in divided doses orally but if no satisfactory clinical improvement is achieved, the dose is increased by 20 mg, and once the condition is controlled the dose of prednisolone is tapered off gradually so as to be withdrawn within another fortnight.

The patient is given appropriate antibiotic, in cases of secondary bacterial infection.

In *Stevens-Johnson syndrome* beneficial effect may achieve from administration of corticosteroids, such as prednisolone, 10 mg three times daily orally. In addition, the patient is also given antibiotics such as erythromycin or amoxycillin, 250-500 mg six to eight hourly.

TOXIC EPIDERMAL NECROLYSIS

It is an acute but rare life-threatening dermatological disorder and is characterised by rapid subepidermal blebbing and exfoliation of skin. The aetiology of its development is not known precisely known. In a large number of cases its development may be related to severe type of drug allergy due to a wide variety of drugs, such as sulphonamides, penicillin, non-steroidal anti-inflammatory drugs (NSAIDs), barbiturates, phenytoin, allopurinol and many more, while in others it follows during the medication for severe type of internal disease. In other instances the development of the condition is idiopathic.

It can affect any man and woman of any age.

Presumably it is variant of erythema multiforme that results diffuse necrosis and sloughing of cutaneous and mucosal epithelial surfaces. Histopathologically the early lesions show superficial, perivascular, lymphocytic infiltration. Later, there is upward migration of lymphocytes, causing discrete and confluent zone of epidermal necrosis with concomitant blister formation. Finally there is epidermal sloughing, leading to formation of shallow erosions.

Clinical Manifestations

Typically the condition begins with localised erythema, which is painful and disseminates rapidly. Soon flaccid blisters develop over the erythema or the epidermis peels off that analogue to an extensive third degree burn. The patient complains of chills, malaise, fever, and other constitutional symptoms. Within 24 to 72 hours there is diffuse necrosis and sloughing of cutaneous as well as of mucosal epithelial surface and the patient appears gravely ill.

Case fatality develops due to infection, and fluid and electrolyte imbalance.

Diagnosis

Diagnosis of the condition is made on clinical grounds.

It is however differentiated from erythema multiforme, drug allergy, Stevens-Johnson syndrome and, in children, from staphylococcal scalded skin syndrome.

Treatment

The patients should be hospitalised immediately for better care, management and observation. All kind of medication that is used by the patient should be withdrawn instantly. The affected areas are treated as per schedule specified under extensive burn. If there is septicaemia, appropriate care is taken accordingly.

Oral corticosteroids may be helpful in cases when the condition develops due to drug allergy. Otherwise, the patient is given parenteral administration of corticosteroids, for example methylprednisolone, 500 mg-1 g daily by IV injection and continued till the control of the condition.

ERYTHEMA NODOSUM

It is an inflammatory reaction of the dermis and subcutaneous tissue. Perhaps the condition occurs as a secondary manifestation of an underlying systemic disease due to infection, such as streptococcal infection, systemic fungal infection, sarcoidosis, tuberculosis, leprosy, or of certain drugs, such as sulphonamide and dapsone.

It occurs at all ages but rare in early childhood and in the elderly persons. It is however more common in young women.

It produces oedema and panarteritis in the corium with dense infiltration of polymorphonuclear leucocytes, histiocytes, occasional eosinophils and plasma cells. There is swelling of the epidermal cells of some blood vessels.

Clinical Manifestations

Prior to the development of skin lesions the patient usually presents with fever, malaise, aches and pains. Following this several nodules appears in crops usually over the anterior surface of the legs. The lesions may however also develop on the extensor surface of the forearms, on the thighs and, very occasionally, on the trunk and the face. The nodules are red, hot, tender, usually discrete, and multiple, distributed symmetrically. Size of the individual nodule may vary between 1 and 10 cm in diameter, and may even coalesce together. Skin over the nodules is smooth and shiny, and appears stretched. Sometimes the nodules may fluctuate but they do not suppurate, nor cause any ulceration. Lesions may last for about 6 weeks and resolve without scarring.

The condition however causes recurrences.

Diagnosis

History of underlying condition is available. Diagnosis of the condition is however comparatively easy but needs a thorough search for identification of the underlying disorders. Biopsy of skin is helpful for diagnosis.

Blood shows raised ESR.

It is differentiated from erythema induratum, which gives raise to lesions occurring on the posterior surface of the legs and the lesions show ulcerations; from nodular vasculitis, which produces pruritic lesions on the calves; and from syphilitic gumma, which shows unilateral involvement with positive STS. Cutaneous rheumatic nodules are differentiated for having entirely different clinical features. Erysipelas is differentiated for having unilateral distribution of the lesions, while the causative organism may be identified. Cellulitis is differentiated for involving deeper tissues and presenting the lesions with diffuse borders, frequently accompanying lymphangitis and regional lymphadenopathy.

Treatment

As the condition by itself has no clinical entity, nor is reckoned as to be a disease process, but a secondary manifestation of another disease pattern, no treatment is available for the development of the erythema nodosum. Specific is therefore aimed for the treatment and control of the underlying condition responsible for producing the lesions.

However some treatment may be given for symptomatic relief.

The patient is given analgesic, aspirin, 300-900 mg four times daily orally, for the relief of aches and pains. Ampicillin, 250 mg every six hours or other appropriate antibiotics re given for the control of infection. Oral corticosteroids appear extremely beneficial in the management, and the patients are given prednisolone, 20-30 mg daily divided doses orally, or dexamethasone, 0.5-1 mg three times daily orally.

ACNE VULGARIS

The condition is also popularly known as acne and pimples, and appears to be extremely common dermatological condition that most people very often encounter with. Aetiology of the condition is however not known. The condition represents chronic inflammatory disorder of the pilosebaceous follicles but how the lesions are produced is far from clear. There however exists several theories based on the intensive investigations, some appear even convincing, and yet nothing could establish the facts conclusively. From the investigations the basic cause of its development appears to be the activation of the sebaceous glands at the time of puberty. It is also suggested that enlarged and hyperactive sebaceous glands show leakage and thus, pour fat into the perifollicular regions when an inflammatory process is induced, resulting development of papules that may later change to pustules. Similarly, hormonal imbalance, particularly sex hormones, may play a significant part in its development. On the other hand, the condition may be induced from consumption of oral corticosteroids, or from heavy use of cosmetics or pomades can also produce the condition, while it may be the presenting manifestation of Cushing's syndrome.

Acne is a disorder of adolescents, and is more common in males than in females. Some cases may however develop in females in their mid-30s.

Pathological changes are brought over from the obstruction of the pilocebaceous duct, which leads to abnormal microbial activity, resulting intrafollicular hyperkeratosis, follicular and perifollicular inflammation with polymorphonuclear leucocytes, round cells and giant cells. Keratin plug when seals of the pilosebaceous orifice, causing extrusion of the plug and forming open comedone (blackhead), or may fail to dilate when the expanding plug may rupture the wall of the pilosebaceous duct (closed comedone, whitehead). Later, retention of sebaceous material and dilatation of the follicles lead to the formation of the cyst. In severe cases, the sebaceous glands may be partly or completely destroyed. In pustular cases, there are abscesses surrounded by dense inflammatory exudate of polymorphonuclear leucocytes and lymphocytes. Resolution of inflammation causes regeneration of the pilosebaceous duct.

Clinical Manifestations

It presents with lesions (Fig. 3.15) occurring chiefly on the cheeks, forehead, chin, nose, and temporal regions and, in severe cases, on the shoulders, back or upper chest. There may be open comedones (blackhead), closed comedones (whitehead), inflammatory papules, and pustules containing yellowish or whitish pus. In some cases, however, there may be inflamed nodules and deep granulomatous infiltration, pus-filled cysts, scars and keloids. Severe form of the cases may give rise to irregular shaped depressed areas due to scarring. Otherwise, there may be no symptom, or the patient may complain of mild soreness, pain or itching, and varieties of emotional disturbances, including embarrassment. Most commonly however there may be worsening of the condition just before the menses due to cyclic activity in the females.

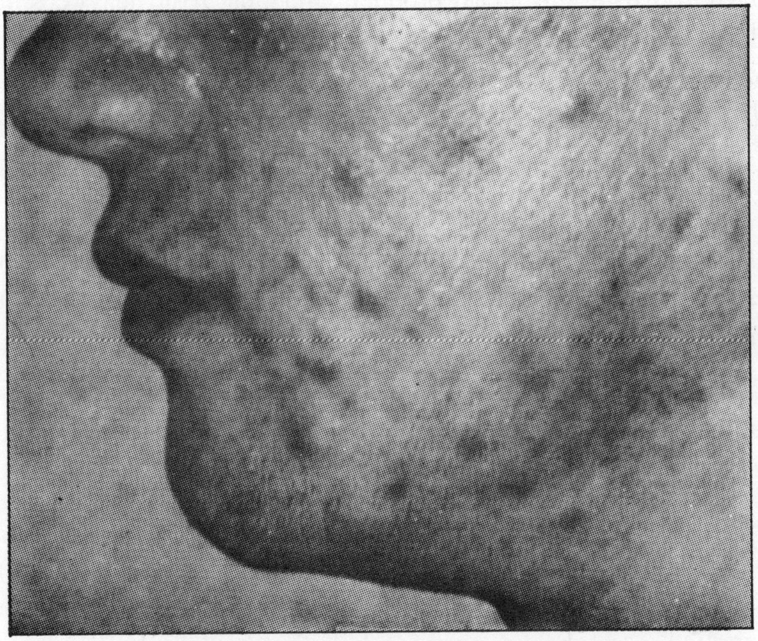

Figure. 3.15. Mild form of acne vulgaris

In severe cases there may be irregular shaped depressed scars due to scarring, and may cause systemic upset and polyarthralgia in its acute stage.

Sometimes, though rarely, the acne lesions may assume large size in the form of papules and pustules, with large indolent abscess, cyst and connecting sinuses (**acne conglobata**), and cause considerable tissue destruction. The lesions however heal slowly, leaving hypertrophic scars.

In addition, much scarring of the affected area may develop due to neurotic habit of picking at the lesions and squeezing out the blackheads. When this type of scarring occurs in ordinary acne vulgaris cases, the lesions are then referred as **acne excoriee**.

Varieties of stimuli, mostly from drugs, can sometimes produce the lesions, which may resemble acne. This lesion is then referred as **acneform eruptions**.

Scarring, disfigurement and psychological trauma are its usual complications.

Diagnosis

It is always diagnosed on clinical grounds.

It may be differentiated from other acneform lesions produced by some chemicals and drugs.

Treatment

Management of the condition is however tricky and may take quite a long time. The patient is strongly prohibited from using any greasy products, and must avoid heavy cosmetics. Cleanliness of the affected area plays a significant role in its cure and prevention. The affected area is therefore washed rigorously with plenty water. Use of any non-abrasive toilet soap may appear beneficial in cleaning the area. Ordinary hair shampoo, particularly lemon, can do much better trick. Rubbing of lemon over the affected area may also be beneficial, more so in the oily type of skin.

Management of the condition principally requires psychological confidence and assurance. Every effort is made so as to make the patient appreciate that the condition is a natural phenomenon, and self-limiting. Unless undue picking or squeezing is done, the condition is moderately benign.

Large comedones may be removed mechanically using the forceps, and cysts are opened and drained.

Mild cases may not require any medical therapy. Otherwise, mild and moderate cases with open and closed comedones, and a few papules and pustules are effectively treated with topical comedolytic agent of vitamin A derivatives, such as isotretinoin, 0.05% gel, or tretinoin, 0.02% cream, applied sparingly once or twice daily for 6 to 8 weeks, or adapalene, 0.1% gel or cream, apply thin film once daily at bedtime after washing and drying the affected area and reassess after 3 months. Resorcinol, 2%, along with sulphur, 8%, cream is also effective and is applied sparingly once daily. Otherwise, the patients are treated with potent bacteriostatic and comedolytic agent, benzoyl peroxide, 2.5%-10% gel, cream or lotion, applied once or twice daily, starting from weak concentration and progress to the higher concentration, as required.

Salicylic acid is also effective and is given as 2% solution lather in warm water and then massage onto the skin two or three times daily, and then rinse. Azelaic acid, 20% cream, applied gently but thoroughly massaged into the affected areas twice daily, in the morning and evening, is also effective. However, when the condition is accompanied by inflammation, treatment may be given with topical preparation of benzoyl peroxide with potassium hydroxyquinoline sulphate or antibiotic. Topical antibiotics, such as tetracycline, erythromycin, or clindamycin, though frequently used with varying success but benzoyl peroxide appears to be more potent.

Moderate cases may require treatment with topical application. Severe cases are usually treated with both topical agents and systemic corticosteroids. Very severe cases may however require vitamin A derivative, isotretinoin, 0.5 mg/kg of body-weight as a single dose or in two divided doses with food for 4 weeks, and adjust according to response in the range of 0.1-1 mg/kg body-weight daily for a further 8-12 weeks. Repeat of the treatment is not recommended.

In severe cases with pustules, cysts, nodules and scarring, the patient is given systemic antibiotic, such as tetracycline or erythromycin, 500 mg twice daily orally, and continued for 4 to 6 months, in addition to the topical therapy. Minocycline, 50 mg twice daily or 100 mg once daily for minimum 6 weeks, is also effective.

In women, moderate to severe cases refractory to prolonged oral antibiotic therapy are however treated with co-cyprindiol (a combination of ethyloestradiol, 35 μg, along with cyproterone acetate, 2 mg,), once daily orally for 21 days starting on the first day of cycle and repeated after an interval of 7 treatment-free days.

Systemic administration of vitamin A derivative, isotretinoin is extremely effective in very severe and nodulocystic cases and in cases that remained irresponsive to antibiotic therapy. It also prevents extensive scarring but has several side effects, including teratogenic effect. Hence, pregnancy must be excluded before starting the treatment, and the patients of childbearing potentials are given oral contraception for one month before, during, and for, at least, 4 weeks after therapy. In such a case isotretinoin is given as 0.5 mg per kg of body-weight daily as single or in two divided doses orally with meals for 4 weeks and then adjusted according to response to 0.1 mg/kg daily for a further 8 to 12 weeks. The drug is not however repeated.

Cysts may be operated and drained.

Better result can however be achieved when the treatment of moderate and severe cases are supplemented by a potent antibiotic, such as erythromycin, 500 mg twice daily orally, or tetracycline, 250 mg four times or 500 mg two times daily orally.

Emotional stresses will however require counselling and assurance.

Some patients may however occasionally require other form of treatment, such as ultraviolet radiation or plastic surgery.

ROSACEA

It is a chronic inflammatory disorder of skin and its aetiology is unknown. It is however related with hormonal effects on the sebaceous glands, and the condition perhaps develops due to hyperplasia and over activity of the sebaceous glands of the face. There are however several factors which can precipitate the development of the condition, and include excessive hot drinks, consumption of alcohol, gastrointestinal or menstrual disturbances, emotional disturbances, incorrect use of potent topical corticosteroids, and exposure to strong sunlight or to cold.

Although the condition can effect any age, it usually affects the middle-aged and elderly persons. It is more common in women than in men, and is often worse at menopause.

Histopathological changes the condition produce are vascular dilatation, low-grade inflammation, hypertrophy of sebaceous glands, and formation of fibrous connective tissue.

Clinical Manifestations

Characteristically the condition presents with localised lesions on the areas of the flush area of the face, involving the nose, cheeks, forehead and chin, but may also occasionally on the extremities, as recurrent episodes of erythema and hot flushes, which later become persistent with chronic dilatation of the superficial capillaries (telangiectasia). There may also be acneform papules or pustules, or hypertrophic nodules on the nose (**rhinophyma**). The lesions cause itching, soreness, burning or stinging.

The condition also produces several ocular manifestations, including the development of nonspecific keratitis.

It generally tends to improve after several years but otherwise, persists indefinitely unless it is suppressed by treatment.

Diagnosis

Diagnosis is made on clinical grounds. Red, shiny, papular or pustular areas on the forehead, cheeks, chin and nose is diagnostic.

It is differentiated from acne vulgaris that presents with comedones, involves younger age group of people and does not give rise to telangiectasia, while the lesions may also develop on the chest or back. Drug eruption is differentiated for having a history of exposure to an offending agent, while lupus erythematosus gives rise to infiltration and hyperkeratosis.

Treatment

Management of the condition requires certain restrictions and it is hopefully believed that imposition of such restrictions may not cause any amount of social inconvenience. Patients are therefore advised to restrict or avoid the aggravating factors of the condition, such as hot and spicy foods, strong tea, strong alcoholic beverages, and emotional stresses.

Topical application of a soothing lotion, such as calamine lotion, may be quite helpful. Even repeated cold water compression can be highly beneficial. Massage of the area with an astringent agent is equally effective. A mild tranquilliser, diazepam, 2-10 mg daily in divided doses orally, may also be given to allay tension.

Severe case is treated with tetracycline, which appears to be the drug of choice. It is given at 500 mg twelve hourly orally for 1-3 months and the dose is then reduced and continued over the subsequent 2 to 3 months. Other alternative drugs are erythromycin, minocycline, co-trimoxazole, and metronidazole. The patient may be given topical treatment with metronidazole, 0.75% gel or 1% cream, to be applied as thin film twice daily for up to 8-9 weeks or longer (children, not recommended). Cream of sulphur and salicylic acid is also effective as topical application. Topical corticosteroids are best avoided but hydrocortisone may be helpful in cases of pruritus.

Within a few months the erythema subsides and the patient shows improvement. If however this does not happen, the patient is given repeated course of treatment with systemic antimicrobial agents.

A substantial proportion of cases relapse within 2 years and require further course of treatment, while a small proportion of cases may need indefinite maintenance therapy.

Telangiectasias are treated with superficial electro-dissection or by freezing with CO_2 snow under moderate pressure.

Radiotherapy is of value in resistant cases and for the hypertrophic nodules on the nose.

URTICARIA

It is an acute or chronic allergic reaction of the dermis in which functional disturbances in cutaneous vessels results due to histamine release from dermal mast cells. This causes vascular dilatation and increased vascular permeability, and produces accumulation of plasma in the superficial connective tissue of the skin and development of urticarial lesions. This phenomenon is an immunological reaction of hypersensitivity of IgE type. Several allergens therefore give rise to the condition, including consumption of certain drugs, injection of sera and vaccine, ingestion of certain foods, use of preservatives, dyes or other food additives, insect stings or bites, and from physical factors such as exposure to excessive heat or cold, and psychological disturbances. It may also accompany several viral infections, such as rubella and viral hepatitis. In others, the cause may remain obscure.

Pathological changes the condition produce are swollen superficial layer of corium, oedema in the corium, wide separation of collagen fibres by oedema, widening of dermal papillae, flattening of rete pegs, proliferation of prickly cells, and enlargement of lymph spaces in the subpapillary zone.

Angio-oedema or **angioneurotic oedema** is however called when the condition develops involving large areas in subcutaneous structures and dermis with oedema.

Hereditary angio-oedema may be a variant of the condition and is inherited as an autosomal dominant trait and is associated with a deficiency of serum inhibitor of the activated first component of complement. There may no be any urticaria, and the oedema customarily univocal, indurated and painful.

Clinical Manifestations

The condition may be localised or generalised. There may be intense itching and a burning sensation, which may however be absent in some cases. This is followed by spontaneous eruptions of evanescent wheals or hives with rings of erythema and oedema. The erythema fades on pressure. The wheals may coalesce to form larger wheals. Crops of hives come and go. The eruptions are generalised but may also be localised, and are distributed symmetrically. In general, the lesions tend to develop on the covered areas of the body, such as trunk, buttocks and thighs. Most incidences are however acute and self-limiting, but a chronic form may also exist.

Severe cases may however be associated with headache, nausea, vomiting, and abdominal pain.

Most incidences of urticaria are acute but a chronic form of the condition may also exist. In fact, whenever urticaria persists over 3 or 4 weeks, it is reckoned as chronic urticaria. Hives may however be present constantly or intermittently during that time.

In *angio-oedema*, there is diffuse swelling in the loose subcutaneous tissue and dermis, usually of the eyelid, often associated with swelling of the lips or tongue. When it involves upper respiratory tract, there may be respiratory distress and stridor.

In hereditary angio-oedema attacks are often precipitated by trauma and viral infection, and are aggravated by emotional stress. It however often presents with gastrointestinal disturbances with nausea, vomiting, and abdominal pain, which may even mimic intestinal obstruction.

The condition can cause infection, laryngeal oedema, and pharyngeal oedema as complications. So hereditary angio-oedema may cause fatal upper airways obstruction.

The terms **dermatographism** is applied when even light stroking on the skin produces urticarial wheals, though there may not be any urticaria. This reaction can also be seen in a proportion of normal individuals. It is therefore not pathognomic for urticaria.

Diagnosis

The condition is diagnosed on clinical grounds.

In hereditary angio-oedema sometimes there may not be any family history. Measuring C4 makes diagnosis of it.

It is differentiated from contact dermatitis in which lesions occur on the exposed parts of the body, while the lesions are not wheals or hives but erythematous papular, macular or papulomacular, and there is always a history available on exposure of the offending agent.

Treatment

If the cause is known, that should be removed immediately preventing further exposure to the cause. If any drug is the cause of urticaria but avoidance to such a drug is not feasible, suitable alternative drug may be given instead.

Mild cases require no treatment, perhaps except local application of soothing agent and the condition subsides in them gradually. Other cases are treated with oral antihistamines, for example, promethazine, 10-25 mg two or three times daily (children: 2-5 years, 5-10 mg; 5-10 years, 10-25 mg twice daily), trimeprazine, 10 mg two to three times daily and increased up to 100 mg a day depending on the clinical response (children: over 2 years, 2.5-5 mg three or four times daily; elderly, 10 mg once or twice daily), or acrivastine, 8 mg three times daily (children not recommended). or. Other effective oral antihistamines are clemastine, 1 mg night and morning, or hydroxyzine hydrochloride, 25 mg at night increasing as necessary to 25 mg three or four times daily (children: 6 months-6 years, 5-15 mg at night increasing to maximum 50 mg daily In severe cases, oral antihistamine must precede by ingestible antihistamines, for example, promethazine, 25-50 mg by IM injection or in an emergency by slow IV injection after dilution, or chlorpheniramine, 10-20 mg by IM or SC injection.

Chronic idiopathic cases may be given antihistamine, loratadine, 10 mg once daily orally, or cetrizine, 10 mg daily or 5 mg twice daily (children 2-6 years, 5 mg daily or 2.5 mg twice daily).

The patient may also be given sedative, diazepam, 5-30 mg daily in divided doses orally.

In cases of severe reaction, a short course of systemic corticosteroids may be given, but otherwise, depending upon the severity of the condition, may also be given parenterally. In this respect prednisolone, 20-30 mg daily in divided doses orally, or dexamethasone, 8-40 mg by slow IV injection of infusion, may be given.

Angio-oedema is a very serious condition if laryngeal oedema is present. However, in cases of pharyngeal or laryngeal oedema, life threatening angio-oedema and anaphylactic shock, the patient is given oxygen inhalation, and adrenaline, 0.5-1 ml (infant under month, 0.05 ml; child 6 months-6 years, 0.12 ml; 6-12 years, 0.25 ml) of 1:1000 solution by IM or SC injection and 0,5 ml are repeated every six hours if necessary, followed by hydrocortisone, 50-100 mg by IV or IM injection and 50 mg may be repeated every six hours if necessary, and promethazine, 25-50 mg by deep IM or slow IV injection after dilution, and once the condition settles down, the patient is then given oral medication. More severe cases may however require tracheostomy and oxygen inhalation.

In many cases administration of systemic corticosteroids may appear unnecessary, and effective control of the condition can be achieved with antihistamine alone. Nevertheless, systemic corticosteroids have a special value in severe cases and in cases that developed due to IgG antibody mediated hypersensitivity. In such cases the patients are given prednisolone, 30-40 mg daily orally, or hydrocortisone, 50-100 mg by IV or IM injection and 50 mg repeated after every 6 hours, if needed.

In cases of pharyngeal or laryngeal angio-oedema and anaphylactic shock, the patient is given adrenaline, 0.5-1 ml of 1:1000 solutions, by IM or SC injection and 0.5 ml repeated every 20-30 minutes in severe cases, followed by injectable antihistamine and then followed by oral medication.

In addition, as emergency measure tracheal intubation and other measures should be taken into consideration instantly.

Specific desensitisation of the patient is also possible through administration of specific antigens.

Administration of C_1 esterase inhibitor (in fresh frozen plasma or in partially purified form) may terminate acute attacks of *hereditary angio-oedema*, but is not practical for long-term prophylaxis. The cases are therefore deal with as per angio-oedema, as detailed above.

In all cases intravenous administration of calcium and oral vitamin A may be found beneficial.

DRUG ALLERGY

Drug allergy or **drug eruptions** are a type II hypersensitivity reaction of skin produced by some drugs when applied topically or administered systemically. The long list of such offending agents includes amongst many more, such as antibiotics, sulphonamides, barbiturates, bromides, chlorothiazide, arsenic, gold, bismuth, all of which are well recognised. The hypersensitivity reaction therefore occurs from any drug in which case the drug may act as antigen or a hapten in the production of allergy.

Pathological changes the condition produce however depend upon the lesions it produce.

Clinical Manifestations

When the condition develops due to topical application of a drug, there may be worsening of the manifestations for which the drug has been used, or there may be formation of skin eruptions at the site of application. In general, the reactions may be variable and may give rise to varieties of urticarial, erythematous, exfoliative, eczematoid, bullous, pruritic or xanthomatous lesions in case of the condition develop from systemic administration of a drug. Otherwise, the allergic reaction may be manifested by photosensitivity, angio-oedema and anaphylactic shock.

On the other hand, Herxheimer reaction may develop following commencement o treatment with any potent trepenomacidal agent in cases of treponemal infection. In this condition development of both the subjective and the constitutional disturbances vary according to the severity of hypersensitivity in which the original lesions may be fiercely intensified and the skin eruption may become worse or be apparent for the first tie.

Diagnosis

Diagnosis of the condition is made on clinical grounds.

Its differentiation from other conditions does not usually pose any problem, more particularly as the condition is self-limiting. Drug allergy due to local application of a drug is easily revealed from careful history taking and the existence of some skin lesions to which a topical preparation of a drug has bee used.

Contact dermatitis may however sometimes cause confusion but it presents with localised lesions on the exposed part of the body, which has come in contact with the offending agent.

Treatment

Management of the condition requires immediate withdrawal of the offending drug and, if needed, substitution by other suitable non-offending drug.

In cases of Herxheimer reaction no withdrawal or substitution of the drug is ever required, rather the reaction is harmless and reckoned as a favourable sign of effective therapy, for which the reaction is also known as ***therapeutic shock***.

When the condition develops from topical application of a drug, the affected part is washed thoroughly with plenty water and soap. The patient is then given antihistamine, such as chlorpheniramine, 4 mg every four to six hours (maximum: 24 mg/day), or corticosteroids, for example, prednisolone, 20-40 mg daily in divided doses orally. Local reactions can also be effectively treated with topical corticosteroids.

When the condition develops from systemic administration of a drug and gives rise to urticarial lesions, the condition is treated with systemic antihistamines or corticosteroids.

Other cases are treated with systemic corticosteroids but acute or anaphylactic reactions are treated with parenteral preparation of corticosteroids.

In addition, the patients may be given supportive treatment, as required.

INSECT BITES AND STINGS

Bites and stings of a wide variety of insects can produce an allergic manifestation. The reaction may develop almost instantly or within a few hours, for example, from bites of bed bugs, or may develop after a prolonged time, for example, from the bites of the fleas.

Clinical Manifestations

It may give rise to just itching or burning, or may produce localised pruritic erythematous macules or wheals at the site of contact. In other instances, the reaction may be very severe and may give rise to anaphylactic shock, restlessness, generalised urticaria, and may even lead to dyspnoea, cyanosis and collapse.

Persistent scratching of the area may lead to secondary bacterial infection.

Diagnosis

It is made on clinical grounds.

Treatment

Many cases do not require any form of therapy, or just cool wet compression of application of calamine lotion may be sufficient. Otherwise, the patient is given antipruritic and antihistamine preparation, such as cream or lotion of calamine, diphenhydramine hydrochloride, applied locally three times a day.

The patient may be given antihistamines, such as chlorpheniramine, 4 mg every four to six hours orally. Systemic corticosteroids, such as prednisolone, 20-40 mg daily in divided doses orally, may also be extremely beneficial, and is given either alone or in association with antihistamine.

In cases of anaphylactic reaction, immediate measures are taken to combat the shock.

In cases of chronic exposure, applying insect repellents, such as diethyltoluamide, may protect the patients.

CHAPTER 4

Disorders due to Keratinisation and Collagen Defects

PSORIASIS

It is a common, chronic, recurrent, non-infectious disorder. The aetiology of the condition is unknown. In some cases, however, there may be a family history reflecting an autosomal dominant character. In others, trauma or irritation to the skin, hypocalcaemia, endocrine changes in puberty and menopause, streptococcal sore throat, stress, and consumption of certain drugs may trigger the formation of the lesions. Characteristically the condition undergoes spontaneous reemission and recurrences at varying intervals.

Although no age or sex is exempted, the condition commonly occurs between the ages of 10 and 40 years.

Pathological changes the condition produce are parakeratosis, thinning of subpapillary parts of the Malpighiii rete, elongation of rete ridges, clubbing of the papillary bodies, thickening of epidermis (acanthosis) and papillomatosis, dilatation and tortuosity of capillaries. There are perivascular infiltration with polymorphonuclear leucocytes and lymphocytes in the upper dermis, and formation of microabscesses of Monroe in stratum corneum or just beneath it.

Clinical Manifestations

Psoriatic lesions appear slowly but may also be very extensive, changing to exfoliative dermatitis, and may appear as a solitary spot or as innumerable patches. The lesions are sharply demarcated, slightly raised, plaques, and are covered with loosely adherent, greyish-white or silvery-white scales (Fig. 4.1). The size and shape of the lesions vary greatly, and the lesions may be small erythematous papules (guttate), coin-shaped or nummular (Fig. 4.2), or may be quite irregular shaped plaques but in severe cases, may give rise to generalised erythroderma. The lesions may extend peripherally and may coalesce to form large plaques (Fig. 4.3), to the extent that the size of the lesions grow extensively, giving rise to an appearance of geographical pattern (Fig. 4.4).

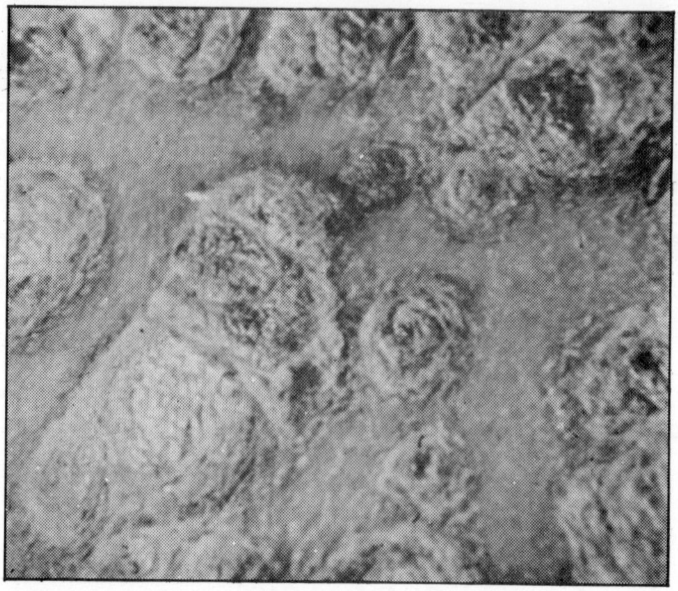

Figure 4.1. Psoriatic lesions (magnified).

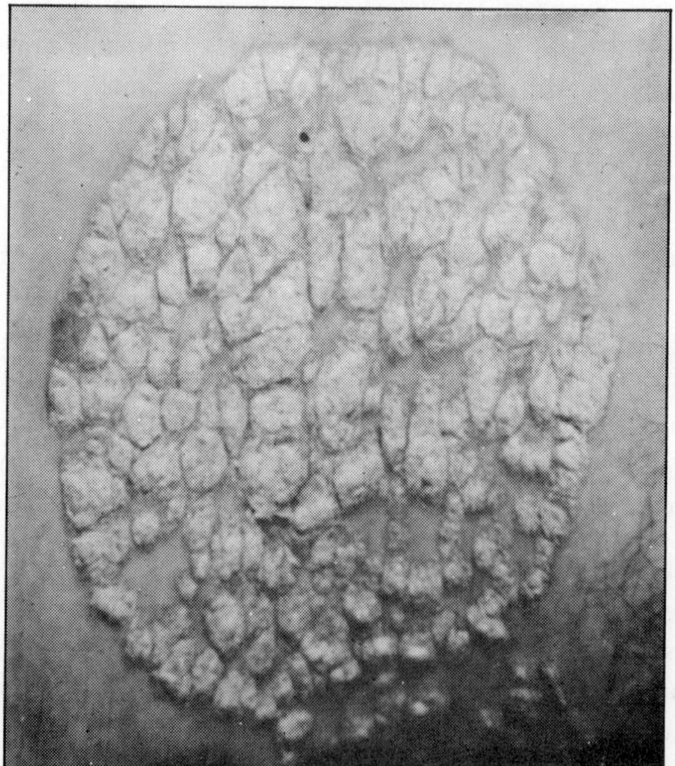

Figure 4.2. Nummular lesions of psoriasis (magnified)

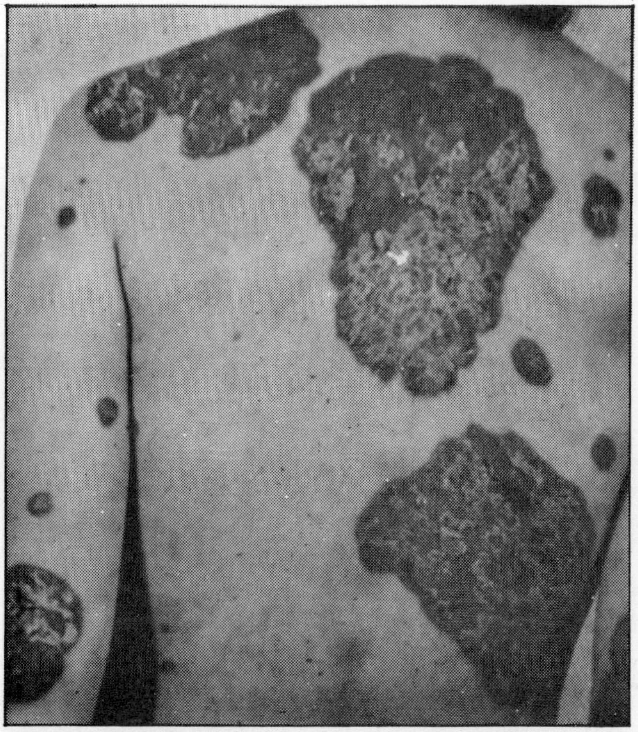

Figure 4.3. Large psoriatic lesions on the back.

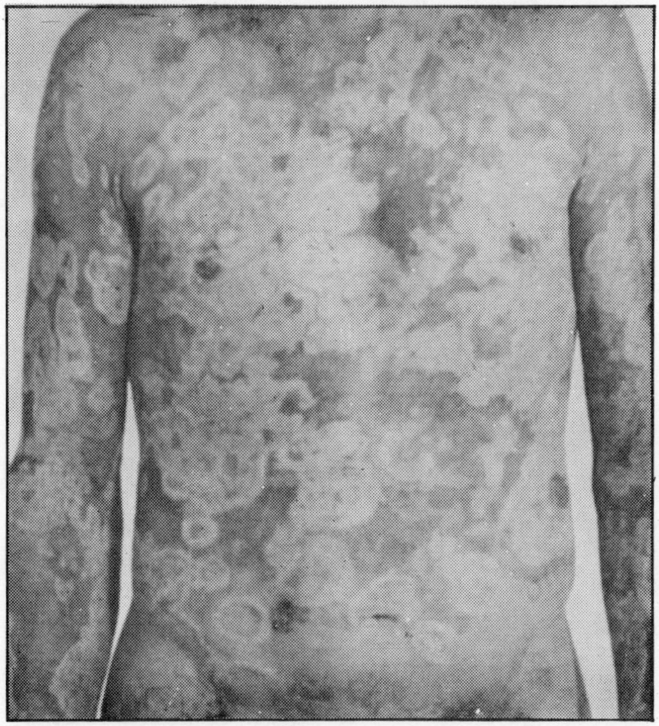

Figure 4.4. Geographical pattern of distribution of psoriasis.

The lesions may occur anywhere and all over the body but show a predilection for the extensor surfaces of the extremities, sacral region of the back, scalp and nail, and often on elbows and knees (Fig. 4.5). When the lesions develop on the back, they show an annular configuration over the upper back (Fig. 4.6). The lesions also involve the sides of the body.

Figure 4.5. Psoriasis on the knee.

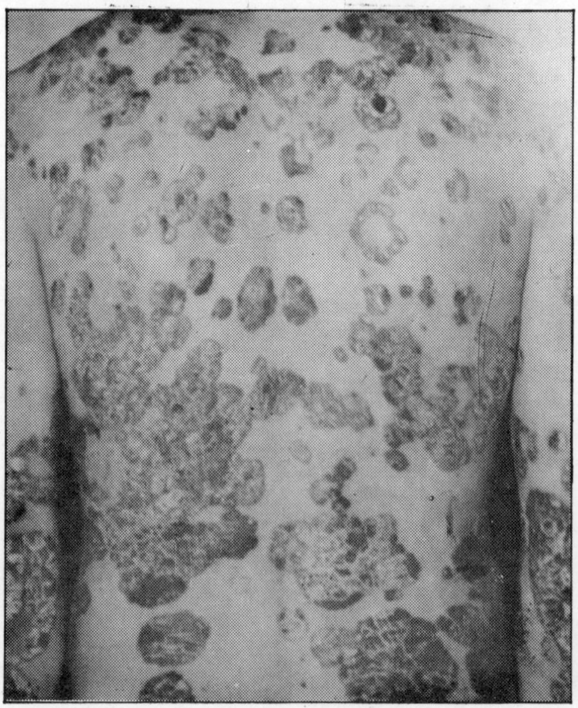

Figure 4.6. Psoriatic lesions showing annular configuration over the upper back.

Characteristically, psoriatic lesions are distributed symmetrically, and when the covering scales are removed on pressure, they leave multiple tiny (pinpoint) bleeding points over the base. Long standing cases however present with tough and thickened lesions covered with lamellae of scales. Psoriatic lesions are generally asymptomatic and only occasionally may give rise to itching and burning.

Scalp is often involved and the lesions present with thicker scaling than those are seen elsewhere on the body. The lesions are however do not involve the hair, nor cause their fall out. In scalp involvement, often there is an extension of erythema and scaling on the forehead, ears and retroauricular area.

Lesions on the palms and soles develop as hyperkeratotic and fissured patches with erythema. The lesions are usually sharply marginated but may not be scaly. They involve the palms more commonly than the soles. Pustular lesions are usually seen on the palms and soles.

In mild cases, the nails show pinpoint pitting but later stripling, cracking of free edges, lifting of nail plates from the bed (**onycholysis**), and thickening, brownish discoloration and irregularity of nail plate (**onychodystrophy**) on fingernails and toenails. The nail bed also becomes hyperkeratotic.

The lesions however do not involve the mucous membrane.

Psoriasis often runs a chronic course, with spontaneous remissions and exacerbations at extremely variable intervals.

There are a few clinical variants of the condition, classified upon the nature of the lesions.

In **guttate psoriasis** the skin eruptions develop as multiple, small, erythematous, macules or maculopapules. These eruptions are generally short-lived. It is more common in children than in adults, and often precipitated by group A β-haemolytic streptococcal infection.

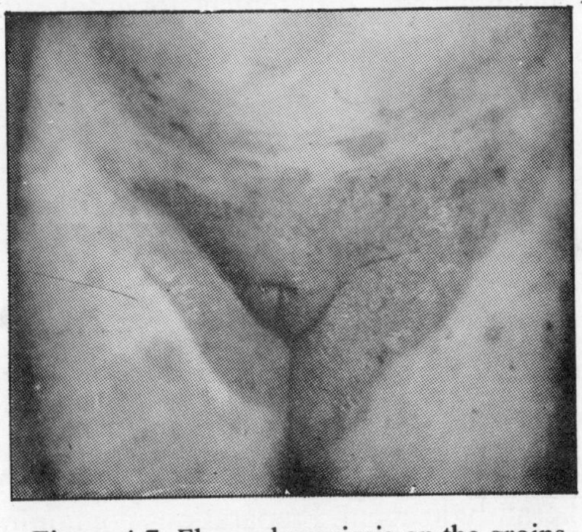

Figure 4.7. Flexural psoriasis on the groins.

Annular psoriasis is called when the lesions appear as ring-shaped circular area with central clearing (involution).

Pustular psoriasis gives rise to superficial pustules that may develop over the psoriatic plaques or on the normal skin.

Sometimes psoriatic lesions may develop on the flexures instead of the usual extensor surface. This variety is referred as **flexural psoriasis** and involves the axillae, groins (Fig. 4.7) and submammary folds. Unlike general psoriatic lesions the lesions in the flexural psoriasis are not dry and are less scaly.

Rarely, in a small proportion of cases rheumatoid-like arthritis may develop (**psoriasis arthropathica**). This affects the joints of the hands and feet, ankles, knees and sacroiliac joints. Unlike rheumatoid arthritis the cases show a positive antigen for HLA B27.

The condition produces chronicity with relapses.

Diagnosis

Characteristic appearance of the lesions makes the diagnosis easy. Köbner's phenomenon (a reaction in which any injury can produce a typical lesion at the site of trauma as it is seen in conditions, such as psoriasis, lichen planus, infected eczematoid dermatitis and verruca plana) can establish the diagnosis by producing typical lesions of the condition at the site where the trauma is made. Diagnosis of the condition can however be established from skin biopsy.

It is differentiated from atopic dermatitis which presents with itchy lesions with less well-defined margins and the lesions show predilection for flexural areas, from seborrhoeic dermatitis which produces little poorly defined lesions with greasy scales, from fungal infection in which the causative organisms can be isolated and identified, and from lichen planus which presents with severely itchy lesions covered with thick, hyperkeratotic scales which when removed forcibly do not leave bleeding bases. Discoid lupus erythematosus is differentiated for having atrophy, follicular plugging and different histopathological characteristics. Pityriasis rosea gives rise to lesions with slightly raised margins, which begin with herald patch and the condition, shows spontaneous remission but recur only very rarely. Secondary syphilis is differentiated for having a history of suspected sexual contact and of the presence of primary chancre, identification of causative organism from the lesions and positive serological tests for syphilis.

Treatment

No curative treatment of the condition is available. The treatment is therefore aimed at decreasing the cell turnover and the hyperkeratosis. It is evident that there is a peculiar tendency for which a particular efficient drug soon looses its efficacy. Most cases however respond well to local application of lubricating keratolytic agent. Preparations containing crude coal tar or dithranol in Laser's paste are also used with good benefit. In this regime patient's compliance is however poor because the drug causes serious stains on both skin and clothing. If the problem can be overcome and thus patient's compliance can be assured, the patient may be given the treatment with cream or lotion of dithranol, applied sparingly over the lesions once daily and then wash that off. The treatment is started initially with the weakest possible concentrations, for example, 0.1% and then washes off after 10 minutes. Gradually the strength of dithranol is increased and so the time of exposure so that the drug can be left for up to 30 minutes with 2% strength, or up to an hour with less strength, for example, 0.5%.

Ointment containing 3% salycylic acid and 6% benzoic acid, applied three to four times daily, may be beneficial. Similar benefit may be obtained from topical corticosteroids, such as betamethasone or triamcinolone, 0.1% cream or ointment applied two to four times daily, or clobetasol, 0.5% cream or ointment applied once or twice daily.

Coal tar is also effective and it is used as cream or lotion of various strength. It is applied liberally two to four times daily. Otherwise the patient is given topical application with preparation containing one or more elements of coal tar, ichthammol, wood tar and crude oil.

Vitamin D analogue, calcipotriol, can be given satisfactorily and unlike naturally occurring vitamin, it has less risk of hypercalcaemia and hypercalciuria. It is therefore given at 50 µg per g, applied sparingly twice daily for one or two weeks (maximum: 100 g a week) and then reduces the dose and continued for 6 to 8 weeks, also give good result. Some cases may however require maintenance with less frequent application. The ointment should not be used on face. It has however dose-related certain mild adverse reactions, which disappear following withdrawal of the ointment.

Vitamin A, given in large dose, is also beneficial, though the result may be inconsistent. Some cases may however respond well with vitamin A, etretinet, 30 mg daily orally for 2-4 weeks but severe cases may need 75 mg or more daily, and then maintenance at 30 mg per day for a further 6 to 8 weeks. Synthetic vitamin A, tazarotene, a water-based topical retinol gel, is also effective and can safely be used even on face. Although improvement with the drug is evident in most cases within 4-6 weeks, its beneficial effect is seen in as little as one week, with a relief lasting for up to 12 weeks. Tazarotene can however occasionally produce dose-related mild to moderate adverse reactions that disappear on reduction of the dose.

Patients inadequately responsive to usual therapy may be given etanercept 25-50 mg (for adults over 18 years) twice weekly by SC injection for up to 12 weeks then reduce to 25 mg twice weekly; max. treatment duration 24 weeks but discontinue if no response after 12 weeks.

More severe cases may however need ultraviolet radiation therapy or a therapy with cytotoxic drugs, such methotrexate, 30-40 mg daily in divided doses orally.

Scalp lesions are treated with similar preparations but in the form of shampoo, such as coal tar distillate to be used as shampoo one to three times in a week, and calcipotriol scalp solution for application twice daily in the morning and evening. Alternatively, a gel of dithranol and salicylic acid can be used and removed with shampoo after 10-20 minutes.

Nail lesions are however quite difficult to treat. Use of topical corticosteroids may be of some value in this situation. More resistant cases may be treated with systemic corticosteroids, in addition.

In cases of less satisfactory regression of the psoriatic lesions, the usual treatment may better be given under occlusive bandage.

Severe cases of refractory psoriasis may be treated with vitamin A derivative, acetretin, 25-30 mg daily for two to four weeks and then titrate against response up to maximum 75 mg daily. The usual maintenance dose is 25-30 mg daily, and the treatment is continued for 6 months.

In severe cases where standard treatment appears ineffective or inappropriate, the patient may then be given immunosuppressant, such as cyclosporin, initially 1.25 mg per kg of body-weight twice daily and, if needed, increased after one month gradually up to maximum 5 mg per kg/body-weight daily, but discontinued if ineffective within 6 weeks with the maximum dose.

Nonspecific treatment, such as intravenous administration of calcium and oral vitamin A, is sometimes found quite beneficial in decreasing the cell turnover and hyperkeratoses.

In cases of psoriasis arthropathica the patient is given non-steroidal anti-inflammatory drugs, such as ibuprofen, 600 mg twice daily orally. Some authors also suggest that a treatment with psoralen, for example, ammoidine, followed by exposure to sunlight or ultraviolet light may be quite effective.

PARAPSORIASIS

It is a chronic condition of erythrodermic or scaly maculopapular dermatoses of unknown origin. The term parapsoriasis is however applied loosely to include several uncommon dermatoses,

The condition generally occurs during the fifth decade of life, and is more common in men tan in women.

Histopathological changes that are evident in this condition are nonspecific. There are however parakeratosis and acanthosis of the epidermis, and infiltration with monocytes and, occasionally, with eosinophils. In other cases there may not be any parakeratosis but hyperkeratosis.

Clinical Manifestations

The condition presents with erythematous, slightly elevated, sharply marginated, flat-topped, papules or plaques (Fig. 4.8), with scanty scaling anywhere on the body but usually show a predilection for the trunk, thighs, arms, and sides of the neck. The lesions however never involve the face and the scalp. In other cases, the lesions present as macules, papules and even vesicles with crusting, necrosis and haemorrhage. Sometimes there may also be generalised lymphadenopathy. The condition does not give rise to any subjective symptom but in some, there may be mild constitutional symptoms.

The condition persists for years with remission and occasional exacerbations.

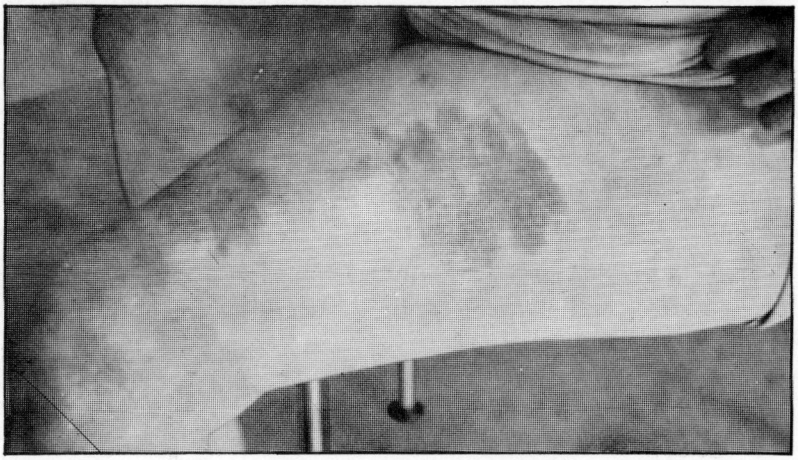

Figure 4.8. Parapsoriasis.

Diagnosis

Clinical diagnosis of the condition is often sufficient. Biopsy of skin can however confirm the diagnosis.

It may however at times need to be differentiated from psoriasis, lichen planus, seborrhoeic dermatitis, mycosis fungoides, and secondary syphilis.

Treatment

No effective therapy of the condition is available. Acute cases are however treated with ultraviolet radiation. Topical application of keratolytic agent, such as coal tar solution with tar and salicylic acid, has beneficial affect and may be massaged onto the area twice daily. Some cases may respond well with tetracycline, 250 mg every six hours orally. In other cases, systemic or topical corticosteroids may be given.

PITYRIASIS RUBRA PILARIS

Pityriasis rubra pilaris is a rare but chronic dermatological disorder. It is however suggested that there may be an inherited metabolic disorder, which perhaps acts as an underlying cause.

The condition becomes worse in summer.

Pathological changes it produces show hyperkeratosis, acanthosis, formation of keratotic follicular plugs, and perhaps patchy parakeratosis around the hair follicles in the epidermis. In general, there are dilatation of the blood vessels and infiltration with round cells and occasional mast and plasma cells.

Clinical Manifestations

It presents with follicular, conical, pinhead sized, papules covered with scales or horny plugs, and erythema. The lesions show predilection for the sides of the neck, trunk and extremities, particularly the dorsal aspects of the hands and fingers. Sometimes however more lesions appear which may involve any part of the body or may even involve the entire body surface. Scalp is diffusely involved. The lesions are initially diffuse, distributed symmetrically, and the skin between the patches appears normal. Much later, generalised erythema and scaling develop. Skin looks glazed and atrophic with increasing sensitivity to any change in weather. The lesions on the palms and soles present with hyperkeratosis and fissuring. Nails are rough, thickened and striated, which may crack or break. The condition is asymptomatic except of varying degree of pruritus.

The lesions may persist for years or disappear spontaneously.

Diagnosis

It is diagnosed on clinical grounds.

The condition is differentiated from psoriasis and lichen planus. Although the latter may pose no problem, clinical differentiation with the former is often difficult.

Treatment

The patient is given soothing compression with normal saline or potassium permanganate solution. Compressions with cold water are also soothing. The patient is given oral antihistamine for the relief of pruritus, in addition.

The patient is also usually given large doses of vitamin A for specific therapy purposes. Other cases may need systemic administration of corticosteroids and supplement of thyroid.

PALMO-PLANTAR KERATODERMA

The condition is also known as **keratosis palmaris et plantaris**, and is a congenital or acquired disorder of keratotic thickening of the palms and soles. It is often a familial disorder showing both autosomal dominant and recessive types. Acquired variety develops from constant pressure and friction, and may develop as an occupational hazard in certain occupations. The condition may also develop in association with ichthyosis and other congenital anomalies.

In pathological changes the condition presents with epidermal horny layers in the palms and soles show marked thickening.

Clinical Manifestations

The whole or part of the palms and soles (Fig. 4.9) show heavy thickening, distributed symmetrically. The surface of the lesions appears smooth, pitted or verrucous. The arch of the soles is however spared. Otherwise, the lesions develop with uniform thickening and end abruptly at the periphery of the palms (Fig. 4.10). In addition, there may be erythema, fissures, and hyperhidrosis. Nails may also become thickened, opaque, and malformed.

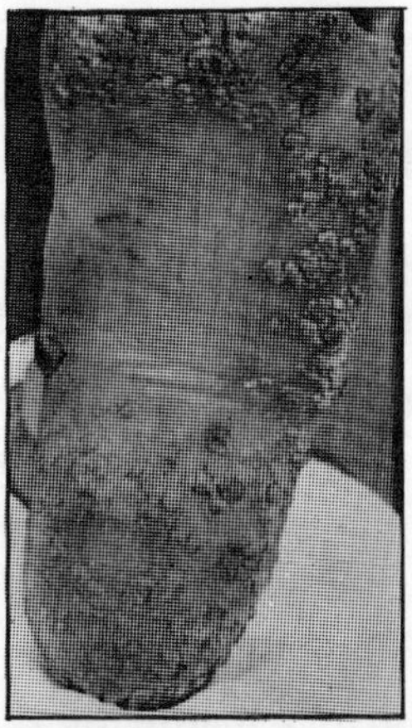

Figure 4.9. Palmo-plantar keratoderma showing lesions on the foot.

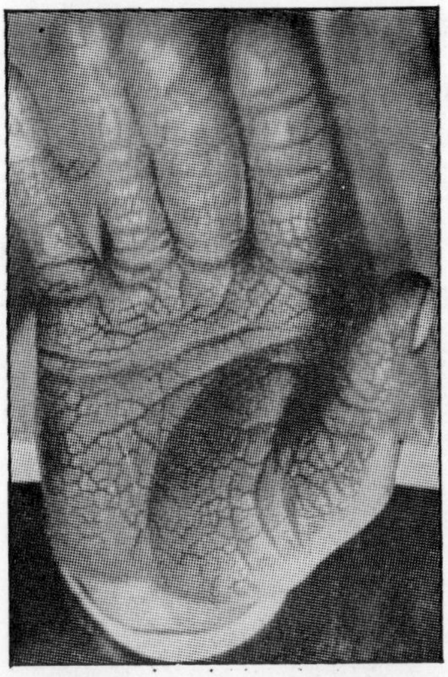

Figure 4.10. Palmo-plantar keratoderma showing lesions of the palm.

Diagnosis

Although clinical presentation of the conditions is highly suggestive, diagnosis is however made on skin biopsy.

Treatment

The lesions are treated with daily application of keratolytic agent such as 40% urea or 10% salicylic acid. Otherwise, the application is made under occlusive bandage and renewed after a few days.

The patient is also given vitamin A derivative, etrotinate, 0.75 mg per kg of body-weight daily in divided doses orally and adjusted according to response, or acitretin, 25-30 mg daily orally for two to four weeks and titrated against response.

Some patients may however benefit well with Granz ray therapy.

ICHTHYOSIS

It is a hereditary disorder that usually occurs during birth but the clinical features may be delayed to early childhood. When the condition develops in a mild form, it is then known as **xeroderma.**

Pathological changes include absence of granular layer, homogenous horny layer directly from the rete, and thickened epidermis and collagen. There is reduction of sebaceous and sweat glands, dilatation and horny plugging of the follicles, and cellular infiltration.

Clinical Manifestations

It presents with dirty looking, brownish, dry scaling on skin, and has a few recognised clinical variants.

Ichthyosis vulgaris or **autosomal dominant ichthyosis** is the commonest variety. In this the lesions do not usually appear at birth but develop during the first year of life. The lesions present with fine scaling, usually affecting the extensor surfaces of the limbs and on the trunk. It can also affect the whole body surface but spare the antecubital and popliteal fossae and other flexural areas. Hyperkeratosis causes exaggerated creases and thickening of the palms and soles. Plugged follicles (**keratosis pilaris**) are common, especially over the upper arms and thighs. The lesions become worse in winter. When the patient attains puberty, the lesions may show some improvement but otherwise persist for life. The patient however does not complain for any other symptom.

X-linked ichthyosis is transmitted by the females but manifested by the males. The lesions usually appear during the first year of life, and resemble ichthyosis vulgaris in many respects. It gives rise to profuse keratinisation and the scales may be fine or large and dark. The lesions however do not spare the flexural parts of the body, and there is no plugging of the follicles or hyperkeratosis of the palms and soles. The patient usually develops asymptomatic cornel opacity by the age of 30 years.

In **lamellar ichthyosis** the clinical features are present at birth, and begins with diffuse erythema and scaling that also involve the flexural areas of the body. Most of the body surface shows large and coarse scales. Skin looses its elasticity and looks shiny with fine wrinkles as the age advances. In adult life the condition however shows little improvement. Although uncommon, **ichthyosis congenita**, a severe variant of the condition, may develop in which some babies may born with severe hyperkeratosis as if encased in a thick sheet cover. The encasement therefore interferes and prevents every bodily movement, to the extent the infant fails to have feeding even. The condition therefore rapidly ends to fatality, and the infant dies. Occasionally however, the covering sheet of hyperkeratosis is shed off and the infant then presents with milder form of lamellar ichthyosis.

Epidermolytic hyperkeratosis or **bullous ichthyosis** is an extremely rare but a severe clinical variant. It presents with generalised erythema, with bullous lesions and denuded areas with hyperkeratosis. Later, the bullous lesions subside and the patient presents with thickened hyperkeratosis on most parts of the body, and warty growths at the skin folds. In early childhood the condition can be quite disabling, and may be associated with mental retardation, corneal abnormalities, and short stature.

Diagnosis

It is diagnosed on clinical grounds, while family history can serve as a helpful guide. Skin biopsy can also confirm the diagnosis.

Treatment

No effective or specific therapy of the condition is available. The patient is therefore given supportive treatment through, for example, topical application of greasy materials such as oil and cream, or of soothing agent. Glycerine however appears quite potent for its property of retaining moisture. In addition, the patient is given local application of keratolytic agents, such as 5-10% salicylic acid and 10-40% urea. This form of palliative treatment is continued for life.

Topical application of vitamin A is another effective method of palliative treatment. In addition, or alternatively, vitamin A, 50,000 IU, once on alternate days may be given orally for 2 to 3 months. Vitamin A derivatives, acitretin, 25-30 mg, once daily orally for 2-4 weeks, increasing up to 75 mg daily if required and then adjusted the dose according to the response to a maintenance at 25-50 mg, may be given and the treatment is continued for maximum of 6 months.

Systemic corticosteroids may be of some value, particularly in cases of lamellar ichthyosis. Prednisolone, 10 mg daily orally, may therefore be given for some months. The drug is however given at 10-20 mg daily in cases of ichthyosis congenita, and its administration is preferred through IM injection rather than through oral route.

Systemic or topical antimicrobial or even antifungal agent is considered whenever there is any infection or a suspicion of existing infection. It however forms a compulsory regimen in cases of bullous lesions present in epidermolytic hyperkeratosis. In this condition, use of both systemic and topical corticosteroids is also needed, in addition.

DARIER'S DISEASE

Darier's disease or **keratosis follicularis** is a rare, chronic, intractable, inherited (autosomal dominant) disorder.

It usually begins early in life, and is more common in boys than in girls.

Histological studies show formation of large epidermal cleft with free lying acantholytic cells and irregular proliferation of epidermal cells. Epidermis is thickened, with marked hyperkeratosis.

Clinical Manifestations

It presents with small follicular and intrafollicular, keratotic, brown-red papules, which quickly become confluent to form plaques, covered with brown or black crusts, and finally lead to the development of dirty black warty papules. The lesions chiefly develop behind the ears and on the extremities, trunk, buttocks and groins, but may also involve any part of the body. The lesions increase in size and coalesce to form large malodorous vegetations. The plaques produce fissuring and ulcerations and discharge offensive purulent exudates. The lips may be crusted, fissured and swollen. Scalp is covered with greasy crusts. Nails are brittle, hyperkeratotic and striated longitudinally. Palms and soles demonstrate patchy horny thickening. Involvement of mucous membrane is however very rare. The condition becomes worse during summer months.

The lesions cause intense itching and bleed easily. There may also be discomfort and pain.

Diagnosis

It is diagnosed clinically, aided by the family history. Skin biopsy can confirm the diagnosis.

Treatment

No effective therapy is available. The patients are therefore given symptomatic treatment with topical application of greasy ointment or lotion. Topical vitamin A is also effective and can be given either alone or with emollient.

Vitamin A derivative, acetretin, 25-30 mg daily orally for four to six weeks, titrated against response to maximum 75 mg daily, and then adjusted to the maintenance at 25-50 mg daily, may be given with benefit. The treatment can however be continued for a maximum of six months.

Other cases may need Granz ray therapy.

DISCOID LUPUS ERYTHEMATOSUS

It is a chronic and recurrent disorder of collagen. The aetiology of the condition, also known as **chronic discoid lupus erythematosus**, is not known. Cutaneous manifestations may, however, occur form exposure to sunlight or ultraviolet light, infections, trauma, stress, exposure to cold, and pregnancy may precipitate the condition.

It commonly occurs between the ages of 30 and 40 and affects more women than men.

Pathological changes show hyperkeratosis with horny plugs in pilosebaceous orifices, epidermal atrophy, and focal infiltration with lymphocytes, dilated blood vessels, hyalinisation, and oedema.

Clinical Manifestations

The condition is usually asymptomatic, and gives rise to single, but may also be multiple, sharply demarcated, localised, erythematous papule or plaques, initially with smooth surfaces but later covered with adherent, grey scales, and gives rise to horny, follicular plugging and pigmentary disturbances, commonly occurring on the exposed part of the body, such as malar prominence and bridge of the nose, scalp, pinna, neck and hands. The lesions may coalesce to form large patches, which may have annular pattern with fairly well demarcated border and atrophic centre, showing telangiectasia. Margins of the lesions usually show hyperpigmentation. On the face the lesions may assume the shape of butterfly due to coalescence of the lesions. Involvement of the scalp may sometimes cause irreversible scarring alopecia. There may also be varying degree of oedema. In addition, there are follicular plugging and pigmentary disturbances.

Very rarely the lesions may involve the mucous membrane and other parts of the body, though not exposed to sunlight and thus, become generalised. The lesions extend peripherally, and show healing in the centre leaving atrophy, scarring and depigmentation. There may also be alopecia. Only a small proportion of eases may develop multisystem manifestation after many years, but there may be mild transient arthralgia.

The condition can produce complications such as recurrences, systemic dissemination and scarring.

Diagnosis

Blood shows leucopenia. Only a small proportion of cases may show LE cells in the serum. Some cases may show positive antinuclear antibody test. The condition is diagnosed by skin biopsy, which like systemic lupus erythematosus shows deposition of immunoglobulin and C3 at dermoepidermal junction but with much fluorescence.

The condition is differentiated from systemic lupus erythematosus, which may be difficult, but the lesions may be generalised, while the condition also shows multisystem involvement. Seborrhoeic dermatitis is differentiated for having yellowish greasy scales without follicular plugs, while the lesions have no distinct margin and atrophy. Psoriasis gives rise to lesions covered with greyish-white or silvery-white scales which when removed forcibly leave minute bleedings behinds behind. Rosacea is differentiated for the absence of atrophy, while lupus vulgaris presents with hyperpigmented, irregular-shaped patches of minute translucent and indurated nodules, and the lesions produce tissue paper scaling on healing. Lichen planus is differentiated as that presents with tiny papules with greyish-puncta or streaks, arranged in a fine network, occurring commonly on the flexures of the wrists and hips, trunk, shins, mouth, glans penis and vaginal mucosa, and gives rise to itching. Drug allergy may also e confused but there is always a history available of exposure to the offending drugs. Sarcoidosis is differentiated for having different histopathological changes.

Treatment

Avoidance to the exposure of sunlight or ultraviolet can often give relief in mild cases. In other instances, patients are given sunscreen.

The lesions are treated with topical corticosteroids. In cases of resistance or of extensive lesions, treatment is given with antimalarial drugs such as chloroquine, 150 mg daily orally, max. 2.5 mg/kg daily, or hydroxychloroquine sulphate, 400 mg daily in divided doses; maintenance 200-400 mg daily.

Systemic corticosteroids, such as prednisolone, 20-30 mg daily orally, or cortisone, 12.5-50 mg daily orally, may be given in more difficult situations.

When the lesions are only few in numbers, they may be treated by freezing with liquid nitrogen or carbon dioxide snow, or through application of phenol.

SYSTEMIC LUPUS ERYTHEMATOSUS

The aetiology of the condition (**SLE**) is still obscured but three may be disturbances in the immune regulation. There may also be the involvement of genetic factors (certain types of human leucocyte antigens and null complement alleles), and the condition shows an increased prevalence of histocompatability antigens HLA-B8 and HLA-DR-3 and, in some, inherited deficiency of complement components, especially C2. The condition shows an increased prevalence in males with Klinefelter's syndrome and in fertile women taking oral contraceptives. Environmental factors may act as predisposing factor, and exposure to ultraviolet ray may exacerbate the condition in some. Sex hormones appear to exert an important influence in its causation, and the incidence of the condition is several-folds higher in women in reproductive age than in other women, and the condition shows exacerbation during normal menses and pregnancy. Several drugs such as isoniazid, D-penicillamine, procainamide and phenothiazine, can produce drug-induced lupus erythematous, while HLA-DR4 antigen makes one more prone to develop the condition with hydralazine.

The incidence and prevalence of the condition varies across ethnicity and geographic regions. It is predominantly a disease of women affecting 90% of them of all ages, having a peculiar predilection for young women, most sufferers being between the ages of 20 and 40 years.

The pathophysiology of the condition is still remains misunderstood. The production of abnormal antibodies by B cells remains the hallmark sign of the condition, while some antibodies, such as anti-double-standard DNA ant anti-Smith, remain specific.

Pathological changes are therefore extremely variable. The small arteries and arterioles show acute necrotising vasculitis, with fibrinoid deposits in vessel walls. There is fibrous thickening with luminal narrowing of the vessels in chronic stage, and frequently there is perivascular infiltration with lymphocytes. Joints show nonerosive synovitis. There is heavy deposit of fibrin and exudation with neutrophils in the synovial membrane. Skin shows liquefaction degeneration of the basal layer of epidermis, oedema at dermal junction, varying degree of fibrosis in the dermis, perivascular infiltration with mononuclear cells, and deposits of immunoglobulin and complement along the dermoepidermal junction. Kidney shows deposits of C3 and IgG on basement membrane, and causes tubulointerstitial lesions, and wire-loop capillaries of the glomeruli. Heart shows Libman-Sacks type of endocarditis. There are small, warty excrescence or friable, berry-like masses of vegetation on the mitral and tricuspid valves. Pericardium and other serosal cavity may become thickened, opaque, and coated with shaggy fibrous tissue. Initially there is perivascular infiltration with inflammatory mononuclear cells but later, infiltration with lymphocytes and plasma cells. Spleen may be markedly enlarged, with capsular thickening. Pulp shows numerous plasma cells and deposits of IgG and IgM. There may be pleurisy with effusion, interstitial pneumonitis and diffuse fibrosing alveolitis. Lymph modes are enlarged and contain hyperactive follicles, and plasma cells. Other organs and tissue also show changes due to active vasculitis.

Clinical Manifestations

It may begin insidiously with nonspecific symptoms of vague rheumatic pain. Otherwise, there may be an explosive onset with multisystem involvement and constitutional symptoms. The condition may therefore produce symptoms and signs accordingly.

Characteristically it affects mucocutaneous system in 80% to 90% cases, while about 30% cases present with classic erythematous "butterfly" rash or dusky red discoloration of skin of the nose and cheek, and discoid and other varieties of skin lesions on the neck, upper chest, back and other areas of skin exposed to sunlight. The characteristics of skin lesions vary and may include discoid lupus eryhematosus-like lesions or the lesions may be pruritic, urticarial or bullous. Atrophy, scarring and pigmentary changes may occur but rarely. The condition however does not give rise to any subjective symptom when the skin is involved but may well be itchy. The patient shows hypopigmentation of skin. Generalised alopecia is frequent during active stage of the condition and constitutes an important feature. There may also be periungual erythema with oedema, purpura, and bullous eruptions. The condition also produces ulcers on the legs, and erythema over the palms, knuckles and phalangeal joints, and dilatation of nail bed capillaries. Painful ulcerations of the mucous membrane of the mouth and nasopharynx may be encountered occasionally.

Drug-induced lupus erythematosus gives rise to fever, skin lesions, polyarthritis, and pulmonary infiltration, but renal and CNS involvement are rare.

Involvement of other systems may however lead to impairment of vital structures, e.g. renal failure, vision problems and blindness, peritonitis, pancreatitis, protein-losing enteropathy, as complications.

Table 4.1

Criteria for diagnosis of Systemic Lupus Erythematosus.

- Malar rash
- Discoid rash
- Oral ulcers
- Photosensitivity
- Arthritis
- Pleuritis/Pericarditis
- Evidence of immunological disorder
    - LE cells
    - Antibodies against double standard DNA
    - False positive VDRL
    - Antibodies against Smith (Sm) antigen
- Evidence of blood disorders
    - Haemolytic anaemia
    - Leucopenia (WBC <4000/mm3)
    - Lymphopenia (lymphocytes <1500/mm3)
    - Thrombocytopenia (platelets <100,000/mm3)
- Evidence of renal disorder
    - Proteinuria (protein >0.5 g/day)
    - Cellular casts
- Evidence of neurological disorder
    - Seizures
    - Psychosis
- Antinuclear antibodies

Diagnosis

The condition is diagnosed on clinical grounds, supported by the determination LE cells in the serum. Alopecia is considered to be useful diagnostic pointer. Blood shows normochromic normocytic anaemia, raised ESR, leucopenia, lymphopenia, thrombocytopenia, and hypergammaglobulinaemia.

A criteria has now been made that the diagnosis of the condition can be confirmed when a patient fulfils no less four of those criteria (Table 4.1).

The dermatological lesions of the condition are differentiated form discoid lupus erythematosus.

Treatment

The patients are strongly advised to avoid sunlight and ultraviolet light for the prevention and control of the cutaneous manifestations. Protection can also be given through the use of topical sunscreen.

Management of the condition is done with corticosteroids. The patient is therefore given prednisolone, 40-60 mg daily as a single dose orally in the morning after breakfast and reduces the dose for maintenance to minimum effective dose with disease control.

Mild to moderate cases are also sometimes treated with antimalarial agent, such as chloroquine, 150 mg daily orally, max. 2.5 mg/kg daily, or hydroxychloroquine sulphate, 400 mg daily in divided doses; maintenance 200-400 mg daily.

In severe cases cyclophosphamide, 1-1.5 mg/kg daily orally, may be given, often in conjunction with corticosteroids in patients with severe or progressive renal disease.

No treatment is usually needed for the drug-induced condition, which resolves after withdrawal of the offending drugs.

SCLERODERMA

The condition is a chronic and generalised disorder of connective tissue, and is also known as systemic sclerosis and progressive systemic sclerosis.

The aetiology of it is not known. It may however be associated with a variety of immunological abnormalities, changes in the microvasculature, and excessive fibrosis. It most commonly involves the skin and may remain so even for years, but soon involve other internal organs.

It occurs more frequently between the ages of 30 and 50 years, and is extremely rare in children. It also shows an increasing incidence amongst the workers exposed to silica dust. The condition is four times more prevalent in women than in men.

Progressive systemic sclerosis practically involves all organs of the body.

In skin involvement, there is firm, white patches, changing to diffuse, sclerotic atrophy of the skin, initially on the skin of the fingers and distal regions of the upper extremities, and extends proximally to involve the upper arms, shoulders, neck and face. In the early stage the affected skin are oedematous and have a doughy consistency. There is oedema and perivascular lymphocytic infiltration; with swelling and degeneration of collagen fibres. Capillaries and small arteries show thickening of the basal lamina, and partial occlusion.

Clinical Manifestations

It gives rise to symmetrical oedema and thickening of the fingers and hands, or Raynaud's phenomenon-like symptoms of vasoconstriction of arteries and arterioles. There is pigmentation and telangiectasia of skin of the face, limbs and trunk. The lesions usually appear as circumscribed or diffuse, hard, smooth, thickened, and depigmented or darkened area. The face becomes taut and 'mask'-like, causing difficulty in opening of the mouth. Stiffness of skin and tightening of skin over the bony prominence generally results to flexion contractures.

Diagnosis

There may be normochromic normocytic anaemia. ESR is raised. Test for antinuclear antibodies is usually positive.

Diagnosis of the condition is made from biopsy of the indurated skin. Antinuclear test is usually positive. Radiological investigations may reveal calcification of the skin (**calcinosis**).

Dermatological lesions may need to be differentiated from systemic lupus erythematosus and dermatomyositis.

Treatment

No effective treatment of the condition is available. The condition is therefore treated symptomatically. The patients are advised to avoid exposure to cold and to keep the affected parts warm. Corticosteroids may appear helpful.

Mild cases are therefore treated with systemic corticosteroids, such as prednisolone, 10-20 mg daily orally, and the treatment is continued for years together or as long as required. Along with this the patients are also given calcium channel antagonist, nifedipine, 10 mg three times daily orally, or nicotinic acid derivative, inositol nicotinate, 1 g three or four times daily orally.

MORPHEA

Morphea is not a clinical entity but a localised form of scleroderma. As it is with scleroderma, so the aetiology of the condition is not known.

It is more common in women, particularly the young women, than in men.

Histopathological changes in the condition are the same as described under scleroderma.

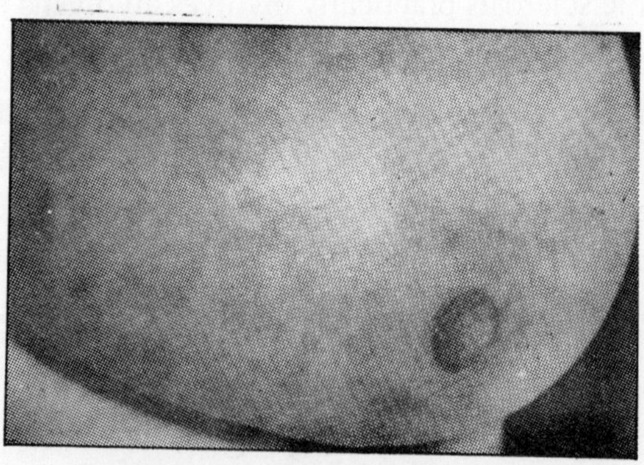

Figure 4.11. Morphea on the breast.

Clinical Manifestations

It presents with one or more, well-defined, deeply indurated, hard, thickened, oval, round or elongated, white or yellow-white plaques, patches or spots, sometimes surrounded by dusky red borders or telangiectasia (Fig. 4.11). The lesions generally occur chiefly on the forehead, face, scalp, chest, abdomen, back, thighs, and legs. The affected skin appears rigid, inelastic, atrophic, and smooth, and looks shiny. The lesions may spread slowly, or remain stationary or regress spontaneously, leaving varying degree of atrophy. The skin however never regains its normal appearance.

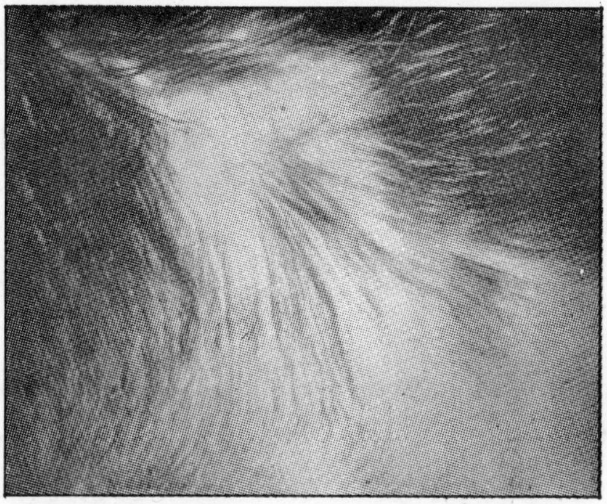

Figure 4.12. Band-like morphea on the scalp.

When the lesions involve hairy parts, the band-like lesions produce patch of cicatricial alopecia (Fig. 4.12).

Full movement of a joint becomes restricted when the condition develops over a joint.

The condition however does not give rise to any symptom except perhaps slight irritation.

Diagnosis

Diagnosis of the condition is made on the evidence of skin biopsy.

It is differentiated from lupus erythematosus and vitiligo.

Treatment

No effective therapy of the condition is available. Topical corticosteroids may however be helpful. In cases of less satisfactory response, topical corticosteroids may be given under occlusive dressings.

Administration of systemic corticosteroids may be considered in cases of increasing size of the lesions.

DERMATOMYOSITIS

It is a rare, acute or slowly developing scleroderma-like condition of both skin and muscles, including other systems of the body. It is also known as polymyositis. The aetiology of the condition is not known. It is however frequently seen to develop following some infection, trauma, immunisation, and use of some drugs. In addition, it appears to have certain distinct association with internal malignant diseases. Although no conclusive evidence is yet available, suggestion also favours of its autoimmune origin.

It is more common in women than in men, and generally involves children below 10 years old and adults aged between 40 and 60 years. Reversal of the pattern is however occurs and it becomes more common in men when it develops in association with internal malignant disease.

In cases of cutaneous involvement the condition gives rise to epidermal atrophy, oedema and hyalinisation of the collagen bundles. There are liquefaction and degeneration of basal cell, vascular dilatation, and infiltration of the dermis with lymphocytes and occasional plasma cells. Sometimes calcification develops in the late stage of the condition.

Clinical Manifestations

The condition may be acute or subacute, and may present with fever, malaise, weakness, muscle pain and cutaneous eruptions. In other cases there may not be any preceding symptom.

In cases of cutaneous involvement, the condition may give rise to scaling erythematous maculopapular or papular eruptions or dusky red patch on the face and eyelids. The patient shows oedema of the face with heliotrope discoloration around the eyes. Small, flat-topped, dusky red papules may be seen clustered over the dorsal aspects of the hands. In addition, the lesions usually occur on the extremities and can also involve the neck, upper chest and back. The affected skin shows non-pitting oedema, and appears firm and tender on touch. There may be erythematous lines on the base and sides of the fingernails. The affected skin later shows plaques, atrophy, telangiectasia, and disturbed pigmentation. Later, subcutaneous deposits of calcium may become palpable, some of which may be extruded through the skin surface. The skin lesions may persist and result in brown pigmentation, depigmentation, or scarring. Calcification of the skin and muscle occur late in the condition.

In addition, there are varying degree of skeletal muscle involvement, which constitute a constant feature of the condition and include pain, tenderness, dysphagia, polyarthralgia, weakness, and even paralysis of the muscle.

Other systemic manifestations may develop rarely, and may include any system of the body.

Diagnosis

The condition is diagnosed on clinical grounds, and is confirmed by histopathological studies. Electromyography can also aid the diagnosis.

Various laboratory investigations are however available but generally nonspecific and serve no purpose in the diagnosis of the condition in cutaneous involvement. Peripheral blood frequently shows an elevated erythrocyte sedimentation rate. Some cases may show the presence of antinuclear antibodies or LE cells or both. The level of serum creatine kinase (CK, CPK, creatine phosphokinase), transaminases (AST and ALT), and aldose are elevated. These findings are however extremely helpful to assess the therapeutic effect during the treatment of the condition. In this respect creatine kinase (CK, CPK) can act as most sensitive index.

The condition is differentiated from scleroderma, erythema nodosum, systemic lupus erythematosus, contact dermatitis and erysipelas for the cutaneous involvement.

Treatment

In acute condition the patient is kept at bed rest till the constitutional symptoms subside. The underlying condition, if known, must call for an immediate attention for adequate management or correction.

In the management of the condition systemic corticosteroids, such as prednisolone, appear to be the drug of choice. The drug is given at 40-80 mg daily orally in divided doses and adjusted according to response. In addition, the patient is given antacid and supplement of potassium. In cases of failure and in resistant cases, immunosuppressive agent, such as cyclophosphamide, methotrexate or chlorambucil, may be given with success.

POLYARTERITIS NODOSA

It is a condition of necrotising panarteritis affecting the medium-sized and muscular arteries. Although the precise mechanism of the development of the condition is not still known it perhaps occurs due to hypersensitivity reaction. Some cases may show an association with some bacterial, such as streptococcal infection, and viral infections (such as HIV), use of drugs (such as sulphonamides and thiouracil), and vaccines.

It occurs in all age groups but most prevalent in the ages between 20 and 50. It is much common in males than in females.

Pathologically the condition produces thickening of the media and intima of the medium and small-sized arteries, showing a predilection for the points of bifurcation or branching. The lesion initially produces necrotic inflammation, which may extend into the adventitia through the media, and at times may involve the entire circumference of the artery. The lesions initially contain numerous polymorphonuclear leucocytes, eosinophils and mononuclear cells in and often around the arterial wall and may thus, lead to the formation of multiple small aneurysms. Later, the lesions show internal proliferation with secondary thrombosis and occlusion. The lesions show infiltration with large number of macrophages and plasma cells.

Clinical Manifestations

The manifestations may vary widely, and the onset may be insidious or acute. The condition frequently runs a remittent course, with long symptom-free intervals. The patients are usually debilitated, with a history of asthma or ulcerative colitis.

The manifestations of the condition usually include low-grade fever, malaise, and weakness and weight loss. Depending upon the involvement of the multisystem the patient may present with oliguria, proteinuria, haematuria, nausea, vomiting, abdominal pain, bloody diarrhoea, precordial pain, pericarditis, myocardial infarction, tachycardia, and muscular pains and aches, and arthralgia.

Cutaneous manifestations of the condition are not always present but when present it gives rise to several cutaneous abnormalities including mucous membrane lesions and gives rise to livedo reticularis, pupura, petechiae, and urticaria. On the skin that may appear as crops of firm, painful, erythematous nodules or flesh-coloured papules that run along the course of the superficial arteries of the lower extremities. The nodules persist for days or weeks and may sometimes also ulcerate and heal spontaneously leaving scar formation, or get enlarged in size resembling epithelioma. Sometimes vesicles and pustules may also develop.

It produces complications such as glomerulonephritis, renal failure and ruptured aneurysms. If untreated, the condition is often fatal.

Diagnosis

It is diagnosed on the basis of biopsy of the lesion that shows necrotising arteritis. Biopsy is also done of skin, subcutaneous tissue, muscle or kidney. Angiography can demonstrate aneurysms in the medium-sized arteries. There is however no LE cells. Autoantibodies are rarely present.

Blood shows leucocytosis, thrombocytosis, raised ESR, hypoalbulinaemia, and elevated level of immunoglobulin.

The condition is differentiated from systemic lupus erythematosus.

Treatment

No curative treatment is available. The patients are usually given prednisolone, 60 mg daily in divided doses orally, and continued for a long time, and then reduced to the lowest effective dose with disease control. The corticosteroid therapy though effectively suppresses the disease process and symptoms relieved, but it does not give any cure to the underlying cause. Antimalarial drugs, such as chloroquine, may also be helpful. In more severe cases and in cases of unsatisfactory response, immunosuppressive drugs are given either alone or along with corticosteroids. The patient is then given cyclophosphamide, 2-3 mg per kg of body-weight daily orally. The patients are also given symptomatic treatment for other manifestations.

CHAPTER 5

Disorders due to Bullous Eruptions and Tumours

PEMPHIGUS

It is a rare but potentially a fatal and relapsing disorder of skin characterised by blistering within the epidermis and deposition of immunoglobulins and complement within the intracellular space. Aetiology of the condition is however not known but it may be an autoimmune phenomenon.

It usually occurs in adults, with its peak incidence between the ages of 60 and 70. The condition is slightly more common in women than in men.

The bullae are epidermal and histopathologically it presents with intracellular oedema, loss of intercellular bridges, acantholysis, cleft formation, intraepidermal or deep bullae formation, and few inflammatory cells. There may be hyperkeratosis, containing acanothosis and papillomatosis, with formation of microabscesses containing eosinophils and monocytes. In the mucous membrane lesions however acantholysis is not an obvious factor.

Clinical Manifestations

The condition has several clinical variants, and the lesions appear on apparently normal looking skin.

Pemphigus vulgaris is the common variety, and usually begins in the later life. It gives rise to crops of diffusely scattered, fragile, flaccid or tense bullae of varying sizes (Fig. 5.1), and may even reach a very large size in dimension. The lesions may develop on any part of the skin but most frequently seen on the face, scalp and trunk, and also on the mucous membrane of the mouth, larynx, nose, conjunctivae, anus, and genitalia, and show a predilection for areas of friction or pressure. The lesions are usually asymmetric in distribution. The bullae initially contain clear serous fluid, which later become haemorrhagic or seropurulent. The bullae may dry up to form crusts or may rupture, leaving oozing and bleeding superficial erosion, and painful raw surfaces. The lesions cause considerable loss of plasma leading even to negative nitrogen balance, and characteristically take a very long time to heal. The bullae are relatively asymptomatic but otherwise constitutional symptoms vary from mild to severe with a bad prognosis. Rise of body temperature during the time when bullae erupt is also considered to be of bad prognostic sign.

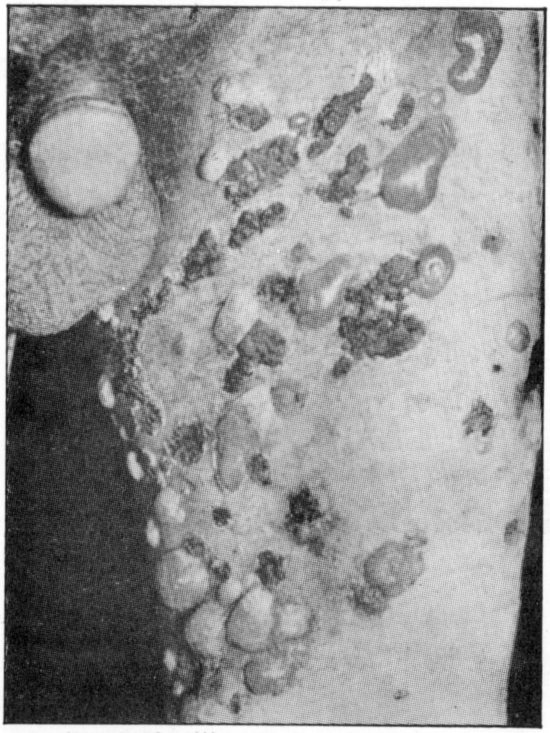

Figure 5.1. Pemphigus vulgaris.

Skin lesions show remissions and relapses at varying intervals, and leave hyperpigmented scars and stains on healing. Case fatality occurs due to secondary infection and toxaemia.

In some cases however formation of bullae may not be apparent. Rubbing on the surface easily results detachment of epidermis from the underlying skin (Nikolsky's sign). In others there may be persistent recurrences of a single bulla at a particular site for months, or one or two crusted lesions, or multiple vesicles may appear insidiously on the palms.

Mucosal lesions produce painful raw areas with hanging epithelium in the mouth, larynx, and nose. Patients may complain of dysphagia and hoarseness of voice. Lips and gums may be swollen.

Pemphigus foliaceous is a rare variant of the condition. It presents with imperfectly formed bullae. The blisters are much more superficial than pemphigus vulgaris, have very thin roofs and are quite fragile. Later, the condition produces generalised exfoliative dermatitis-like moist, red, oedematous, exfoliative and malodorous lesions. The eruptions generally develop on the face, and spread slowly and symmetrically until the entire area integument is involved. Involvement of the scalp may give rise to yellowish granular scales, and the hair may fall out. The lesion may affect the rest of the body. Mucous membrane is not generally involved in this variant but, if it does, the lesions appear lately and never so severely. The patient may also develop diarrhoea and pyrexia. Remissions and exacerbations of the lesions are common. Case fatality often follows an intercurrent infection.

Pemphigus erythematosus (Senear-Usher Syndrome) is a chronic but unusual variant of pemphigus. It presents with early lesions surrounded by erythema and crusting, occurring chiefly as localised lesions on the nose, cheeks and ears, and may resemble lupus erythematosus. When the crusts are removed, the lesions leave moist, raw surfaces. Occasionally the lesions may also occur on the trunk and extremities. The lesions are distributed somewhere symmetrically, and show various remissions and intermissions. The general health of the patient is not affected but there may be intense itching.

Pemphigus vegetans is the rarest variety of the condition and begins as pemphigus vulgaris. It presents with bullae occurring on the nose, lips or in the mouth, and later may also involve the groins, axillae, other flexures, genitalia, perineum, scalp and extremities. The bullae rupture, causing moist superficial ulcers, which produce fungoid vegetations with malodorous discharge, capped with crusts and surrounded by inflammatory zone. The lesions tend to coalesce to form large patches or are arranged into groups or configuration patterns. The condition however gives prolonged remissions with few subjective symptoms. Constitutional symptoms may however develop due to infection.

The condition commonly shows recurrences and exacerbation. Case fatality occurs due to secondary infection and toxaemia. Otherwise, it produces septicaemia, pulmonary congestion with oedema, bronchopneumonia, focal myocarditis, and electrolyte imbalance as complications.

Diagnosis

Peripheral blood shows leucocytosis with eosinophilia and elevated ESR and, in late stage, low level of protein and electrolyte changes. Nikolsky's sign and Tzank test are positive. Direct immunofluorescence test is helpful and shows inter-epidermal deposition of IgG between the cells. Indirect immunofluorescence test is also positive in many cases. Histological picture shows intra-epidermal separation forming a split within the epidermis.

Differentiation of the condition is however easy for the characteristic formation of epidermal blister within the epidermis in pemphigus. Dermatitis herpetiformis is differentiated for having extremely itchy lesions; leave pigmented spots on healing, while the oral lesions are rare. Erythema multiforme bullosum is differentiated for having lesions that are more localised and gives a negative Nikolsky's sign. Bullous pemphigoid is differentiated for having large, tense, subepidermal lesions which when rupture leave large denuded area, the lesions heal spontaneously and the Nikolsky's sign is negative. Bullous contact dermatitis and drug eruptions are differentiated for having a history of exposure to the offending agent.

Treatment

Local lesions are given soothing compression with potassium permanganate, followed by topical application of antibiotic either alone or with corticosteroids. Mild cases may be treated successfully with topical corticosteroids alone. Other cases may need systemic corticosteroids, for example, prednisolone, 80-100 mg daily in divided doses orally and then gradually reduce to a maintenance dose. It is better to add cytotoxic immunosuppressants, azathioprine, 1-2 mg per kg of body-weight daily orally. Treatment with immunosuppressants, such as methotrexate or cyclophosphmide, is also beneficial for better care and management. Treatment with other immunosuppressants, such as methotrexate or cyclophosphamide, may also be beneficial. Some success has also been claimed in the treatment with dapsone, 100-200 mg daily orally, perhaps supplemented by sulphapyridine, 1-3 g daily orally. Similarly some success has been claimed with gold salt, for example, aurothiomalate.

Mucosal lesions are often difficult to treat and may never fully resolve

A few patients may however go into natural remission.

PEMPHIGOID

Pemphigoid or **bullous pemphigoid** is an autoimmune disorder characterised by benign, self-limiting, superficial blistering eruptions on the skin. It may be a chronic variant of erythema multiforme. However the condition develops as an immunological response, the target agent being a protein attached to the hemidesmosomes of basal keratinocytes.

It is a condition of elderly persons, and extremely rare before the age of 50. It is much common in females than in males.

Histopathological changes the condition produce include subepidermal bulla with no acantholysis, infiltration with few eosinophils, necrosis and regeneration of the epidermis, and oedema of the upper dermis with few inflammatory infiltrates.

Clinical Manifestations

It presents with diffusely scattered, large, tense, dome-shaped bullae (Fig. 5.2), usually on the groins, lower abdomen, and thighs or flexures surfaces of the extremities. The lesions appear on the apparently normal skin but may also follow erythematous or eczematous lesions. The lesions remain localised for a few months before becoming widespread but otherwise may be widespread directly. The bullae may remain intact for several days and later may rupture leaving large denuded areas. The lesions however heal spontaneously and more rapidly than those of pemphigus. Mucosal lesions develop in a proportion of patients, and involve the oral mucosa, anus and vagina, and seldom gives rise to any symptom.

Recurrences of the condition are however quite frequent.

The condition has a variant, **cicatricial pemphigoid**, which only affects the mucous membrane, often with scarring.

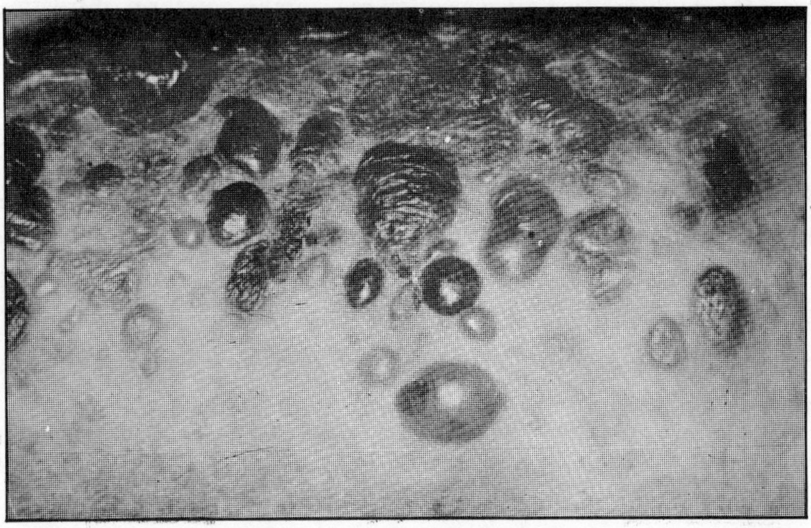

Figure 5.2. Bullous pemphigoid.

Diagnosis

The bullae are subepidermal. Acantholytic cells are usually absent in the biopsy. Nikolsky's sign is usually negative. Direct immunofluorescence test shows deposition of IgG antibodies and/or C3 at the basement membrane. Indirect immunofluorescence can detect IgG or C3 antibodies in the circulating blood.

It is differentiated from pemphigus, which presents with epidermal lesions, and the lesions leave large erosions after rupture and the denuded areas take a very long time to heal. Dermatitis herpetiformis is differentiated for having symmetrically distributed lesions that give rises to intense itching and burning.

Treatment

Localised lesions are given soothing compression with potassium permanganate followed by administration of topical corticosteroids.

Patients are given systemic treatment with corticosteroids, such as prednisolone, 30-60 mg daily in divided doses orally and once the condition is controlled, the dose is then gradually reduced to the maintenance level. The patients can also be treated with dapsone, 100-200 mg daily orally, and sulphapyridine, 1-3 g daily in divided doses orally.

Immunosuppressive drugs, such as azathioprine, cyclophosphamide or methotrexate may also be beneficial but the result is variable. Much better result is however achieved when the patients are treated with both prednisolone and azathioprine, and as soon as the condition is controlled the doses of both the drugs are reduced to the maintenance levels. The treatment is however withdrawn when the condition remits spontaneously, often after 2 to 5 years.

Cicatricial pemphigoid is however often resistant to any form of treatment.

DERMATITIS HERPETIFORMIS

It is a rare, chronic, relapsing, inflammatory eruption of skin occurring due to several immunological abnormalities. There may however be genetic factor involved, and the condition shows a strong association with certain histocompatability type, such as HLA-B8, DR3 and DQW2. The condition also shows a positive association with asymptomatic gluten-sensitive enteropathy in many cases. An increased incidence of thyroid disease is evident in this condition. Non-steroidal anti-inflammatory drugs (NSIDs) may exacerbate the condition even though the symptoms of the condition are well controlled with medical therapy.

It primarily affects the young and the middle-aged persons but in another communities it may occur in childhood. Similarly, although it is usually more common in men but sometimes there may not be sex predilection. The condition is however rare in blacks and Orients.

Pathologically the condition produces subepidermal bullae, oedema and separation of the epidermis from the dermis, collections of neutrophils at the tips of the dermal papillae, formation of microabscesses in the dermal papillae, deposition of IgA at the epidermo-dermal junction, and infiltrations with lymphocytes and eosinophils.

Clinical Manifestations

It presents with vesicular, bullous and pustular lesions on an erythematous base, appearing on any part of the body (Fig. 5.3) but mostly on the buttocks, extensor surfaces of the elbows and knees, and sometimes on the axillae, shoulders, scalp, sacral region and abdomen. The lesions tend to form clusters and are distributed roughly symmetrically. The condition may rarely involve the mucous membrane. In children however the lesions may only be vesicular and bullous. There may be prodromal symptoms of malaise and neuralgic pain. Intense pruritus and burning sensation are the prominent features of the condition and may even precede other symptoms. Insomnia and nervousness are its usual accompaniment. The lesions are often found heavily excoriated. Remissions and recurrences of the lesions at variable intervals are common, and following healing the lesions leave pigmented spots.

The condition shows a close association with coeliac disease, and a proportion of patients present with the symptoms of it. Jejunal biopsy of many patients also clearly demonstrates the evidence of coeliac disease.

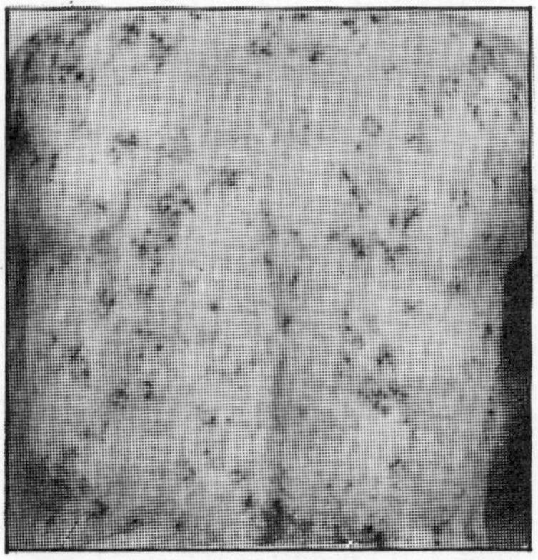

Figure 5.3. Dermatitis herpetiformis.

Diagnosis

The condition is diagnosed on clinical grounds. Typical histopathological changes on skin biopsy are only seen in the early lesions. Nikolsky's sign is negative in the condition. Direct immunofluorescence shows granular deposition of IgA in the dermal papillary tips is always positive and always reckoned as an important diagnostic aid. Serological tests can detect circulating antibodies. Biopsy of small intestine may show gluten-sensitive enteropathy.

The condition is differentiated from pemphigus in which intense itching is not a prominent feature, and the condition presents with intraepidermal bullae while mucosal involvement is quite common, and the condition leaves large denuded areas following rupture of the bullae that takes long time to heal. Bullous pemphigoid is differentiated for involving usually the elderly people, and the condition shows diffusely scattered lesions, usually asymptomatic and shows no association with the gluten-sensitive enteropathy. Erythema multiforme is an acute and self-limiting condition, and the lesions are annular and often arranged in concentric rings, and the lesions are pink coloured, while itching is not intense in this condition. Scabies is differentiated which is often present in other members of close contact, gives rise to nocturnal pruritus, while the characteristic burrows are always evident on the skin.

Treatment

The condition is effectively treated with dapsone, 50-200 mg daily orally, and is cautiously titrated to a minimum effective maintenance dose. As the drug may cause haemolysis, it is essential to monitor blood count regularly after every 2 weeks. Once the condition is stabilised and the drug is given at a minimum effective dose, monitoring of blood count may be done at 4-weekly intervals. Alternatively, though less effective, the patient may be given sulphapyridine, 1-5 g daily in divided doses orally. In the event of less satisfactory response, the treatment is given with, at least, two drugs, such as dapsone and sulphapyridine, or dapsone along with prednisolone, 40-80 mg daily in divided doses orally, and gradually reduced to a maintenance dose.

Although the presence of gluten-sensitive enteropathy in the condition is frequently asymptomatic, the patient is put on strict gluten-free diet, and is continued for life.

SUBCORNEAL PUSTULAR DERMATOSIS

It is a chronic but rare condition of very superficial pustular dermatosis. The aetiology of its causation is yet not known

It however chiefly affects young and middle-aged women.

Pathological changes show pustular blisters on the erythematous skin. The lesions appear on the lower abdomen, groins and axillae, and are arranged in annular and serpiginous pattern. Sometimes vesicular lesions may develop which later change to pustular blebs. The pustules show sterile pus. It however does not cause any oral lesion but, if it does, the involvement is slight.

Diagnosis

It is diagnosed on clinical grounds.

The condition is differentiated from dermatitis herpetiformis in which intense itching is a prominent feature, accompanied by insomnia and nervousness' from bullous pemphigoid that presents with widespread subepidermal bullae; from erythema multiforme which is an acute condition and the lesions usually involve the distal parts of the extremities and the face, while the lesions tend to spread peripherally so as to fuse together; and from pemphigus foliaceous that presents with imperfectly formed flaccid bullae and the lesions usually involve the face and later become widespread like exfoliative dermatitis. Occasionally, generalised pustular eruptions may cause certain amount of confusion but is differentiated easily as the pustular contents show the presence of causative organism.

Treatment

The condition responds well to dapsone therapy. It is given orally at 50-200 mg daily and is titrated cautiously to the lowest effective maintenance dose. Sulphapyridine, 1-3 g daily in divided does orally, is a useful alternative particularly in cases when dapsone produces reaction but least effective.

EPIDERMOLYSIS BULLOSA

Epidermolysis bullosa is a rare, inherited, mechanobullous disorder, usually occurring at birth or early infancy but may also occasionally affects the adults (acquired type). The lesions comprising blisters and erosions appear even on trivial trauma or friction, and affects the parts of the body exposed to trauma, such as knees, elbows, hands and feet, but, in severe form, the condition may also affect the conjunctivae, oral mucosa and genitalia.

The condition has several modes of presentation and is principally classified under 3 major forms on the basis of mode of transmission and clinical features as simplex, junctional and dystrophic. Other forms of the condition are however extremely rare. Simplex form is inherited as dominant autosomal trait, and the condition may develop soon after birth or nay defer till late childhood or adult life. Junctional form is of autosomal recessive inheritance, and becomes evident at or slightly after birth. Dystrophic form is acquired or inherited as dominant or recessive type.

Formation of blisters depends on the type of inheritance and may cause subepidermal split through the epidermal side of the basement membrane (junctional) or below the dermo-epidermal junction (dystrophic) or suprabasal split (simplex). Dermal papillae appear swollen and oedematous, and the blood vessels show great dilatation. Some cases may give rise to paucity or perhaps absence of elastic tissue.

Clinical Manifestations

Epidermolysis bullous simplex (Fig. 5.4) is the benign or simple type of the condition. It presents with vesicles, bullae and epidermal cysts, and involves the skin surface only. The lesions are sparse, and the condition does not cause serious disturbances. The lesions however show worsening in summer. If not subjected to further trauma or friction and if there is no secondary infection, the lesions heal quickly without any atrophy or scarring, but leave pigmentation.

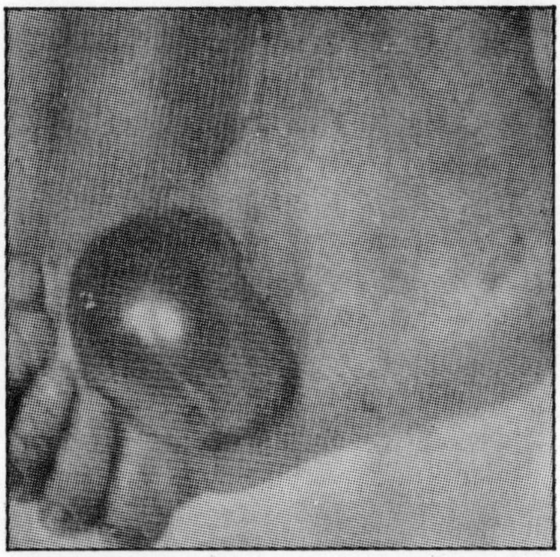

Figure 5.4. Epidermolysis bullosa simplex.

Epidermolysis bullosa junctional in an uncommon but lethal condition. It presents with severe blistering all over the body, including oral and systemic mucosae. The lesions however tend to heal without scarring. In some cases the lesions may also include nails and teeth, causing loss of nails and dysplastic teeth. In some the lesions may not be so severe and may rather show improvement, as the children grow older, while in other cases the lesions may remain localised to the lower extremities. The lesions may how worsening in summer.

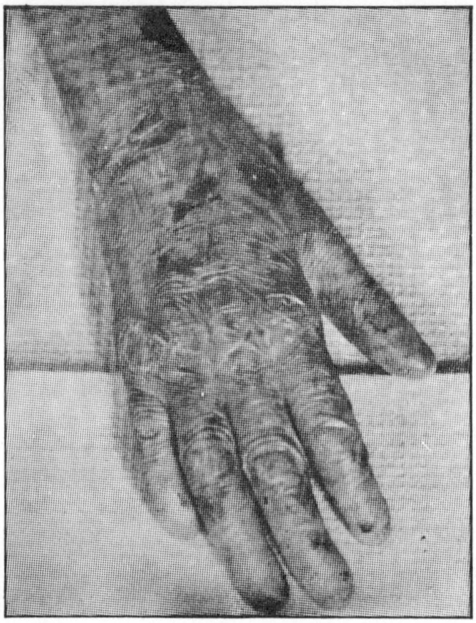

Figure 5.5. Epidermolysis bullosa dystrophica.

Epidermolysis bullosa dystrophica is the severe or dystrophic form of the condition (Fig. 5.5). The lesions may occur independently or any area of friction or trauma, and may occur repeatedly in severe form. The condition is characterised by blister formation which she tendency to be haemorrhagic, followed by development of atrophic scars, leading often to disabling mutilation of the extremities. Mucosal lesions are seen in the buccal cavity, oesophagus, trachea, conjunctiva, cornea and urethra, and cause much discomfort and destruction. Involvement of the nail may cause deformed development or loss of nails. There may also be loss of teeth. Involvement of the scalp leads to cicatricial alopecia. Very severe involvement of the condition may cause fatality.

Diagnosis

Diagnosis of the condition is made on clinical grounds and confirmed by skin biopsy. Family history is a useful diagnostic aid.

It is differentiated from pemphigus, bullous pemphigoid, bullous contact dermatitis, and erythema multiforme.

Treatment

No effective therapy of the condition is yet available. Immediate diagnosis of the condition, prevention and protection against every kind of possible trauma and friction, and a high-quality nursing can all change the outlook of the condition. Emphasis also needs to be made that though mild cases often tend to subside at puberty, without adequate management all cases may turn to fatality.

Many cases are treated with antimicrobial agent given through systemic or topical administration, or both. Some cases may however be treated with systemic corticosteroids in large doses. Dystrophic cases may, in addition, be treated with vitamin E, 100 mg daily orally, for some months.

The purpose of genetic counselling to the affected families need not to be over-emphasised.

MILIUM

Milium is a manifestation of **keratinous cyst** or **sebaceous cyst**. It is a benign, very small-sized epidermal cyst of unknown origin. It develops spontaneously following various types of epithelial trauma or develops the healing of certain bullous conditions.

It is commonly seen in infancy and in middle-aged individuals.

Pathologically there is downgrowth and cystic expansion of the epidermis, and the cyst contains keratin and lipid-containing debris.

Clinical Manifestations

It presents with multiple number of milium as tiny (about pinhead sized) white, slightly elevated, and cystic excrescence. The lesions occur on the eyelids, forehead, temples, below the eyes, cheeks, and on the external genitalia. The lesions are firm in consistency, and when punctured or pressed hard between the fingers, they express white material. The condition is however completely asymptomatic.

Diagnosis

Diagnosis of the condition is made on clinical grounds.

It may sometimes need to be differentiated from hypovitaminosis A, acne, molluscum contagiosum, and other cystic tumours.

Treatment

The condition does not require any form of treatment. Yet, if it is required, particularly for cosmetic purposes, they may be punctured with the fine needle and the content can be squeezed out. Otherwise, and more so when they are numerous in number, they can be destroyed by electro-desiccation.

SEBORRHOEIC KERATOSIS

Seborrhoeic keratosis or **seborrhoeic wart** is senile, benign, pigmented, epidermal hyperplasia. The aetiology of the condition is not known.

It commonly occurs in middle and old persons, and affects more men than women.

Histopathologically it gives a discrete lesion with hyperkeratosis and irregular acanthosis. There are small keratin-filled cysts and downgrowths of keratin into the main rumour mass.

Clinical Manifestations

The condition spontaneously gives rise to raise, sit up on skin surface-type nodular growth or plaque with warty or flat surface, covered by loosely attached greasy crust, and well-demarcated edges. Its size varies from few millimetres to centimetres in diameter, and its colour from skin-colour to tan or dark brown or may even be black (Fig. 5.6). When palpated the growth appears soft in consistency and there is neither induration nor infiltration. It is however more superficial than actinic keratosis. The growth increases in size but slowly and also shows increase in number. The lesions may occur on any part of the body but appears more numerous on trunk and temples. In black women often the lesion appears on the malar part of the face. There is however no symptom but the condition may occasionally give riser to slight pruritus.

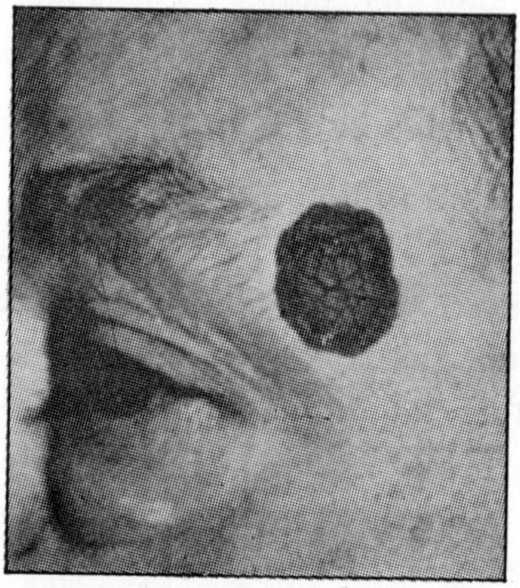

Figure 5.6. Seborrhoeic keratosis.

Diagnosis

It is made on clinical grounds.

The condition is differentiated from actinic keratosis, wart, mole, and verrucous naevi.

Treatment

The condition usually does not require any treatment, while they are not pre-cancerous. Yet sometimes treatment may be needed in some cases for cosmetic problem or when the lesions give rise to irritation and itching, and cryo-surgery often appears to be satisfactory.

KERATO-ACANTHOMA

Kerato-acanthoma is a rapidly growing pseudocarcinomatous hyperplasia and is generally considered to be a transitional change between benign keratosis and definite epithelioma. Although the aetiology of the condition is not known, it is probably a pilosebaceous origin. Exposure to sunlight might have certain aetiological significance for the fact that the often develops on the parts of the body exposed to sunlight. The lesions also occur following exposure to tar, pitch and petroleum oil and hence, they act as predisposing factors. There is also a familial tendency in cases of development of multiple lesions.

Histological changes in the condition show hyperplastic epithelium with a central crater filled with keratin, epidermal proliferation beneath the crater with marked keratinisation, and dense inflammatory infiltrate below the tumour.

Clinical Manifestations

It gives rise to small pimple on the part of the body exposed to sunlight but usually on the face, forearm or dorsum of the hand. The pimple grows very rapidly over a period of 10-12 weeks into a large, firm, skin-coloured, globular tumour with central crater filled with keratin. The tumour reaches the size of 1 to 2 centimetre or may also be enormously enlarged that exceed 5 centimetre even. The epidermis is stretched over the edges if the tumour, and there is telangiectasia between the surface. In the centre of the tumour there is a horny plug.

If left untreated, the tumour undergoes spontaneous resolution, leaving atrophic scar, within a period of six months since onset of the symptom.

Diagnosis

It is diagnosed on clinical grounds and is confirmed by skin biopsy.

The condition is differentiated from squamous cell carcinoma, which is often extremely difficult both clinically and histologically. If there is any confusion on diagnosis the histopathogy is made on the total excised pimple or a cut through specimen over the middle of the lesion.

Treatment

The tumour usually resolves spontaneously even without any treatment. Otherwise, the lesion is treated by surgical excision or curettage. As the spontaneous healing leave scarring, it is wise to give interstitial injection of corticosteroids or cystostatic, fluoroouracil. Alternatively, the lesion is treated cryo-surgery in which the lesion is destroyed by CO_2 snow or liquid nitrogen applied to the lesion for 5 to 30 seconds in cases of small lesion but up to 90 seconds in large lesions.

MALIGNANT MELANOMA

Malignant melanoma or **melanoma** is a group of malignant tumours occurring from the pigmented naevi, particularly junctional naevi, and from melanocytes in apparently normal skin. Occasionally melanomas may also develop from compound or even intradermal naevi. They are the most dangerous of the cutaneous tumours.

Although no age is exempted, the condition shows preponderance to the middle-aged and elderly individuals. It is more common in women than in men. Rarely, it may involve children in whom the condition develops from congenital large pigmented moles.

Histopathological changes show hyperplasia and downward proliferation of he epidermis, and abnormal naevus cells involving all levels within the epidermis initially. Some atypical melanocytes are found proliferating along the basal layer or the epidermis. There are clumps of large tumour cells at the base of the lesion, asymmetrical shape of the tumour, progressive infiltration of pigmented cells into the dermis, and inflammatory infiltrate in band round the tumour. Melanoma cells in the vertical phase of growth possess distinctive antigenic, cytogenic, and biosynthetic abnormalities.

Clinical Manifestations

The condition is divided into four major varieties, such as lentigo maligna, nodular, superficial spreading and acral lentiginous.

Lentigo maligna melanoma is a slow growing intra-epidermal melanoma. It presents with well-demarcated pigmented macule, which is not usually elevated. Colour of the lesion may vary widely, ranging from light to dark brown to blue, black, red or even grey. The lesion is usually found on the face and other parts of the body exposed to sunlight. The lesion grows slowly over several years but can become rapidly invasive melanoma at any stage. The lesion tends to form clusters or groups that spread peripherally. The condition is always associated with marked solar changes in the dermis.

In **nodular melanoma** the existing naevus or a tumour on the normal skin shows an increase in size and later, deepening of colour, presents with formation of crusts, bleeding, ulceration, lymphadenopathy and formation of firm nodule (Fig. 5.7 and 5.8). The tumour may grow further and may become papillary, fungoid or ulcerative. The tumour may develop anywhere on the body but most commonly on the lower legs in females and upper back in males. Involvement of the parts of the body exposed to sunlight is less common. The condition affects children rarely but when it does, it gives rise to brown or even black nodule, more frequently on the face. Other than a change in size, shape and colour of the lesion, the condition is generally asymptomatic but there may be occasional itch or bleeding. Finally metastases occur through lymphatic to the adjacent areas and regional lymph node and later, through bloodstream to other areas and visceras as firm, round nodules, which may be pigmented or non-pigmented (**non-pigmented melanoma**).

Alike nodular melanoma **superficial spreading melanoma** is a common variety, and usually involves the lower extremities Fig. 5.9) in females and upper back in males. It gives rise to small, flat-topped plaques or papules with raised indurated edges and shows multiple hues. The earliest growth however shows lateral extension within the epidermis, giving the appearance of an unusual freckle. The lesions are generally asymptomatic though they can occasionally itch or bleed. The tumour grows slowly and finally present as nodular melanoma, generally with little pigment on them.

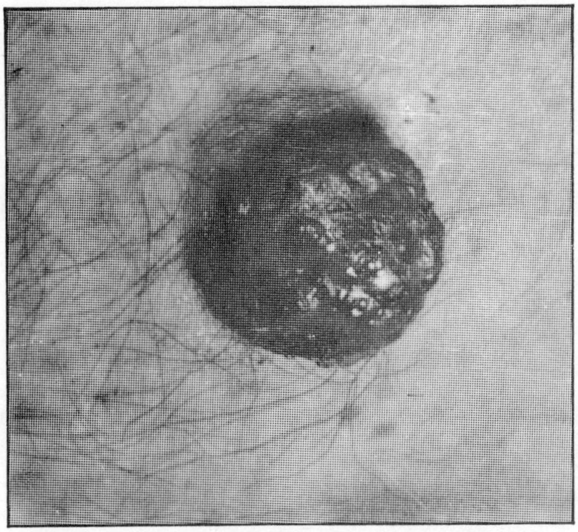

Figure 5.7. Slowly growing nodular melanoma.

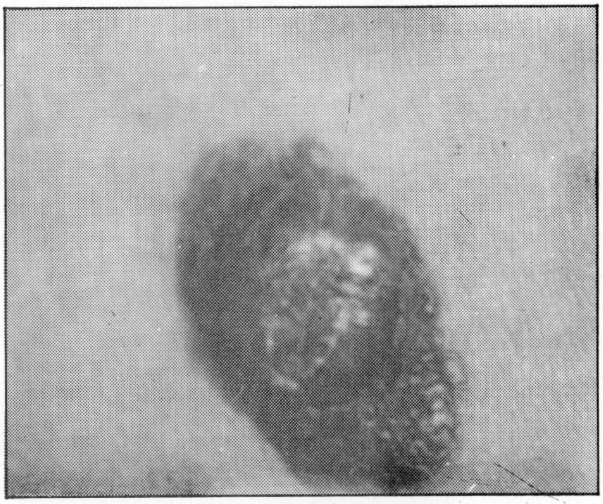

Figure 5.8. Nodular melanoma from old-standing naevus.

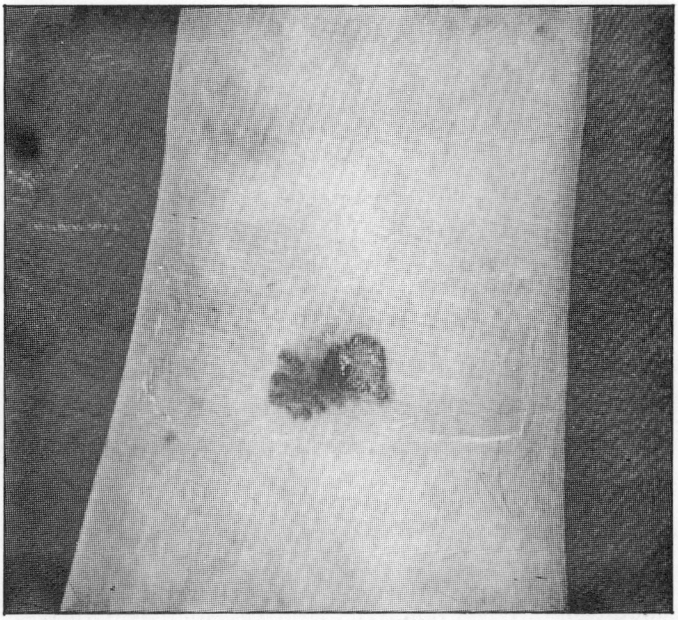

Figure 5.9. Superficial spreading melanoma on the leg.

Acral lentiginous melanoma is similar to superficial spreading melanoma but the tumours develop on the palms, soles and distal phalanges.

Amelanotic melanoma may develop from any one of the above-mentioned four varieties of melanoma, and presents as erythematous papule or nodule, usually having minimum pigmentation.

Occasionally melanoma may effect lateral nail folds or the nails (**subungual melanoma, melanotic whitlow**), and give rise to light brown discoloration of a small spot with erosion, uplifting or furrows of the neighbourhood, and finally lead to the formation of nodule or development of metastasis in axillary or epitrochlear lymph nodes.

Prognosis of the condition depends upon the thickness of the tumour at the time of diagnosis, and it is always worse. So the melanomas have a bad prognosis of those arising from mucous membrane.

Diagnosis

The condition is always suspected whenever a mole or tumour on normal skin shows increase in size and deepening of colour. Nemonic technique used for asymmetry of the lesion, border irregularities, colour irregularity and diameter enlarging; can also diagnose a suspected tumour. Diagnosis is however confirmed by histopathology of the lesion. The nature and extent of the vertical growth phase determined the multiple myeloma.

The diagnostic nemonic and biopsy help the condition to be differentiated easily from other conditions mimicking melanoma.

Treatment

Accurate recognition of early stages of melanoma development has now led to conservative strategies for surgical removal. However, whenever surgery is done it is given as wide excision, with lymph node dissection varying with the depth and location of the lesion and the background. Both surgery and chemotherapy actually alter the prognosis of the condition.

In cases of primary melanoma, surgical excision is the choice of treatment. However, when the malignancy is suspected, wide excision of the lesion and closure of the wound are desirable. In cases of confirmed malignancy, the cases are given wide surgical excision of the lesions with excision of regional lymph nodes and lymphatics, or further depending upon the levels of extension. Palliative treatment with radiotherapy is only suggested in cases, which are not suitable for surgical excision.

Chemotherapy with ankylosing cytotoxic, decarbazine, 2.0-4.5 mg/kg daily by IV injection for 10 days, may give good relief. Similarly, injectable preparation of vinca alkaloid, such as vindesine, or oral preparation of DNA reactive cytotoxic, such as hydroxyurea, is also equally effective. Immunotherapy with BCG vaccination has also been claimed to offer satisfactory result.

The principle criteria of prognosis of the condition are dependent on the histological assessment of the thickness of the tumour, and the thicker is the tumour the worse is the prognosis. This measurement is done vertically from the granular layer of the epidermis downwards. In general, when the lesion is in the intraepidermal, in macular phase, the prognosis is excellent, as in lentigo maligna, but becomes substantially poor when it becomes invasive. It is for this reason whenever possible the tumour should be given complete excision and a treatment with cryotherapy in its macular phase. The prognosis in nodular melanoma and superficial spreading melanoma is not good because the cases are not recognised until the lesions is very thick. So it is the case with amelanotic melanoma. The prognosis is also extremely poor in cases of acral lentiginous melanoma.

So as to overcome the prognostic gloominess general awareness of the people is highly desirable. Emphasis needs to be made for alertness so that whenever there is increase in size or deepening of colour of any mole or tumour occurs, the affected individual must seek immediate medical help. On the other hand, persons who have moles, which are subject to any friction, pressure, or otherwise causes irritation, are strongly advised for immediate surgical removal of them.

BASAL CELL CARCINOMA

Basal cell carcinoma or **basal cell epithelioma** is a most common form of epithelial tumour developing from the epidermis. The precise aetiology of the condition is still not known but chronic exposure to sunlight definitely bears certain aetiological association with it. Genetic predisposition may also play some role in its causation. The incidence is found to be high in persons with immunosuppression and with inherited defects in DNA replication or repair. The condition is also evident in several other conditions, such as chronic leg ulcer and burn scar.

Histological; changes may show tumour cells arising from the epidermis to the skin surface or may grow downward deeply into the dermis as cords or islands of cells with large, deeply basophilic nuclei and no cytoplasm. They are often surrounded by many fibroblasts and lymphocytes. The tumour cell islands are bounded in the periphery by the pallisade of cells. The islands or cords are embedded in a strauma.

Clinical Manifestations

It gives rise to lesion, usually single but may also be multiple, occurring on any part of the body excluding the palms and soles but often on the face. The lesion begins as a small, firm, skin-coloured papule, which later changes to nodule. The lesions slowly increase in size and cause necrosis and ulceration in the centre and thus, destroy large area of tissue. The ulcer has a rolled, pearly white border. This type of lesion is known as **rodent ulcer**.

Depending upon the feature of the presenting lesion the condition has several recognised type in which the lesions may show ulceration (rodent ulcer), while in some the lesion is translucent and often crossed with telangiectic vessels (***nodular type***). In ***pigmented type*** the lesion gives somewhat glassy appearance with pigmentation. In ***multicentric type*** the lesions present as scaly patch, while in ***superficial type*** the lesion appears as scar and increases in size by peripheral extension.

The lesion continues to enlarge slowly, with recurrent crusting or bleeding but otherwise there is usually no symptom.

The condition runs an indolent, chronic course, and causes localised malignancy. It usually does not cause any metastasis.

Diagnosis

It is diagnosed on clinical grounds, and is confirmed by histopathological findings.

It is differentiated from kerato-acanthoma in which the lesion grows very rapidly to assume a large, globular, symmetrical tumour, with horny plug in the centre, while the condition gives a different type of histopathological picture. Cutaneous tuberculosis, particularly lupus vulgaris, may however cause certain confusion for slow development of the lesion but causes hyperpigmented, irregular-shaped patches of minute translucent and indurated nodules, and the patches show healing with tissue paper-like scarring, and the condition may give a positive tubrculin test. Squamous cell carcinoma is differentiated for its rapid growth, absence of pearly nodule, and a different histopathological picture. Lupus erythematosus is differentiated for having lesion with horny follicular plugging and pigmentary changes, and the lesions may coalesce together to form large patches with atrophic centres. In tertiary syphilis, solitary or multiple gumma may occur on the skin and may thus, cause confusion but the lesions are large and destructive with a tendency to spread at the periphery and heal at the centre or the nodule may show ulceration with punched-out edges, and here may be a history of syphilis available and a positive serological test for syphilis.

Treatment

Total destruction of the tumour forms the principle of treatment. Surgical excision of the lesion is therefore preferable. Otherwise, destruction of the growth is done by curettage, supplemented by cautery or cryotherapy. Radiotherapy is also effective, particularly in cases of large superficial growth and in elderly persons.

The condition however carries a good prognosis.

SQUAMOUS CELL CARCINOMA

Squamous cell carcinoma or **squamous cell epithelioma** is a rapidly developing malignant tumour of the epidermis. It is however less common than basal cell carcinoma, and the cells in this condition show keratin formation. Exposure to ultraviolet rays plays a significant role in its causation. Although it can develop on normal skin, practically almost always the condition develops at the site of irritation or as a result of some predisposing skin lesions, such as Bowen's disease, actinic keratitis, actinic cheilitis, chronic ulcers and scars, draining osteomyelitis, exposure to industrial carcinogen (for example, tar and oil), exposure to arsenics, and betel nut or tobacco chewing. Immunosuppressed individuals appear to be more susceptible to the condition.

Histological changes in the condition show proliferation of epidermal cells with penetration of the dermo-epidermal junction, and pleomorphic keratinocytes. In poorly differentiated tumour the cells are anaplastic but otherwise they mature to form a central core of keratin.

Clinical Manifestations

It usually presents with dry, superficial, warty-like outgrowth on any part of the body but shows a predilection to the areas chronically exposed to the sunlight, such as back of the hands, forearms, lower lip, upper part of the face, and pinna of the ears, and less to other sites, such as extremities and external genitalia.

The tumour arises from elevated, firm, frequently dull red or telangiectic, indurated, round base, or the base may be depressed, flat, indurated or infiltrated. The warty growth is strongly attached on the skin. In other cases the lesion appears as firm, nodule (Fig. 5.10), or thickened plaques that ulcerates within a few weeks to produce well-demarcated ulcer with indurated and averted borders, or the lesion may assume cauliflower appearance or may even show fungating character. The lesion bleeds easily.

The condition undergoes metastasis within several weeks and produces regional lymphadenopathy.

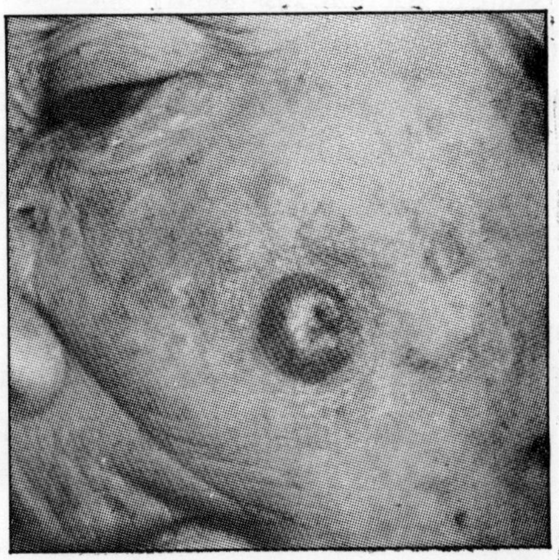

Figure 5.10. Nodular growth in squamous cell carcinoma.

Diagnosis

It is diagnosed on clinical grounds, and is confirmed by histological pictures.

It is differentiated from basal cell carcinoma, kerato-acanthoma, lupus erythematosus, lupus vulgaris, and tertiary syphilis.

Treatment

Destruction of the growth is the only choice of treatment. The patient is therefore treated surgically for the excision. In other cases, radiotherapy can be given quite effectively.

CHAPTER 6

Disorders due to Physical Agent and Nutrition

CALLUS AND CORN

Both callus and corn are benign conditions of cellular proliferation of the epidermis, produced by prolonged or repeated pressure or friction. Frequently callus develops due to certain occupation or habits, while corn develops due to defect in foot or toenails or in the footwear.

Histopathologically the condition produces localised hyperkeratosis and marked thickening of the stratum corneum. The papillae beneath the lesion appear flattened due to pressure, and may show some cellular infiltration. In cases of corn however keratinisation develops as a dense localised plug.

Clinical Manifestations

Cases of callus or **callosity** present with firm, raised, superficial, less demarcated, flattened, plaques or hyperkeratosis, with localised area of thick, compacted scales. The lesions are usually seen on the hands and dorsum of the feet. They are usually painless but can cause irritation or pain due to continued pressure or friction.

Corn is manifested by polished, flesh-coloured, conical, well-circumscribed, hyperkeratotic nodule, occurring usually on the soles, toe joints and at other bony prominences. It appears as 'hard' when occurs on the foot but 'soft' between the toes. It may cause pain and may appear tender on pressure.

Diagnosis

Diagnosis of the condition is made on clinical grounds alone.

Corn may however at times cause confusion with plantar wart which shows papillary acanthosis with marked hyperkeratosis, vacuolisation of the cells of the rete and widening of the rete pegs.

Treatment

Callus often tend to disappear spontaneously if the causative factor is removed. Avoidance to further exposure to pressure of friction may cause further improvement. No treatment is therefore required for the calluses unless they cause much inconvenience or appear unsightly. In such a case the lesions may be painted daily with keratolytic agent, 10% salicylic acid paste. If they repeatedly develop due to occupational hazard, change of occupation or perhaps use of protective device appropriate for the type of work, involved, may lead to a permanent cure.

In cases of corn, correction of the underlying cause is essential. In addition, relief can be given by removal from further pressure by using pads and rings available for the purpose. In other cases, keratolytic agent, such as urea or salicylic acid, 10% paste, may be applied locally once daily which softens the lesions and thus give relief from the pain.

INTERTRIGO

It is a quite common dermatological disorder that results from the effect of moisture, warmth and friction. Poor hygiene of keeping the skin folds perhaps act as predisposing factor. Diabetes and gout also predispose to the condition. Often it is found associated with staphylococcal and candidial infection.

It chiefly affects the obese and overdressed persons with hyperhidrosis, and involves the flexures of the body. Affected area is erythematous, and the epidermis underlying it is macerated. The lesions show erosions, fissures and exudation.

The condition shows maceration of the superficial epidermis.

Clinical Manifestations

It presents with localised erythematous areas of itching, stinging, and burning on the skin flexures, such as creases of the neck, axillae, cubital fossae, submammary folds, groins, popliteal fossae, and umbilicus, producing maceration of the overlying epidermis. There may also be fissures, erosions, and exudation. Lesions over the submammary folds may however give a weeping, glazed appearance.

It can produce moniliasis and secondary bacterial infection as complications.

Diagnosis

Diagnosis is made on clinical grounds.

Sometimes the condition may need to be differentiated from bacterial, candidial, and parasitic infections in which case the causative organisms can always be identified from the lesions. Differentiation from contact dermatitis and neurodermatitis may however pose certain problem though a detailed clinical feature is often sufficient to establish the diagnosis with confidence.

Treatment

The principle of management of the condition is to keep the affected area scrupulously clean and dry, and to keep the skin folds separated so that evaporation of moisture is not obstructed. In fact, exposure of the skin folds to fresh air and sunlight is extremely beneficial in the condition. Care is also taken to avoid further friction of the affected area. In cases of the lesions under the pendulous breasts, emphasis needs to be made for proper use of correct size of brassieres. In all cases the patients are instructed to expose the skin folds of the body to fresh and cool air as frequently as possible.

The lesions are kept cleaned with potassium permanganate solution, and kept dry. Liberal application of dusting powder over the affected area, containing chloroxylenol and aluminium dihydroxyallantoinate, may be beneficial. In cases of troublesome lesions, topical corticosteroid may be applied. Antibacterial agents are however given in cases of secondary bacterial infection but antifungal preparations for fungal infection.

NAPKIN RASH

It is the most common disorder of the infants, and is also known as **napkin dermatitis, diaper dermatitis** and **diaper rash**. It results from the use of wet or soiled napkins. Prolong contact with ammoniated urine can also produce the condition. So it is with the use of napkins that have been washed with abrasive detergent and not washed later thoroughly with sufficient water.

The condition frequently develops in infants aged over 3 months and in infants left overnight with soiled napkins.

It produces a superficial inflammatory reaction.

Clinical Manifestations

The infant presents with erythematous rash over the napkin area (Fig. 6.1), which includes thigh, genitalia, perineum and lower abdomen. The lesions may however also be vesicular or even ulcerative in severe cases. The lesions do not involve the flexures usually but may spread down to the legs and heels from contact of wet napkin.

In male infants, the tip of the penis may become irritated and crusted, and the infant may urinate frequently and may produce spots of blood on the napkin.

The lesions can be secondarily infected with bacteria and candida species.

Diagnosis

Diagnosis of the condition is made on clinical grounds.

It is differentiated from intertrigo that involves the flexures only. Infantile eczema is differentiated for having itchy, weeping and crusted lesions, which principally affect the cheeks and then spread to the groins, frequently involving the extensor surfaces. Thrush is differentiated for having white adherent patches on the buccal mucous membrane, and may give rise to moist, red areas on the groins and intergluteal folds with erosions on the edges. Tinea is differentiated for having erythematous scaling or vesicular and crusted patches with clear centres and active elevated margins. Congenital syphilis is differentiated for having other symptoms and signs of syphilis, including a positive test for syphilis (STS).

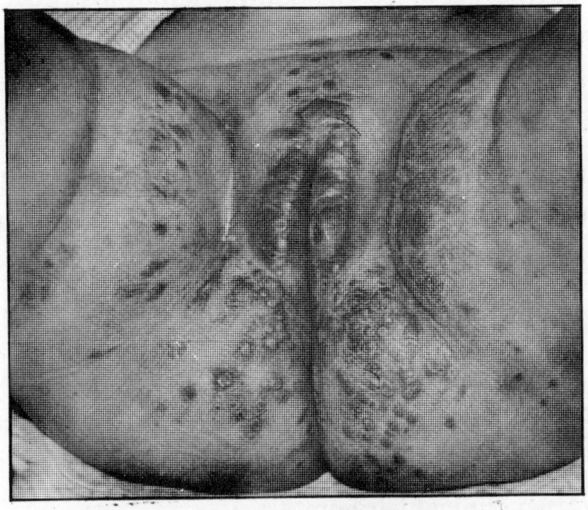

Figure 6.1. Napkin rash.

Treatment

Management of the condition requires immediate correction of the cause, with every emphasis on absolute cleanliness. Care must be taken that the infants are not left over in soiled napkins for any length of time, and the napkins are washed thoroughly with plenty water. The affected part of the skin is kept dry and exposed to fresh air for as long as possible. If the urine is too strong, the infant is given frequent drinks between the feeds.

Cleaning the area with olive oil does treatment of the affected part. Sometimes application of talcum powder is quite sufficient. Otherwise, the affected part is painted thinly with the cream of benzalkonium chloride in combination with dimethicone or cetrimide. Zinc oxide in combination with chamomile extract is also effective. When antiseptic application is required, the affected part may be applied with a cream containing an admixture of zinc oxide, benzyl benzoate and benzyl cinnamate, with anhydrous wool fat. In severely inflamed cases, however, administration of topical corticosteroids may be considered but for a very brief period.

In cases of secondary infection, appropriate antimicrobial or fungicidal agent may be given.

MILIARIA

Miliaria, commonly known as **prickly heat** or **heat rash**, occurs due to failure of sweat to reach the skin surface. In circumstances such as hot and humid environment there may be increased production of sweat. In this circumstances when fails to come out pf the skin due to occlusion of the seat ducts or blocking of the sweat pore, the sweat gets trapped inside the skin and causes the development of the condition. It also occurs as occupational hazard to the workers exposed to such an environment at working place. In addition, it may also develop from local friction or on macerated skin where occlusive clothing prevents adequate evaporation of moisture. Persons who sweat profusely or are obese usually found to be prone for the development of the condition. Wearing undue heavy clothing can produce the condition, in addition

Pathological changes it produces include dilatation of the sweat gland ducts, obstruction of the ducts by horny plugs, and periductal inflammation. Sweat is escaped and entrapped in the stratum corneum of epidermis.

Clinical Manifestations

It presents with acute inflammatory eruptions, chiefly on the trunk, upper extremities and intertrigenous areas, accompanied by severe itching, burning, and irritation. Repeated scratching may lead to excoriation and infection. There may be hyperhidrosis initially but later anhydrosis.

The condition has two clinical variants.

Miliaria crystallina (sudamina) develops in fever, sunburn, and hot fomentation and underneath the plaster casts. It gives rise to transient lesions that appear rapidly. The lesions are superficial, small, pinpoint sized, translucent vesicles, and are discrete and multiple.

Prickly heat or **Miliaria rubra** is the most common variety. It gives rise to pinhead sized macules and papules, or even papulovesicles, surrounded by erythematous halo. The lesions may be confluent. Scratching and secondary infection may cause the lesions to become pustular. In very severe form of the condition there may also be rise in body temperature and heat prostration.

Secondary bacterial infection is its usual complication.

Diagnosis

Diagnosis is easy on clinical grounds.

In case of any confusion it may be differentiated from drug eruptions in which a history of exposure to the offending drugs is available and the rashes are relieved following withdrawal of the drug, while the development of the lesions shows no relation with the environment, obesity, clothing or with any other factors. Chickenpox is differentiated for presenting with constitutional symptoms, while the condition gives rise to pruritic papular rash distributed over the body centripetally and that the lesions change to vesicles, pustules and finally subside with crust formation.

Treatment

The best way of management is to provide a cooler, less humid environment. Otherwise, the patient is removed from the hot and humid weather, and the involved areas are kept cool and dry. The patient can be given frequent cold bath, or placed in air conditioning. The patient is also given antipruritic or dusting powder, or a soothing lotion, such as calamine lotion or hydrocortisone lotion for topical application over the affected areas. In severe cases, anticholinergic drug may be given. Antimicrobial agent is needed in cases of secondary infection.

SOLAR DERMATITIS

Solar dermatitis or **sunburn** occurs from overexposure of skin to sunlight or ultraviolet light, but may also occur due to hypersensitivity. Solar dermatitis is reckoned when its development is associated with a very chronic exposure to sunlight or ultraviolet light. Development of the lesions however depends upon the duration and intensity of light to which the skin is exposed. It usually occurs as occupational hazard amongst the farmers, sailors and out-door workers.

The condition may be acute or chronic, while there is another type of the condition, known as **actinic keratosis.**

The condition affects the light-skinned persons more severely than the dark-skinned, and to individuals who have more frequent exposure to sunlight than those who have less. Actinic keratosis however develops in the middle-aged and elderly persons.

Skin shows intense hyperaemia and varying degree of oedema, and may even blister formation. Later, resolution occurs with desquamation and increase in pigmentation. In chronic exposure, patches of erythema may become rough and scaly, and finally keratosis may develop.

In actinic keratosis however the epidermal change show acanthosis and varying degree of dysplasia. Overlying stratum corneum is often parakeratotic. There may be downward proliferation of the cells in an irregular pattern or infiltration of the cells into the dermis. The basement membrane is however intact.

Clinical Manifestations

Symptom and signs of the condition depend upon the intensity and duration of exposure. The clinical manifestations therefore vary greatly from local redness to swelling, and perhaps blister formation on the exposed parts of the body. The lesions are usually bilateral and symmetrical in distribution. They may show erythema or even maculopapular eruptions, with subsequent scaling and hyperpigmentation. In cases of involvement of the face, the eyelids may appear swollen. The affected person may complain of local burning, feeling of warms, itching, pain and tenderness. In severe cases, there may be nausea, chills, fever, tachycardia and shock, in addition. Oedema may also develop on the ankles, legs, feet and other parts of the body.

Chronic exposure may lead to the development of **chronic solar dermatitis,** and usually occurs as an occupational hazard amongst the farmers, sailors and other out-door workers. The exposed parts of the body, such as face, neck, dorsum of the hands and feet, show regular wrinkling, with shiny and smooth surface, or diffuse pigmentation, telangiectasia and keratotic lesions, with shiny and smooth surface, or covered with scales. The condition frequently leads to give rise to epithelioma.

Cutis rhomboidalis nuchae is another form of chronic solar dermatitis, and the lesions develop on the back of the neck. The skin becomes thickened, tough and tanned, with exaggerated prominent creases.

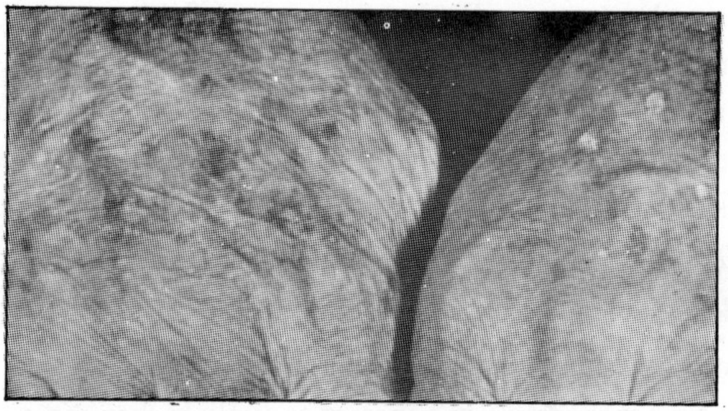

Figure 6.2. Actinic keratosis on dorsum of the hands.

Actinic keratosis or **senile keratosis** develops anywhere on the body exposed to sunlight but most frequently affects the dorsum of the hands, face, and arms, as multiple, small, pink-grey, hyperkeratotic warty lesions. On the dorsum of the hands (Fig. 6.2), it produces patches of hyperpigmentation and depigmentation on an atrophic skin. Involvement of the face (Fig. 6.3) produces small, rough scaling lesions on an atrophic and erythematous skin. The lesions however tend to become near nodular when it involves the ears. In general, the lesions appear to be chronic solar dermatitis in all respects and tend to give rise to epithelioma.

Diagnosis

It is diagnosed on clinical grounds.

The condition my be differentiated from contact dermatitis which has a history of exposure to certain offending agents; from seborrhoeic dermatitis which gives rise to greasy scales and pruritus; from erysipelas that has sharply demarcated localised lesions with raised margins and elevated body temperature; and from other conditions which present with localised lesions and raised body temperature. The condition may however appear indistinguishable from low-grade squamous cell carcinoma.

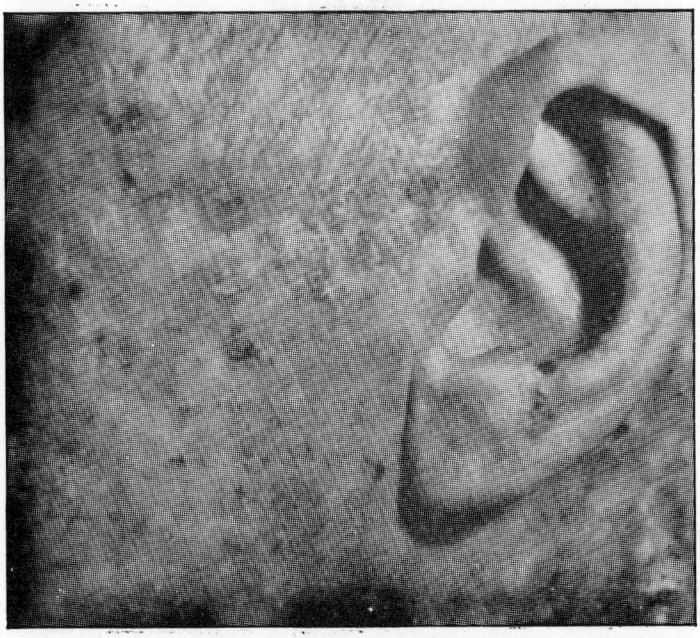

Figure 6.3. Actinic keratosis on face.

Treatment

The principle of management of the condition is to avoid further exposure to sunlight or ultraviolet light. Change of occupation therefore appears to be an ideal preventive measure but at times may well be unavoidable. In such a condition and in other circumstances it is strongly advisable to keep the exposed surfaces of the body well covered with cloth so as to prevent the exposure to sunlight or ultraviolet light. Use of sunscreens may also be beneficial.

Mild lesions usually clear up within a few days, and do not usually require any treatment. Acute lesions are however treated with normal saline or cold-water compression, or by application of lotion or cream containing calamine and diphenhydramine may be applied locally three or four times a day. Topical corticosteroids are also beneficial, particularly in chronic cases, such as cream of 0.1% hydrocortisone, applied liberally locally twice daily, or hydrocortisone cream in combination with crotamin applied topically two or three times daily, for 10 to 14 days. In cases of involvement of large area however the treatment is given with topical 5-flurouracil cream with or without retinoic acid, followed by topical corticosteroids.

Moderate and severe cases are treated with oral antihistamine and corticosteroids. The patients are given rest and correction of fluid and electrolyte balance, if necessary. More chronic cases may however require curettage of the lesions. Cryotherapy with liquid nitrogen is however quite rapid and effective.

BURNS

The condition results from thermal heat, chemical agents, electricity and radiation. The extent of damage thus produced however depends upon the intensity and duration of exposure.

Burns may be superficial or deep, and is therefore classified into first, second and third degree.

In first degree the damage is limited superficially to the dermis. There is hyperaemia and slight oedema of the epidermis. There may be necrosis of the superficial layer of the epidermis.

In second degree the damage is not so superficial and presents with destruction of the epidermis. There is formation of blebs or vesicles between the epidermis and dermis, with some degree of destruction of the dermis.

Third degree burn includes complete destruction of dermis, including the sensory nerves.

Clinical Manifestations

First degree burns presents with erythema, slight oedema of the epidermis. The patient complains of increasing warmth and tenderness on the parts involved. The lesion is superficial with formation of no bleb.

Second degree burns presents with vesicles, blebs or bullae, pain, tenderness and a feeling of warmth. Erythema is present.

In third degree burns, the surface appears pale and leathery, or charred and coagulated, and the condition gives rise to shock. Small blood vessels of the area show dilatation, with increased capillary permeability and oozing of plasma in the burned area. There may also be superimposed infection. As the extent of injury damages the nerves, this stage of burns appears relatively painless.

In severe cases, there may be haemoconcentration. Later, dead tissue sloughs with formation of new epithelium over the affected area but, in deep wound, extensive granulation tissue may develop before re-epithelisation, and may produce scars.

Electric burns may however cause much deeper damage even though the lesions may appear superficial. The wounds are well demarcated, and show progressive sloughing and later, necrosis. Severe cases may however cause respiratory or cardiac failure.

Chemical burns develop due to strong acids and alkalis, and several other chemicals. Characteristically they give rise to necrosis of the area, developing gradually over the hours.

Burns can produce secondary bacterial infection and, in severe cases, shock as complications.

Diagnosis

It is diagnosed on clinical grounds.

The condition my be differentiated from contact dermatitis which has a history of exposure to certain offending agents; from seborrhoeic dermatitis which gives rise to greasy scales and pruritus; from erysipelas that has sharply demarcated localised lesions with raised margins and elevated body temperature; and from other conditions which present with localised lesions and raised body temperature. The condition may however appear indistinguishable from low-grade squamous cell carcinoma.

Diagnosis

It is diagnosed clinically. A history of exposure is always available, which is usually conclusive.

Treatment

In general, the affected parts are cleaned carefully with soap and water. Burns due to chemical agents and, also, the dirty wounds are washed thoroughly with plenty water. Some wound may however need debridment, in addition.

In cases of minor burns of first and second degrees, the blisters are left unruptured but the large bullae may be aspirated aseptically leaving the overlying dermis intact to cover, the wounds. Other wounds are, after cleaning, covered with sterile petroleum gauze and left with pressure dressings. Some wounds are; however, require local application of corticosteroids or dressings with 0 5% solution of silver nitrate. Analgesics are helpful and the patients may be given codeine phosphate, 30-60 mg, or aspirin, 300-900 mg, four times daily orally. Some cases however may even need narcotics, morphine by SC, IM or IV injection, for relief of pain. Larger or widespread wounds may require antimicrobial agents for prevention of secondary infection.

Adequate management is also needed in cases of shock, and for correction of fluid and electrolyte balance, if required.

It is now evident that artificial nutrition can substantially improve the management of critically ill burn patients through enhancing immunity and healing capacity. In such cases, following standard resuscitation for 48 hours, artificial nutrition, such as glucose, crystalline insulin every 8 hours, amino acid (amino sterile) every 12 hours and fat in the form of intralipid every 12 hours, is given intravenously.

In cases of severe electrical burns, adequate cardiopulmonary resuscitation is required.

CHILBLAINS

Chilblains, also known as **pernio,** result from vascular disturbances when arterial spasms develop from exposure to cold weather. The spasm is relieved by warm weather. It usually develops in persons nourished poorly or has disturbances in peripheral circulation.

The condition is more common in women than in men.

In this condition, exposure to cold produces arteriolar spasms and results ischaemia that causes damage to the capillaries and formation of thrombosis.

Clinical Manifestations

It gives rise to painful, burning and itchy erythematous lesions with oedema or blistering on the fingers and toes, but can also involve the ears and face. The lesions are usually associated with local oedema or blistering. The patient complains of a feeling of burning, and the lesions are painful and itchy. The affected part is cold, clammy, and cyanotic but the colour disappears on pressure. A quick warming up of the affected part worsens the condition. There may also be maceration and increased sweating. In addition, the patient may present with other symptoms and signs of peripheral circulatory disturbances.

Recurrences of the lesions are common, and may cause ulcerations, haemorrhage, fibrosis, and atrophy.

Diagnosis

Diagnosis is made on clinical grounds.

It is differentiated from Raynaud's phenomenon, which is relieved by warmth, involves the fingers usually of both hands; pain is uncommon, while it affects the toes only rarely. Lupus erythematosus when involves the hands may also cause confusion but is differentiated for having elevated and scaly lesions along with the characteristic lesions developing on the face.

Treatment

No satisfactory treatment is available. The general principles of management of the condition include gradual rewarming and elevation of the affected part therefore do management of the condition, with protection against further exposure to cold.

The affected part may be massaged with rubefacient, such as admixture of menthol 2%, camphor 4%, methyl salicylate 4% and capsicum oleoresin 0.035% cream, to be used as required, or the affected part is painted with chlorbutol, tannic acid, phenol and camphor. Uses of topical circulatory preparations are used to improve circulation. The patients may therefore be given heparinoid, 0.3% cream or 0.8% ointment. The cream is applied up to four times daily, or the ointment 2-3 times daily.

The patient may be given systemic treatment with vasodilators, such as nicotinic acid derivative, inositol nicotinate, 1 g three or four times daily orally, oxpentifylline, 400 mg two or three times daily orally, class II Ca^{++} antagonist, nifedipine, 5 mg every eight hours orally, selective á$_1$-blocker, prazosin, 500 µg in the evening orally and then 500 µg twice daily for 7-10 days and then adjust according to response, or antihistamine, cinnarizine, 75 mg three times daily orally and maintenance at 75 mg two or three times daily. Alternatively the patient may be given peripheral and cerebral activator, naftidrofuryl, 100-200 mg three times daily orally. Selective á$_1$ blocker, thymoxamine, is also highly effective and is given for short-term therapy. It is given as 40 mg four times daily orally, increasing to 80 mg four times daily if response is poor but discontinued after 2 weeks if remains irresponsive.

Administration of vitamin K may also be beneficial.

In addition, there are several other remedies available, such as galvanic baths or local exposure to ultraviolet ray, which may be tried with varying success.

ACROCYANOSIS

The condition is produced from vasospasm occurring from exposure to cold. Disturbances in peripheral circulation may have certain aetiological influence on its occurrence. The condition however has no association with occlusive arterial disease.

It predominantly affects the young people, and is more common in females than in males.

Vasospasms of the smaller vessels of the skin occurs being triggered by exposure to cold, and result dilatation of the capillaries and venules.

Clinical Manifestations

It presents with cold, clammy, and cyanotic skin of the hands and feet, but can also affect the tip of the nose and ears, accompanied by hyperhidrosis, but the symptoms subside as the parts become warmer. The cyanosis is persistent, painless, and segmental, and symmetrical in distribution. Exposure to further cold intensified the cyanosis. There may be oedema but no pain, and it does not cause ulceration or trophic changes.

Diagnosis

It is made clinically.

It is differentiated from Raynaud's phenomenon for having numbness, tingling or burning in the affected areas. Chilblain and frostbite are differentiated for having pain and burning, and for causing ulcerations or trophic changes.

Treatment

The affected part is kept warm, and the patient is encouraged for exercise of the part involved. No treatment is usually necessary but otherwise, nicotinic acid derivatives, such as nicotinyl, 25-50 mg four times orally, may be give while some cases may need exposure to ultraviolet rays. Few selected cases may however gain from sympathectomy.

FROSTBITE

It results from freezing that causes injury to superficial tissue. The injury however depends upon the degree of coldness and the length of exposure to it.

Involved parts appear bloodless but later, red and swollen. There may be necrosis, with formation of blisters and subsequent desquamation, or may lead to further necrosis and gangrene due to arteriolar spasms, and ischaemia aggravated by stasis of blood in the damaged capillaries.

There are sludging of RBC due to capillary thrombosis and shunting of blood from neurovascular impulses.

Clinical Manifestations

Mild cases present with numbness, pricking and itching in the exposed parts of the body, involving chiefly the cheeks, nose, ears, fingers and toes. In other cases, it gives rise to stiffness, paraesthesia, tenderness, and burning pain. The affected part is initially cold and cyanotic, which change to hard and white when freezing sets in, and later becomes erythematous and painful on rewarming. There may be blisters and bullae and later, necrosis or gangrene.

Diagnosis

Diagnosis is made on clinical grounds.

It is differentiated from chilblains, which presents with itchy lesions but without actually freezing of the tissue. Raynaud's phenomenon is differentiated for being relieved by warmth, while pain in this condition is rare.

Treatment

The principle of management of the condition includes gradually warming up of the affected person, and to remove away from further exposure. The patient is therefore kept in warm environment. The affected person is given hot drinks and hot water bottles for rewarming. In addition, the affected part is protected from trauma, friction and pressure. If there is hypothermia, appropriate measures are taken accordingly. If situation warrants, the patient may also be given oxygen inhalation.

An analgesic may be given for relief of pain, such as aspirin, 300-900 mg three to four times daily orally. In moderate and severe cases, treatment with anticoagulant is essential for prevention of thrombosis and gangrene. The patient is given heparin, 5000 U twice daily by SC injection, and continued for 7 to 10 days. Topical corticosteroids may be applied locally for prevention of inflammation, and antimicrobial agents are given for control of secondary infection.

In cases of developing gangrene, prompt surgical interference is desirable, with special consideration of skin grafting as necessary.

KWASHIORKOR

Kwashiorkor is an example of **protein-energy (calorie) malnutrition (PEM),** which results from inadequate intake of proteins, but the intake of calories may be adequate. However, this nutritional deficiency causes growth failure, skin manifestations, irritability and apathy. Some specific amino acids and deficiency of minerals and vitamins too play some role in its causation. Gastroenteritis, measles and malaria frequently precipitate the condition.

The condition very commonly occurs in the rural areas, and affects the late weaning infants, usually 1 to 4 years old.

Pathologically the condition produces enlargement and peripheral fatty changes in the liver, zymogen depletion in the pancreas, atrophy of the adrenal cortex and skeletal muscles, and fusion of villi of upper part of the small intestine with mucosal atrophy and decrease in the mitotic index in the crypts.

Clinical Manifestations

The child looks apathetic and miserable, and presents with retardation of growth. The child fails to gain weight. There is oedema of the feet, which may also be evident on the hands and face. Little ascites and pleural effusion may also be present. Wasting of muscles is another prominent feature. In cases of gross restriction in both protein and calorie, there will be complete lack of subcutaneous but shows oedema on the feet. On the other hand, the amount of subcutaneous fat may be plenty in children whose diets though show serious deficiency in protein but have otherwise sufficient calories.

In skin involvement the condition gives rise to erythematous and bronzed patches with wavy texture and sharp raised edges on the trunk and limbs, which may show cracks on the flexures. Later, the patches become hard, scaly and distinctly elevated. Skin shows depigmentation along with area of hyperpigmentation, and pallor around the mouth and nose. Curly hair becomes soft and straight, and looses its pigmentation. Otherwise, hair is sparse or depigmented or shows pale band across. Nails are usually thin, ridged and brittle.

The condition produces iron deficiency anaemia, sometimes even megaloblastic anaemia, malnutrition, jaundice, petechiae, and stupor as sequelae. It also causes increased susceptibility to infection, which, in some cases, may lead to tuberculosis.

Diagnosis

Reduced body weight for age in comparison to normal standard is diagnostic for protein-energy malnutrition.

Blood shows anaemia, and low levels of cholesterol, amylase, lipase, alkaline phosphatase, and urea. Plasma protein level is reduced but the level of gammaglobulin is well maintained or may be relatively elevated. Level of total blood potassium is reduced.

It is differentiated form pellagra in which however the lesions do not show wavy texture, while the condition gives rise to itching or burning.

Treatment

The patients are given easily digestible diets with adequate protein, minerals and vitamins, with extra calories. Careful protection is needed for dermatoses, and the associated complaints are managed symptomatically. Adequate supplement is also given for other vitamin deficiencies. In cases of difficulties in oral diet supplements, injectable preparations may be given parentally instead.

HYPOVITAMINOSIS A

Hypovitaminosis A (**vitamin A deficiency**) is a condition of nutritional deficiency of vitamin A due to inadequate or insufficient intake of vitamin A, or its inadequate utilisation. Deficiency of the vitamin is also common in protein-energy (calories) malnutrition.

The pathological changes the deficiency cause is that the epithelial surfaces of tissue become flattened and heaped up from squamous metaplasia. The metaplasia is evident in the mucous membrane of the eye; the mucosa of gastrointestinal, respiratory and genitourinary tracts. The metaplasia is also evident in the epithelium lining of glandular ducts, such as in the pancreas. The sebaceous glands, lacrimal glands and hair follicles are blocked with horny plugs of keratin.

When it involves the skin, it produces follicular hyperkeratosis due to formation of keratin plugs in the sebaceous glands.

Clinical Manifestations

In general, the condition may present with symptoms of other vitamin deficiency or of malnutrition, and the affected persons show increased susceptibility to infection. Children show growth retardation. Otherwise, it presents with night blindness or visual disturbances. Xerosis of bulbar conjunctivae develops with dryness, thickening and muddies pigmentation, and may show foamy patches (Bitot's spots). Later, there may be xerophthalmia and keratomalacia.

The condition causes infection and blindness as complications.

In skin involvement the condition presents with dry, firm, pigmented, keratotic, papules (**phrynoderma, toad skin**) occurring especially on the hair follicles, usually on the extensor surfaces of the lower and upper extremities (Fig. 6.4). The lesions later extend to the buttocks, shoulders, abdomen, back, face and posterior aspects of the neck, and generally spare the hands and feet. The keratotic plugs may protrude from the hair follicles as horny spines or be covered with loosely adherent scales. When the lesions develop on the face, it resembles acne but the skin appears dry.

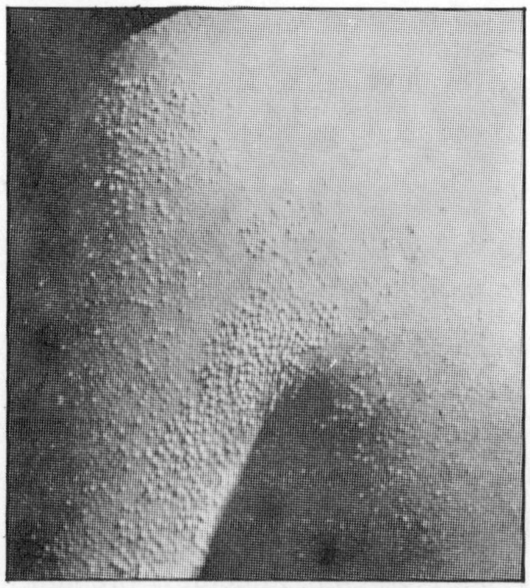

Figure 6.4. Phrynoderma on posterior aspects of arm and back.

Diagnosis

Blood shows decreased level of retinol. Clinical trial with vitamin A can confirm the diagnosis.

When lesions develop on face it is then differentiated from acne vulgaris, which however does not present with dryness of the skin.

Treatment

The condition is treated with vitamin A, 200,000 IU daily for 2-3 days orally or by IM injection, followed by 25,000-50,000 IU daily orally till cure. The patient is also encouraged to have ample supply of the vitamin through diet, and through halibut-liver oil, 400 U; also contain vitamin D.

A combined preparation of vitamin A (5000 U), vitamin D (2000 U) and ascorbic acid (150 mg/ml) to the pregnant and nursing mothers and child, 1 month-5 years as 5 drops daily.

In addition, the patient is given ample supply of vitamins and iron, as required.

RIBOFLAVIN DEFICIENCY

Riboflavin is a constituent of flavoproteins that is responsible for tissue oxidation, and an inadequate or insufficient intake or metabolism of it from dietary sources causes the deficiency **(vitamin B_2 deficiency).**

Pathological changes the condition produce are however neither distinctive, nor pathognomic. In general, it causes atrophy of the skin and mucous membrane when it causes dermatitis and glossitis. In cases of developing cheilosis, the pathological changes include hyperkeratosis of the epidermis and a dermal inflammatory infiltrate.

Clinical Manifestations

In cutaneous involvement it presents with dry scaling and cracking and fissuring of the lips (cheilosis). In addition, it gives rise to erythematous, greasy seborrhoeic scales at nasolabial; folds and also on nose which extend with a butterfly distribution, covering the eyelids and ears.

There may also be other symptoms and signs of riboflavin deficiency, such as malaise, weight loss, interstitial keratitis, photophobia, and dysphagia, and magenta coloured tongue.

Diagnosis

It is diagnosed clinical and is confirmed through therapeutic trail with riboflavin

The condition may at time need to be differentiated from seborrhoeic dermatitis, which is comparatively easy for having characteristic lesions, while riboflavin has no therapeutic effect on it.

Treatment

The deficiency is recovered by giving riboflavin 5-10 mg 3 times daily orally. Addition of vitamin B complex may confer greater achievement.

CHEILOSIS

The condition is also known as **cheilitis** and **angular stomatitis**. Principally it is the first but characteristic symptom and sign of riboflavin deficiency, but it can also develop independently due top deficiency of vitamin B-complex. On addition, drooling of saliva, wearing faulty dentures, and pipe smoking can produce the condition. Sometimes it may also result to candidial infection.

In this condition hyperkeratosis of the epidermis develops at the angle of the mouth, and shows inflammatory infiltrate, with formation of cracks and fissures.

Clinical Manifestations

The condition does not give rise to any symptom except pallor and, moist fissures at the angles of the mouth, radiating downwards and outwards, covered by yellowish crusts. The lesions may however become secondary infected and macerated.

Diagnosis

The condition is diagnosed clinically.

It is differentiated from riboflavin deficiency which gives rise to other symptoms, such as glossitis, interstitial keratitis and dermatitis. Candidial cheilosis is differentiated from identification of the causative fungus. Herpetic stomatitis is differentiated in which the condition presents with erythema, oedema, fever and cervical lymphadenopathy.

Treatment

Management of the condition requires prompt correction of the underlying causes, such as drooling of saliva and faulty dentures, and appropriate treatment with riboflavin in cases of riboflavin deficiency.

The lesions may be cleaned with potassium permanganate solution, and may be pained with 1% silver nitrate solution in water.

In addition, the patient may need ample administration of vitamin B-complex orally.

PELLAGRA

It is a nutritional disorder principally associated with deficiency of niacin and is characterised by 3 Ds: dermatitis, diarrhoea and dementia. It occurs from a dietary habit rich in maize and form deficiency of niacin (nicotinin acid, nicotinamide) occurring due to gastrointestinal disease, cirrhosis of liver, alcoholism, and extra demand due to pregnancy and hyperthyroidism when the extra demand is not supplied adequately. In addition, imbalance of or intolerance to amino acid (tryptophan) may also play a part in its causation. The condition may be associated with protein and vitamin B deficiency.

Pathological changes it produces show thickened and hyperkeratotic skin and shows symmetrical pigmentation and erythema, and oedema and congestion in the dermis. Mucous membrane of the alimentary tract and of vagina shows disappearance of lining epithelium with underlying inflammation, ulcers and small mucous cyst formation in the colon. In the nervous, system there may be chromatolysis of ganglionic cells.

Clinical Manifestations

Characteristically the condition is accompanied by 3Ds: dermatitis, diarrhoea and dementia.

It presents with slightly swollen and well-demarcated areas of erythematous rash, distributed symmetrically on any part of the skin but tend to be more severe and pronounced over the areas of chronic irritation or exposure to sunlight, such as face, neck, dorsum of hands, wrists, elbows, and knees. The lesions show hyperkeratosis and scaling, and may itch and give a burning sensation. Later, the lesions may become vesiculated, exudative, cracked and crusted with ulcerations. The affected skin appears depigmented. In chronic state, skin becomes markedly thickened due to subcutaneous fibrosis and scarring, and produce roughening and fissuring of the skin with alternating areas of hyperpigmentation and depigmentation. Otherwise, the lesions may become chronic atrophic with scales, and the skin may appear dry, shiny and atrophic. Development of secondary infection is quite frequent.

In addition to the cutaneous manifestations, the condition characteristically presents with fatigability and weakness. Diarrhoea is common, though sometimes it may as well as be absent. Diarrhoea is usually watery or the stools may contain mucus and blood. Patient complains of anorexia, nausea, vomiting, excessive salivation, cheilosis, dyspepsia, and soreness of mouth, dysphagia, abdominal pain, proctitis and vaginitis. Tongue is swollen and painful, with raw beefy appearance. There may also be weakness, spastic or flaccid paresis in the legs, anxiety, depression, irritability, failure of concentration, delirium and, in chronic state, dementia. There may also be coexisting symptoms of other vitamin B deficiency.

The condition can cause infection and malabsorption as complications.

Diagnosis

Diagnosis of the condition is easy from clinical manifestations in fully developed cases. Dietary habit is another helpful guide. There may also be coexisting vitamin B deficiencies.

Scaly lesions of the condition may at times however cause confusion with seborrhoeic dermatitis but is differentiated from its distribution pattern, while it presents with greasy scales, and the characteristic symptoms of pellagra is absent.

The condition may also need to be differentiated from other causes of diarrhoea, and glossitis.

Treatment

As dermatological features are not the only manifestations of the condition, nor has such involvement any specific therapy, and as dementia develops in the late stage, it is always highly advisable that the cases are treated in the hospitals.

Rest and well balanced diet with high protein content are the first line of management of the condition. Specific therapy is however given by nicotinamide, 400-600 mg daily in divided doses orally. The patient is also given zinc oxide or calamine lotion for topical application in cases of cutaneous involvement. Protection of the affected area is needed against further exposure to sunlight.

In addition, adequate management is required for other vitamin B deficiencies, and folic acid, iron and vitamin B_{12}, if there is also anaemia. The patients are also given well-balanced diet with high protein content.

XANTHOMATOSIS

It is a form of hyperlipidaemia that occurs due to abnormalities in lipid metabolism, resulting elevated levels cholesterol and/or triglyceride carrying lipoproteins in the plasma. This is represented by tumour-like collections of foamy histiocytes seen in the subepithelial connective tissue and in the tendons. It may occur as primary hyperlipoproteinaemia inherited as an autosomal dominant trait, or may occur as secondary to hypothyroidism, haemochromatosis, biliary cirrhosis and obstruction in the common bile duct. Cutaneous xanthomatosis may also develop in cases of hyperlipidaemia as that results in renal disease, diabetes and pancreatitis, while in others there may not be any association with blood lipid.

Pathological changes it produces intracellular accumulation of histiocytes with foamy cytoplasm and Touton giant cells within macrophages, and yellowish-brown growth consisting connective tissue cells, greatly distended with lipid droplets.

Clinical Manifestations

The condition has several clinical variants.

Xanthelasma is the commonest variety of the condition and is associated with types IIa and III hyperlipoproteinaemia but may also occur without any lipid abnormality. The condition affects the elderly persons, and presents with soft, flat, slightly elevated, round or oval, yellowish plaques on the eyelids, usually near the inner canthus (Fig. 6.5). The lesions are multiple, distributed symmetrically, and tend to coalesce. There is however no subjective symptom.

Tuberous xanthoma and **tendinous xanthoma** are associated with types IIa and III hyperlipoproteinaemia, though other types may rarely be associated with. Tuberous xanthoma presents with flat or rounded, multiple, yellow or yellowish-brown, infiltrated, tumour-like growth anywhere on the skin but more commonly over the bony prominences of the hands, elbows Fig. 6.6) and knees. Tendinous xanthoma is similar like tuberous xanthoma but have lighter colour, and occurs over the tendons and tendon sheaths, frequently on the Achilles tendon, patellar tendon and extensor tendons of the digits. Although xanthomas do not give rise to any subjective symptom but as cardiovascular complications are closely associated with type II hyperlipoproteinaemia, the patients may therefore also present with symptoms and signs of the complications.

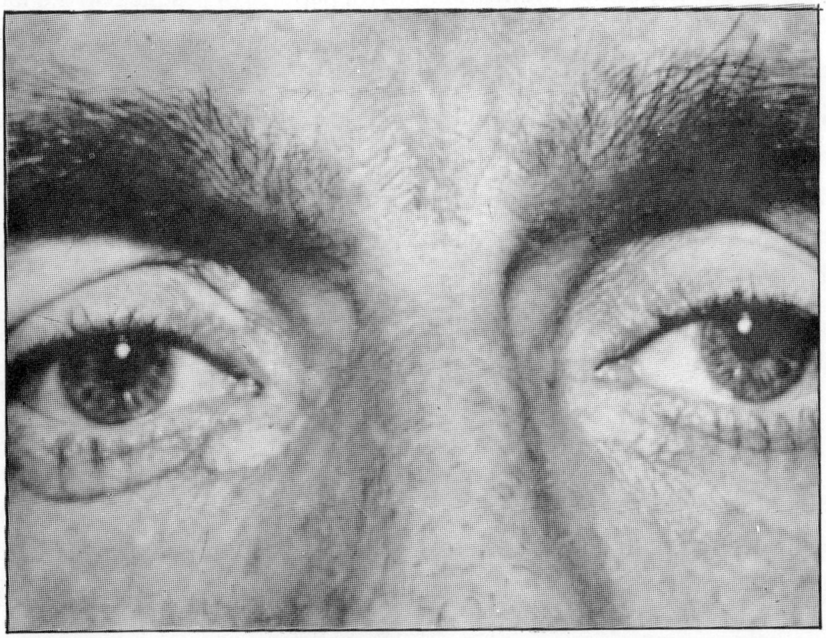

Figure 6.5. Xanthelasma.

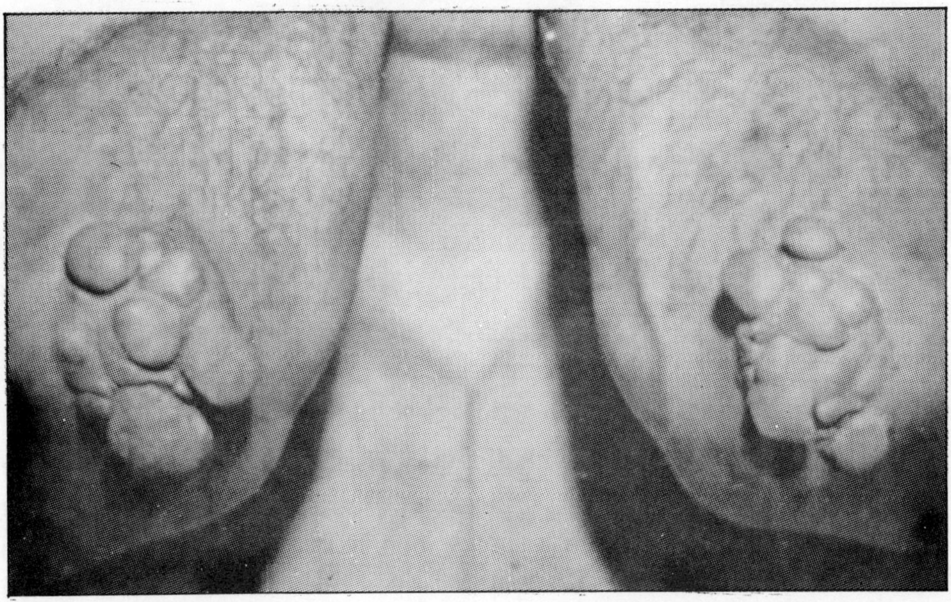

Figure 6.6. Tuberous xanthoma on elbows.

Disseminated xanthoma is perhaps a variety of tuberous xanthoma but shows no abnormality in cholesterol and lipid metabolism. It is also not associated with cardiovascular complication. It presents with small, yellowish-brown papules or plaques on the face, neck, and other parts of the body, including mucous membrane, but shows a predilection to the flexures, especially the axillae.

Eruptive xanthoma is associated with several types of hyperlipoproteinaemia. It gives rise to sudden showers of yellow papules on an erythematous base. The lesions are scattered over the body but show some predilection for the buttocks, posterior thighs, knees and elbows. Some patients may also have cardiovascular complaint. Many patients may have abnormal glucose metabolism or even diabetes mellitus.

Plane xanthoma is associated with primary biliary cirrhosis and types IIa and III hyperlipoproteinaemia. It presents with linear, yellow lesions on the skin, especially the palmer creases.

Diagnosis

Primary xanthomatosis shows elevation of cholesterol and triglyceride carrying lipoproteins in the plasma but the level of neutral fat is normal. In secondary xanthomatosis there is an elevation of neutral fat. In general, however, diagnosis of the condition is comparatively easy on clinical grounds.

At times the condition may cause confusion with tuberculoid leprosy, which presents with anaesthetic lesions, thickened nerves and shows a positive reaction to lepromin test. Urticaria pigmentosa is differentiated fo: having itchy, hyperpigmented macules, papules or nodules with urticaria, and the lesions become red and swollen from scratching.

Treatment

Every effort is made to lower the blood cholesterol level. Management of the condition therefore requires elimination of all foods with high-saturated fatty acids (for example, meat, eggs, butter, cooking oil) and to replace them by foods with less saturated fatty acid (for example, fish, poultry products, vegetables). The patient is also encouraged to loose weight.

In addition, management of the condition calls for immediate correction or management of the underlying conditions having certain aetiological influence.

If the condition is not controlled with diet therapy and management of the underlying conditions, drug therapy can only then be considered with hypolipidaemic agents. The patient is therefore given bile acid sequestrant, such as cholestyramine, 1 sachet of 4g daily orally initially increasing gradually over 3-4 weeks to 3-6 sachets daily in single or divided doses (maximum: 9 sachets daily), or colestipol, 5-30 g (5 g per sachet) daily in 1 or 2 divided doses orally in liquid. Nicotinic acid derivative, such as acipimox, 500-750 mg in divided doses orally with meals, is also effective. Otherwise, the patient may be given isobutyric acid derivatives, such as clofifibrate, 20-30 mg per kg of body-weight daily in 2 o3 divided doses orally after meals, bezafibrate, 400 mg daily orally after food at night or in the morning, or gemfibrozil, 600 mg twice daily orally.

Resistant cases and other cases may be treated with cauterisation but bigger lesions may need surgical excision.

CUTANEOUS AMYLOIDOSIS

It is a complex disorder arising from accumulation or insoluble fibril protein (amyloid) in the tissues causing interruption or interference of organ specific function The mechanism and cause of amyloid production and its deposition in the tissues are not known but there may be a defect in protein metabolism responsible for the condition.

The condition may develop as a *primary type* that is idiopathic in origin or as a *secondary type* when it develops secondary to systemic amyloidosis, while some cases may develop independently as a cutaneous condition.

Hereditary or *familial type* develops from heterogeneous groups and shows a distinctive pattern of organ involvement.

Amyloidosis is also seen associated with multiple myeloma, Hodgkin's lymphoma, medullary carcinoma of thyroid and other malignancies. The condition may develop in persons with long-term dialysis. There may be deposition of amyloid in the synovium, joints and tendon sheath. Deposition of amyloid also occurs in the heart or in the cerebral blood vessels in the elderly, and in the pancreas in adult-onset (type II) diabetes mellitus.

Involvement of amyloidosis is usually generalised but may also be localised. There is however no consistency or distinctive pattern of amyloid deposits in various organs and tissue. It generally involves kidneys, liver, spleen, adrenals, thyroid, and lymph nodes, and many other tissues. Large deposits of amyloid cause the affected part swollen, waxy in appearance, and of increased consistence.

In skin involvement there is deposition of amyloid in the papillae, destruction of elastic tissue, and moderate infiltration with leucocytes. Epidermis may show hyperkeratosis.

Clinical Manifestations

Its manifestations are very variable and often nonspecific inasmuch as the features may be so obscured that a case fatality may develop prior to the identification of the condition. In general, however, it gives rise to weakness and loss of body weight. There may also be syncope.

Localised nodular mass in the tongue, depending upon its size, may cause difficulty in speech and swallowing.

In the skin the primary condition gives rise to shiny, smooth, flat-topped or spherical, waxy or translucent patches, occurring usually over the eyelids but may also develop elsewhere on the face. Often purpura develops from amyloidosis in small cutaneous vessels. The condition is however asymptomatic. Secondary amyloidosis presents with extremely itchy small, normal skin coloured or slight yellowish-brown coloured, waxy or translucent papules. The lesions tend to coalesce and cause infiltration over the shoulders and anterior tibial surfaces. Purpura develops but less frequently. When the condition develops independently (**lichen amyloidosis**) the lesions also develop in macular and nodular forms.

Diagnosis

The presenting manifestations may cause suspicion of the condition, while a history of pre-existing illness is suggestive. Diagnosis of the condition is however always made on biopsy and Congo red skin test.

Differentiation of the condition depends upon the system or organ involved, and may include several conditions mimicking amyloidosis.

Skin lesions are however differentiated from lichen planus and lichen simplex chronicus but in both cases the lesions are neither waxy, nor translucent.

Treatment

Appropriate care and treatment of the underlying conditions must receive prompt attention for the management of the condition. There is however no specific treatment of the condition is available. The patients are therefore given symptomatic relief and by the treatment schedules as specified under each specific condition.

Treatment with corticosteroids and immunosuppressive agents may be encouraging but give inconsistent results.

In cutaneous involvement treatment with corticosteroids may be beneficial. Resistant localised lesions may also be treated with fractional radiotherapy.

CHAPTER 7

Disorders due to Infections and Infestations

HERPES SIMPLEX

The condition, with formation of vesicles and ulcers on the skin surface and mucous membrane, is produced by herpes simplex virus (herpesvirus hominis) and may produce several clinical entities. The virus has two strains, and types 1 virus (HSV-1) is responsible for most of the clinical entities. The virus is intermittently present in the oropharynx of the normal healthy persons, and the infection spreads from direct contact of saliva and through contaminated utensils of the patients. Transmission of infection occurs more readily in crowed and lower hygienic living environment. The infection can also cause transplacental spread to the foetus and thus, may produce congenital malformations.

Type 2 virus (HSV-2) causes genital infection and has been described under sexually transmitted diseases in Chapter 11.

Pathological changes in the infection show proliferation, ballooning degeneration, multinucleated giant cells, and intracellular eosinophilic inclusion bodies in the cutaneous and mucosal lesions. There may be perivascular infiltration and nerve cell destruction in fatal cases.

Clinical Manifestation

The condition may be acute or recurrent, and may present with different clinical entities. In general, the lesions give a sensation of burning or itching, but occasionally may also be painful when the vesicles are ruptured or produce ulcerative lesions on mucous membrane.

Herpetic gingivostomatitis (herpetic stomatitis, Vincent's stomatitis) is the commonest clinical entity of the condition. It frequently involves children aged 1 to 3 years old, and presents with extensive vesiculoulcerative lesions as small, discrete, superficial ulcers or as white plaques in the oral cavity, sometimes extending to posterior pharynx, accompanied by erythema and oedema. The lesions are painful in severe cases, and may as well be haemorrhagic.

The affected children may have fever and the temperature may rise up to 103oF (39.4°C) and may persist for about a week. There are also malaise, irritability, and secondary bacterial infection. There may also be cervical lymphadenopathy. The illness is usually self-limiting and runs for about 1 to 3 weeks.

Herpes labialis (**herpes febrilis, fever blister, cold sores**) is a quite common condition, in which clusters of localised vesicles occur, usually on the mucocutaneous junction of the lips (Fig. 7.1). The lesions are commonly bilateral. Sometimes the vesicles may however extend to involve the skin of the chin, nose, cheeks, and ears. The vesicles rupture leaving painful ulcers, frequently causing secondary infection to take place. The lesions heal without scarring generally in 2 to 7 days.

In some cases, the condition may appear following short febrile episodes, common respiratory infection, trigeminal neuralgia, minor gastrointestinal disturbances, physical exertion, and emotional stress. The lesions develop due to extracellular oedema and ballooning degeneration of epithelial cells. Old age, exposure to sunlight and occasionally some underlying serious illness or malignancies may act as predisposing factor of its development.

Regional lymph nodes may be enlarged and tender.

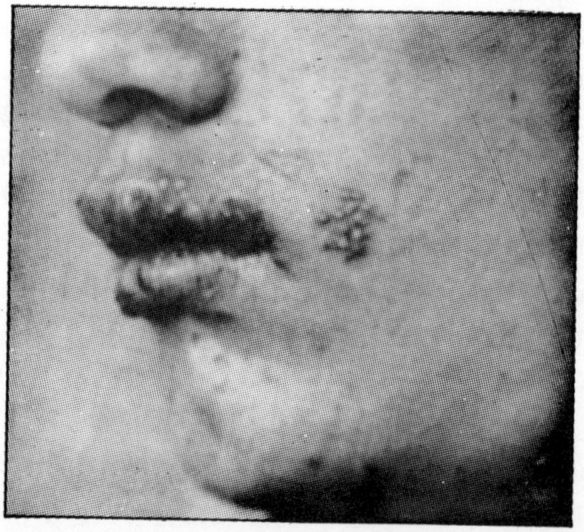

Figure 7.1. Herpes labialis.

Eczema herpeticum (**Kaposi's varcelliform eruption**) may develop in persons with immunodeficiency and with chronic eczema. The condition gives rise to extensive vesiculation in eczematous lesions with high fever, even sometimes causing fatality. Similarly, when eczematous children receive any vaccination, the condition gives rise to sudden widespread papulovesicular eruptions, frequently umbilicated with a surrounding zone of erythema. The lesions appear in crops, often produce severe constitutional disturbances, and may eventually lead to encephalitis or death.

Occasionally the infection may be inoculated accidentally through trauma or injury (**traumatic herpes simplex, inoculation herpes simplex**), and is usual seen amongst the laboratory personnel. The infection therefore causes formation of large vesicles or papules at the site of inoculation. The lesions may however cause excruciating pain, malaise, fever, and regional lymphadenopathy.

Herpes simplex infection not only can cause secondary infection but can also produce encephalitis, cervical cancer, and other malignancies as sequel.

Diagnosis

Diagnosis of the condition is made by isolation of the virus. Secretions and swabs from early herpetic lesions show multinucleated giant epithelial cells, surrounded by acantholytic balloon cells. Diagnosis of the condition is also made by detection of fluorescence antibody, complement-fixing antibody, and by cell culture. Tzanck test may yield a positive result.

Depending upon the clinical entity and the site of involvement, the condition may be differentiated from a large number of disorders. For example, sometimes the condition may cause confusion with herpes zoster which is however more painful and presents with larger lesions, distributed along the course of the sensory nerve. Chickenpox has a distinctive pattern of itchy lesions that are generalised and become numerous on the trunk and face but relatively sparse over the extremities, and the flexor surfaces appear to be more affected than the extensor surfaces. Impetigo is a condition of bacterial infection, affects chiefly the children and gives rise to itching. The lesions of erythema multiforme are often annular and arranged in concentric rings, usually develop on the distal parts of the extremities and face, and tend to extent peripherally and fuse together. Herpangina results due to coxsackievirus but also due to other enteroviruses, and presents with papular and vesicular lesions, more frequently seen on the tonsillar pillar, tonsils, soft palate, uvula and tongue. Pyoderma results from bacterial; infection and in persons in whom the natural protective mechanism of the skin is deficient, and presents with infected, inflamed or denuded areas on the skin.

Treatment

In the management of herpes simplex infection every care is taken so as to eliminate or restrict every predisposing factor, which can reactivate the latent virus.

For systemic administration and in severe cases, the patients are treated with antiviral, such as nucleoside analogue, aciclovir, 200 mg (400 mg in immunocompromised or if absorption impaired) five times a day orally, omitting the nighttime dose, usually for 5 days (child under 2 years, half adult dose). The corresponding dose in children is 100 mg for children aged less than 2 years, but children over 2 years are given the full adult dose. Otherwise, the patient may be given valaciclovir, 500 mg twice daily for 5-10 days.

Herpetic gingivostomatitis, herpes labialis, and other superficial lesions are treated with topical application of 5% solution of idoxuridine four times daily for four days. The patient is also given palliative treatment with normal saline for local application, or for mouthwash.

For skin lesions, 5% aciclovir cream may be applied topically at four hourly intervals for 5 days, and the application may be continued for another 5 days if healing is not complete. Alternatively, the patients may be given idoxuridine, 5% solution, applied topically four times daily for 4 days.

In addition, vigorous supportive treatment is given in cases of systemic involvement.

HERPES ZOSTER

Caused by varicella–zoster virus herpes zoster (**zoster, zone, shingles**) is a sporadic but incapacitating condition characterised by an inflammatory reaction of posterior nerve roots and ganglia, accompanied by crops of vesicles over the skin supplied by the affected sensory nerve. Local lesions involving the posterior root ganglion in Hodgkin's lymphoma, systemic disease, or from use of immunosuppressive agents can also activate the infection. Emotional stress, febrile illness, and physical injuries can trigger the predisposing factors.

Herpes zoster affects both sexes equally but is quite common among the adults, particularly aged 50 or over. Children are affected only occasionally. The severity of the infection however increases with the age and, also, in immunocompromised individuals. One attack generally confers life-long immunity.

The incubation period of the condition is not precisely known.

The cutaneous lesions are histopathologically identical to those of chickenpox. In addition, it produces inflammatory reactions at the posterior nerve roots and sensory ganglia corresponding to the skin lesions, cellular infiltration, necrosis of nerve cells, and inflammation of the ganglion sheath.

In cutaneous involvement, there is swelling of the epithelial cells, ballooning degeneration, and accumulation of tissue fluid, resulting vesicle formation.

Clinical Manifestation

Initially the condition gives rise to a boring pain with hyperaesthesia and later, fever, malaise, and severe pain in the distribution of the affected nerve root. This is followed after a few days by the appearance of crops of vesicles over the skin supplied by the affected nerve, surrounded by inflammatory region. The eruption is usually unilateral and is distributed along the cutaneous distribution of one or more posterior nerve ganglion, frequently affecting the thoracic and lumbar roots.

The patient presents with pain in the ears with vesicular eruptions on pinna and external auditory canal. Vesicles also develop on skin over the mastoid area, on palate and anterior pillar of fauces. There is also facial paralysis. The patient also complains of vertigo and deafness.

The condition may also involve other nerve roots and may lead to trigeminal herpes, meningoencephalitis, or may cause visceral herpes giving rise to pleurisy, cystitis, and arthritis.

Skin lesions develop like those of chickenpox from maculopapules to deep-seated vesicles and then to pustules. Regional lymph nodes may be enlarged and tender.

If it involves the eye, scarring of cornea may occur.

In most instances spontaneous resolution of cutaneous lesions and disappearance of pain occur within 2 to 3 weeks.

The complications the condition can produce are persistent and intractable neuralgia, anaesthesia of the affected area, facial and other nerve paralysis, and blindness.

Diagnosis

Diagnosis of the condition is made from isolation of the virus in culture. Serological tests such as complement-fixing and indirect immunofluorescence antibodies can also establish the diagnosis. Scrapping or swab of base of the vesicular lesions shows multinucleated giant cells. Tzanck test may also be positive.

It is often difficult to differentiate the condition from other disorders during the pre-eruptive stage, but comparatively easy after the appearance of skin lesions. At times herpes simplex may however pose problems but the condition tends to recur while the recurrence is unusual in herpes zoster. Chickenpox presents with centripetal distribution of pruritic rash and, in general, painless. In trigeminal neuralgia there is paroxysms of sharp, stabbing pain and absence of skin lesion. Bell's palsy produces unilateral facial paralysis and there is no skin lesion. Pleurisy may however at times mimic herpes zoster but has no skin lesion or multinucleated giant cells.

Treatment

Locally applied calamine lotion or wet compressions may have soothing effect on the lesions. Analgesic, such as aspirin, 600-900 mg, alone or with codeine, 30-60 mg, four times daily orally, may be given for relief of pain. To combat the nervous tension the patient may be given barbiturates, such as, phenobarbitone, 14 mg three or four times daily orally, or tricyclic antidepressants, such as, amitriptyline, 75 mg daily orally in divided doses increasing if required to 150 mg daily. In cases of seventh nerve involvement, surgical decompression may be needed occasionally. Systemic corticosteroids may be beneficial in some cases.

Specific therapy is given through antiviral, which can reduce the severity and the duration of pain, reduce complications, and reduce viral shedding. Treatment with antiviral should be started within 72 hours of the onset of rash and is usually continued for 7-10 days. The patient is therefore given nucleoside analogue, such as aciclovir, 800 mg five times daily orally (omitting nigh-time dose) for 7 days. Immunocompromised patients at high risk of disseminated or severe infection should be treated with a parenteral preparation, for example, aciclovir, 5 mg/kg every

8 hours by intravenous infusion usually for 5 days; doubled to 10 mg/kg every 8 hours in the immunocompromised patients Otherwise, the treatment may be given with famciclovir, 250 mg three times daily orally for 7 days, or valaciclovir, 1 g three times daily orally for 7 days. Tricyclic amine inhibits viral replication and hence may be beneficial in the condition. The patient may therefore be given amantadine, 100 mg twice daily orally for 14 to 28 days. In addition, the patient may also be given idoxuridine, 5% solution, for topical application over the lesions four times daily for 4 days but severe cases may need up to 40% solution on lint and change every 24 hours for 4 days.

Immunosuppressed patients are however treated with aciclovir, 10 mg per kg of body-weight every eight hours by IV injection for 7 days, or vidarabine, 10 mg/kg daily by slow IV infusion for 5 to 7 days.

Application of topical local anaesthetic may be helpful in some patients, and the patient may be given capsaicin, 0.075% cream, apply a small amount up to 3-4 times daily.

VERRUCA

Verruca (*pleural*: **verrucae**) is a benign condition of epithelial outgrowth produced by human papilloma virus. The condition is also popularly known as **warts**. This section however includes general warts (verrucae) but excludes genital wart that is described under chapter 11. The infection spread through direct or indirect contact, while autoinoculation of the condition is also possible. Genital warts however spread through sexual intercourse, while perianal area and rectum from rectal intercourse.

It usually affects the children but genital warts (*see chapter 11*) in adult females and uncircumcised males.

The condition produces capillary acanothosis with marked hyperkeratosis and parakeratosis in the epidermis, and cellular infiltration in the dermis. There may be vacuolisation of the cells of the rete and widening of the rete pegs.

Clinical Manifestations

Several clinical variants of the condition is recognised and the lesions, often multiple but may also be single, grow very slowly, generally giving rise to no subjective symptom.

The commonest form of the warts, **common warts (verrucae vulgaris)** occur as multiple (but may also be single), sharply demarcated, small, brown or skin-coloured, round or oval, papules or nodules (Fig. 7.2), involving any part of the body, including tongue and nails (**periungual warts**) The warts however more commonly occur on the exposed parts of the body, such as hands (Fig. 7.3), elbows, knees and feet. On the scalp the wart may assume the shape of cauliflower. The lesions grow slowly and become dirty and irregular surfaced.

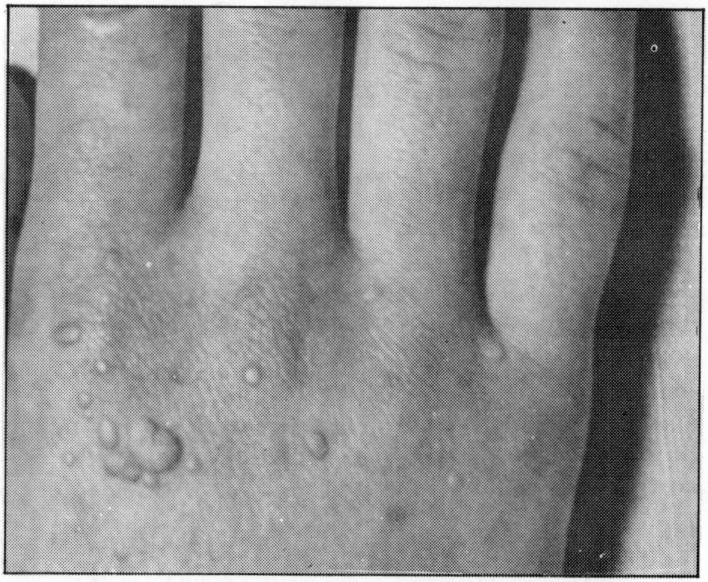

Figure 7.2. Common warts.

Filliform warts (verrucae filliformis) present as thread-like projection, usually single, on the neck and scalp.

Plane warts (verrucae plana), a variety of common warts, occur mostly in children and occasionally in young adults, particularly women. They occur as multiple, pinhead-sized or little larger, flesh-coloured, smooth, scarcely raised, flat-topped papules, frequently seen on the back of the hands, face, neck, wrist and knee.

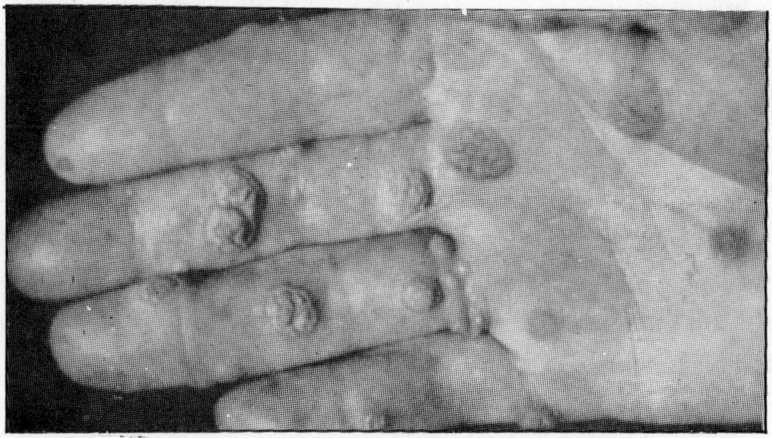

Figure 7.3. Common warts on palm and fingers.

Plantar warts (verrucae plantaris) develop usually on the pressure points of the sole (Fig. 7.4) and on the palms as flat corn-like warty growth. As they are deeply embedded in the dermis, the warts are painful and tender on touch.

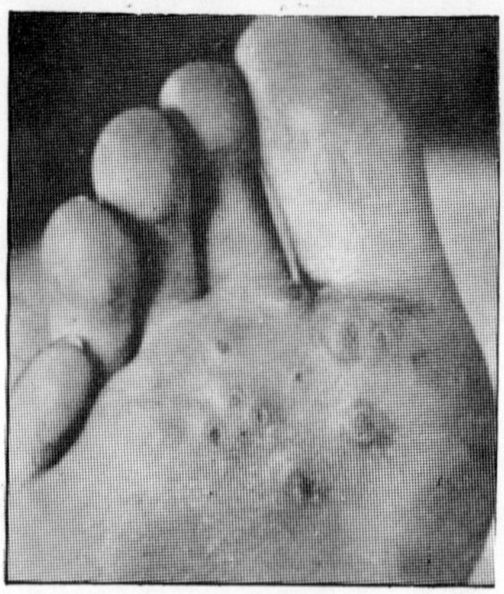

Figure 7.4. Plantar warts on sole.

Diagnosis

Diagnosis is made on clinical grounds and may be confirmed by skin biopsy.

At times common warts may be confused with seborrhoeic warts, which are covered with greasy scales. Plane warts can be differentiated from molluscum contagiosum that presents with almost transparent, waxy, umbilicated papules which when squeezed hard express cheesy material.

Treatment

As no antiviral agent is still readily available yet, treatment of the warts indeed creates certain problem. The only treatment appears to be destruction of the lesions with an emphasis that if the warts are not destroyed completely, warts may reappear at the same site. On the other hand, many warts do not require any treatment and after some time they subside spontaneously.

Warts are treated with keratolytics, such as pad of silver nitrate, 95%, with caustic pencil, and cover the abraded wart and moisten tip of the pencil and apply for 1-2 minutes, covered with dressing, and repeat after 24 hours, up to 3 treatments per week, or ointment of salicylic acid, 16.7%, and lactic acid, 16.7%, applied twice daily and abrade between the applications.

Plantar warts are treated with keratolytics, such as salicylic acid, 11-12%, along with lactic acid, 4%, paint and applied one or two-drops on the wart at night after soaking the area and the elastic film is removed in the morning and re-apply, and the warts are abraded between the application. Alternatively, ointment of salicylic acid, 25%, and podophyllum, 20%, is applied to the warts and cover with a plaster two or three times weekly, or formaldehyde solution, 0.75% gel, applied twice daily, cover with a plaster, and abrade between the applications, or salicylic acid, 50% ointment, applied once daily and cover with plaster and abrade between the applications.

Local application with podophyllum, 50% in water, with tincture benzoin or spirit, and left for 6 hours and then wash away thoroughly with soap and water, is also effective.

On the other hand, warts can be treated by gel of glutaraldehyde, 10% solution, applied twice daily under occlusive dressings and abrade between the applications.

Filliform warts are removed by shaving off.

Otherwise, the warts are treated with CO2 snow or liquid nitrogen. Cauterisation of the warts can also be done with liquefied phenol or trichloracetic acid. Electric cauterisation is also effective. Cryosurgery or lasers is equally effective. Single or just a few warts can also be removed by electrocoagulation with surgical diathermy.

IMPETIGO

Impetigo is a superficial infection of skin and is caused by *Staphylococcus aureus* and less frequently by group A β-haemolytic streptococci. The condition may also develop secondary to eczema and other exudative, pustular or itchy dermatitis, herpes simplex infection, insect bites, scabies and pediculosis.

It is a contagious disorder and spread by overcrowding and unhygienic living environment.

It chiefly affects the children, and adults only rarely.

The condition gives rise to vesicle that changes to pustule between the stratum corneum and rete Malpighi. There therefore develops intracellular oedema in the rete, dilated capillaries in the upper corium and infiltration with polymorphonuclear leucocytes. The pustule ruptures leaving a crust.

Clinical Manifestations

It presents with vesicle that changes to pustule between the stratum corneum and rete Malphigii. The condition however has several recognised forms.

Impetigo contagiosa presents with pea-sized or larger, macular, maculopapular, bullous, pustular, or honey-coloured, crusted, circinate lesions. The lesions usually appear on the face (Fig. 7.5), arms, legs and other exposed parts of the body. Infrequently however the lesions may also develop on other parts of the body, such as back (Fig. 7.6). The intervening area of the skin remains unaffected and normal. There is no other symptom other than perhaps itching. The condition may give rise to constitutional symptoms but only in extensive involvement. The infection may spread to other parts of the body. The lesions usually heal within 2 or 3 weeks, without any scarring.

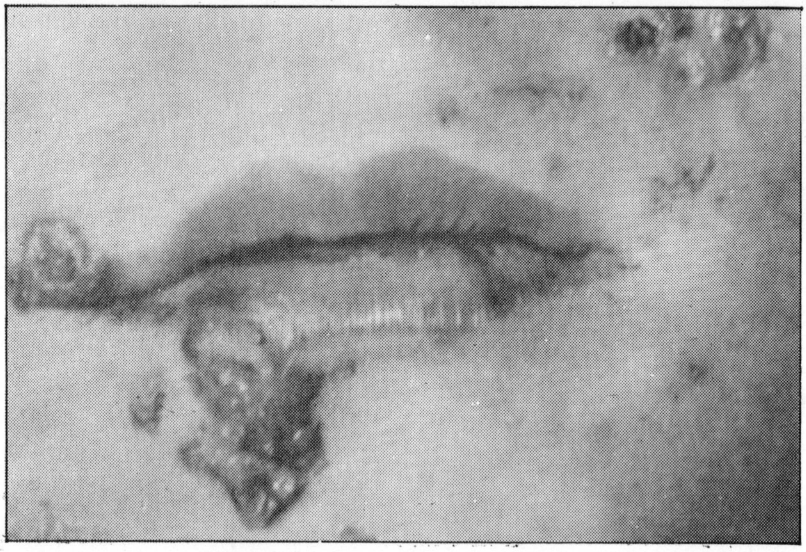

Figure 7.5. Impetigo contagiosa.

Sometimes the lesions may appear as superficial bullae (**bullous impetigo**) containing seropurulent matter, which coagulate and produce honey-coloured crust with epidermal tags at the periphery, or the bullae my rupture leaving circinate lesions (**impetigo circinata**). Sometimes the bullae heal in the centre and spread at the periphery with circinate lesions.

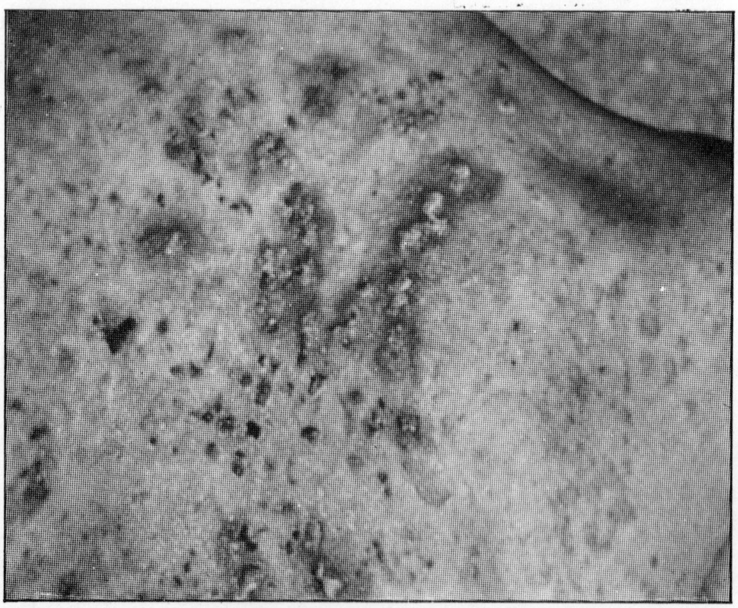

Figure 7.6. Impetigo on back.

Impetigo neonatorum occurs in the newborn infants and presents with tense bullae on the exposed parts of the body, usually on the limbs, trunk, face, and neck but spares the palms and soles. Sometimes the lesions may develop on the mucous membrane, with constitutional disturbances. Sometimes the bullae may rupture to produce superficial raw surfaces with overlying epidermal tags but crust formation is not frequent. The condition may finally become complicated with bacteraemia, pneumonia, meningitis and glomerulonephritis.

In Bockhart's impetigo (follicular impetigo) the lesions develop as superficial folliculitis, covered with yellow crusts. The lesions usually occur on the thighs, legs, and pubic area, forearms and body flexures.

When the lesions appear much deeper and larger, perhaps with inflammation, it is then called **ecthyma**. It frequently occurs on the legs, buttocks and trunk, and gives rise to pus stained with blood, and shows dark brown or black crusts. The lesions heal slowly leaving permanent scars. This variety of infection is generally seen amongst the persons with cachexia ands in debilitated state.

Diagnosis

The condition is diagnosed on clinical grounds.

It is differentiated from chickenpox, which has a characteristic pattern of skin eruptions with all stages of development at a particular site, and the lesions are fragile. Herpes simplex is differentiated for having lesions, which cause pain and show the presence of herpesvirus. Contact dermatitis gives a history of exposure to certain offending agents and show remission after their withdrawal. Dermatitis herpetiformis gives rise to symmetrically distributed and extremely itchy and burning lesions. Scabies may at times be able to cause confusion but the condition gives rise to intense nocturnal itching and shows evidence of burrows, and the mite or the ova may be detectable. Pediculosis causes itching and excoriation, and the louse may be detected.

Treatment

The lesions are treated with broad-spectrum antibiotics, such as mupirocin, 2% ointment, applied three times daily for up to 10 days. If there is however no satisfactory response, the patient is given appropriate systemic antibiotic, for example, cephalexin, 25-50 mg per kg of body weight (adult: 1-4 g) daily in divided doses orally, cloxacillin, 250 mg for children aged over 2 years (adult: 500 mg) every six hours orally, or flucloxacillin, 125 mg for children aged over 2 years (adults: 250 mg) four times daily orally.

ERYSIPELAS

The condition is an acute inflammatory condition of skin and subcutaneous tissue characterised by massive brawny oedema with rapidly advancing margins. It is produced by group A β-haemolytic streptococci and, occasionally, by other streptococcus, staphylococcus and pneumococcus. Bacteria presumably gins entry into the human skin by way of small or unapparent break in the skin, and also through wounds, surgical incisions and via the patches of eczema.

The condition may be recurrent.

The infection spreads upward from the site of inoculation, producing an indurated area with a sharp margin and acute inflammation with swelling of the lymphatics of the skin. This results intense oedema, vascular dilatation, enlargement of the lymphatic spaces crowded with the organisms and lymphocytes or mononuclear cells. In severe cases, deeper tissues may be involved with thrombosis, cellulitis, and suppuration.

Clinical Manifestations

At the site of inoculation initially there may be itching and discomfort, followed by development of small area of erythema, spreading to form a tense, sharply demarcated with elevated margin, glistening, smooth, tender, hot, oedematous area with elevated margins. The condition often involves the face (for example, cheeks), bridge of the nose and, occasionally, arms or legs (Fig. 7.7). Vesicles or bullae often develop on the surface.

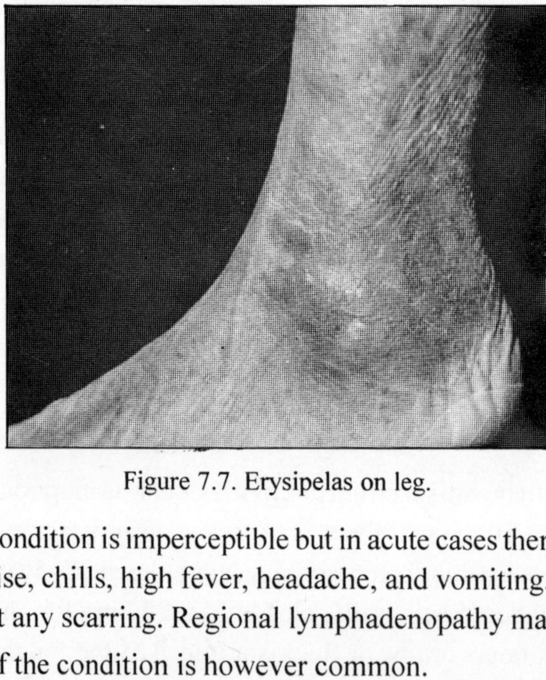

Figure 7.7. Erysipelas on leg.

The onset of the condition is imperceptible but in acute cases there may be severe systemic disturbances with malaise, chills, high fever, headache, and vomiting. The patch usually heals by 1 or 2 weeks without any scarring. Regional lymphadenopathy may develop occasionally.

Recrudescence of the condition is however common.

If the condition is not controlled properly, it may eventually lead to toxaemia with systemic involvement. Death may result in very young or old patients due to toxaemia.

Excluding that of toxaemia the condition however seldom causes any complication except lymphoedema.

Diagnosis

It is usually made on clinical grounds. Causative organism can however be isolated and identified from the lesion and blood. There may be leucocytosis, and a raised ESR.

It is differentiated from cellulitis in which the lesions involve deeper tissue and the margin of the lesion is less distinct, and from erysipeloid in which redness of skin of the fingers or back of the hands occur usually amongst the fishermen and meat handlers, reflecting an associated with occupation. Herpes zoster presents with painful lesions over the skin supplied by the affected nerve. In contact dermatitis, there is always a history of exposure to the offending agents, which make the differentiation much easy. Angio-oedema may also cause confusion but there is welling in loose subcutaneous tissue and dermis elsewhere in the body, particularly of the eyelids, lips or tongue, and usually there is a history of allergy.

Treatment

Appropriate management of the condition is often sufficient with oral penicillin (phenoxymethylpenicillin) or erythromycin, 250 mg every six hours for 2 weeks if penicillin-allergic). Add flucloxacillin, 250-500 mg every 6 hours, half-an-hour to 1 hour before meal.

Acute cases may however be treated with penicillin G sodium, 0.5-1 million U four times a day by IV injection and then institute oral medication. Azithromycin, 500 mg once daily orally for 3 days, or ciprofloxacin, 250 mg twice daily orally, is also effective.

Application of cold pads over the affected area can give some comfort. The patient is also given oral analgesics, aspirin, 600 mg, with or without codeine, 30 mg, four times daily, for the relief of pain and fever.

ERYSIPELOID

It is a rare but acute bacterial infection of the skin characterised by development of tender lesions, and is the clinical form of **erysipelothricosis**. The condition develops due to Gram-positive microaerophilic bacteria, *Erysipelothrix insidiosa* (*Erysipelothrix rhusiopathine*), an infection of a variety of animals, for example, fish, shellfish, birds, mammals and insects. Human beings only become infected when the organism come in contact with abraded skin.

Human beings only become infected when the organism come in contact of abraded skin. It therefore develops as an occupational hazard amongst the handlers of fish and animal tissue, such as fisherman, fishmonger, and butcher and meat handlers.

Clinical Manifestations

It presents with erythema and less prominent swelling, usually on the fingers or back of the hands that slowly progresses to form sharply demarcated, purplish-red coloured, indurated maculopapules, which are raised but not vesiculated. The lesions may spread by continuity or may spread from one area to another. The affected area appears swollen and tender. When it involves all the fingers, movements of the hands may become difficult. The patients complain of pain, itching and burning. There may be mild constitutional symptoms but may also be severe occasionally. In some cases however the eruptions may be diffuse or generalised, and may be associated with fever and joint pains.

The condition is self-limiting but may lead to bacteraemia as sequel.

Diagnosis

The characteristic purplish-red coloured lesions, clinical manifestations and the occupational history are often sufficient to make the diagnosis with confidence. The causative organism can also be isolated and identified from biopsy of the lesions and culture.

It is differentiated from erysipelas in which the lesions develop at different sites, vesiculation is common, and there is no suggestive occupational history. Cellulitis is differentiated for its frequent accompaniment with lymphangitis and regional lumphadenopathy, while the lesions involve deeper tissue.

Treatment

The condition is adequately treated with penicillin G, 1.2 million U by deep IM injection daily, erythromycin, 500 mg four times daily orally, or with any other appropriate broad-spectrum antibiotic.

FOLLICULITIS

It is a superficial or deep infection of the hair follicles produced by microorganisms, most common being Gram-positive *Staphylococcus aureus*. It also develops from fungal infection, scabies, pediculosis, and contact of irritant chemicals. The condition develops rapidly on the area with coarse hair, and involves more and more hair follicles.

It usually affects adult males but females only occasionally, and spares the children.

The condition produces varying degree of inflammatory changes, vascular dilatation, formation of intrafollicular abscesses, and perifollicular infiltration.

Clinical Manifestations

The involvement may be superficial or deep.

Superficial folliculitis presents with tiny pustules around the coarse hair, surrounded by small erythematous zone. The lesions spread rapidly to other hair follicles, and may be pruritic or painful. Usually the lesions form crusts and heal without scarring.

Deep folliculitis gives rise to erythematous papules around the coarse terminal hair. There are always deeper and larger abscesses communicating the skin lesions. The lesions cause epilation and scarring.

The chronic form of folliculitis, known as **sycosis**, may present as small, superficial pustules, surrounded by small zone of erythema, which may rupture and discharge beads of pus or may dry up to form crust or may present as erythematous papule around the hair follicle on any part of the body. It causes burning and itching, but usually there is no pain. The lesions persist with chronicity, and the area looks congested, swollen and infiltrated.

The condition has several clinical forms, and **folliculitis barbae** or **sycosis barbae** is one of them. In this the lesions involve the beard area (Fig. 7.8), usually the chin but may also involve other shorthaired areas, such as eyebrows and thighs. The lesions develop as papules or pustules. Later, the eruptions spread to other parts of the body. The lesions however do not cause oozing or weeping, but the hair of the affected area can be pulled out easily.

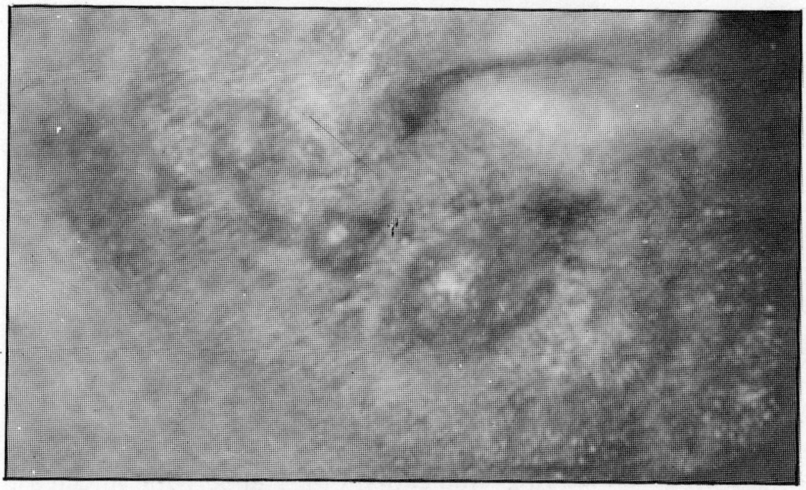

Figure 7. 8. Folliculitis barbae.

In **sycosis nuchae** the lesions develop on the back of the neck as small papules and pustules, and lead to keloidal thickening and cicatrisation. The lesions show a tendency of becoming chronic and relapsing. Hairs on the affected area appear twisted and tangled. The condition gives rise to marked itching but may also painful.

Folliculitis decalvans involves the scalp and is characterised by the development of furuncles. It presents with cicatricial alopecia (Fig. 7.9), and show pustules, erythema and scaling, producing smooth, shiny, depressed scars. Development of furuncles is however common.

In **sycosis lupoides** the lesions very rarely may involve both the scalp and the beard regions. It may then give rise to small, smooth, atrophic patches of alopecia with pustules and crusts forming a brim at the periphery. The condition is usually progressive in course.

Diagnosis

It is diagnosed on clinical grounds.

It is differentiated from follicular eczema, which causes oozing and weeping. Impetigo presents with large lesions, tense bullae and honey-coloured crusts. Bockhart's impetigo may sometimes cause confusion but is differentiated for having lesions involving large areas of the body, usually the thigh and the body flexure, and the condition chiefly affects the children. Tinea barbae is differentiated for having deep-seated, indurated, boggy swelling, and the causative fungus can be identified from the lesions. Acne is differentiated for the presence of comedons on the lesions.

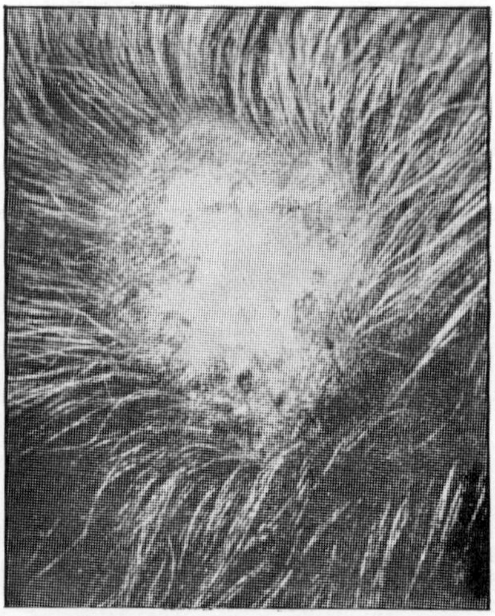

Figure 7.9. Folliculitis decalvans.

Treatment

Management of the condition requires eradication of the underlying infected foci, if known, and to avoid trauma. The lesions may be cleaned thoroughly with soap and water or with potassium permanganate solution.

Mild cases are treated with topical application of appropriate antibiotic. Concurrent administration of systemic broad-spectrum antibiotic is considered for severe infection. In cases of involvement of the beard area, the patient is given either topical application of both antibiotic and corticosteroids, or systemic broad-spectrum antibiotics and topical antibiotic concurrently.

Resistant cases may be treated with fractional radiotherapy.

In cases of alopecia, local infiltration with hydrocortisone or prednisolone may be tried, in addition to the treatment schedule specified above.

ERYTHRASMA

It is a superficial infection of the intertriginous areas of the body, and is caused by Gram-positive rod, *Corynbacterium minutissimum*. Its incidence is usually high in the tropics, and in the persons suffering from diabetes mellitus.

It is common in summer and monsoon period.

Clinical Manifestations

It presents with well-demarcated, dry, brown or reddish, slightly scaly patches. The lesions generally develop on the moist areas of the body such as toe-webs. On the groins it gives rise to irregular and pink patches, which later become brown with thin scales. The lesions may also involve axillae, trunk, abdominal folds, perineum and underneath of pendulous breasts, particularly in the obese middle-aged women and the diabetics. The lesions tend to show fissuring and slight maceration. There is however no other symptom, perhaps except mild itching.

Diagnosis

Diagnosis of the condition is made from identification of the causative organism in the material obtained from smear and culture. Exposure to Wood's light causes coral-red fluorescence of the lesions due to the presence of *Corynbacterium minutissimum*.

It is differentiated from tinea infection that is itchy and the causative fungus can be identified. Intertrigo may at times cause certain confusion but is differentiated for the lesions do not show any specific predilection for moist areas only, and the condition often affects the obese and overdressed persons with hyperhidrosis.

Treatment

The cases are effectively treated with appropriate antibiotics such as erythromycin, 250 mg four times daily orally for 14 days, or cefixime, 200-400 mg daily as single or two-divided doses orally for 7 to 14 days.

CUTANEOUS DIPHTHERIA

It is an acute infectious childhood condition characterised by formation of tenacious grey pseudomembrane, which usually attacks the respiratory tract but may also involve any mucous membrane, such as conjunctiva and vagina, and may produce wound on the skin. It is caused by Corynbacterium diphtheriae, a nonmotile, nonsporforming, Gram-positive rod, with club shaped ends and irregularly stained granules. The infection spreads through respiratory secretions from direct contact or indirectly through contaminated fomites.

Children aged between 1 and 5 years are the usual victims of the condition.

The incubation period is 1 to 4 days, and the infection persists for 2 to 3 weeks.

Cutaneous diphtheria occurs due to direct contact with the organism, usually secondary to the wounds, including eczematous, vesicular, pustular and ulcerative skin eruptions, or its occurrence may be independent.

The condition is not however serious because the absorption of toxin is slight and the systemic effects are negligible.

Clinical Manifestations

Cutaneous diphtheria may develop without any systemic involvement nut otherwise it may occur in association with general diphtheria. It is characterised by acutely spreading lesions or chronic non-healing punched out ulcers with swollen, rolled and elevated, hard edges, and shows formation of dirty grey membrane. The ulcers are usually round or oval in shape but may also be linear in an infected scratch. The condition usually develops on pre-existing dermatosis, and frequently affects lower extremities, upper extremities, head or trunk.

Diagnosis

Diagnosis of the condition is usually made on clinical grounds and is supported by isolation of the causative bacteria. The organism can be cultured on special fibrin-containing media, which also eliminates other organisms of the throat flora to grow. Isolation and identification of the organism is however essential as similar membranous respiratory or cutaneous infection can be caused due to fungal or fusospirochaetal infection. Even so when the organism is identified, its toxicity is also tested by gel diffusion because the throat specimen may contain commensal diphtheroids.

Presence of pseudomembrane makes it easy to differentiate the condition from other similar skin disorders.

Treatment

In cases of cutaneous diphtheria, administration of 10,000-20,000 U of diphtheria antitoxin may be sufficient. In addition, the patient is given treatment with antibiotic, for example, erythromycin, 50 mg per kg of body-weight daily in four divided doses orally or by IV injection for 7 days, or procaine penicillin G, 600,000 U by IM injection every twelve hours for 10 days.

CUTANEOUS TUBERCULOSIS

Cutaneous tuberculosis or **tuberculosis cutis** is a rare condition and occurs due to acid-fast bacillus, *Mycobacterium tuberculosis*. Occasionally the infection may also result from bovine strains of *M. bovis*, In fact, skin is resistant to tuberculous infection and hence development of the condition is not possible in an intact skin surface. The infection may therefore gain entry through abraded skin from contact of contaminated material or through infected droplets coughed on to the skin, or the infection may reach the skin surface through lymphatic or bloodstream from an existing tuberculous focus. Abrasion of skin may occur from varieties of reason ranging between scratching and ear piercing, tattooing, and intramuscular injection. The condition may also develop

Pathological changes in cutaneous tuberculosis however vary a little from one variety to another.

Primary tuberculous complex shows marked inflammatory reaction initially with polymorphonuclear leucocytes but later with lymphocytes and epitheloid cells, and development of tubercles at the site of inoculation and in the regional lymph nodes.

In *lupus vulgaris* there is cellular infiltration in the stratum corneum, formation of tubercles with lymphocytes and plasma cells at the periphery, perhaps hypertrophy of the epidermis with flattened cells, and necrosis of the elastic tissue.

Tuberculosis verrucosa cutis shows development of tubercles, caseation, overgrowth of granulation tissue, formation of new blood vessels, acanthosis and hyperkeratosis.

In *scleerofuloderma*, there are caseation necrosis, liquefied debris filled cavities, and sinus formation. *Tuberculosis cutis orifacialis* shows localised lesions at mucocutaneous borders with inflammatory process, while tuberculosis *miliaris disseminata* shows widespread miliary lesions.

Papulonecrotic tuberculides shows liquefaction necrosis at the dermis.

In *erythema induratum* there are the development of epitheloid cell tubercles in the vessel walls consisting epitheloid cells, lymphocytes, plasma cells and, occasional, multinucleated giant cells, destruction of elastic and collagen tissues, and thickening of the veins and arteries.

Clinical Manifestations

This condition may be localised or generalised, and has several clinical entities.

Primary tuberculous complex occurs chiefly in the children, and presents with painless, brownish-red papule, usually on the face and extremities, and is known as **tuberculous chancre**. The condition is associated with lymphadenopathy. The papule later develops into indurated nodule or plaque, and ulcerates. The ulcer later heals spontaneously but lymphadenopathy persists and breaks down finally.

Lupus vulgaris is the commonest form, and runs a very prolong protracted course. It usually begins in childhood and causes extensive destruction of the tissue. Lesions appear as painless, reddish-brown macule which changes slowly over the months and years, and finally presents with raised or flat, hyperpigmented, irregular-shaped patches of minute translucent and indurated nodules, covered with very fine adherent scales. The most commonly occur on the exposed parts of the body, usually face, and affects the children and young adults. Affection to other unexposed parts of the body, such as breasts (Fig. 7.10), is however not unusual. The patches show healing with tissue paper-like scarring at one end and progression with formation of more translucent granulomatous nodules at the other. Eventually large patches are formed with coalescence of the lesions and development of new nodules. The nodules may ulcerate, causing atrophic depigmented scars, or the lesions may produce hard, thick, depigmented, usually crusted or exudative, warty vegetative growth. There may be accompanying oedema, hypertrophy, lymphangitis, and regional lymphadenopathy.

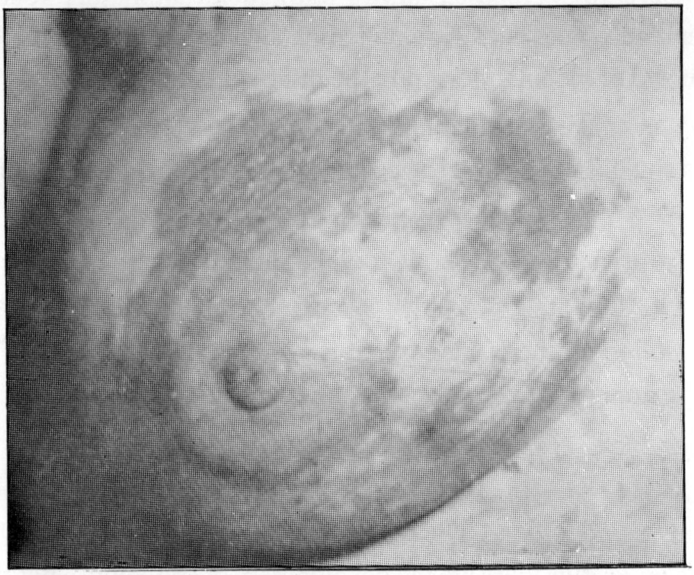

Figure 7.10. Lupus vulgaris on breast.

Sometimes similar warty growth but with more vegetations (**tuberculosis verrucosa cutis, verruca necrogenica**) may occur. The lesions develop as firm, indurated papule, which may extend to form large patches. Surface of the lesions become crusted and later verrucous. The lesions more frequently develop on the hands (Fig. 7.11) and other parts of the extremities, usually in the adults, perhaps from inoculation of the causative microorganism, for example, in persons engaged in autopsies and in handling tuberculous meat. The eruption is superficial, and may also assume serpentines shape (Fig. 7.12). The lesions do not ulcerate, while lymphangitis and regional lymphadenopathy are not common. The lesions seldom heal spontaneously.

Scrofuloderma runs a chronic course and generally occurs secondary to existing tuberculosis, and involves the lymph nodes, most frequently the cervical group, bone or joints in children and young adults. The lesion presents as purplish induration of skin overlying the lymph nodes usually the neck and groins but can also occur on any part of the body. It appears as dermal nodule or swelling which over the months softens and ruptures to discharge purulent and sanguineous exudate, leading to the formation of sinus or ulcer with irregular undermined edges, and formation of granulation tissue. The lesion produces thin atrophic or retracted scar on healing.

Tuberculosis cutis orificialis (tuberculous ulcerosa) almost always occurs secondary to the existing extrapulmonary tuberculosis in young adults. It presents with localised lesions at the mucocutaneous junction of the mouth, nose, urethra, vulva and anus, and occasionally on the skin, as round or oval, shallow, discrete ulcers, with crust formation, showing little tendency of spontaneous healing.

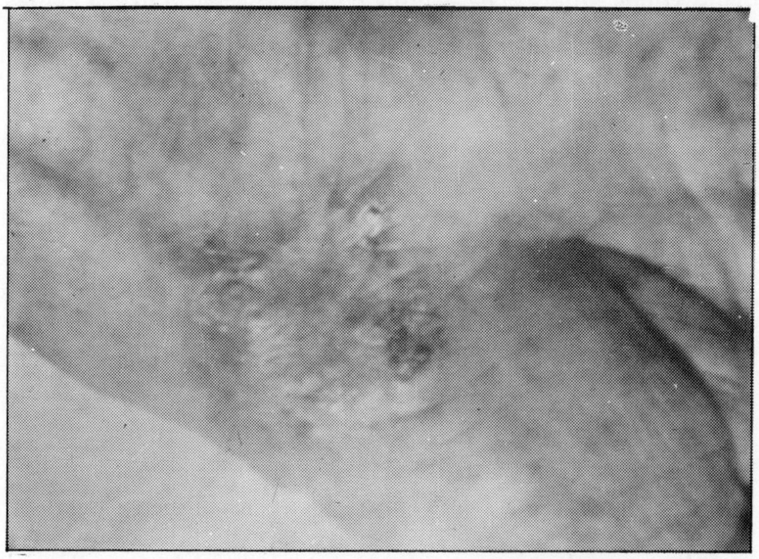

Figure 7.11. Tuberculosis verrucosa cutis.

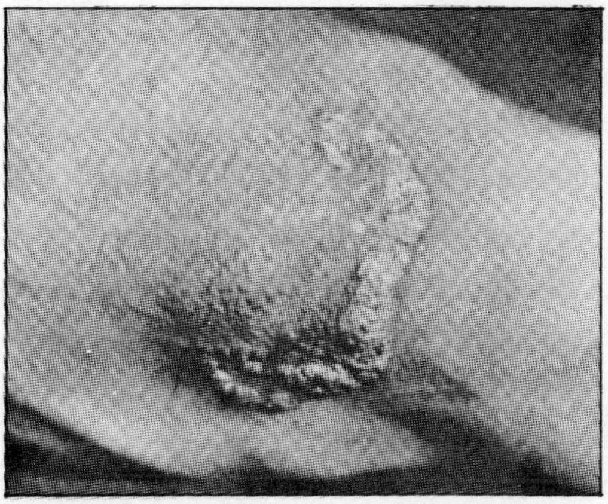

Figure 7.12. Tuberculosis verrucosa cutis on elbow (seringinous lesion)

Tuberculosis miliaris disseminata is a rare form of acute generalised eruptions of indolent, brownish-red papules. The condition presents with multiple, superficial papules, which form minute, circular ulcers with seropurulent exudate and dull red margins and miliary tubercles at the base and the edge of the ulcers. Similar lesions may also occur with bilateral distribution and in crops, affecting the facial region only, known as **lupus miliaris disseminata faciei** (Fig. 7.13).

Papulonecrotic tuberculoid presents with sudden development of crops of pin-head to pea-sized, firm, papules or nodules, usually bilateral and symmetrical in distribution Eruptions occur in successive crops and usually involve the extensor surfaces of the extremities (Fig. 7.14), especially on the elbows, knees, dorsal aspects of hands and feet, and also on the face and trunk in children and young adults. The lesions become necrotic in the centre, discharge pus, and finally heal spontaneously, causing hyperpigmented pitted scars.

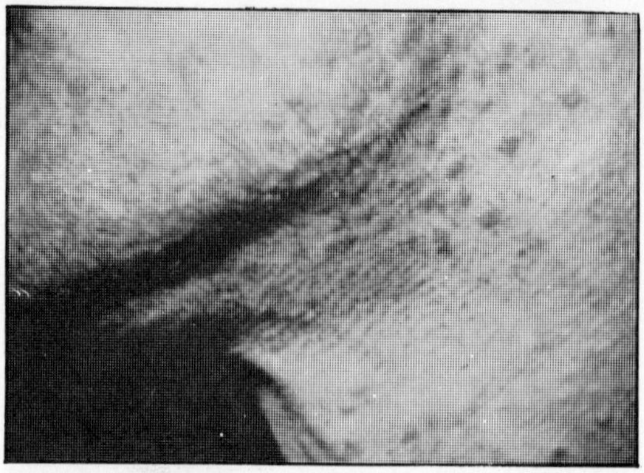

Figure 7.13. Lupus miliaris disseminata faciei.

Lichen scrofulosorum develops as minute, pinhead sized or smaller, and skin-coloured reddish-brown, firm, flat-topped, keratotic, follicular, indolent papules, affecting the trunk and extremities in children with tuberculosis of the lymph nodes or of the bone. The lesions are surrounded by tiny pustules or scales, and are arranged in annular groups. The lesions may persist for a long time without any symptom, except perhaps slight itching, and disappear spontaneously with recurrences.

Erythema induratum (tuberculosis indurativa, Bazin's disease) is a chronic benign tuberculous vasculitis. It usually affects young women with tuberculosis of lymph glands and acrocyanosis. The condition gives rise to indolent, recurrent, bluish-red, soft nodules, distributed symmetrically about the subcutaneous vessels of back of the lower parts of the legs but may also, on rare occasions, affect the front of the legs, or on the arms or elsewhere. The nodules usually persist for a few months and then lead to dry up and heal, and then recur. The lesions produce slightly tender erythematous induration and the nodules gradually become deep. Much later, the overlying skin becomes dusky or bluish in colour, and the nodules later. soften at the centre, produce deep ulcers with steep or undermined edges, and finally heals spontaneously, leaving depressed depigmented scars. The lesions are however painless. With recurrences the condition persists for years.

Diagnosis

Evidence of existing tuberculosis elsewhere in the body may be available and can make the diagnosis easy. Tuberculin test may also be helpful. Diagnosis is however confirmed by skin biopsy.

Depending upon the presenting features it may cause confusion with a number of skin disorders but the differentiation is easy from tuberculin test and skin biopsy.

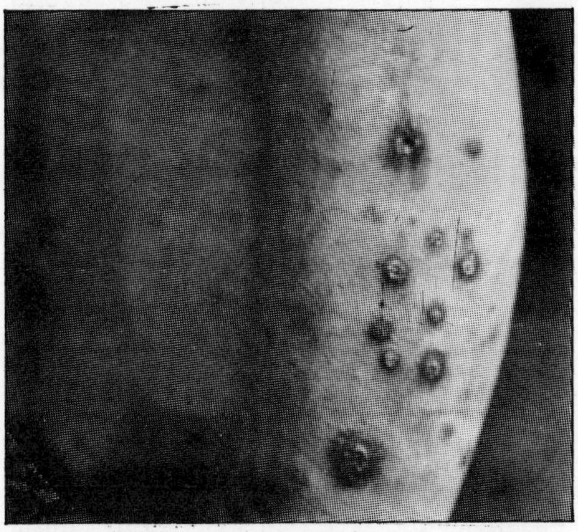

Figure 7.14. Papulonecrotic tuberculoid on leg.

Treatment

All cases are treated with antituberculous drugs, and the duration of treatment, choice of drugs and combination of antituberculous drugs, all depend upon the nature of the lesions and concurrent evidence of tuberculosis elsewhere. In cases when cutaneous involvement is a concomitant manifestation of an active primary lesion, no extra treatment is perhaps as the primary condition might be receiving appropriate antituberculous therapy.

In other cases, antituberculous therapy is given as per treatment schedule laid under pulmonary tuberculosis.

The common drugs are now used for treatment purposes are isoniazid (INH), 200-300 mg (children: 3 mg per kg of body-weight) daily in the morning as a single dose orally; streptomycin, 1 g but 0.75 g for adults weighing less than 50 kg (children: 30 mg/kg, maximum: 1 g) daily by IM injection; ethambutol, 25 mg/kg daily as a single dose orally (divided doses in older children but not recommended for children under 13 years of age) for 8 weeks or till the sputum is negative and then the dose is reduced to 15 mg/kg for prolonged or unsupervised use; rifampicin, 450 mg for patients weighing less than 50 kg but 600 mg for those weighing more (children: 10-20 mg/kg) daily as a single dose orally; pyrazinamide, 20-35 mg/kg daily as a single dose orally; sodium para-aminosalicylic acid (PAS), 10 g (children: 300 mg/kg) daily in two divided doses orally; and thiacetazone, 150 mg (children: 4 mg/kg) daily as a single dose orally.

The principal criteria of treating tuberculosis are never to give any drug alone but to treat the cases with combination of more than one potent antituberculous drug. The minimum requirement for this purpose is adopted as to give the treatment with, at least, two drugs in simple cases but in severe cases, the treatment schedule must include not less than three drugs.

Administration of antituberculous therapy follows several schedule, and Table 7.1. illustrates two such schedules of nine and inexpensive twelve months as example. In general circumstances however, though a satisfactory level of success can be achieved with potent antituberculous drugs continued for 12 months, the treatment is preferred to be continued for 18 to 24 months so as to achieve greater success and, also, in advanced cases.

Table 7.1. Two Regimen of Antituberculous Therapy

Regimen	Therapy
Nine-month regimen	2 months: Ethambutol or Streptomycin + Isoniazid* + Rifampicin 7 months: Rifampicin + Isoniazid*
Inexpensive twelve-month regimen	Daily: Isoniazid*+ thiacetazone Twice weekly: Streptomycin + Isoniazid + Pyrazinamide

* Pyridoxine, 10-20 mg daily orally should be supplemented with isoniazid

If economy does not pose any debarring factor, expensive treatment schedule can however substantially reduce the length of period of chemotherapy and thus, reducing the length of suffering and the risk of spreading the infection. In such a treatment schedule (Table 7.2) daily treatment is given with isoniazid and rifampicin for 6 months, with an addition of pyrazinamide during the first two months.

Table 7.2. Daily recommended regime of six months' Chemotherapy.

Body-weight	Initial intensive : 2 months	Continuation : 4 months
Adults below 50 kg (110 lb)	Rifampicin, 450 mg, + Isoniazid*, 300 mg, + Pyrazinamide, 1.5 g, + Ethambutol**, 400 mg, or Streptomycin, 0.75 g by IM injection	Rifampicin, 450 mg, + Isoniazid, 300 mg
Adults 50 kg (110 lb) and over	Rifampicin, 600 mg, + Isoniazid*, 300 mg, + Pyrazinamide, 2 g, + Ethambutol**, 400 mg, or Streptomycin, 1 g by IM injection	Rifampicin, 600 mg, + Isoniazid*, 300 mg

* Supplement of pyridoxine, 10-20 mg daily orally.

** Sero-positive cases are preferably be given ethambutol during the initial period, particularly where the prevalence of initial drug resistance is high.

LEPROSY

Leprosy (**Hansen's disease**) is a slowly progressive disorder causing granulomatous lesions that develops due to acid fast, obligatory, intracellular bacillus, *Mycobacterium leprae*. Although the organism can be found in cooler tissue of body, such as skin and mucous membrane, and in endothelial cells in blood vessels and in mononuclear cells, it has never been cultured extracellularly in laboratory media. Human beings are the only known source of the infection. Armadillos in the American continent however found to be naturally infected with an organism, indistinguishable from *M. leprae*.

The organism is present in the nasal secretions as well as in the cutaneous lesions. Patients with active disease shed large amount of the organism through coughing, sneezing, and even in normal speaking. There is therefore no doubt that the transmission of the infection occurs through respiratory droplets when respiratory tract is the portal of entry of the infection, and from direct contact in which the organism is inoculated. The causative organism may also be transmitted through breast milk, by arthropod vectors and also by tattooing needles.

According to Madrid classification the condition has clinically two polar or ends of the spectrum, lepromatous (LL) and tuberculoid (TT) leprosy, with two intermediate forms clinically classified as borderline and indeterminate form.

Infection occurs directly from the active cases, more so in the lepromatous leprosy. In tuberculoid leprosy, however, there exists vast confusion as to its transmissibility. Otherwise, the clinical type of tuberculoid leprosy may be less, or not at all, contagious and may usually develop subclinically.

Transmission of infection is common in the endemic areas but almost majority of individuals, having an immune response, does not develop clinical leprosy, and only a negligible fraction of people does. On the other hand, persons may be infective for years before diagnosed and thus, they serve as a reservoir of the infection in the community. The organism produces antibodies in the body but shows no association with host resistance. Rather the host resistance shows an association with cellular immunity of the body.

However, the condition is definitely not non-infectious, and yet our present knowledge cannot specify its contagiousness. As it is seen that the tissue may be teeming with leprae bacilli and yet shows no obvious clinical changes. It is therefore confirmed that the infectivity and virulence of the organism is extremely low. Yet, despite this low communicability the condition is still endemic in the tropics and subtropics.

The infection principally involves the skin, superficial nerves, nose, pharynx, larynx and eye. It is also capable of involving any organ or tissue, including liver, spleen, kidney, adrenal, testes, lymphoid tissue, bone marrow, hands and feet.

In lepromatous leprosy, the lesion appears as xanthoma with nodules or masses of cellular granulation tissue, composed mainly of large mononuclear cells (*lepra cells*) with pale foamy appearance due to high lipid contents, and covered by acid-fast bacilli. The nodules may assume any size, and may be quite large enough. Ulceration of the superficial nodules is common, causing great destruction and disfigurement, including autoamputation of fingers and toes. Lymph nodes show foamy histiocytes in the paracortical areas and enlargement of the germinal centres. Similar macrophages can also be seen in liver and splenic red pulp. Extensive involvement is seen in tissues, causing destruction of seminiferous tubules. The peripheral nerves are enlarged. There is also fibrosis of the nerves and visceral amyloidosis.

In tuberculoid form, the lesions are sarcoid-like, appearing as macules on the skin with an indurated border. The peripheral nerves are thickened. Leprae bacilli penetrate the nerve bundles, and cause formation of loose granulation tissue, followed by fibrosis, and later by motor and trophic disorders. There are little or no leprae bacilli.

Apart from these two ends of the spectrum of the condition, there is the borderline form in which the lesions and the pathological changes are as such that they fall neither in the clinical type LL nor in the TT. They rather occupy the middle of the spectrum. This type of infection is quite unstable and the condition may downgrade near the LL form, better described as near-lepromatous form, or may undergo a reversal reaction, becoming more nearly TT form, described as near-tuberculoid form.

Once acquired the infection runs an extremely slow course, involving years together.

The incidence of the condition is greater in males than in females, frequently affecting young adults, but the susceptibility to the condition may generally be controlled by HLA determinants.

The incubation period of the infection is not known but may extend over many years, perhaps ranging between 5 and 15 years.

Clinical Manifestations

The condition begins insidiously. Skin lesions may develop anywhere of the body at a particular area with impaired sensation, or as anaesthetic (may initially be paraesthetic), hypopigmented or erythematous macules, frequently with loss of hair over the lesions or as nodules with thickening of cutaneous tissue. The lesions may be diffuse or discrete erythematous plaques, or may form large plaques or may cause generalised macular eruptions (Fig. 7.15), or produce indolent ulcers covered with seropurulent exudate, or may cause ulceration and necrosis, mutilating with extensive scarring. The condition rarely affects central nervous system.

Lepromatous leprosy (LL) runs a malignant and progressive course. It presents with numerous, small, hypopigmented, erythematous macules, papules or nodules, with ill-defined margins, on the skin (Fig. 7.16). The lesions show a predilection for the face, ears (Fig. 7.17), elbows, wrists, buttocks and knees. The lesions are widely scattered all over the body symmetrically and diffusely. Sensitivity to the skin is however not impaired. As the condition progresses the skin lesions become more infiltrative, with thickening of the skin. Loss of body hair and other skin appendages are common. Nerve involvement appears late in the course, and is slow and symmetrical. The lesions are hypoanaesthetic or anaesthetic. It gives rise to anhidrosis, which starts from the dorsal aspects of the forearms and lower legs, and involves the whole body. Axillae, groins, palms and soles however escape anhidrosis.

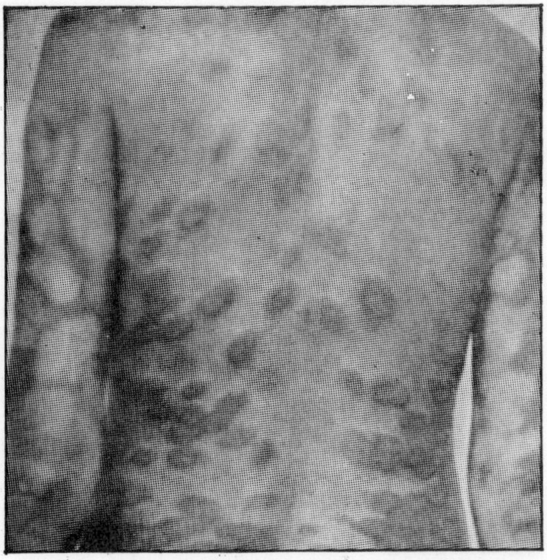

Figure 7.15. Generalised macular eruptions.

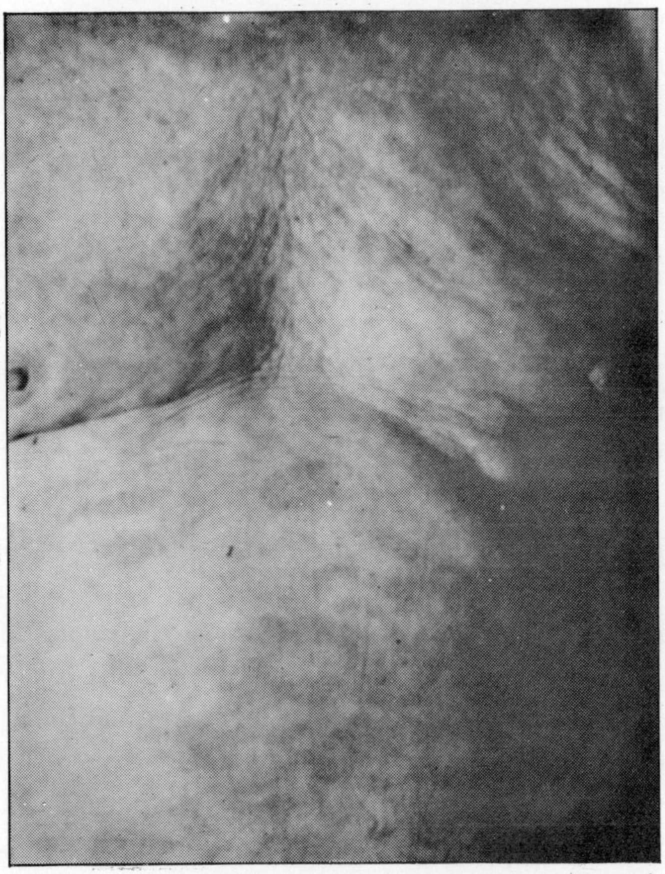

Figure 7.16. Lepromatous leprosy.

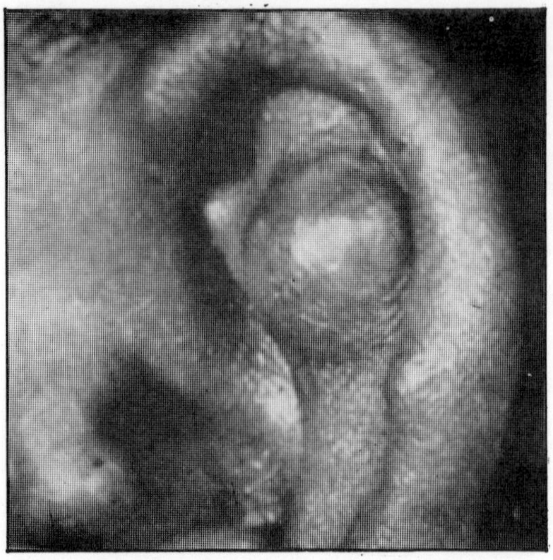

Figure 7.17. Typical ear nodules in lepromatous leprosy.

In the advanced stage of the condition, loss of eyelashes and eyebrows occur, and nodular lesions of varying size develop. Mucous membrane of nose, mouth and pharynx may produce ulcerations and cause necrosis of cartilage and bone, resulting in nasal deformity and collapse, or perforation of the septum, and may lead to airway distress. The nerves, especially ulnar and peripheral nerves nearing the skin surface, may show infiltration and thickening, with resultant anaesthesia, neuritis, trophic ulcers, bone resorption and shortening of digits. Consequently extensive disfigurement and deformity may result from skin infiltration and peripheral nerve destruction.

Involvement of eyes is common and there may be punctate keratitis and corneal ulcer. Testes may be destroyed, resulting sterility, and gynaecomastia may develop. In more advanced case, the peripheral lymph glands may be enlarged and may later produce abscesses. The lesions may also involve the spleen, liver, kidney and other organs. Amyloidosis develops occasionally.

Tuberculoid leprosy (TT) runs a benign and non-progressive course. It presents with localised lesions on skin and peripheral nerves. The skin lesions appear as hypopigmented macules, or as large, well-defined, elevated, erythematous plaques of irregular sizes, and induration (Fig. 7.18). They are few in numbers and are distributed symmetrically. The lesions usually show markedly diminished sensation to touch, temperature and pain. Skin lesions are dry or may be covered with fine scales. The lesions occur anywhere on the body, particularly the lateral aspects of the arms, legs and buttocks. Nerve involvement is sudden and asymmetrical, and usually affects a large peripheral nerve, particularly ulnar nerve above the elbow, radial nerve at the wrist, median nerve, posterior tibial nerve around the medial malleolus, common perineal nerve at the popliteal fossa, and popliteal nerve. Nerve involvement causes enlargement, thickening, and anaesthesia and muscle weakness. Characteristically necrosis occurs which destroys the nerve bundles and causes paralysis of the part supplied by the particular nerve involved. Otherwise, the lesions may heal spontaneously but slowly without residual disability, or the peripheral nerve may remain damaged or destroyed. Involvement of facial nerve produces paralysis of the eyelids, and lead to keratitis and corneal ulcer. Development of trophic ulcer is common. Later, there may be contracture, and autoamputation of fingers and toes.

Borderline leprosy, including ***near-lepromatous*** and ***near-tuberculoid*** forms, gives rise to variable manifestations, and the lesions may be either progressive or regressive. The symptoms and signs the condition presents with depend upon the encroachment of either end of the spectrum. The manifestations may then resemble near-lepromatous or near-tuberculoid. Otherwise, borderline leprosy may present with mild or transient manifestations.

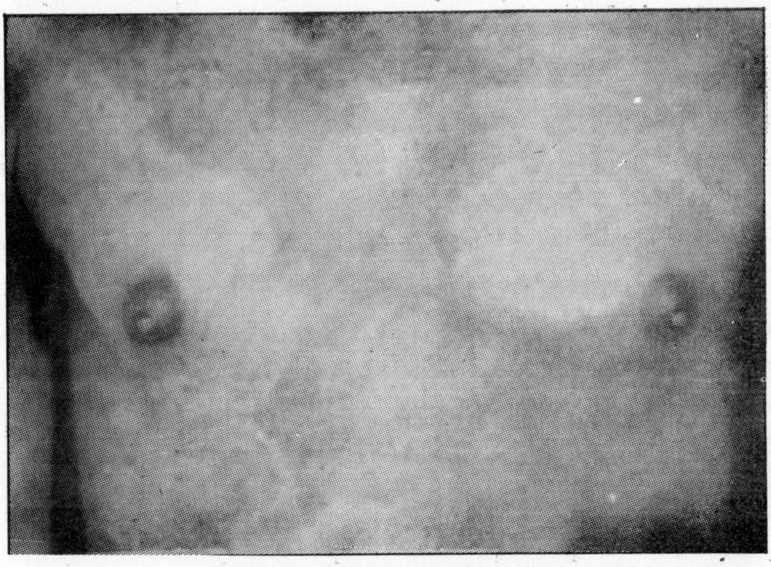

Figure 7.18. Tuberculoid leprosy.

Indeterminate leprosy, as the term implies, remains inconclusive. This form sometime develops as an early benign and unstable condition, and gives rise to ill-defined hypopigmented macules. There may or may not be sensory impairment. Nerve thickening is, however, usually absent. The condition may finally evolve towards tuberculoid, lepromatous or borderline form but otherwise, get healed up spontaneously.

Sometimes there may be an additional form, **primary neuritic leprosy**, in which there is enlargement of peripheral nerves. This may occur with or without damage on nerves, and there is no skin lesion.

In intercurrent pulmonary tuberculosis and amyloidosis are the principal complications of leprosy. Otherwise, the condition produces complications due to peripheral nerve involvement.

In addition, the condition can cause secondary infection, various eye complications and, in lepromatous leprosy, deformity and disfigurement.

During the later part of initial year of treatment, lepromatous leprosy may give rise to **erythema nodosum leprosum** due to antigen-antibody complex deposits on the skin and other tissues. They appear suddenly in crops as tender, inflamed, subcutaneous nodules, last for 2 to 7 days, and then disappear without leaving any trace. In severe cases however, the nodules may become pustular and show necrosis at the centres. In such a reaction the patient may present with fever, malaise and arthralgia. Sometimes there may also be neuritis and nerve palsies, orchitis, iritis, albuminuria, and oedema of extremities and lymphadenopathy.

Tuberculoid and borderline leprosy may however give rise to a reversal reaction, causing skin patches to become raised, oedematous and tender. Nerve damage is however an important feature. There may also be fever, arthritis, and oedema of the extremities and lymphadenopathy.

Diagnosis

Anaesthetic hypopigmented macules on skin surface are typical of the condition. It is also suspected in persons coming from endemic areas and presenting with unexplained macules, plaques, nodules, and infiltration or erythema nodosum. In cases of nerve involvement, diagnosis can be made on clinical grounds, and even if the diagnostic provisions fail to identify the causative bacillus, histological changes in the peripheral nerve is considered to be pathognomic.

Confirmation of diagnosis is made from isolation and identification of acid-fast bacillus from the scrapings of cutaneous lesion or nasal mucosa. Biopsy of skin lesions show characteristic vacuolated macrophages and lymphocytes and a heavy crowd of acid-fast bacilli in lepromatous leprosy and in some cases of borderline leprosy, including near-lepromatous form, but show granulomas containing lymphocytes and epitheloid cells in tuberculoid leprosy and also in near-tuberculoid form.

Intradermal test, lepromin test, has no diagnostic value but is of much help in differentiating the known cases of leprosy. The test yields a negative result in lepromatous leprosy that is not linked with T-cell mediated immunity even though the skin and the nasal mucous membrane lesions show abundant acid-fast bacilli. In tuberculoid leprosy the lesions show a few or no acid-fast bacillus and yet the test is positive because of its association with vigorous T-cell mediated immunity.

Diagnosis of the condition usually does not pose any problem and yet, at times, if it causes any confusion, the condition may need to be differentiated from sarcoidosis, lupus erythematosus, erythema multiforme, erythema nodosum, syphilis, scleroderma and syringomyelitis.

Treatment

Management of leprosy requires prolonged treatment and a special care for anaesthetic extremities. It also needs identification and even, if possible, isolation of the lepromatous, near-lepromatous and borderline cases until finding of acid-fast bacilli in them becomes few or scarce. To achieve this the patients are energetically treated with a combination of 3 antileprotic drugs for no less than 2 years period or until bacteriological cure is achieved. Other cases are however treated for a short period with 2 antileprotic drugs simultaneously.

For the purpose of treatment with multi-drug, leprosy is classified into two groups: multibacillary which includes lepromatous leprosy along with near-lepromatous and borderline leprosy, and paucibacillary which includes tuberculoid leprosy, near-tuberculoid and indeterminate leprosy.

The basic treatment of the condition is given by sulphone, such as dapsone, 1-2 mg per kg of body-weight daily orally. The drug is quite safe but can occasionally cause high fever, haemolysis, frank anaemia and allergic dermatoses. Rifampicin, 600 mg once in a month or 10 mg/kg as a single dose daily orally, though expensive and has certain hepatotoxicity, is also highly effective. Other antileprotic drugs used are clofazimine, 50 mg daily or 100 mg three times weekly orally increased to 300 mg daily for maximum of 3 months, and ethionamide, 250-500 mg daily orally.

Multibacillary type of the condition, which also shows abundance of acid-fast bacilli, is given 3-drug regimen, with rifampicin, 600 mg once-monthly orally, supervised (450 mg for adults weighing less than 35 kg), dapsone, 100 mg daily orally, self-administered (50 mg daily or 1-2 mg/kg daily for adult weighing less than 35 kg), along with clofazimine, 300 mg once monthly, supervised, but 50 mg daily (or 100 mg on alternate days), self-administered. In cases of less satisfactory response, the dose of clofazimine is increased to 100 mg six times in a week or even much higher as 300 mg daily. Rifampicin, 600 mg, is given daily for 2 to 3 days and then on the consecutive days in each month. In cases where dapsone-resistance has developed, the patient may alternatively be treated with ethionamide. The drug is however not frequently tolerated due to its gastrointestinal irritability. In addition, it can cause liver dysfunction. However, the treatments are continued for at least two years or till. Multibacillary leprosy should be treated for at least two years or till bacteriological cure is achieved, and is followed up for no less than five years time after cessation of therapy. The treatment should be continued unchanged during both type I (reversal) or type II (erythema nodosum leprosum) reactions. However, during reversal reaction when neuritic pain or weakness can herald the rapid onset of permanent nerve damage, treatment with prednisolone, initially 40-60 mg daily, should be instituted instantly. Mild type II reactions are adequately managed with aspirin or chloroquine, but severe type II reactions may require corticosteroid. Otherwise, thalidomide may be given under strict supervision of specialist physician but exclusively to men and post-menopausal women only who have developed corticosteroid dependency. Increased doses of clofazimine (100 mg 3 times daily) for the first month with subsequent reactions, are also useful but to attain full effect it may take 4-6 weeks time.

The paucibacillary type is treated with 2-drug regimen, and the patient is given dapsone, 100 mg, daily, self-administered (50 mg daily or 1-2 mg/kg daily for adult weighing less than 35 kg) and rifampicin, 600 mg, once in a month, supervised (450 mg for persons weighing less than 35 kg) and the treatment is continued for six months. If however treatment is interrupted the regimen should be recommended where it was left off to complete the full course. Follow up after cessation of therapy is needed for at least two years.

As emphasised earlier in cases of erythema nodosum leprosum, administration of antipyretic and analgesic, such as paracetamol, 500 mg-1 g four times daily orally, is often sufficient in mild cases. Severe cases will however need corticosteroid, such as prednisolone, 60-80 mg daily in divided doses orally, and once the condition is controlled the drug is tapered off gradually as soon as feasible. Thalidomide is also a most effective drug and is given at 200 mg twice daily orally and then tapered off to levels of 50-100 mg daily. The drug is however contraindicated in pregnant women.

In cases of any reaction that occurs in tuberculoid and borderline cases with near-tuberculoid type, and causes pain and tenderness in the nerves, the patient is then given prednisolone, initially 60 mg or more daily in divided doses orally, followed by 20 mg daily for some weeks and then tapered off gradually over months.

When however reversal reaction develops in lepromatous, near-lepromatous and borderline cases, the patient is given prednisolone as specified above along with increasing dose of clofazimine, 200-300 mg daily orally for a few weeks.

In any cases, if there is any reaction and that is of mild nature, the patient is kept at rest and analgesic, such as aspirin, 300-900 mg every four to six hours orally, is given.

Under no circumstance the antileprotic drug should be ever discontinued for any reason. If there is any reaction, appropriate treatment is given simultaneously, in addition.

In cases of ocular involvement, the patient must need ophthalmologist's care. Until then, or if such a service is not readily available, the eyes may be instilled with atropine, 1% drop or ointment applied twice daily, or hydrocortisone, 1% drop or ointment, for the time being so as to prevent further ocular deterioration.

In cases of dry skin due to anhidrosis, passive therapy is given by soaking hands and feet in cold water daily for about 30 minutes.

In cases of nerve involvement simple manoeuvre may be made to release the nerve compression before any surgical interference is sought for.

The patient will however need surgical interference, plastic surgery and physiotherapy, as the situation warrants, for contracture, ulcers and other mutilating or disfiguring features.

TROPICAL ULCER

The condition produces acute or chronic ulcerative lesion characterised by rapid destruction of tissues, and occurs due to anaerobic bacteroides, *fusospirochaetes*, and other bacteria. Most of these organisms are however found to be normal inhabitants of upper respiratory tract bacterial flora, while some are seen in intestinal and female genital tracts.

The mode of transmission of infection is not precisely clear. Minor trauma, under-nourishment, debility, concurrent infections and poor hygiene are known to act as predisposing factors. The ulcerations may also be resulted from several disease conditions as well. It occurs in hot and damp climate, and involves the exposed parts of the body, such as feet, lower parts of the legs and the arms.

The condition commonly affects people aged up to 30 years, and is more common in males than in females.

The initial lesion appears as a bleb with sanguineous fluid, which rapidly spreads in the skin and subcutaneous tissue, sloughs, releases offensive discharge, and the necrotic tissue separates and leaves an ulcer.

Clinical Manifestations

Initially there is a small abraded or ulcerated area on the part of the body exposed to trauma, which later forms a deep circular ulcer with undermined edges. The lesion is usually solitary and presents with foul-smelling pus. When the base of the ulcer is peeled off, it bleeds readily. General constitutional symptoms are slight and, in absence of any secondary infection, there is also no lymphadenopathy. The damage is usually limited to superficial tissue but may, in severe cases, involve the underlying deeper structure or even the bone. The ulcer heals slowly but may persist for months.

The possible complications the condition can produce are bacteraemia, endocarditis, and malignancy.

Diagnosis

The condition is diagnosed on clinical grounds.

In cases of any confusion, the condition may need to be differentiated from other causes of cutaneous ulceration, such as anthrax, which presents with a necrotic ulcer associated with region al lymphadenopathy, and the condition tend to suppurate. Other bacterial infections cause pain and perhaps lymphadenopathy.

Treatment

The ulcer is cleaned thoroughly, and the treatment is given with antibiotics for example procaine penicillin G, 400,000 U twice daily by IM injection, or tetracycline, 500 mg every six hours orally. The patient may also be given antimicrobial agent, such as metronidazole, 400 mg three times daily orally for 7 days.

Chronic ulcers and ulcers larger than 3 cm in diameter may require surgical treatment.

ANTHRAX

Caused by Large, nonmotile, sporeforming, aerobic, Gram-positive rods, *Bacillus anthracis*, anthrax (also known as **malignant pustule, Woolsorter's disease**) is an infection principally of cattle, sheep, goats, horses and swine. Transmission of infection in human beings is possible from entry of spores through abraded skin or mucous membrane and, rarely, by inhalation or by ingestion. Spread of infection from human to human is though possible but rare.

In wool sorter's disease it produces haemorrhagic necrosis of alveolar septa, with overwhelming abundance of organism within the inflammatory exudates. There may be thrombosis of small veins and arteries, with profuse endothelial vascular damage.

As this condition develops from contact of the infected animals, their skin, tissue, bone and carcasses, it constitutes as an occupational hazard usually of farmers, butchers, woolsorters, felt-makers, and veterinarians.

Its incubation period is 12 hours to 5 days usually 12 to 36 ours.

Skin lesion shows oedema, haemorrhage, necrosis, and various degree of inflammation. When the organism gains entry into blood, it involves all organs of the body, causing septicaemia, with enlargement of spleen and other organs.

Clinical Manifestations

A small erythematous macule appears on the exposed part of skin, usually the face, neck, forearm or hand. The macule enlarges in size and becomes oedematous to create a papule, which soon becomes vesicle, containing clear serous or bloodstained fluid swarming with anthrax bacillus, often surrounded by a zone of secondary vesicles. The vesicle later changes to a pustule, and then finally to a necrotic ulcer with slough and eschar. The surrounding area appears reddened, oedematous and indurated but there is no pitting on pressure. The eschar gradually extends to cover the secondary vesicles. The lesion is necrotic but not very tender. Regional lymphadenopathy occurs with tenderness. In severe cases reddened lymphatic are seen along the course of lymphatic drainage. There may also be variable constitutional symptoms and rise in body temperature.

High fever, prostration, shock, cyanosis, sweating, collapse and ever death may occur from septicaemia due to haematogenous spread occurring when the eschar sloughs.

In woolsorter's disease, diffuse pneumonia develops with extensive serofibrinous exudation. Frequently septicaemia develops and ensues death within a short time.

In other cases, the condition may present with primary pneumonia due to inhalation of spores. It then gives rise to mild fever, malaise, headache, and cough. Haemoptysis is usually evident. The patient complains of dyspnoea, and gives rise to cyanosis. Systemic disturbances are usually profound. Haemorrhagic meningitis and haemorrhagic mediastinitis may also occur. Chest X-ray and auscultation of lungs reveal signs of pneumonia. The condition often leads to fatality.

Ingestion of spores causes gastrointestinal anthrax. It then presents with anorexia, nausea, vomiting, and abdominal pain with bloody diarrhoea. The patient rapidly develops septicaemia and shock.

The usual complication of the condition is bacteraemia, while pulmonary anthrax produces pleural effusion.

Diagnosis

Occupational history of the patient often serves as a helpful guide. The causative organism can be identified from smear of local lesion, and culture of blood and sputum. Precipitation or haemagglutination test can also detect antibodies.

The condition may be differentiated from furuncle, glanders, primary syphilis, bacterial pneumonia, subarachnoid haemorrhage, and cardiovascular accidents.

Treatment

Most antibiotics are effective in the management of the condition. In mild localised condition, the patient is given benzylpenicillin, 2.4 g every 4 hours (child, 150 mg/kg daily in 4 divided doses) by slow IV injection or infusion, along with another antimicrobial agent such as ceftriaxone, 1 g daily (2-4 g in severe cases) by IV infusion. Streptomycin may also be a good alternative and it is given at 1 g by IM injection, daily for 10 to 12 days.

Pulmonary and other severe cases are treated with penicillin G, 20 million U daily through continuous infusion. In addition, the patient is given streptomycin, 0.5 g every eight hours daily by IM injection.

GLANDERS

Glanders is an infection of horses, mules and donkeys, and is caused by small, nonmotile, aerobic, Gram-negative rod, *Pseudomonas mallei*. Human beings are infected from nasal and other secretions of glandered animals by inhalation or accidental ingestion, or through mucous membrane or skin abrasion. Abscess on skin spreads through lymphatic and invades bloodstream, and produces metastatic abscesses in lungs, bones, and elsewhere in the body. There are cellulitis, necrosis, abscesses and thrombosis with septic embolisms.

Persons engaged in handling animals, including laboratory personnel, can acquire the infection as an occupational hazard. Transmission of the infection is also possible from human to human.

The condition is known as **farcy** when the infection is limited to skin only.

The incubation period of the condition varies between few days and months.

The condition gives rise to lesions on the skin, which spreads along the lymphatics and invades the bloodstream and produces metastatic abscesses in the lungs, bone and elsewhere in the body. There are cellulitis, necrosis, abscesses and thrombosis with septic embolism.

Clinical Manifestations

The lesion begins as an ulcer on the skin or mucous membrane. In skin involvement it presents with an inflammatory papule or vesicle, usually on the face and hands. The papule or vesicle soon changes to nodule, pustule, and form irregular ulceration with undermined edges, and covered with purulent and serosanguineous exudate. Later, more nodules appear along the lymphatics, and eventually ulcerate. The condition may also give rise to constitutional symptoms or may occur as a chronic indolent disease with fever, chills, aches and pains, and prostration.

There is ulceration on nasal mucosa with a foetid, bloodstained discharge. Nasal septal perforation occurs due to necrosis. There is also palatal and pharyngeal ulceration.

In cases of dissemination of infection, there may be subcutaneous and muscular abscesses, destructive polyarthritis, osteomyelitis, meningitis, and pustular skin lesions over the joints and face. Prostration and stupor may develop, and followed by death in 2 to 3 weeks.

The condition often results to a fulminating course, and death. It also produces amyloidosis as complication.

Diagnosis

Occupational history may be a useful guide. Identification of the causative organism from focal lesions is possible through culture but is hazardous. Diagnosis is therefore usually made by demonstration of rising agglutination titre and a positive mallein skin test.

The condition may need to be differentiated from mycotic and staphylococcal infection, streptococcal cellulitis, pneumonia, and melioidosis.

Treatment

The infection responds well to sulphonamides, and a treatment with sulphadimidine, 3 g initially followed by 1.5 g every six hours orally, is often sufficient. Addition of another antibiotic, for example, streptomycin, 1 g daily by IM injection, or chloramphenicol or tetracycline, 250-500 mg every six hours orally, may be of some advantage.

The patient is also given supportive treatment as necessary.

YAWS

It is an endemic, non-venereal, contagious tropical disease, affecting the people living in humid, equatorial countries. The causative organism of yaws (**framboesia, pian**) is *Treponema pertenue*, an organism morphologically indistinguishable from *T. pallidum*, and the causative organism of syphilis. The infection spreads from person to person through intimate body contact but not through sexual contact. The organism gains entry through the abraded or excoriated skin surface, usually on the exposed parts of body, particularly legs and arms. Contaminated flies and insects can also play part in its transmission. Overcrowding and poor hygienic living environment therefore favours the spread of infection.

The condition is endemic in areas with warm and humid weather, usually near the Equator, and generally affects the children. Adults become infected only rarely from the infected children.

Incubation period of the infection varies between 2 and 6 weeks but usually 3-4 weeks

Treponema pertenue shows cross immunity with *T. pallidum*. Histopathologically, the lesions resemble those of syphilis, with particular involvement of the small blood vessels. Treponemas are seen in abundance in between the epidermal cells in both primary and secondary lesions.

The condition behaves like venereal syphilis in all respects but produces mucous patches only occasionally. It spares the cardiovascular and central nervous systems, and other viscera. It also does not cause any transplacental transmission. Alike syphilis the clinical manifestations of the condition are divided into primary, secondary and tertiary (late) stages. Secondary stage usually appears 4-12 weeks after the primary lesion and is non-destructive. Tertiary stage occurs 1 year after healing of secondary lesions or after a latent period of some years. Spontaneous cure may however occur in some cases during the period of latency. The lesions in tertiary stage are destructive.

Clinical Manifestations

Primary stage of the condition presents with an initial lesion (**mother yaws**) at the site of inoculation as a single, large, raised, painless ulcer or as itching papule that develops into a granular mass. The lesion is covered with a yellow crust which when removed leaves a pink, granular surface resembling strawberry and bleeds easily. There may also be accompanying headache, fever, painless regional lymphadenitis, and bone pain, worse at night. The skin lesion heals within a few weeks leaving an atrophic scar but may also persist for months together, in cases of secondary infection.

Secondary stage of the condition is characterised by the development of papillomata of varying sizes. The overlying skin of them becomes eroded and forms several, raised, pink 'mother yaws'–like granular surface, covered with yellow crusts. The lesions tend to grow on the moist and warm areas such as axillae, groins and perineum but less on the trunk, and particularly spare the scalp. The lesion occurring at mucocutaneous junctions such as around the mouth, vulva and anus, tend to be warty, hypertrophic and confluent mimicking condylomata lata of syphilis. In addition, alike secondary syphilis, a wide variety of skin rashes usually develop. The lesions show recurrences and several crops may erupt during the first 2 to 3 years of the condition. The lesions heal leaving faint, wrinkled scars, and changes in pigmentation. There may be painful papillomata on the palms and soles, or the skin may be thickened with cracks and fissures, causing painful condition of the foot. Due to this painful ulceration from keratotic lesion results a peculiar waddling crab-like gait (**'crab' yaws**), a characteristic feature of the condition.

The condition commonly produces generalised lymphadenopathy. Bone involvement gives rise to tenderness, pian and swelling of bones, osteitis, periosteitis, anterior bowing of tibia, and multiple dactylitis. Bone tumours (***goundou***) may occur at the sides of nose and may cause rhinitis in children with purulent nasal discharge, headache, bone pain, obstruction to breathing is late cases and, if extended further, may interfere with vision or may cause destruction of eye.

In its tertiary (late) stage the condition gives rise to solitary or multiple nodular lesions that ulcerate like gummatous ulcers with well-demarcated margins, having rough dirty bases. The superficial and deep ulcers on the skin heal with scarring on one part and extension on another or with keloid formation and contractors, with depigmentation. Occasionally, there may also be elephantiasis. The palms and soles become hyperkeratotic with painful fissures and erosions, which on healing leave pitting with moth-eaten appearance and depigmentation. There is also destructive gummatous and hypertrophic periosteitis, osteitis, osteoperiosteitis, spontaneous fracture, and shortening of a digit. Hard fibrous nodules (*juxta-articular nodule*), often symmetrical in distribution, and affect subcutaneous tissue with no attachment to skin or deeper structures, occur close to the joints, particularly in the region of knees, hips and elbows, and cause painless swelling with or without effusion. Occasionally, the nodules may however be attached to the overlying skin and may produce pressure symptoms. There may also be arthritis. Gummatous ulceration in the nasopharynx may cause perforation of both soft and hard palate and nasal septum, and finally may lead to complete destruction of the palate and nose (***gangosa, rhinopharyngitis mutilans***), causing pain, purulent nasal discharge and foetid breath. Infrequently however the ulcerative process may be limited to nasal septum and may thus cause collapse of the bridge of the nose.

It causes chronicity, recurrences and mutilating disfigurement as complications.

Diagnosis

The condition is diagnosed on clinical grounds. The organism can be identified by dark-field microscopy in the material from the initial and secondary lesions and lymph node aspirates but poses a serious problem in differentiation from *Treponema pallidum*. The condition also gives positive STS from few weeks since acquiring the infection, and the sero-positivity may persist through latency, to the extent even after successful treatment.

The condition is therefore extremely difficult to differentiate from syphilis and endemic syphilis, and there is no specific test to rule out the case. Otherwise, depending upon the lesions it produces, the condition may need to be differentiated from several other conditions as described under syphilis.

Treatment

The condition is successfully treated with Benzedrine penicillin, 2.4 million units as a single dose by deep IM injection. Children and adults weighing less than 45 kg are given 600,000 units. Patients having a history of hypersensitivity to penicillin are treated with erythromycin or tetracycline, 500 mg every six hours orally for 10 days.

If there is any open wound, the wound is cleaned with antiseptic agent and kept dry.

ENDEMIC SYPHILIS

Endemic syphilis or **non-venereal syphilis** is an infectious disorder of chronic nature, mimicking venereal syphilis in all respects but occurs non-venereal in origin, and is caused by treponema, which is both morphologically and serologically indistinguishable with *Treponema pallidum*, and may well be a modified strain of *T. pallidum*, that causes venereal syphilis. The organism is present in the oral mucosa and in the moist lesions of the infected persons. Transmission of infection therefore occurs non-venereally from direct contact (such as kissing) or from contamination on abraded or excoriated skin surface and mucous membrane. Indirect spread through the use of contaminated communal eating and drinking utensils, pipes and toothpicks, is also possible. Flies and insects may also play some role in its transmission.

Pathological changes the condition produce follows the same pattern, as those are evident in venereally acquired syphilis. The lesion usually starts as grey patches on buccal mucous membrane followed by papular eruption on the moist areas of the body. Venereal involvement is practically non-existing. It also does not affect the cardiovascular and nervous system.

The condition is prevalent in dry climates of the Middle East (**bejel**) and also in Africa, Southeast Asia and elsewhere and is common amongst the nomadic tribes and amongst those living in a poor social and economic condition. It runs within the families, affecting the whole community. The condition however most often develops in childhood, and adults may acquire the same from the children.

A similar variant of treponema, *Treponema carateum*, however causes a very mild condition, **pinta**, that occurs in some limited local rural foci in Latin America, and also in the Philippines and some other areas of the Pacific, and appears to be restricted in dark-skinned races. Unlike endemic syphilis the condition is principally a skin disease, causing unsightly pigment disturbances. Excluding the usual spread from direct contact, transmission of the infection also occurs through a fly, *Hippelates*.

Endemic syphilis behaves like venereal syphilis and gives rise to primary, secondary and tertiary stages.

Clinical Manifestations

The symptoms and signs of endemic syphilis, including bejel, are same as those are evident in venereal syphilis but a primary chancre is extremely rare. Rather the primary sore develops in the childhood as a mucous patch or may however appear as ulcerative papule on the nipples of the mother of the children sucking breasts. Otherwise, the condition presents with skin, mucosal and bones lesions, as those are evident in secondary syphilis. It also runs a latent phase, and finally in the late stage, gives rise to gummatous lesions, destruction of nose, nasal septum, soft palate and pharynx from nasopharyngeal ulceration, hyperkeratosis of palms and soles, and depigmentation of skin. There may also be periosteitis of long bones, painless synovitis, and firm, fibrous subcutaneous nodules around the joints, often symmetrically arranged and not attached to the skin or deeper structures (*juxtra-articular nodules*).

The condition usually leads to chronicity, relapses and disfigurement as complications.

Primary lesion in ***pinta*** develops as non-ulcerating papule on the skin of the exposed parts of the body, which several months after change to erythematous, flat and hyperpigmented papule, usually on the extremities, face and neck. Later, perhaps the lapse of several years, the lesions appear depigmented. Hyperkeratosis commonly develops on the palms and soles.

Diagnosis

Diagnosis of the condition is usually made n clinical grounds. The organism can however be isolated from the lesions and identified on dark-field microscopy. Serological tests for syphilis are also positive.

Depending upon the site of involvement and the stage of the condition, it may need to be differentiated from a large number of conditions as stated under venereal syphilis. There is however no way of differentiating it from venereal syphilis as well as from yaws. This may therefore at times cause enormous problem, more particularly in communities where neither endemic syphilis nor yaws is endemic.

Treatment

It is effectively treated as per schedule recommended under secondary syphilis. Benzathine penicillin G, 1.2 million U (2.4 million U in adults) as a single dose by IM injection, is usually quite sufficient.

DERMATOPHYTOSIS

Dermatophyte infection that produces dermatophytosis (**ringworm, tinea**) is the species belonging to the genera *epidermophyton, microsporum* and *trichophyton.* The dermatophytes are capable of living in keratinised tissue. Some of the organisms are found in the soil (geophilic), while some infect domestic and other animals (zoophilic). Transmission of infection occurs through contact of infected persons or animals, and from sharing materials used by the infected persons, such as comb, shaving razors and barbers' instruments. It also affects persons receiving systemic corticosteroid or other immunosuppressive agents, in whom the infection becomes generalised. Hot and humid environment favours the growth of dermatophytes. It is also evident on skin test that chronically infected persons frequently develop decreased cell mediated immunity and therefore predispose them to acquire the infection.

The condition manifests itself differently in different parts of the body, giving rise to a number of clinical entities, and presents with distinctive features, characterised to the part involved. The infection may occur at any age and sex but tinea capitis occur mainly in children, tinea cruris in adults but mainly in the males and in persons who are obese or perspire heavily, tinea pedis in adults who wear shoes and nylon socks in summer, and tinea barbae in adult males only.

Fungi attack the keratinised, dead layers of skin, nail and hair, and produce loca inflammatory reaction, either as a result of alternating the defensive properties of keratin or as the result of sensitisation. The lesion spreads in circle leaving a healing, scaly portion in the centre. The lesions include inflammation, scaling, hyperkeratosis, vesiculation, pustulation, maceration, and ulceration.

Clinical Manifestations

The condition characteristically produces circular type of lesions with raised active borders and a healing central portion. The presentation however varies depending upon the clinical variant and thus, the site of involvement.

Tinea corporis (tinea circinata, ringworm of body) generally involves the exposed parts of the body, usually non-hairy areas, usually face, neck, trunk (Fig. 7.19) and hands, with the exception of certain localised areas, for example, palms, soles and groins. It also quite commonly affects the waist area, especially in women. It presents with circular or irregular shaped patches of varying sizes, measuring one to many centimetres in diameter, with well-defined, raised and active margins of papulovesicles and healing hyperpigmented scaly centres (Fig. 7.20). The lesions spread to the periphery by direct extension, and cause intense itching. Inflammation is usually present, and follicular involvement often produces pustules. In persons who have used topical corticosteroids, the lesions tend to be widespread with reduced scaling, in which case the margins of the lesions may not be raised or clearly defined (**tinea incognita**). Occasionally the surrounding area may appear hyperpigmented.

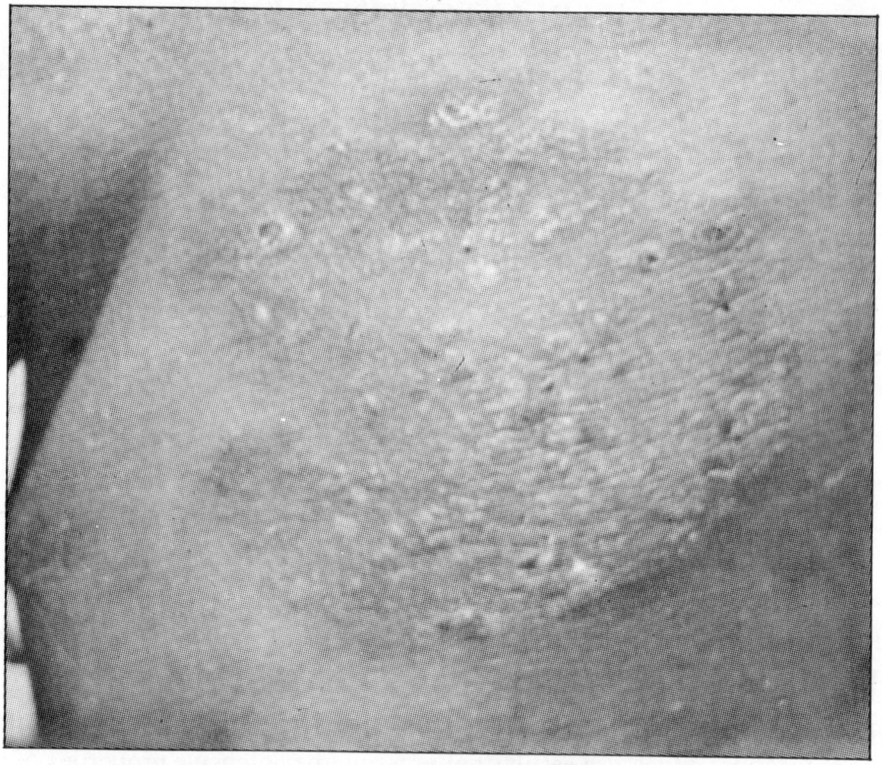

Figure 7.19. Tinea corporis.

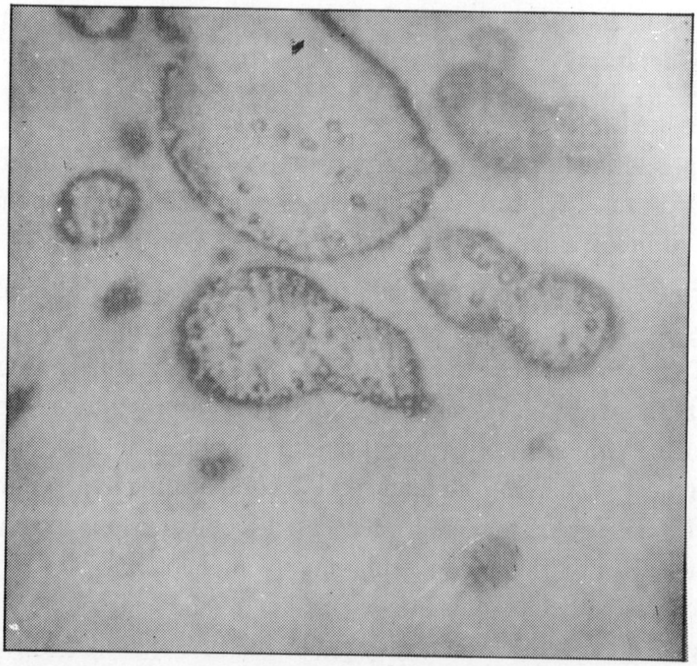

Figure 7.20. Typical lesions of tinea corporis.

Tinea capitis (tinea tonsurans, ringworm of scalp) involves the hair more so than the scalp, usually on the occipital and temporal regions. It is manifested by circular patch or patches of partial alopecia with broken stumps of hair, or matting of hair in the crusts, with thin, grey scales. Otherwise, there may be eruption of small lesions with oozing but without any pus, followed by localised, red, painless, boggy swelling. Hair appears dry, lustreless and brittle. It is a common cause of hair loss. On the other hand, the patches present with indolent abscesses. In fact, it is a common cause of hair loss. The condition does not usually give rise to any symptom except perhaps slight itching. The lesions heal spontaneously or may result scarring, with localised permanent alopecia. Regional lymphadenopathy is a common feature. So is the case with secondary bacterial infection.

Tinea barbae (tinea psychosis, ringworm of beard, barber's itch) develops on the beard area. It presents with localised boggy swelling with or without abscesses, and the lesions show loss or absence of beard hair. In other instances the lesions may appear as patch or patches of vesicle or vesicopapules with inflammation and itching. The lesions are usually unilateral and may extend to the face and neck. In the affected area pus may be expressed through the follicular opening.

Tinea cruris (dhobi's itch, ringworm of upper and inner thigh) commonly occurs in summer and affects the groins and upper part of the inner thighs (Fig. 7.21). The lesions spread to the genitalia, pubic area and perineal skin, and later to the buttock and trunk. The condition is infrequent in males before puberty and affects females less commonly. It develops as sharply marginated, erythematous macules and annular plaques, with clear centres and active raised margins, spreading peripherally in intertrigenous areas with scaling or crusting. Formation of satellite vesicular lesions and vesicle formation are however rare. Follicular pustules may also be evident. It causes severe itching, after changes of dress following continuous use of few hours, when the part is exposed to general environment, and at night. Occasionally, however, the lesions may also be asymptomatic. Heat and sweating often enhance the development of the lesions for which the condition is often known as **jock itch**. Characteristically once the lesion starts itching, the process of itching and scratching continues, causing every inconvenience and irritation.

Tinea axillaries produce similar lesions like tinea cruris but involve the axillae and undersurface of the pendulous beasts in women.

Tinea mannum (ringworm of soles and palms) involves the palms and soles, and gives rise to circumscribed areas of papulovesicular or pustular eruptions with confluent erythema, scaling, fissuring, and itching. When it involves the palms, intact vesicles may be seen on the dorsum of the hand (Fig. 7.22) but broken vesicles produce erythema and peripheral scales. Similarly it also affects the soles. There may be blistering lesions, often few in number, on the plantar surface of the toes and foot. Sometimes the lesions extend to cover the entire pal and sole. There may also be burning, stinging or other sensation. The lesions my also spread to the medial aspect of the thigh and perineal skin in males.

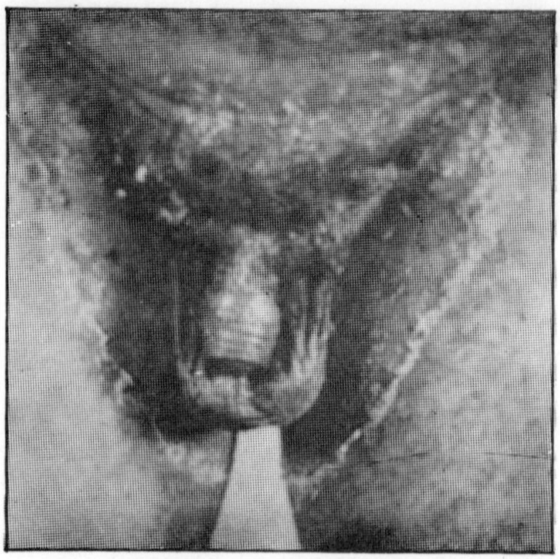

Figure 7.21. Tinea cruris.

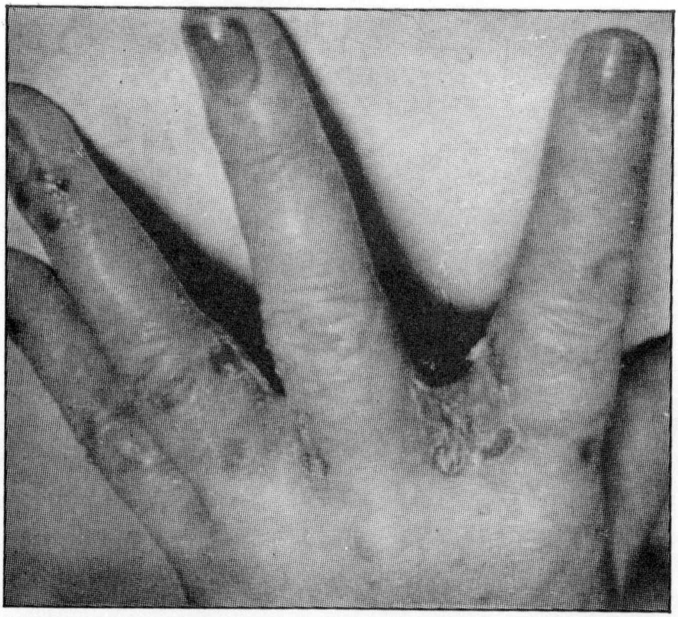

Figure 7.22. Tinea mannum.

Tinea pedis (athlete's foot) presents with scaling and fissuring on the fourth interdigital toeweb. There may also be varying degree of inflammation. Later, it involves the interdigital spaces of the foot with white sodden areas that may become eroded or may show marked scaling and fissuring (Fig. 7.23). Sometimes the lesions may extend from the plantar surface of the foot to the lateral margin, and the ruptured vesicles can cause erythema and peripheral scaling (Fig. 7.24). Often there is however no symptom.

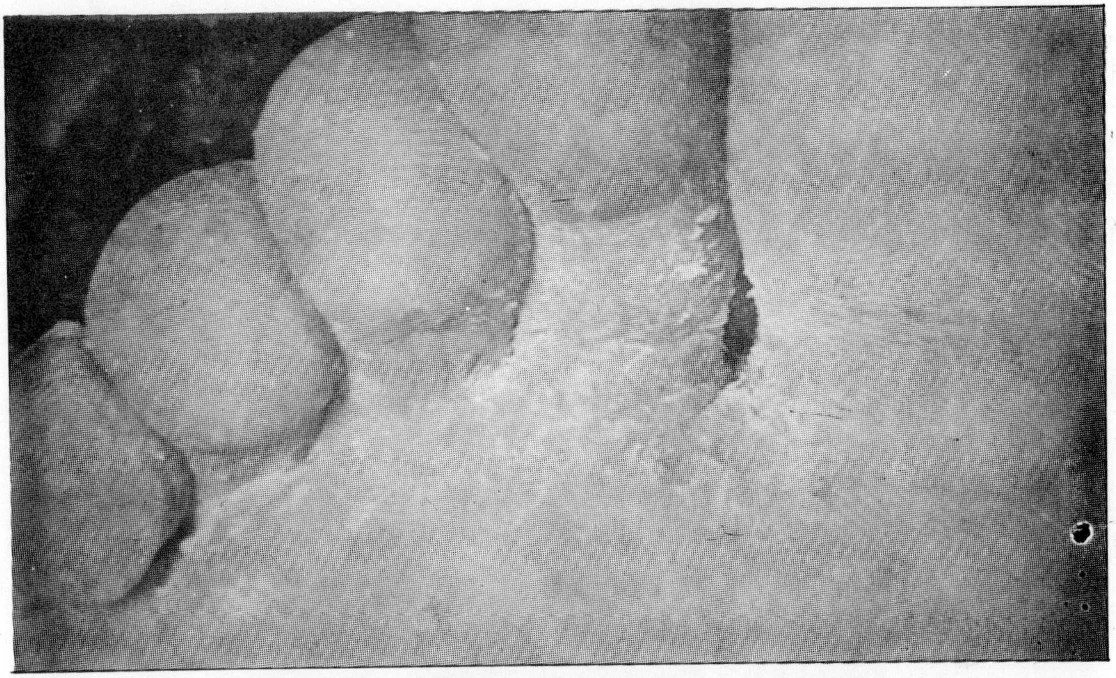

Figure 7.23. Tinea pedis.

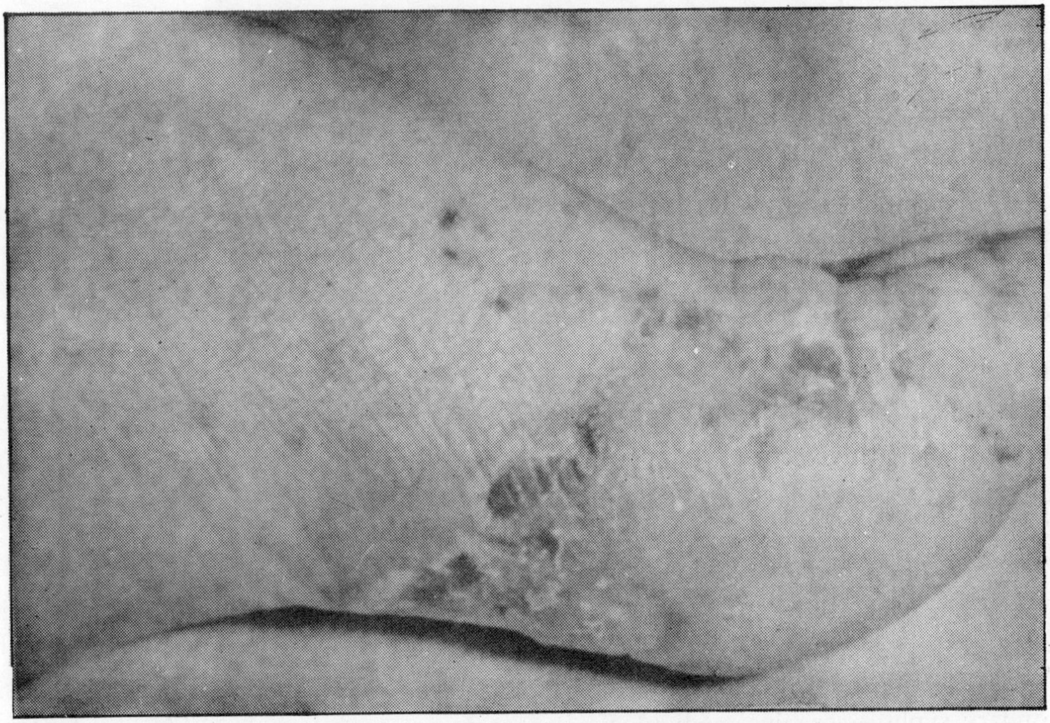

Figure 7.24. Tinea pedis with erythematous base and peripheral scaling.

Tinea unguium (ringworm of nail, onychomycosis) involves the nails, and most commonly affect the great toenails but can also involve other nails. The lesions usually starts under the free margin or along the lateral portion of the nail and grows backward into the nail bed, causing discoloration, chalky ridging and fissuring with black streaks. The nail plate becomes loose, brittle, separates from the bed, and breaks off. Fingernails (Fig. 7.25) do also show similar changes but are affected less frequently. The lesion may resemble candidial onychomycosis.

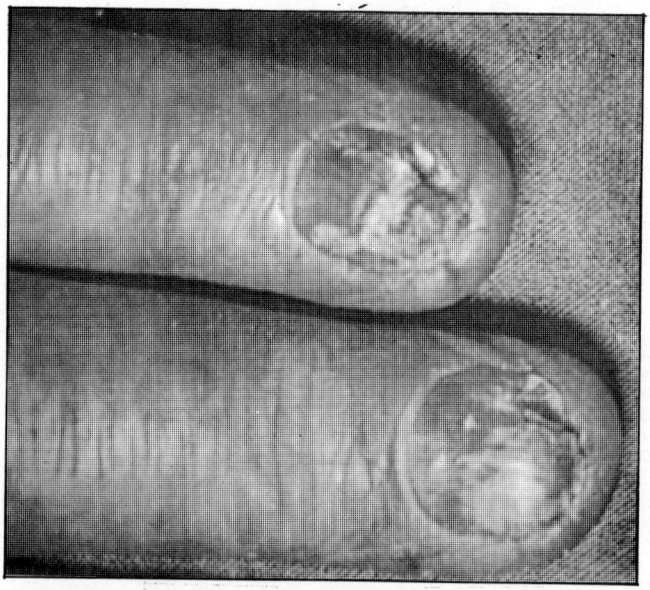

Figure 7.25. Tinea unguium.

Dermatophytes may lead to secondary infection, kerion and dermatophytid as complications. In addition, over-treatment may also lead to chronic dermatitis.

Diagnosis

Diagnosis is often possible on clinical grounds, supported by the identification of the organisms or their hyphae. The fungus can be isolated from the scrapings of skin, nail and hair, depending upon the site of involvement and clinical nature. Microsporum infection of hair can be identified through use of Wood's light in the dark. Some species can also be cultured, which is often necessary for the confirmation of diagnosis.

Depending on the clinical variant of the condition, it needs to be differentiated from several conditions, depending upon the clinical variant involved. Tinea corporis is therefore differentiated from psoriasis, eczema, seborrhoeic dermatitis, erythema multiform, erythrasma, secondary syphilis, scabies, pediculosis and drug reaction; tine capitis from seborrhoeic dermatitis, atopic dermatitis, and psoriasis; tinea barbae from folliculitis, pyoderma, and pediculosis; tinea cruris and tinea axillaries from contact dermatitis, psoriasis, candidiasis, other lesions involving intertrigenous areas, and pediculosis; tinea pedis and tinea mannum from interdigital erythrasma, candidiasis, intertrigo, contact dermatitis, and eczema; and tinea unguium from candidiasis and psoriasis.

Treatment

Systemic treatment is given with antifungal, griseofulvin, 125 mg four times or 500 mg once daily orally (children: 10 mg per kg of body-weight daily). The drug however requires long-term administration because of its low affinity for keratin. Its spectrum of activity is also narrow. In addition, not only it has several adverse side effects, it is also moderately hepatotoxic. Ketoconazole, 200-400 mg once daily orally (children: 3 mg per kg of body-weight daily) for 2 to 8 weeks but 1 to 12 months for onychomycoes, may be a suitable alternative but also has several side effects and interference with testosterone synthesis. It also has severe hepatotoxicity for which its administration requires monitoring of liver function test. Although not recommended for the children and elderly persons, itraconazole is however a triazole agent, with broad-spectrum antifungal activity. It is also non-hepatotoxic and has very few side effects. It is given as 100 mg daily orally for 7 days in cases of tinea corporis and tinea capitis but 30 days in cases of tinea pedis and tinea mannum. Fluconazole is another triazole agent like itraconazole, and is given as 150 mg once in a week orally for 4-6 weeks or 50 mg daily for 14-28 days in cases of all tinea infection, but 150 mg a week for up to 12 months in cases of onychomycosis. Allylamine antifungal, terbinafin, is another potent drug that is more superior to griseofulvin, It is however not recommended for the children, and is given as 250 mg daily orally for 2-6 weeks in tinea pedis, 2-4 weeks in tinea cruris, 4 weeks in tinea corporis, 6 weeks to 3 months in fingernail infections and 3-6 months in toenail infections.

Topical application of lotio iodine, salenium sulphate, Whitfield ointment, etc., is however of no help when the fungi have penetrated into the deep layers of epidermis. On the other hand, they need prolonged application for several weeks or even months. Yet, if needed, topical application of miconazol 2%, econazole 1%, terbinafine 1% or ketoconazole 2%, twice daily, may be given. In cases of tinea cruris, topical application of Lugole's iodine, once daily, though little traumatic and cause staining on the cloth is quite beneficial. In tinea pedis, alcoholic Whitfield lotion or coal tar solution or paste may also be beneficial. Interdigital lesions are kept clean and dry. Onychomycosis may however needs local application of antifungal agent continuously for some months.

In cases of severe itching, the patient may be given antihistamine. Appropriate antibiotic is also given in cases of secondary infection.

CANDIDIASIS

It is an acute or chronic condition that usually affects the skin and mucous membrane and genital tract, and occasionally causes systemic involvement. The condition is also known as **candidiosis** and **moniliasis**, and results due to oval, budding yeast, *Candida albicans*. In the tissue, the yeast however appears as non-branching, chain of tubular cells (pseudohyphae) from which small yeast forms bud off (blastospores). It is saprophytic yeast often found as a commensal in the mouth and gastrointestinal tract, and is commonly present in the female genital tract. The yeast can also be recovered from the soil, hospital environment, foods and other substances. There are several factors, which may influence the carriage of the yeast, and pregnancy is a good example thereof. Again, oral colonisation of the yeast is found more common in hospital environment than in non-hospital environment. Acquiring the infection is usually endogenous, though cross-infection is also possible. However, susceptibility to the infection increases in infancy, pregnancy and old age, and in persons undertaking broad-spectrum antibacterial or corticosteroid therapy. It also develops frequently in persons suffering from diabetes mellitus, in debilitated or dehydrated state, carcinoma, and from defects in immunity (primary T cell or phagocytosis), such as leukaemia, chronic granulomatous disease, and in cytotoxic therapy in organ transplantation. On the other hand, subcutaneous candidiasis frequently develops in hypothyroidism, hypoparathyroidism and hypoadrenalism, while oral contraceptives cause vaginal candidiasis. Other predisposing factors of the condition include local epithelial defects or occlusion, intravenous narcotic abuse, constant immersion in water, malabsorption, iron deficiency and zinc deficiency.

Use of common bathroom, swimming pool or sharing personal belongings of the affected person, such as washing towels, caps, etc. can favour the spread of the infection. Direct inoculation of the infection can also occur, particularly in immunocompromised individuals, though peritoneal dialysis, catheters and cardiac surgery can even cause severe disseminated candidiasis.

Other species of Candida, such as *C. tropicalis*, *C. pseudotropicalis*, *C. parapsilosis* and *C. guilliermondii*, can also cause superficial infections, but are less common.

Other yeast, such as *Torulopsis glabratea*, may also be pathognomic and may produce systemic disease as well.

However, candida causes superficial infection or deep invasion from surface lesion. It therefore causes a variety of clinical syndromes and is categorised by the site of its involvement.

Skin and mucosal lesions show inflammatory changes with microabscesses but granulomas in their chronic state. In lung involvement, there are extensive, spherical or irregular lesions, often haemorrhagic, with patchy infarction. Renal involvement shows innumerable microabscesses in the both cortex and medulla, with pseudohyphae in the centre of the lesion, surrounded by necrotic areas and infiltration with polymorphonuclear leucocytes. Brain, heart, thyroid, adrenals, liver, pancreas or joints may also be involved in cases of dissemination, and will show miliary abscesses.

Clinical Manifestations

Cutaneous candidiasis is rarely a primary condition and is almost always secondary to intercurrent skin or systemic disease. Superficial infection usually present as oral mucositis (oral thrush) or as vaginitis (vaginal thrush).

In the skin involvement, warm and moist parts of the body, such as axillae, groins, intergluteal folds, especially in the obese, and underneath the pendulous breast may be affected. The lesions may become red and weeping, and may give rise to vesicles, which leave eroded areas and show a tendency of fissuring. Similarly, wet napkins in infants may encourage the development of the cutaneous lesions. The lesions however appear as oval shaped macerated area with raw fissures, surrounded by overhanging detached epidermis in the interdigital area (Fig. 7.26). In between the toes the lesion produces white sodden areas.

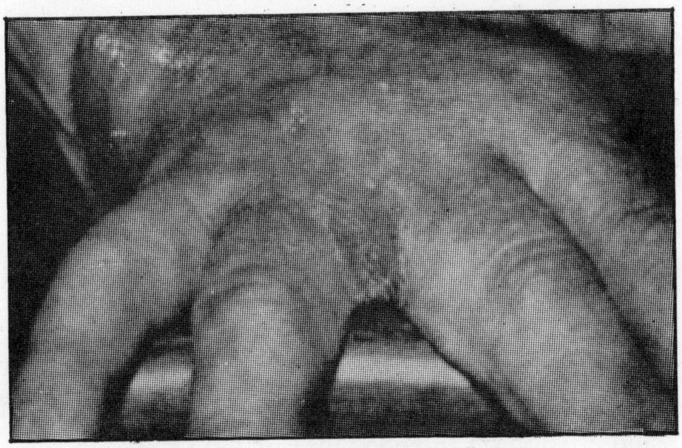

Figure 7.26. Interdigital candidiasis.

The condition may produce generalised cutaneous lesions, particularly in the adolescents, and give rise to vesicles and vesiculopapules, which rupture to form, denuded areas, surrounded by fringe-like detached epidermis. Generalised cutaneous lesions may even involve the palms (Fig. 7.27). The condition can also produce erythematous patches at and around the mouth and nose.

In nail involvement (**candidial onychomycosis**) it causes painful, reddened swelling of the nail fold, leading to thickening and transverse grooving of the nails, and eventual loss of the nail. The condition however resembles tinea unguium (ringworm of nail) in all respects.

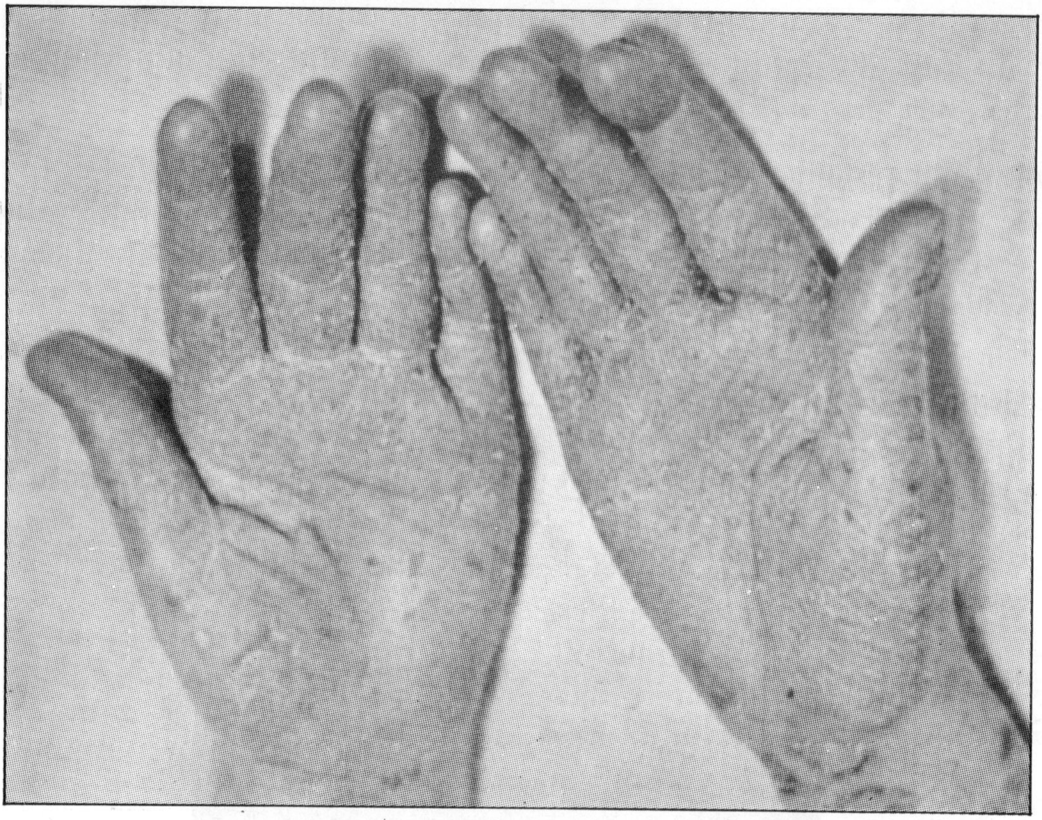

Figure 7.27. Generalised candidiasis involving both palms.

Involvement of mouth (**thrush, acute pseudomembranous candidiasis**) occurs usually in the infants as superficial white patches, or as large fluffy membranous lesions that are easily detached, leaving a reddened, underlying surface. The lesions may become confluent on the buccal mucosa, tongue, palate and gingiva, and may give rise to pain and dysphagia. Similar lesions with vesicles and erosion on the edge and irritation may occur on the buccal mucous membrane of the adults, especially in debilitated, hospitalised, elderly persons, and on the mucous membrane of the rectum (**candidial proctitis**) or of vagina and cervix.

Unlike thrush candidial leucoplakia (chronic hyperplastic candidiasis) however presents with firm, raised, white or translucent, adherent patches on the buccal mucosa or tongue (Fig. 7.28), with surrounding erythema.

Due to dentures however the condition can give rise to chronic erythema and oedema of the palatal mucosa that contacts the dentures (**chronic atrophic candidiasis**). Development of angular stomatitis is common.

The infection also produces cheilosis (**candidial cheilosis**) and presents with erythema, fissuring, maceration and soreness at the angles of the mouth.

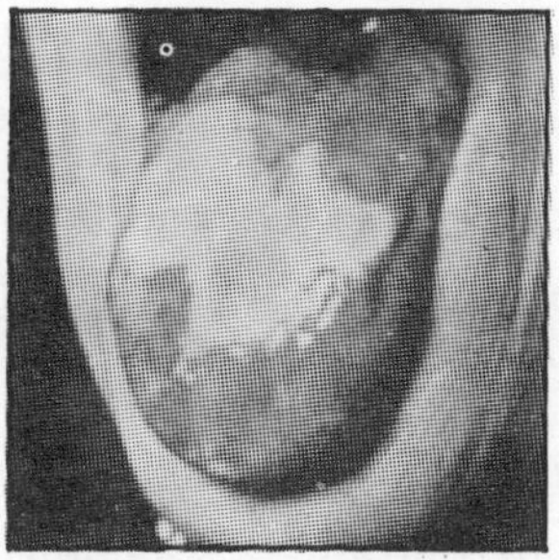

Figure 7.28. Candidiasis of tongue.

Involvement of genitalia causes vaginal thrush in adult women with irritation (**candidial vulvovaginitis**). The patient complains of vaginal discharge, frequency of micturition and intense itching. The vulva appears swollen and reddened, with excoriation and fissure (**pruritus vulvae**). Sometimes white creamy material may be seen to cover the vaginal wall. In men, the condition produces **candidial balanoposthitis** and **candidial balanitis** in the circumcised (Fig. 7.29). The condition is manifested by localised area of superficial ulceration on glans penis, covered by translucent or white cheesy material. The condition is however generally acquired through sexual intercourse.

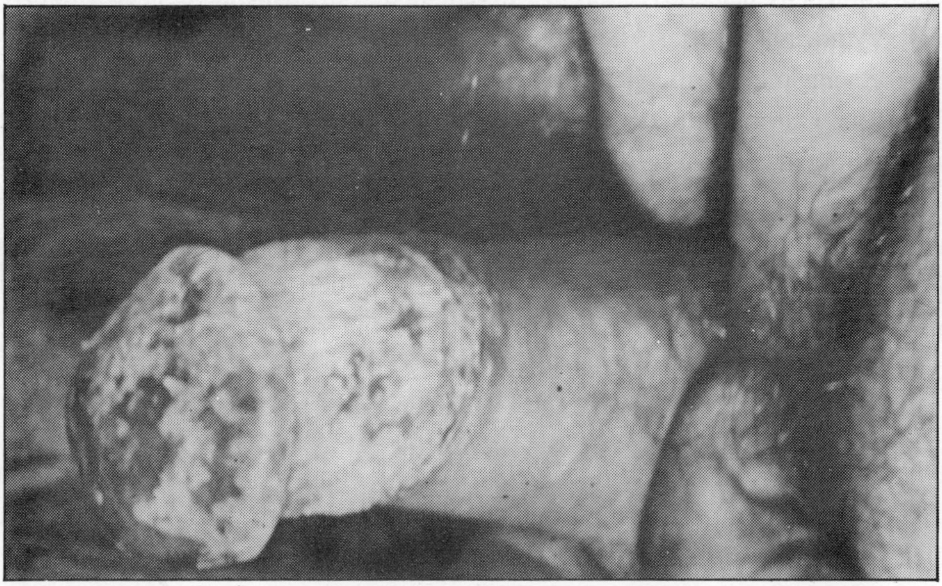

Figure 7.29. Candidial balanitis.

The infection can cause urinary tract infection (**candidial urethritis**), causing dysuria and frequency in micturition. In men, it is however often symptomfree but otherwise there may be irritation or soreness of penis, especially after intercourse. Sometimes there may also be slight urethral discharge. Vesicles or erosions may be present, and the glans and prepuce may appear reddened. White creamy material may be seen on the undersurface of the prepuce.

The organism may occasionally invade tissue directly or distant tissue haematogenously and, depending upon the site of involvement, may produce symptoms and signs of septicaemia, ocular infection, bronchopneumonia, renal failure, gastrointestinal bleeding, thrombophlebitis, endocarditis, meningitis, shock, coma and death. Occasionally it may also produce osteomyelitis.

The sequelae of candidiasis are chronic oesophagitis, oesophageal stricture, phimosis, and systemic involvement.

Diagnosis

Diagnosis of the condition is made on clinical grounds and by identification of the organism from surface lesions, sputum, exudate and aspirated material. In systemic involvement with skin lesions, diagnosis can be made from histopathology and culture of skin biopsy. Serological tests such as agglutination, direct immunofluorescence and precipitation are available, and though detection of their high antibody titres may suggest continuing activity of the infection, they do not serve any purpose for diagnosis. Similarly, skin test may not also be of any help.

Depending upon the site of involvement the condition may need to be differentiated from a number of ailments. Cutaneous cases are differentiated from tinea infection, eczema, seborrhoeic dermatitis, erythrasma, psoriasis and intertrigo. Oral lesions are differentiated from herpetic infection, erythema multiforme, lichen planus, pemphigus, leukoplakia, secondary syphilis and hiistoplasmosis. Chronic mucocutaneous cases are differentiated from tinea and bacterial pyoderma. Candidial cheilosis is differentiated from iron deficiency state, riboflavin deficiency and secondary syphilis. Nail involvement us however difficult to differentiate from tinea unguium but otherwise it is differentiated from bacterial paronychia and from similar conditions that occur in Reiter's syndrome, hypoparathyroidism and coeliac disease. Systemic candidiasis associated with cutaneous manifestations are differentiated from bacterial sepsis, seep fungal infection, aspergillosis and pseudomonous ecthyma.

Treatment

Prior to treatment of the cases, removal, correction or control of the underlying predisposing factors, if known, is essential. Depending upon the site of involvement and severity, the conditions are treated with specific antifungal agent either systemic or topical or both.

Systemic treatment is given for systemic involvement, including oropharyngeal, gastrointestinal and urinary tract infections, or as an adjunct to other treatment. The drugs commonly used for such purposes are amphotericin, 100-200 mg (100,000-200,000 U) every 6-hours orally (infant and child, 100 mg four times daily) for gastrointestinal infection, or 0.25-1.5 mg per kg of body-weight daily by slow IV infusion. For systemic candidiasis amphotericin is given as 1 mg over 20-30 minutes by IV infusion then 250 μg/kg daily, gradually increase if tolerated 1 mg/kg daily (max. 1.5 mg/kg daily or on alternate days in severe cases), fluconazole is given as 400 mg once orally on first day followed by 200 mg daily for 28 days or more, or by slow intravenous infusion at a rate of 5-10 ml per minute. It is also given as 50-100 mg once daily orally for 14 –30 days in mucosal infection, 200 mg on the first day followed by 100 mg daily for 14 days in cases of oropharyngeal candidiasis but for 14-30 days in oesophageal candidiasis, 150 mg as a single dose in acute or recurrent vaginal candidiasis, and 150 mg once weekly for 12 months in onychomycosis. For systemic infection flucytosine can be given as an adjunct to amphotericin or fluconazole as 200 mg/kg daily in 4 divided doses by IV infusion over 20-40 minutes usually for not more than 7 days. Itraconazole is given as 100 mg once daily for 15 days in oropharyngeal candidiasis but 200 mg twice daily orally for 1 day in vaginal candidiasis. Ketoconazole is given as 200-400 mg once daily orally and the treatment is continued for at least one week after the disappearance of the symptoms but 400 mg once daily for 5 days in chronic vaginal infections. Miconazole is another effective drug and is given as 250 mg four times daily orally for oropharyngeal and gastrointestinal infections.

Most cutaneous and vaginal lesions can adequately be treated with 1% gentian violet paint but it causes unsightingly severe staining on both skin and clothing. Otherwise, the patients are given topical application of an azole agent with or without hydrocortisone or nystatin and steroid.

Involvement of nails however requires much long time for treatment. Most topical agent used for cutaneous lesions is also effective in cases of nail involvement. The treatment is therefore given with azole lotion or amorofine nail lacquer but the cure rate is often highly unsatisfactory.

Vaginal candidiasis are treated with clotrimazole, 500 mg vaginal tablet inserted intravaginally as a single dose or 200 mg nightly for 3 consecutive nights or 100 mg nightly for 6 nights, econazole, 150 mg pessary inserted high into the vagina nightly for 3 consecutive nights, miconazole, 1,200 mg pessary vaginal capsule inserted high into the vagina as a single dose or 100 mg pessary intravaginally twice daily for 7 days, isoconazole, 600 mg intravaginally as a single dose, or nystatin, 100,000-200,000 U vaginal pessary or 4-8 g of cream intravaginally for 14 consecutive nights.

Candidial balantitis and balanoposthitis are cleaned thoroughly with soap and water, dried and then given topical nystatin (100,000 U) twice daily for 7 to 10 days, 1% econazole cream morning and evening, 2% miconazole cream twice daily, or clotrimazole 1% cream two to three times daily, for at least 2 weeks.

PITYRIASIS VERSICOLOR

Pityriasis versicolor or **tinea versicolor** is a trivial, often unsightly, superficial mycosis produced by *Pityrosperum orbiculare* (previously known as *Malassezia furfur*), normally commensal yeast on the skin. Severe perspiration and wearing of too heavy clothes may favour the development of the infection. Use of systemic corticosteroids may aggravate the condition. So it is with some cases in summer.

The condition develops more commonly in early childhood.

Stratum corneum shows growth of clusters of spherical, thick-walled budding cells and short bent hyphae. There are no other pathological changes

Clinical Manifestations

The patient presents with brown, tan or white, but in coloured skin, hypopigmented or depigmented, macules, plaques or sheets. The lesions are delicately covered with fine or brawny scales, and show a tendency to coalesce. They occur (Fig. 7.30) principally on the trunk, upper part of the arms and neck but can also affect abdomen, groins and, occasionally, face. The lesion can develop anywhere but hands and feet are usually spared. The lesions do not tan on exposure to sunlight. Other than cosmetic importance the lesions do not produce any symptom. They may however rarely cause mild itching. The lesions may persist for some time or may resolve spontaneously.

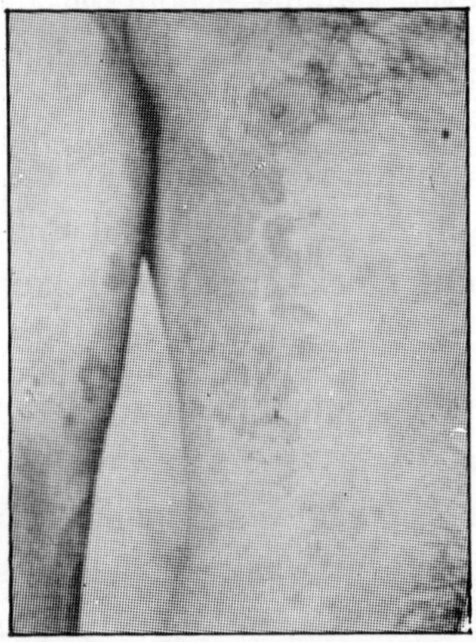

Figure 7.30. Pityriasis versicolor on trunk and arm.

Diagnosis

Diagnosis of the condition is made on clinical grounds. Identification of thick-walled budding spore and short hyphae of *Pityrosporum orbiculare* is diagnostic. When viewed by Wood's light, the lesions give a distinct yellow fluorescence.

It is differentiated from seborrhoeic dermatitis, which presents with lesions having erythematous yellowish tint and covered with soft and greasy scales, involves the scalp and face, shows oozing and fissuring, and causes pruritus. Erythrasma may however cause certain confusion as that also produces pink fluorescence on Wood's light. Macular eruptions in syphilis present with irregularly round or oval lesions, principally distributed on the sides of the trunk and flexures of extremities, and the condition lymphadenopathy and positive serological tests for syphilis. Vitiligo is differentiated for having large totally depigmented patches from fusion, has no scales, does not resolve spontaneously, and looks much whiter than the surrounding normal skin, while the condition is completely asymptomatic. The condition is also differentiated from pityriasis simplex for having sharply defined hypopigmented macules covered with fine, adherent scales, and from leprosy for having slightly atrophic lesions with no scales, and the lesions though initially may be hyperanaesthetic or mildly anaesthetic but always anaesthetic later and do not resolve spontaneously.

Treatment

It is treated with 2.5% selenium sulphide in a detergent base, leathered on affected areas, dried and left overnight and wash off in the next morning, and repeated 7 days after. This is not only effective but also relatively cheap. Otherwise, the cases are treated with sulconazole, 1% cream, massaged into the area twice daily and continued for 2 to 3 weeks after healing of the lesions, or clotrimazole, 1% cream or solution, applied sparingly two or three times daily until 2 weeks after clinical cure. Topical application of other antifungal preparation, such as econazole, 1% cream, applied morning and evening, or ketoconazole, 2% cream, applied once or twice daily. is also effective.

In cases of unsatisfactory response or in cases of widespread lesions, the patient may be given a short course of systemic treatment with ketoconazole, 2 mg once daily orally for 2 days, itraconazole, 200 mg once daily orally for 7 days, or fluconazole, 400 mg as a single dose orally for 1 day.

SPOROTRICHOSIS

The condition affecting subcutaneous tissue results from *Sporothrix schenckii*, a saprophyte of plants or wood. Infection occurs through implantation of the organism on the skin, or through inhalation. It is therefore reckoned as an occupational hazard to the horticulturists, farm workers, miners and others who come in contact with the plant or wood.

It gives rise to chronic inflammation and granulomas that undergo necrosis and result in formation of deep abscesses, sinuses and ulcerations. The centre of the lesion contains collection of neutrophils, eosinophils and macrophages, surrounded by epitheloid and giant cells, with plasma cells, lymphocytes and connective tissue in the periphery. The epidermis is thickened and oedematous.

The disease is however prevalent worldwide and yet it is more common in Central and Southern Africa.

Clinical Manifestations

A small, movable, non-tender, subcutaneous papule develops at the site of inoculation, generally on finger, hand or arm. The lesion slowly enlarges and adheres to the skin, and finally causes necrosis and ulceration. Subsequently multiple subcutaneous nodules and ulcers occur along the lymphatic draining the area. General symptoms such as local pain, heat, chills, fever, malaise and anorexia are usually absent. The lymphatic channel draining the area becomes thickened and palpable.

Sometimes the infection can gain entry through respiratory tract, and may give rise to pneumonia, localised infiltration, or cavity formation. The condition runs a chronic course but the symptoms are usually mild.

Haematogenous dissemination of the infection is however quite rare. Yet, when it occurs, it affects any part of the body but involvement of liver, spleen, kidneys, genitals and central nervous system is extremely uncommon.

Diagnosis

Isolation and identification of the organism make diagnosis of the condition. The fungus can also be identified from discharges. Identification of the organism from biopsy material is however extremely difficult. Agglutination test shows high titre with sera of infected persons.

The condition is differentiated from chromomycosis, blastomycosis, histoplasmosis and candidiasis.

Treatment

Although chronic in nature, most infections are however self-limiting. Cutaneous cases are treated with potassium iodide diluted with water or any other drink. Potassium iodide is given as 1 ml three times a day orally, increasing by 1 ml daily till its optimal dose of 3-4 ml three times a day. The treatment can however at times gives rise to iodism in which case, the dose is decreased or even the treatment is discontinued temporarily, and the treatment is continued as soon as the symptoms of iodism subside.

Systemic involvement cases need treatment with antifungal, such as amphotericin, 100-200 mg (100,000-200,000 U) four times daily orally (children: 100 mg four times daily orally).

CHROMOMYCOSIS

Chromomycosis, also known as **chromoblastomycosis**, a slowly progressive granulomatous infection of skin that causes blocking of the lymphatic channels. It is caused by several species of black moulds of which *Phialophora verrucosa*, *Cladosporium carrionii* and *Pansecaea pedrosoi* are most common. The fungi are dark-brown, thick-walled, with round cell, usually arranged in clusters, but the colour may vary in pigmentation. The fungi are available on vegetation and soil as saprophytes, and gain entry into human being's body through trauma or broken skin surface. It therefore commonly affects barefooted farm workers, and the condition is prevalent in warm, rural areas, particularly in Latin America.

The condition commonly occurs in persons aged between 30 and 50 years, and affects more men than women.

It produces granulomatous lesions. Pigmented round fungal cells are found inside the leucocytes or giant cells. There is granulomatous reaction with formation of tubercles containing giant cells and a focal round cell infiltration in the subcortical portions of the corium.

Clinical Manifestations

Infection begins on the foot or leg or on exposed part of the body where the skin has somehow become broken. The early lesion, often unilateral, appears as dull red or violaceous, sharply demarcated, patch with an indurated base, containing small itching papule resembling ringworm at the site of inoculation. New crops of lesions may appear over the path of lymphatic drainage after several weeks or months. Slowly hard, greyish or dull red cauliflower-like warty growth occurs along the lymphatic of the affected area, which slowly develop into large papillomatous vegetation with a tendency to ulcerate. These cauliflower-like nodules with crusting abscesses eventually occur over the affected area. The lymphatic may be blocked. There may also be itching. Over the course of a few years a whole extremity may be affected.

Secondary bacterial infection is a common complication of the condition and leads to regional lymphadenopathy. Extensive fibrosis, ulceration and secondary infection can cause lymph stasis, resulting elephantiasis.

Diagnosis

Diagnosis of the condition is made on clinical grounds. Occupational history of the patient may be a helpful guide. Diagnosis is however made by identifying the dark brown septate bodies in the pus and biopsy. The organism grows rapidly in the culture media but is difficult to identify.

It is differentiated from dermatophytosis and sporotrichosis. Warts are however easily excluded on clinical grounds.

Treatment

Appropriate management of the condition requires surgical resection, including skin grafting.

Medical treatment is however given by antifungal, such as amphotericin, 20 mg (0.3 mg per kg of body-weight) by IV injection daily perhaps along with 100-200 mg four times daily orally. Fluconazole is also effective and is given as 400 mg on the first day and then 200-400 mg once daily orally or by intravenous infusion at a rate of 5-10 ml per minute. Depending upon the severity of the condition a single or two antifungals may be given. Flucytosine is another effective drug and is given at 200 mg per kg of body-weight by intravenous infusion over 20-40 minutes daily usually for not more than 7 days

In addition, or alternatively, the patient is treated with surgical excision and skin grafting. Electrocoagulation may also be helpful.

ACTINOMYCOSIS

Actinomycosis is a chronic suppurative disorder, localised chiefly to the neck, lung or abdomen, causing formation of multiple indurated abscesses and sinus tracts. It is causes by anaerobic, non-acid fast, gram-positive, filamentous bacteria, *Actinomyces israelii*, found in normal bacterial flora of oral cavity. Other species such as *A. viscosus*, *A. odontolyticus* and *A. naeslundii*, rarely affect human beings. However, the condition occurs due to spread by direct extension into the contiguous tissue. Haematogenous dissemination of the organism also occurs. The condition is however never communicable.

Pathological changes the condition produces are abscess formation with central necrosis, surrounded by granulation tissue and fibrous tissue, and the pus contains 'sulphur granules' and may drain to outside through the sinuses.

Clinical Manifestations

Classically the condition presents as cervicofacial, abdominal or thoracic form but can also frequently present in other atypical form. Cervicofacial form of the condition is however quite common, and presents with red, hard, relatively non-tender, swelling occurring on the cervicofacial area, involving the face, tongue, mandible or neck. The lesion develops slowly, becomes fluctuating, points to the surface, and finally breaks down to form chronic sinus with little tendency of healing, and drains 'sulphur granules' or pus. The lesion by extends by contiguity. There may be a large, woody swelling, characteristically over the angle of the jaw. Periosteitis and osteomyelitis with extensive destruction of bone are common accompaniments. The condition also produces serious constitutional disturbances with sinus formation.

In cases when the lesion involves the thorax or abdomen, it presents with chills, fever, and cough with sputum formation, night sweats, anorexia, malaise, pleural pain, dyspnoea, dysphagia, and abdominal colic.

It produces secondary infection, septicaemia and perforating ulcer as complications.

It is a slowly progressive disease with worse prognosis in CNS involvement.

Diagnosis

Presence of large fistula-forming inflammatory mass is a clinical clue of diagnosis of the condition. Blood shows leucocytosis, anaemia, and elevated level of ESR. Identification of the causative organism from pus and sputum is possible through smear examination and culture. Diagnosis can also be established by biopsy of the tissue.

The condition is differentiated from other fungal infections, pulmonary tuberculosis, osteomyelitis, and malignant diseases.

Treatment

Management of the condition is done with procaine penicillin G, 10-20 million U daily by IM injection. Otherwise, the patient is given amoxycillin, 1 g eight hourly orally, or tetracycline,

500 mg every six hours orally. Most cases respond well with such medical treatment but needs the treatment for months together, ranging between 3 months and 1 year, till after apparent cure.

The condition also needs extensive and repeated surgical interference. Small abscesses are aspirated, surgical drainage of large ones, and resection and repair of the sinus are good therapeutic measures.

MADURAMYCOSIS

The condition is also known as **mycetoma**, and is caused by a variety of fungi and filamentous bacteria (actinomycetes) such as *Nocardia brasiliensis*, *Madurella mycetomy*, *M. grisea*, *Acromanium falciforme*, *Phialophora jeanselmii* and *Actinomadura madurae*, occurring on the soil and vegetation. Eumycetoma however occurs from true fungi of many different genera. The organism gains entry into the human subcutaneous tissue through trauma.

The condition may therefore be reckoned as an occupational hazard and usually affects of the barefooted farm workers. It is prevalent in the tropics.

The lesions resemble those of actinomycosis, with abscess formation, granulation tissue, necrotic foci, and fibrosis. The lesions show numerous sinuses, connecting with the abscesses of the skin, subcutaneous tissue or bone. Characteristically there are tightly clusters of colonies of fungi within the network of burrowing abscess and sinus. Fungal cells may also be found in the pus, or with the macrophages of giant cells.

Clinical Manifestation

The lesion appears most commonly on the foot (**madura foot**) but may also occur at other exposed parts of the body, such as leg, hand, back and face. The lesion appears as painless papule at the site of inoculation which later changes to deepened nodule, vesicle or abscess that over months or years rupture and produce fistula discharging viscid, oily or serosanguineous exudate, containing yellow or white and, rarely, back or red granules. The entire area gradually becomes indurated like wood, and is covered with open sinuses or atrophic scars. There is no other generalised symptom and, in the absence of secondary infection, the lesions are non-tender. In some cases, however, elephantiasis may develop due to extensive fibrosis of the tissue. In the late stage of the condition, muscle, tendon and fascia may be destroyed. The patient becomes disabled due to deformity or muscle wasting.

The condition usually leads to sepsis and intercurrent infections as complications.

Diagnosis

Occupational history of the patient along with the clinical features may be a helpful guide. The colour and characteristic morphology of granules of the organism in the draining material aid diagnosis. The fungus and the filamentous bacteria may also be isolated and identified. Radiological examinations may reveal bone lysis and periosteal proliferation in cases of bone destruction.

The condition may at times need to be differentiated from other fungal infection, tuberculosis, yaws and neoplasms.

Treatment

When the condition develops due to actinomycetes, the condition may respond with a combination of chemotherapy given for a prolonged period of time. In this regime the patient is given streptomycin, 1 g daily by IM injection. In addition, the patient is given either trimethoprim, 160 mg, along with sulphamethoxazole, 800 mg, twice daily orally, or dapsone, 100 mg twice daily orally after meals, or any other sulphone. This treatment is given for a long time and continued for several months after clinical cure, which may take as long as 2 years even. Emphasis needs to be made that eumycetoma seldom respond to antifungal therapy. Their occasional use in rare instances may however result remission or cure. In this respect the patient may be given griseofulvin, 500 mg-1 g, preferably after seals in divided doses daily orally, amphotericin, 100-200 mg four times daily orally, miconazole, 250 mg four times daily orally, or ketoconazole, 200-400 mg once daily orally.

Surgical dressings of the wound may assist healing.

Otherwise, surgical excision or even amputation of the limb may be the only choice of treatment.

POST-KALA-AZAR DERMAL LEISHMANIASIS

Caused by *Leis mania donovani* it occurs after a prolonged period, usually 1 to 5 years or more, of acquiring kala-azar. Inadequate or incomplete treatment of kala-azar can also produce the condition. Occasionally, however, the affected person may not give any history of kala-azar.

Pathological changes show oedematous subpapillary layer, and the vessels are enlarged, dilated and infiltrated with macrophages. Early lesion may not show large number of parasites. Cutaneous nodules however show numerous histiocytes, stuffed with *L. donovani*.

Clinical Manifestations

The condition does not give rise to any symptom but presents with hypopigmented or erythematous macules occurring on the cheeks, nose, lips, back, upper and lower extremities, and abdomen. Later, the lesions become depigmented. The macules generally increase in size and may be replaced by nodules, or there may be diffuse nodular eruptions reminiscent of lepromatous leprosy.

The condition is however benign, and produces no complication.

Diagnosis

History of kala-azar, if available, may be a helpful guide. Diagnosis is however made from identification of the organism or the LD bodies from the lesions.

It is differentiated from leprosy that presents with anaesthetic lesions, macules with loss of hair and nodules with subcutaneous thickening, and the lesions may show presence of acid-fast bacillus or show a positive lepromin test. Vitiligo is differentiated for having large depigmented patches and looks much whiter than the surrounding normal skin on Wood's light. Pityriasis versicolor is differentiated for having slightly hypopigmented macules, patches or sheets covered with fine or brawny scales, and the lesions may resolve spontaneously. Leucoderma is differentiated for having lesions, which may be surrounded by hyperpigmented skin, while there is not history of kala-azar.

Treatment

The patients are treated with full regimen of kala-azar therapy. The patient is therefore given pentavalent antimony compound, such as sodium antimony gluconate (sodium stibogluconate), 20 mg per kg of body-weight daily by slow IV or IM injection for 20 days. In other instances, the patients may be given pentamidine isothionate, 3-5 mg/kg (maximum: 250 mg) by IV or IM injection on alternate days for 15 injections. If required, either treatment schedule may be repeated after treatment-free intervals as specified under kala-azar.

CUTANEOUS LEISHMANIASIS

It is also known as **oriental sore**, **tropical sore**, **Delhi boil**, **Baghdad boil** and **Aleppo boil**. *Leishmania tropica* or *L. major* causes it, and the infection is transmitted through the bites of sandfly (*Phlebotomus species*), which are the natural vector of the organism. Direct inoculation of the organism is also possible through broken skin. The condition is prevalent in Southern Asia and parts of Africa. One attack confers solid immunity against it.

Its incubation period varies between days and months.

Following inoculation of the organism, infiltration of corium with lymphocytes, plasma cells and large endothelial macrophages produce a nodule. The overlying epidermis becomes thin and atrophic. Later, ulcer develops with granulation tissue base and surrounding zone of inflammation. Leishmania is seen at the margin of the lesion and in the scrapings of the floor.

Clinical Manifestations

It presents with chronic, single or multiple, sharply growing papule on the exposed part of skin, which may remain dry or ulcerate, and covered with crust that exudes a sticky secretion. Removal of the crust reveals moist, freely bleeding ulcer. Secondary infection is common and may lead to greater tissue destruction. Healing of the lesion occurs by granulation, leaving a depressed fibrous scar, following adequate treatment, or spontaneously in 2-18 months, if left untreated.

Diagnosis

The site of the lesion and the presence of sandfly may serve a helpful guide in the diagnosis of the condition. The organism can however be identified from the scrapings of the side or base of the ulcer, or aspirates, and from culture.

It is differentiated from tertiary syphilis, yaws, leprosy, tuberculosis and blastomycosis but it is often easy on clinical grounds.

Treatment

In cases of single lesion or of a very few lesions, the lesions are generally cleaned, curetted, covered and left to heal. In other cases, intralesional instillation of pentamidine antimony compound is given for four times daily. Application of heat also appears to be effective. Other suitable local therapies are cauterisation with carbon dioxide snow or liquid nitrogen, electrocautery, infrared therapy or radiotherapy.

In cases of indolent ulcers, treatment regime of kala-azar is given effectively but with half the doses and for a short duration.

Appropriate antibiotics are also given in cases of secondary bacterial infection.

MUCOCUTANEOUS LEISHMANIASIS

The condition is also known as **American leishmaniasis** and **espundia**, and is caused by *Leishmania braziliensis* and perhaps by several other *Leishmania species*. It may develop by itself as cutaneous ulceration.

The condition is prevalent in South Africa.

Initially there is mixed inflammatory infiltrate with histiocytes stuffed with numerous parasites along with lymphocytes and plasma cells. Later, granulomatous reaction becomes evident with declining parasitation.

Clinical Manifestations

It presents with cutaneous leishmaniasis-like localised chronic cutaneous ulcer on the face, forearm, legs or trunk. There is however no other symptom. Before the lesion heals up, which may take even years, secondary moist, localised, ulcerating or non-ulcerating lesion may develop at the mucocutaneous junctions, such as nose, pharynx, anus or vulva. The ulcer is destructive and disfiguring, and tends to undergo spontaneous exacerbation and remission. Chronicity of the lesion is usual. Later, regression of the lesion occurs with healing and scar formation.

Secondary bacterial infection is common and may even cause death.

Diagnosis

It is diagnosed by isolation and identification of the causative protozoon from culture of ulcer-edge aspirates, and from biopsy.

It is differentiated from cutaneous leishmaniasis, syphilis and yaws.

Treatment

The cases are treated as per schedule detailed under cutaneous leishmaniasis.

In cases of single lesion or of a very few lesions, the lesions are generally cleaned, curetted, covered and left to heal. In other cases, intralesional instillation of pentamidine antimony compound is given for four times daily. Application of heat also appears to be effective. Other suitable local therapies are cauterisation with carbon dioxide snow or liquid nitrogen, electrocautery, infrared therapy or radiotherapy.

In cases of indolent ulcers, treatment regime of kala-azar is given effectively but with half the doses and for a short duration.

Appropriate antibiotics are also given in cases of secondary bacterial infection.

CREEPING ERUPTION

The condition is also known as **larva migrans** and **creeping myiasis**, and result due to migration of the parasitic larvae in the epidermis. The larvae of some insects and nematodes of human and animal origin when come in contact can gain entry into the human body through penetration of the skin. It therefore commonly affects those who walk barefooted or work barehanded on the contaminated soil.

Clinical Manifestations

It presents with papule at the site of inoculation followed by slightly raised thread-like erythema associated with itching and irritation. The papule may sometimes be slightly painful.

Scratching of the area may cause secondary infection.

Diagnosis

It is diagnosed on clinical ground.

It however does not need any differentiation from any other condition.

Treatment

It is treated with freezing of the larvae with CO_2 snow or ethylchloride.

Oral antihistamine may also be given in cases of pruritus, and appropriate antibiotics for secondary infection.

SCABIES

The mite, *Sarcoptes scabie*, causes the condition, which live upon the skin and is barely visible through naked eyes (Fig. 7.31). Occasionally similar parasites are also found in the domestic animals, which can infect human beings as well. The infection is transmitted through close bodily contact, such as sleeping or sitting together. The modern tendency has therefore grown to include the condition as one of the sexually transmitted diseases for better management and care. The infection can also occur through use of clothes and bedding of the infected persons.

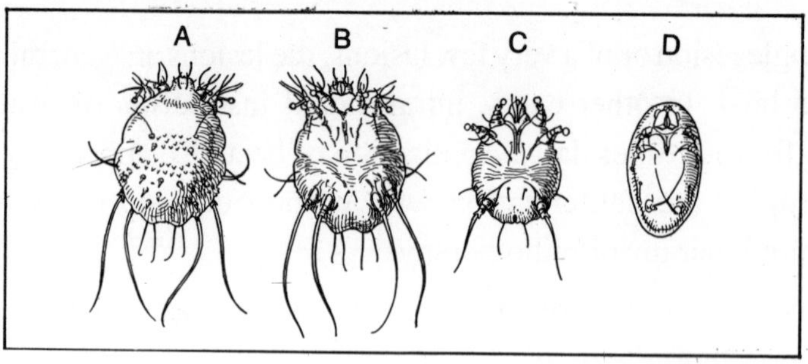

Figure 7.31. Sarcoptes scabie. (A) Dorsal aspect of adult female mite, (B) Central aspect of female mite, (c) Larva, (D) Embryo.

When fertilised the female mite burrows into the stratum corneum and lays and deposits eggs along with her irritating excreta in the burrows, and after hatching, young larvae leave the burrows.

Pathological changes the mite produces as reddish, elevated, curved, dark tracts on the surface of the skin, with translucent vesicular swelling along with course. The vesicles may become secondarily infected due to scratching.

Clinical Manifestations

It gives rise to papular or papulovesicular lesions on the skin anywhere in the body but spare the head and neck, except in infants and immunocompromised persons. There may be characteristic burrows, which are greyish, linear, scaly lesions usually of about 5 mm long, that are generally seen in the inierdigital spaces (Fig. 7.32) but can also be seen on the flexures of the wrists and elbows, axillary folds, nipples, the naval area and lower abdomen. The burrows are seldom seen on buttocks and male genitalia but when they do, they appear usually as firm, deep and red papules. In infants, however, the burrows may be seen on the face and there may be pustular papules on the soles. Itching is the usual complaint, which is more intense in the night. Scratching may cause secondary infection and pyoderma.

It produces impetigo and furunculosis as complications.

Diagnosis

The condition is diagnosed by identification of the mite or its ova. The mite can also be detected by probing the fresh end of the burrow or by shaving off the entire burrow.

It may need to be differentiated from pediculosis, dermatitis herpetiformis, and other causes of pruritus.

Treatment

The condition is effectively treated by scabicides, which selectively kill the mite that invades the epidermis. The patient is therefore given benzyl benzoate, 25% emulsion, applied after a hot bath to whole body except head and face and repeat within 5 days if necessary or applied on 3

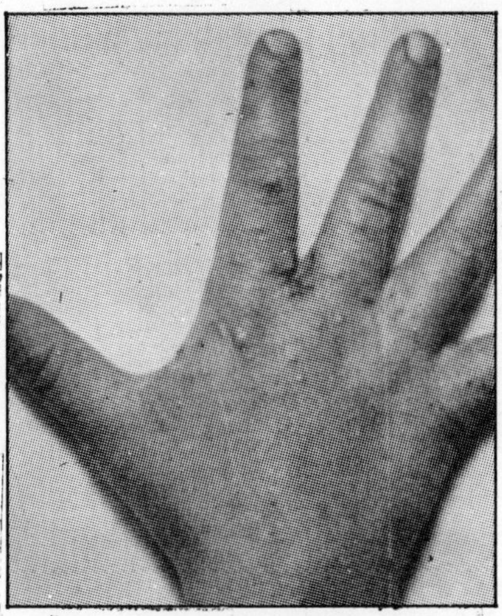

Figure 7.32. Scabies showing interdigital burrows.

occasions after 12 hours intervals followed by hot bath 12 hours later, melathion, 0.5% aqueous liquid, applied to whole body except above neck and left for 24 hours and then wash off on the following day, or lindane, 1% lotion, applied to whole body except head and face and left for 24 hours before washing off and repeat after 7 days if necessary (wash after 9 to 12 hours in infants aged between 1 month and 6 months). Crotamiton however has antiscabetic activity and a mild antipruritic effect, for which the drug is useful for follow up treatment. However the patient is given 10% lotion or cream of crotamiton to be applied after a hot bath to whole body except face and head and repeat after 24 hours and then wash off on the following day. It is essential that following treatment all the clothing and bedding of the infected person should be changed and properly washed.

The itch and secondary eczematous changes, if any, may persist for 1 to 2 weeks or even up to 3 weeks after successful treatment.

The infected persons are also given appropriate antibiotics in cases of secondary bacterial infection.

PEDICULOSIS

Pediculosis (**louse infestation**) occurs due to three varieties of lice. *Pediculus corporis* (body louse), *P. capitis* (head louse) and *Phthirus pubis* (pubic louse, 'crabs'). Human louse lives on human body and feeds on blood. The body lice are not always found on the skin surface as they keep themselves concealed and only frequent to the skin surface for blood-meal and thus, the louse can be transmitted through close contact or from sharing dresses and underclothing of the infected persons. Head lice are transmitted through sharing combs and caps, but can also spread from sitting or sleeping head to head together. Pubic lice live in the pubic area but may also be found in other hairy areas. They are transmitted through close or intimate body contacts, such as sexual contact.

In general, louse infestation occurs most commonly amongst people living in overcrowded condition with inadequate hygienic provisions.

The condition only causes local irritation of skin and excoriation. In severe infestation, there may be induration and pigmentation of skin.

Clinical Manifestations

The condition does not give rises to any symptom except that of itching, which may even is very intense. Scratching may lead to excoriation over the affected areas. Prolong infestation with head lice may however lead to malaise and poor mental performance. On the other hand, body lice may produce papular eruptions.

The condition can produce secondary bacterial infection, and transmission of louse-borne disease such as typhus and relapsing fever as complications.

Diagnosis

Diagnosis is easy and is made by detection of the louse.

The condition may however at times need to be differentiated from scabies, seborrhoeic dermatitis, and anogential pruritus.

Treatment

It is treated by topical application of dichlorodiphenyl trichloroethane (DDT) and gamma-benzene hexachloride for 2 to 3 days and is found quite effective. There are also several preparations now readily available. Of them phenothrin, 0.2% lotion, and permethrin, 1% conditioner, are highly effective insecticidal neurotoxins and are effective against head lice and their eggs. Phenothrin is rubbed on hair and dry naturally, shampoo after 2 hours and combed wet hair. Permethrin is used to saturate hair and scalp following normal shampooing and towel drying of hair, and the conditioner is left for 10 minutes and then rinses and dries. Carbaryl, 0.5% lotion, is given for head and pubic lice, which is rubbed into hair and dry naturally, left for 2 hours but preferably overnight and then shampoo, and repeated after 7 to 9 days if re-infested, but 1% lotion for single application to dry hair for head lice and left for 12 hours. Melathion, 0.5% aqueous liquid, is also effective and is applied liberally for head lice and left for 12 hours but for 1 to 12 hours in cases of pubic lice and the lotion is applied to all areas including beard and moustache, and wash off. Lindane, 1% shampoo, is also effective against head and pubic lice and is applied to dry infested areas, rubbed well, left for 4 minutes, then shampoo and combed through before drying.

For body lice benzyl benzoate, 25% emulsion, is applied to affected area and cleanse after 24 hours and repeat two or three times if necessary. In addition, the treatment may require removal of the louse, picking up by fingers or by forceps, followed by its destruction.

In cases of distressing itching, the patient may also be given oral antihistamine, such as chlopheniramine, 4 mg four to six hourly, trimeprazine, 10 mg two or three times daily, or clemastine, 1 mg night and morning.

FILARIASIS

Thread-like nematodes, *Wuchereria bancrofti* and *Brugia malayi* produce the condition. The infection is transmitted by the bites of Culex and Aedes Mosquitoes in cases of bancrofti infection and by certain Mansonian and Anopheles mosquitoes in cases of malayi infection. Mosquitoes are the intermediate host of the nematodes, and human being is the only vertebrate host for W. bancrofti, but the list may include cats, monkeys, and other animals as well for *B. malayi*. The microfilariae found in the human peripheral blood (Table 7.3) may show a periodicity, which is generally nocturnal in cases of *W. bancrofti*, but *B. malayi* may be nocturnal or present at all times with a slight nocturnal rise. Bancrofti infection is distributed worldwide in all tropical countries. Malayi infection is however limited to Southeast Asia.

Table 7.3. Characteristics of Microfilariae.

Organism	Size	Availability	Prevalence
Wuchereria bancrofti	225-300 × 8-10 μm	Blood, Lymph, Hydrocele fluid	Nocturnal or no periodicity
Brugia malayi	160-260 × 5-6 μm	Blood, Lymph, Lymphatic node	Nocturnal or sub-periodical
Loa loa	200-300 × 6-9 μm	Blood	Diurnal
Onchocerca volvulus	300-500 × 5-9 μm	Skin and connective tissue lymphatic	No periodicity

Its incubation period is quite long and may extend up to 3 months or more.

Wuchereria bancrofti is thread-like worm, measuring up to 100 mm in length, with sexes coiled Which can only be separated with difficulty, and cretified after death. The male worm is coiled with corkscrew-like tail, while the anterior end tapers, ending in swelling, in female worm. *Brugia malayi*, measures 25 mm in length, is practically identical and shows slight variations when compared with *W. bancrofti*.

In human body, the worms mature in or near the lymphatic and lymph nodes. The female produces large number of motile larvae (*microfilariae*) which travel via lymphatic into the bloodstream whence they are ingested by the biting mosquitoes, the intermediate host, in which they complete part of their life cycle and become infective. When the mosquitoes bite the humans, the infective microfilariae break through terminal portion of proboscis sheath, wriggle into human skin, and gain entry into human body by penetration through the puncture of mosquito bite, migrate by way of blood vessels and lymphatic to mature in the lymphatic vessels and glands, and thoracic duct.

The pathological changes they produce in human body vary widely. Microfilariae are apparently harmless. They however produce specific lesion in the lymphatic glands as fibrosis, focal necrosis and giant cell inflammation, lymphatic varix by obstruction of the main channels, compensatory lymphatic circulation, and living, dead or cretified adult worms in the lymphatic. In chronic stage, the cellular necrosis and oedema are replaced by fibroblastic hyperplasia, absorption and replacement of the parasites by proliferative granulation tissue, and extension of lymph varices.

Clinical Manifestations

Clinical features vary widely, and most residents in the endemic area run indefinitely asymptomatic. Otherwise, there are episodes of fever with or without inflammation of the lymphatic and glands that come and go. There may also be chills, headache, malaise and urticaria. Inflammation of the spermatic cord, epididymitis and orchitis are common, and abscesses may form at the sites of lymphatic inflammation. Later, interference to normal lymphatic flow may produce hydrocele and scrotal lymphoedema in males, and lymphatic varices and elephantiasis is both sexes. The lymphatic varix may rupture and produce chyluria, associated with suprapubic oppression, and general debility. There may be arthritis, synovitis, and elephantiasis of the legs, scrotum (Fig. 7.33), vulva and other parts of the body.

The condition can produce infection and septicaemia as complications.

Diagnosis

Blood shows eosinophilia in early stage. Diagnosis of the condition is made from demonstration of microfilariae in the blood. If no microfilaria is available, complement fixation test may be done. Intradermal test for filariasis may be helpful.

The condition may need to be differentiated from venous thrombosis, multiple lipomatosis, cardiac failure, hernia and non-filarial elephantiasis.

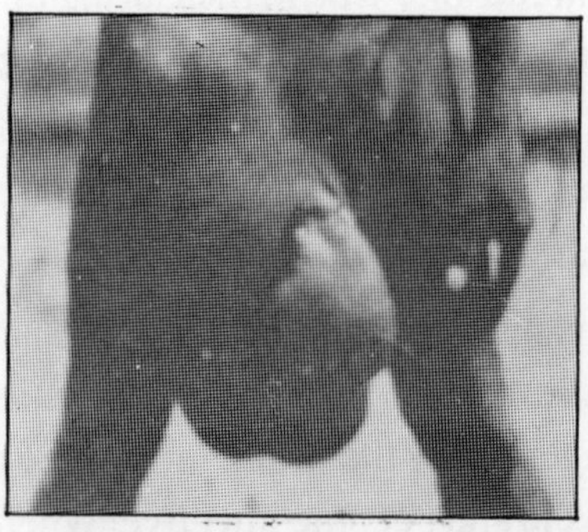

Figure 7.33. Scrotal elephantiasis in filariasis.

Treatment

It is treated with anthelmintic, for example, diethylcarbamazine, 6 mg per kg of body-weight (initially starting from 1 mg/kg and increases gradually over 3 days) daily in three divided doses orally for 3-4 weeks and repeat, if necessary, after a treatment-free interval of 3 to 4 weeks. In endemic areas, however, the dose of diethylcarbamazine may be increased to 9 mg/kg.

Administration of antihistamine or corticosteroid is considered whenever there are any allergic manifestations. In cases of orchitis, epididymitis and scrotal lymphoedema, the patient is given suspensor bandage as general measure. Bed rest, use of elastic stockings and elevation of foot-end of the bed are needed in cases of mild oedema of the limb. Bed rest is also given for chyluria. Elephantiasis however needs surgical interference.

LOIASIS

It is caused by filaria, *Loa loa*, and the blood sucking deer flies of genus Chrysops transmits the infection. The condition is common in Equatorial Africa.

Loa loa is almost indistinguishable from *W. bancrofti* in all respect except that the former is stout than the latter, with chitinous bosses on cuticle. Alike *W. bancrofti* the organism undergoes development in the deer flies and finally the larvae congegrate at the root of proboscis, and when the fly feed on blood, the microfilariae gain entry into the skin and migrate. The microfilariae circulated in the peripheral blood and show a diurnal periodicity (Table 7.3).

Migration of microfilariae in the subcutaneous tissue produces oedematous swelling (calabar swelling). The adult filaria usually parasites the subcutaneous tissue.

Clinical Manifestations

It gives rise to pricking or creeping sensation, and transient, localised calabar swelling on the arms, legs and face. The calabar swelling when situated near a joint, it can give rise to pain. The swelling usually disappears after a few days, but may also persist for a few weeks, and a succession of calabar swellings may appear at irregular intervals. Some times, there may be urticaria, pruritus, and allergic dermatitis. Occasionally, a worm may cross the eye under the conjunctiva, and may give rise to conjunctivitis, irritation and photophobia. Occasionally there may also be severe unilateral headache.

Diagnosis

Presence of calabar swelling in persons of endemic area or coming from endemic area is highly suggestive. Usually Loa loa microfilariae can be detected from peripheral blood and the filaria is strictly diurnal. Live filaria may occasionally be also seen wriggling under the skin, particularly of eyelid, or a calcified dead worm may be seen on X-ray. Diagnosis can also be made by complement fixation and indirect fluorescent antibody tests. Intradermal test is also helpful.

The condition is differentiated from filariasis and other allergic and urticarial conditions.

Treatment

Treatment is given by diethylcarbamazine, 9-12 mg per kg of body-weight daily in three divided doses orally for 3 weeks. The drug is however liable to precipitate severe reaction. If there is allergy, the patient is given antihistamine, such as chlorphenramine, 4-8 mg three or four times a day orally, and prednisolone, 4-8 mg daily in divided doses orally, during the first 4 days of the treatment.

ONCHOCERCIASIS

Onchocerciasis or **river blindness** is caused by *Onchocerca volvulus*, the largest human filariae (Table 7.3), measuring up to 50 cm in length. The filaria undergoes development in the black flies of genus Simulium that live mostly in well-watered areas of trees and forests. Man is the only host of the infection and becomes infected from the bites of the infected Simulium flies. The condition is common in Equatorial Africa, Central and South America, and Southern Arabia.

The filaria is white, filiform, with cuticular striations, tapered at both ends. The female filaria lays eggs and microfilariae are hatched. The worm maintains its life cycle in the body of Simulium black flies. When black flies bite human beings, the microfilariae are then introduced into the skin, which gain their maturity in the subcutaneous and connective tissue. Lodgement of adult filaria may produce nodules from fibrosis.

Pathological changes in the skin include development of subcutaneous nodules, epidermal thickening and hyperkeratosis and later, fibrosis and dermal atrophy. The reaction of adult filaria becomes granulomatous and fibrotic, and later calcification. Live microfilariae show infiltration with mononuclear and eosinophil cells.

Clinical Manifestations

The condition may remain asymptomatic. Otherwise, there is pruritus and dermatoses, which run a chronic course, causing the skin to become rough and thickened. There may be one or several subcutaneous fibrous tumours, 1 cm or more in diameter. They usually occur in the axilla, popliteal fossa, elbow, suboccipital region and intercostal spaces. Tumours may also be seen on the scalp and in occipitofrontaol and temporal regions. The tumours may produce no symptom or may be painful. The superficial lymph nodes are enlarged, and the sclerosed femoral and inguinal lymph glands may hang down in folds of loose skin at the groin. There may also be enlargement of scrotum, hydrocele, enlargement of testes, elephantiasis, and femoral hernia.

In heavy infestation, involvement of the eyes may be common, and may present with itching, lacrimation, conjunctivitis, sclerosing keratitis, impaired vision, iritis, and choroidoretinitis.

The condition can produce blindness and epileptiform attacks as complications.

Diagnosis

Presence of characteristic nodules in the endemic area and eosinophilia are highly suggestive. Diagnosis of the condition is however made by identification of the microfilariae in skin snips or excised nodules. Slit-lamp examination of the eye may at times show moving microfilaria. The diagnosis may be supported by a test trial with 50 mg of diethylcarbamazine, which worsens the dermatitis. Diagnosis can also made by complement fixation and immunofluorescence tests. Intradermal tests are also a diagnostic aid.

It is differentiated from other filariasis.

Treatment

It is treated by diethylcarbamazine. The drug is given orally initially at a low dose of 25 mg and increased gradually to the tolerance of the patient up to 12 mg per kg body-weight daily in three divided doses, and the final tolerated dose in continued for 3 weeks time. Suramin is also effective to kill the adult filariae. It is given at 1 g by IV injection and repeated after 5 to 7 days for a total dose of 6 g. An antihistamine, such as chlorpheniramine, 4-8 mg three or four times daily orally, is given for allergic manifestations but in severe cases, corticosteroid is recommended for systemic administration and also by eye drops.

Subcutaneous nodules may need surgical excision for removal.

DRACUNCULIASIS

Dracunculiasis (**guinea worm infection, dracontiasis**) occurs due to *Dracunculus medinensis*. The worm inhabits in the subcutaneous tissue and body cavities in man. Human beings acquire the infection from ingestion of water containing crustacean in which the larva of the worm reaches to its infective form.

Dracunculus medinensis is an extremely large human worm, measuring 40-80 cm in length. It has cylindrical, smooth, white body with pointed tail, forming blunt hook. Its embryos have rounded head, bulbous oesophagus, with flattened long slender tail.

In human beings, the gravid female worm migrates to the skin surface, especially of the legs and feet which when come in contact with water, the worm penetrates through the subcutaneous tissue, and produces a cutaneous blister that ulcerates. On contact with water the worm discharges large number of larvae, which are ingested by the crustacea (*cyclops*), and the larvae there attain infectivity. When human beings swallow such water containing infected cyclops, larvae emerge, penetrate the intestinal wall and eventually migrate to the subcutaneous tissue to attain maturity.

It produces slight inflammatory reaction. However, there may be severe inflammatory reaction if the worm dies. The worm then becomes calcified.

Clinical Manifestations

Penetration of gravid female worm causes cutaneous blister that ulcerates, which, in absence of secondary infection, heals in 4 to 6 weeks. The patient complains of nausea, vomiting, diarrhoea, dyspnoea and giddiness, and urticaria during the formation of blister. Thereafter as the blister ruptures the symptoms subside. Bacterial contamination of the ulcer may however produce cellulitis and subcutaneous abscesses. There may also be arthritis, synovitis, epididymitis, tendinous contraction and ankylosis of joints.

The condition may produce abscess, septicaemia, ankle and knee joint infections and deformity.

Diagnosis

Peripheral blood shows moderate eosinophilia.

Diagnosis is made on the presence of cutaneous ulcers and worms in the subcutaneous tissue. When no worm can be seen in the ulcer, splashing water over the ulcer may bring forth typical larvae. Skin test may be helpful for diagnosis. X-ray may show calcified worms.

It is differentiated from bacterial infections and urticaria.

Treatment

Daily cleaning and dressing of the ulcer is an important part of management of the condition. The worm may be removed surgically. Otherwise, gentle traction through winding up the worm on a stick is maintained on several days to ease out the emerging worm. Appropriate antibiotics are given to combat secondary bacterial infection.

Specific therapy is however given with thiabendazole, 25 mg per kg of body-weight (1.5 g for persons weighing over 60 kg) twice daily orally, or niridazole, 25 mg/kg daily in three divided doses orally, for 3 days.

CHAPTER 8

Miscellaneous Disorders

PRURITUS

Pruritus or **itching** is not a clinical entity but a common manifestation of many dermatological disorders as well as several other disease pattern, such as multiple sclerosis, chronic renal failure, tabes dorsalis, cholestasis, biliary obstruction, hypothyroidism, hypoparathyroidism, diabetes mellitus, brain tumours, Hodgkin's lymphoma, late stage of neoplasms, parasitic infestation, and in a number of psychological disorders. Several drugs also produce generalised pruritus. In polycythaemia the pruritus may however be generalised or localised, and may also be episodic. In pruritus ani and pruritus valvae the pruritus is just localised.

Clinical Manifestations

The patient only complains of itching. It therefore gives rise to scratching and rubbing, which eventually may produce excoriated papules, fissures, and elongated crusts along the scratch line. There may also be lichenification and pigmentation due to persistent scratching and rubbing. Severe itching may cause disturbances in sleep and even insomnia.

It can cause secondary bacterial infection as complication.

Diagnosis

It is made clinically. Scratch test may however help to identify the cause of pruritus.

Treatment

Pruritus is a manifestation of underlying something. Management of it therefore requires correction, or appropriate measures, of the underlying or existing factor, which give rise to pruritus. Control of such coexisting factor often made the specific treatment for pruritus unnecessary.

Otherwise, the patient is given relief through a soothing lotion, such as calamine lotion. Crotamin, 10% solution or cream, or a combined preparation with antazoline, cetrimide and calamine, is also quite satisfactory and is applied topically.

For the relief of itching the patient may be given oral antihistamine, such as such chlorphenamine, 4 mg every four or six hourly (children: 1-2 years, 1 mg twice daily; 2-5 years, 1 mg every four or six hours; 6012 years, 2 mg every four or six hours), promethazine, 10-25 mg two to three times daily (children: 2-5 years, 5-15 mg twice daily; 5-10 years, 10-15 mg twice daily), or timeprazine, 10 mg two or three times daily (children: 2-5 years, 2.5-5 mg three or four times daily), or the patient may be given mild tranquilliser, such as diazepam, 6-30 mg daily orally in divided doses, or chlorpromazine, 10 mg three times daily orally. diazepam, 5-30 mg daily in divided doses orally.

Localised lesions may be treated with topical corticosteroids.

HIDROSIS

Hidrosis or **sweating** is a natural physiological activity of human body. At times however this normal activity may be interfered for any reason, causing diminished or profuse sweating.

In **anhidrosis** the secretion of sweating is greatly reduced or may even be absent due to reduction in number of, damage of or absence of sweat glands. This sort of situation is encountered with in a few congenital abnormalities, while a few disorders, for example, leprosy and scleroderma, may cause local anhidrosis.

Hyperhidrosis represents excessive sweating which often develops due to varieties of psychological elements. In normal health it is also evident following great physical effort, and consumption of hot and spicy foods. It may an accompaniment of several endocrine dysfunctions or other ailments, for example, hyperthyroidism, ands central nervous system disease, including debility and wasting diseases. . On the other end, localised hyperhidrosis may develop due to hereditary, excessive intake of tea and alcohol, and localised deformity, such as flat feet.

Local hyperhidrosis may sometimes cause offensive sweating (**bromhidrosis**) due to decomposition of sweat and cellular debris by the bacteria or fungus. It may also develop from prolonged use of nylon socks and tight shoes, ingestion of large quantities of onions and garlic in foods and, also, in certain disease process, for example, diabetes. On the other end, use of various chemicals and drugs may cause sweating containing black, blue or red pigment (**chromhidrosis**).

Clinical Manifestations

Anhidrosis presents with a sensation of peculiar dryness of the body. The patients complains of too little or absence of sweating, and shows an intolerance to heat.

In *hyperhydrosis*, profuse and excessive sweating cannot only cause certain amount of embarrassment, including perhaps insomnia and varieties of psychological disturbances, along with other factors; it may also at time cause imbalance in body fluid. The sweated skin may show maceration, and the constantly soaked and wet skin can eventually give rise to bacterial or fungal infection.

Localised hyperhidrosis principally affects the palms, soles, axillae, undersurface of the breasts, and groins. Perspiration of palms or soles causes great inconveniences to the patient, while, like generalised hyperhidrosis, local involvement can also produce maceration of skin and can also be a great affection to kind of microorganisms.

Bromhidrosis however presents with soul smelling sweating that cause a great amount of inconvenience and annoyance.

Diagnosis

It is diagnosed on clinical grounds.

Abnormality in hidrosis however by itself does not require any differentiation except for the underlying conditions.

Treatment

No satisfactory treatment is available for anhidrosis, nor does it cause much inconvenience. In cases of its origin due to any congenital factor, the patient is kept away from exposure to heat and from excessive physical activity. As far as possible the patient is kept in air-conditioned environment, and the exposed parts of the body are frequently sponged with wet towels and handkerchiefs. The patient is also given frequent cold drink and ice foods. The patients are also strongly advised not to use any clothes made of synthetic fibres. Anhidrosis cases of non-congenital origin may be treated with corticosteroids, such as prednisolone, 20 mg daily in divided doses orally and continued for 2 or 3 months, following which the drug is tapered down slowly till withdrawal. In spite of such a treatment schedule if the condition remains unresponsive, the patient is then protected as per schedule for the congenital type of anhidrosis.

Adequate management and control of the underlying factor must end the problem of generalised hyperhidrosis, while a change in environment may stop localised hyperhidrosis in some cases. Some cases may however need surgical interference through sympathectomy but the beneficial effect is much variable, and may well be temporary or even disappointing.

Antiperspirant, aluminium chloride hexahydrate, can however give some symptomatic relief by reducing the volume of sweat produced. This is however quite effective in cases of localised hyperhidrosis, including bromidrosis, and the patient is given 20% solution or powder of aluminium chloride hexahydrate for application at night on dry axillae, hands and feet, and wash off in the morning. Initially the application is given daily and thereafter the number of such topical administration is reduced as sweating diminishes. The patient however must not bathe immediately before use of antiperspirants. Localised hyperhidrosis can also be satisfactorily controlled through immersion of the affected part in cold water, added with small quantity of formaldehyde, and kept half-an-hour every morning.

In more severe cases glycopyrronium bromide, 0.5% solution, in the iontophoretic treatment of hyperhidrosis of palmar and plantar areas. The solution is applied at only one site at a time, maximum 2 sites treated in any 24 hours, and the treatment must not be repeated within 7 days.

In severe hyperhidrosis of the axillae unresponsive to topical antiperspirant or other antihidrotic treatment, injection of botulinum A toxin-haemagglutinin complex may be given intradermally.

Dusting powder containing chloroxylenol, 0.5%, and aluminium dihydroxyallantoinate, 0.2%, along with cellulose, 46%, or a preparation containing aldioxa, 0.22%, along with chloroxylenol, 0.5%, applied liberally as required can also control both hyperhidrosis and bromhidrosis.

In addition or alternate to the use of dusting powder bromhidrosis can be treated effectively through maintaining scrupulous cleanliness of the parts affected. If required axillary hair may be shaved off. The patient is also encouraged to avoid using nylon socks and to change the socks as frequently as opportunity arises. The patient can also be given deodorant for use.

In other instances, much benefit may be gained by reducing the psychological tension and anxiety of the patient; the patient may therefore be given anxiolytics.

ALOPECIA

Alopecia represents partial or total loss of hair and occurs due to abnormal atrophy of hair follicles. Although, in general, a familial factor is often involved in the causation of alopecia or **baldness**, several infections and disorders, for example, tinea, folliculitis, typhoid fever, syphilis, lupus vulgaris, lupus erythematosus, exfoliative dermatitis and myxoedema, can produce the condition. Use of certain drugs, for example, methotrexate and selenium, can also cause alopecia, while there are some cases where the causation of the condition remains obscured or idiopathic.

Clinical Manifestations

The loss of hair may present with sharply demarcated round or oval bald patches (**alopecia areata**), leaving a smooth, shiny patch of normal coloured skin on the scalp, beard, eyelashes or any other hairy area of the body. The baldness may be widespread and may involve the whole scalp (**alopecia totalis**) or the whole body (**alopecia universalis**). In other cases, the baldness may be cicatricial (**cicatricial alopecia**). General form of alopecia however occurs on all over the frontal and vertex in men (**man-pattern alopecia, alopecia androgenetica**). Occasionally women may also present with thinning of hair on the frontal and parietal region.

Diagnosis

It is diagnosed on clinical grounds. Examination of hair and hair follicle can help the diagnosis.

Treatment

No effective therapy other than surgical transplantation is yet available in cases of familial baldness. Alopecia developing due to the result of varieties of causes does not generally require any form of treatment and the process is reversible with the control of the underlying condition. In all other cases, corticosteroids may be tried intralesionally or systemically or both. Transplant of hair is also possible

In cases of man-pattern (alopecia androgenetica) hair-restorer, minoxidil may be tried with varying success. In this situation 1 ml of 2% (for 1 ml of 5% strength) liquid minoxidil is massaged on the dry hair and scalp twice daily for minimum 4 months and continue till hair loss do not recur but discontinue if no improvement after 1 year. The drug may however cause irritant dermatitis and allergic contact dermatitis. Selective 5-alpha reductase inhibitor, finasteride, is also quite effective, and it is given at 5 mg daily orally, review treatment after 6 months (may require several months before benefit is obtained.

HIRSUTISM

The condition is often idiopathic, racial or familial in origin but, in some cases, it may occur due to endocrine disturbances. The condition also develops as side-effect of drugs from systemic treatment with corticosteroids, minoxidil, danazol, anabolic steroids, or androgen steroid and, also, in menopause.

When the distribution of coarse hair is more generalised, the condition is then known as **hypertrichosis.**

Clinical Manifestations

The patient complains of the presence of hair on the beard region and on the upper lip. Hair may also be seen on the chest and abdomen. The hair stuffs tend to be uniform in texture and calibre, and the growth of hair is always terminal.

Sometimes the growth of hair may be generalised or occur at other unusual areas, for example, neck, ears and forehead.

The condition may also sometimes accompany acne vulgaris.

Diagnosis

It is easy on clinical grounds alone.

Treatment

Cytotoxic-induced reversible hair loss is a common complication and the degree varies between drugs and individual patients. Otherwise, no remedy is available therapeutically.

In other cases management of the condition immediately requires adequate control of the underlying factors, if known. Drugs, which are reckoned to contribute to the development, require withdrawal or replacement of substitute.

In cases when it co-exists with acne, the patient may be adequately treated with co-cyprindiol, a mixture of cyproterone and ethinyloestradiol.

Temporary relief may be given by removal of the hair through plucking, shaving or wax epilation.

Male-pattern baldness is treated by finasteride, 1 mg daily orally. The treatment is continued for 3-6 months before benefit is seen, and effects are reversed 6-12 months after treatment is discontinued. Both male and female patients may also benefit in man-pattern baldness from minoxidil, 2% solution, apply 1 ml twice daily to dry hair and scalp (5% solution is for the use of males only) but discontinue if no improvement after 1 year. The drug is effective only for as long as it is used. On the other hand, if irritant dermatitis and allergic contact dermatitis develop and if hair loss persists for more than 2 weeks, application of minoxidil should be discontinued.

Oral administration of oestrogen in small doses is also rewarding. Progression of the condition can be prevented through anti-androgen drugs. Electrolysis however appears to give permanent cure though such a therapy may also leave varying degree of scarring, often trivial in nature.

DECUBITUS ULCER

Decubitus ulcer is a disorder of ischaemic necrosis and ulceration of the skin and tissue resulting from unusually prolonged pressure from bed, wheelchair, etcetera, or from trophic changes in cases of paralysis Depending upon the mode of presentation the condition is also known as **bedsore**, **pressure sore** an **trophic ulcer**. Prolonged and continuous pressure over the cartilaginous or bony prominences of the body, depending upon the duration of the pressure, can cause localised impairment of circulation. This, in addition to the physical and nutritional status of the person involved, can cause tissue anoxia, which progresses further and finally results to necrosis of the skin and subcutaneous tissue. Similar situation also arises in spasticity and in conditions which give rise to loss of pain and pressure sensation. The entire process however depends upon the combination of several contributory factors that include nutritional state, general health and resistance status of the person, vascular resistance and circulatory state, thickness of the muscle and fat padding between the weight-bearing prominences of the body and the surface, and duration of the pressure.

It involves the bony and cartilaginous prominences of the body, most common sites being the sacrum, the buttocks and the heels, and generally affects the old, debilitated, bedridden or paralysed persons.

Clinical Manifestations

It initially presents with erythema over the pressure points of the body. The erythema blanches or disappears on pressure. Later, the erythematous area shows oedema and induration. At this stage there may be evidence of epidermal blistering or desquamation. Progression of the condition leads to superficial necrosis and ulceration of the area which, if not prevented or not seriously taken care of, become deeper involving the whole extent of skin, fat and muscle. Progression further even causes bony destruction.

Diagnosis

It is diagnosed on clinical grounds alone.

The clinical manifestations are so obvious that it does not cause any confusion and yet if it does, the condition may be differentiated from other ulcers and gangrenous conditions.

Treatment

The principle of management of the condition includes improvement of general condition of the patients, frequent changing in position of the bedridden and paralysed persons, and appropriate arrangements of the bed, wheelchair, etcetera, so that the weight-bearing parts of the body are not left for long under pressure. Conscientious appreciation is needed to combat the contributory factors leading to the development of the condition.

The superficial ulcers may not perhaps need any form of treatment, but otherwise, application of a soothing agent, such as semi-permeable hydrocolloid or calcium alginate dressing, is often quite sufficient. In other cases, the ulcers are regularly cleaned thoroughly and dressed with topical antimicrobial agents. Severe form of ulcers may however need surgical interference and care.

SARCOIDOSIS

Sarcoidosis is a rare, benign disorder of skin, often occurring with systemic involvement. The cutaneous condition can however appear independently. The aetiology of the condition is not known yet.

It usually affects young and middle-aged women.

Histologically it shows packed collection of epitheloid cells, surrounded by lymphocytes. The early lesions show giant cell reaction but fibrosis in the older lesions.

Clinical Manifestations

It gives rise to varieties of lesions ranging from macule, papule, and nodule to plaque and tumour, with granulomatous infiltration, of varying size and colour. The lesions are usually multiple, though may also be single, and appear firm and elastic on palpation. The lesions occur on any part of the body but often involve the face, particularly around the eyes (Fig. 8.1), nose and mouth, and external aspects of the arms and feet in one variety, but trunk in another variety. Sometimes lesions may show miliary distribution or may appear as annular pattern. The condition runs a very chronic course, often with relapses. The lesions tend to involve the centre and spread in a raised ring at the border but eventually at times heal spontaneously, leaving practically no trace even though there may be some atrophy or scarring in occasional cases. The condition is frequently manifested with erythema nodosum.

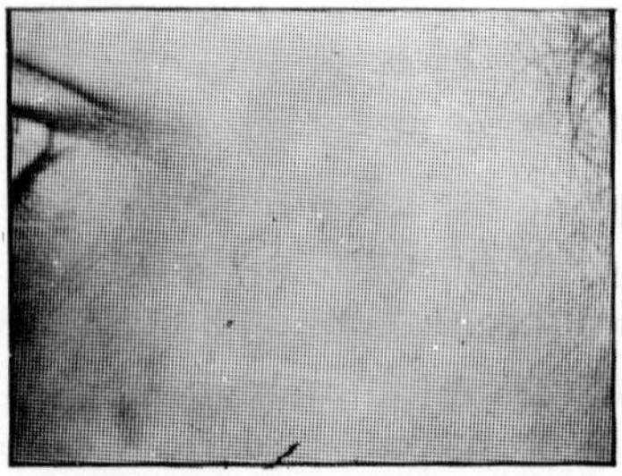

Figure 8.1. Granulomatous papules of sarcoidosis on face.

Cutaneous involvement of the condition is however completely asymptomatic. It only presents with other symptoms and signs of systemic involvement of the condition.

Diagnosis

The condition is diagnosed on clinical grounds, and is confirmed by the histological findings Intradermal test (Kvein test) though nonspecific but may be an aid to diagnosis. Tuberculin test is however negative. The condition also gives rise to increased level of serum globulin but a decreased level of serum albumin, and hypercalcaemia.

It is differentiated from nodular vasculitis, erythema induratumn, leprosy and granulomatous lesion of syphilis.

Treatment

No specific therapy of the condition is yet available. Therefore no form of treatment appears satisfactory. Care is taken for improvement of health of the patient. In addition, treatment may be given with corticosteroids or ACTH, which may give varying success.

NODULAR VASCULITIS

Nodular vasculitis is a chronic or recurrent nodular lesion of the subcutaneous tissue. The condition may often follow trauma, septic focus or use of certain drugs. Often there may be history pf phlebitis.

The condition is more common in adult women than in men.

Histopathology of the nodule shows vasculitis with thickening and obliteration of the blood vessels, and fibrosis of the subcutaneous tissue.

Clinical Manifestations

It presents with slightly painful and tender erythematous nodules, occurring chiefly on the calves of the leg but can also develop on the anterior surface of the legs, thighs and, occasionally, elsewhere on the body. The nodules usually subside following bed rest and reappear on standing. New nodules may appear at varying intervals. The nodules do not cause ulceration but when they do, they produce dirty, indolent ulcers. Later, there may be brown pigmentation along the course of the superficial veins. The lesions heal leaving pigmented scars. The condition however does not give rise to any constitutional symptom, nor is there any systemic involvement.

Diagnosis

The cases are diagnosed from biopsy of the nodule.

It is differentiated from erythema nodosum, which presets with symmetrically distributed lesions appearing in crops, and the nodules may coalesce together and may fluctuate and show different histological picture. Erythema induratum usually affects young women with tuberculosis of lymph glands and acrocyanosis, and gives rise to symmetrically distributed soft nodules which later produce deep ulcer with steep or undermined edges.

Treatment

Management of the condition essentially requires treatment or correction of the underlying factors. The affected part is kept at rest. The patient is given treatment with corticosteroids and antibiotics. Treatment with alkalyting cytotoxic, such as cyclophosphamide, is also found effective in some cases

In cases of ulcerations, the wound is given surgical dressings.

MYCOSIS FUNGOIDES

Mycosis fungoides is a T-cell Lymphoproliferative disorder that primarily invades the skin but may evolve into generalised lymphoma. It is caused by the malignant proliferation of dermal reticuloendothelial cells but the precise aetiology of its causation is not known. Recent investigations however suggest that the condition may have an infectious causation.

It occurs at an age but most commonly affects persons aged 40 years or more.

Progression of the condition generally occurs through three stages: premycotic, infiltrative and tumour, but, though rare, a case may develop directly to tumour stage skipping two intermediary stages in between.

Histopathological changes the condition produce are however not specific in the premycotic stage but otherwise the condition gives a uniform picture of pleomorphic collection of large abnormal reticulum cells, together with histiocytes, neutrophils and eosinophils.

Characteristically the condition shows T-helper cells that form band-like aggregates with the superficial dermis and invades the epidermis as single cells and small clusters which, in tumour stage, grow deeply in the dermis.

Clinical Manifestations

The condition usually follow a protracted course extending over years or even decades together, giving rise to generalised persistent itching until the condition becomes recognisable or, very rarely, the condition become rapidly fatal.

In *premycotic stage* it gives rise to a variety of lesions, such as macules, papules, urticarial, plaques, scaly patches, and occasionally bullous eruption mimicking large number of dermatoses, including eczema, seborrhoeic dermatitis, psoriasis, parapsoriasis, erythema multiforme, exfoliative dermatitis and poikiloderma. In this stage, the lesions however do not show any distinctive characteristic of the condition. The lesions may however be transitory or may persist for some time. The lesions may remain localised or be generalised, or coalesce and form extensive well-defined patches with more or less exudation and scaling. The lesions show both regression and progression.

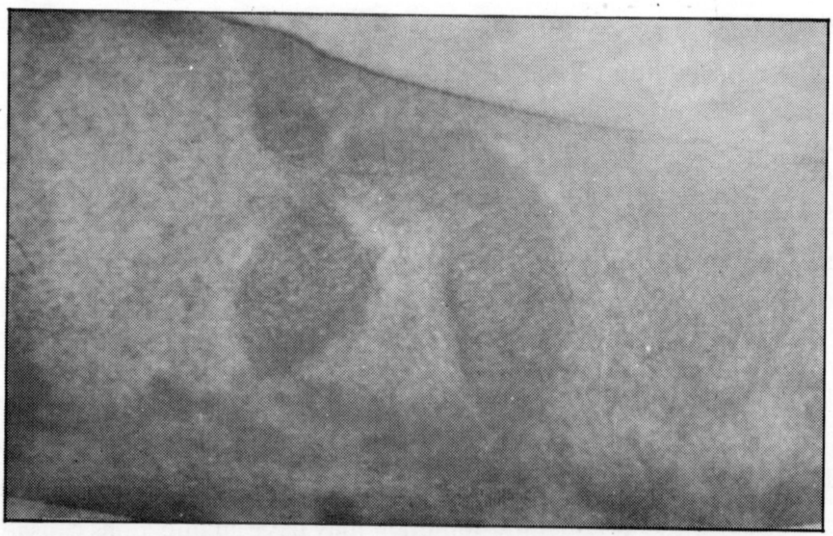

Figure 8.2. Mycosis fungoides involving annular infiltration on foıearm.

In *infiltrative stage*, the lesions give rise to well-defined areas on infiltration on the skin (Fig. 8.2), sometimes even resembling psoriasiform patches (Fig. 8.3). Development of bullous and vesicular lesions from the infiltrated nodules and plaque is extremely rare. The lesions may ulcerate at this stage. Development of exfoliative dermatitis appears to be a complimentary of the condition. Hairs become scanty, and nails dry and ridged. Splenomegaly and enlargement of the lymph nodes are also common.

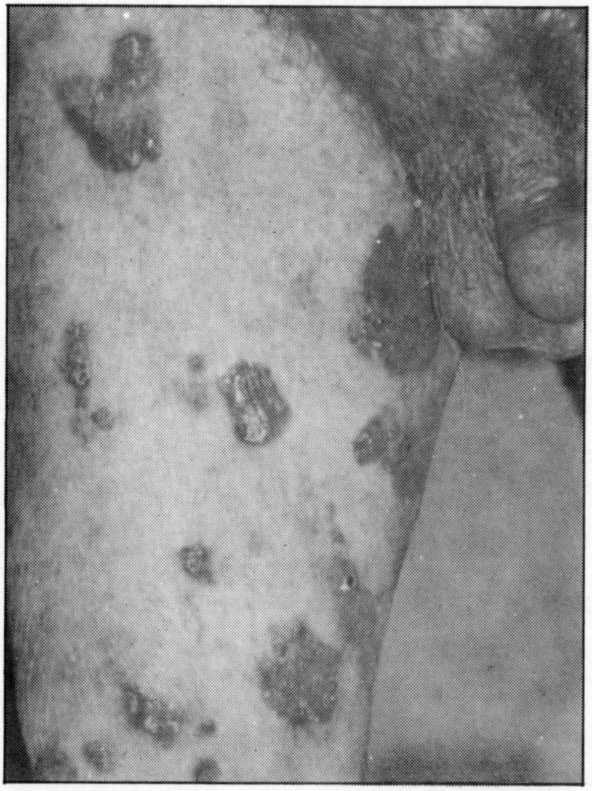

Figure 8.3. Psoriasiform patches of mycosis fungoides.

In the *tumour stage* there are nodules of various size and shape that develop on the infiltrated patches as well as on the normal skin. The nodules tend to break down in the early stage and produce deep oval ulcers with necrotic greyish base; the edges of the ulcers are often rolled. This stage of the condition may be mild but otherwise may become fatal.

Diagnosis

Diagnosis of the condition in its premycotic stage is practically impracticable. Otherwise, the condition is diagnosed on clinical grounds, supported by the histology of the lesions.

The condition needs to be differentiated from almost all kind of dermatosss, lymphomas and lymphocytic leukaemia.

Treatment

So far radiotherapy appears to be the only effective treatment of the condition, and the patient is given the same. Much better result may however be achieved through addition of nitrogen mustard. Folic acid antagonist, such as methotrexate, can achieve regression of the transient lesions through treatment with ankylating cytotoxic, for example, cyclophosphamide, busulphan or decarbazine, and. The plaques of lesions can also be treated with topical corticosteroids, supplemented by exposure to sunlight.

EXFOLIATIVE DERMATITIS

Exfoliative dermatitis or **erythroderma** in a severe and generalised form of dermatitis. In most cases the aetiology of it is not known but in others, its development may be the end stage or secondary to some preceding dermatoses, such as psoriasis, lichen planus, and generalised contact dermatitis that can involve the entire integument by them or due to overtreatment with irritant application and may thus, lead to the development of the condition. Cutaneous manifestations of reticulosis, particularly lymphatic leukaemia, Hodgkin's lymphoma and, rarely, mycosis fungoides, can produce the condition. Certain drugs, such as penicillin, sulphonamides, chloroquine, barbiturates, phenylbutazone, isoniazid, para-aminosalicylic acid (PAS), arsenic, gold, mercury and certain irritant agents can also produce the condition.

There is oedema in the upper part of the corium and the epidermis, parakeratosis, acanthosis, dilatation of vessels and infiltration with lymphocytes and eosinophils. The papillae become enlarged and thickened.

Clinical Manifestations

It presents with generalised reddening of the skin, covered with varying degree of lamellared scales, distributed virtually all over the body (Fig. 8.4). In some cases the scaling may be minimum and the greatly inflamed epidermis may show oozing. Regional lymph nodes, particularly inguinal, become enlarged. Skin appears thickened and the patient looks uncomfortable and irritable. The patient complains of intense irritation and profuse sweating. Insomnia is a quite common accompaniment. The patient appears to be sensitive to cold. In late stage, there may also be loss of hair and nails.

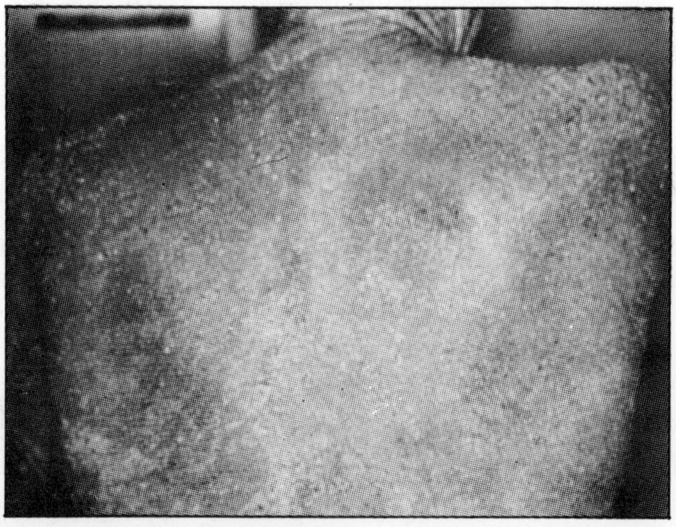

Figure 8.4. Exfoliative dermatitis covering the entire back.

In some cases there may be malaise, fever, chills, rigors, fluid and electrolyte imbalance, hypoproteinaemia, and congestive heart failure. The patient develops anaemia and shows an interference with body temperature regulation.

When it presents as an acute condition, it shows improvement after several weeks but otherwise, it may be extremely chronic and may give rise to repeated attacks.

Diagnosis

It is made on clinical grounds.

The condition may be differentiated from psoriasis, seborrhoeic dermatitis, and lichen planus.

Treatment

Avoidance of unnecessary medication and removal or treatment of the underlying causes is most important in the management of the condition. Management of the condition also principally requires removal, control or adequate treatment of the underlying factors.

For relief of subjective symptoms, soothing local compressions with saline or potassium permanganate is beneficial. The patient is given systemic corticosteroids and the condition often responds to prednisolone, 40-60 mg daily in divided doses orally and then reduce the dose gradually by 2.5 mg every three or four days to a most effective maintenance dose. In cases of secondary infection, the patient is also given appropriate antibiotics.

URTICARIA PIGMENTOSA

It is a rare familial disorder associated with dermal accumulation of mast cells due to unknown aetiology. Occasionally there may be widespread proliferation of mast cells throughout the body, causing systemic involvement, and the condition is then known as **mastocytosis**. The systemic involvement may however be trivial or severe. The condition runs a chronic course.

It appears in infancy or in adult life, the former being however more common.

Histological changes the condition produce are strands or columns of closely packed mast cells in the upper corium, increased amount of pigment in the epidermis and corium, and dilatation of the lymph vessels.

Clinical Manifestations

The condition has two recognised types: childhood and adult.

In *childhood type* the lesions appear soon after birth or during the first year of life. The condition then gives rise to generalised, hyperpigmented, macular, papular or nodular eruption, but characteristically however they are usually large, brown-red nodules (Fig. 8.5). Sometimes there may also bullae formation. The lesions may occur on any part of the body but more commonly on the front and back of the trunk, and less commonly on the neck, face and limbs. Itching is the only complaint. Any amount of scratching makes the lesions to become red, swollen and enlarged resembling urticarial wheals. Fresh lesions may continue to appear in crops. The condition however runs a benign course and hardly persists till the patient gains puberty, and the lesions subsides without any recurrences.

In *adult type*, though similar lesions develop and there is practically no difference of the condition with that of childhood type, characteristically the lesions are usually flat brown macules. Occasionally the lesions may also be haemorrhagic. Scratching or stroking the lesions or consumption of certain drugs, such as codeine, can immediately produce urticarial wheals.

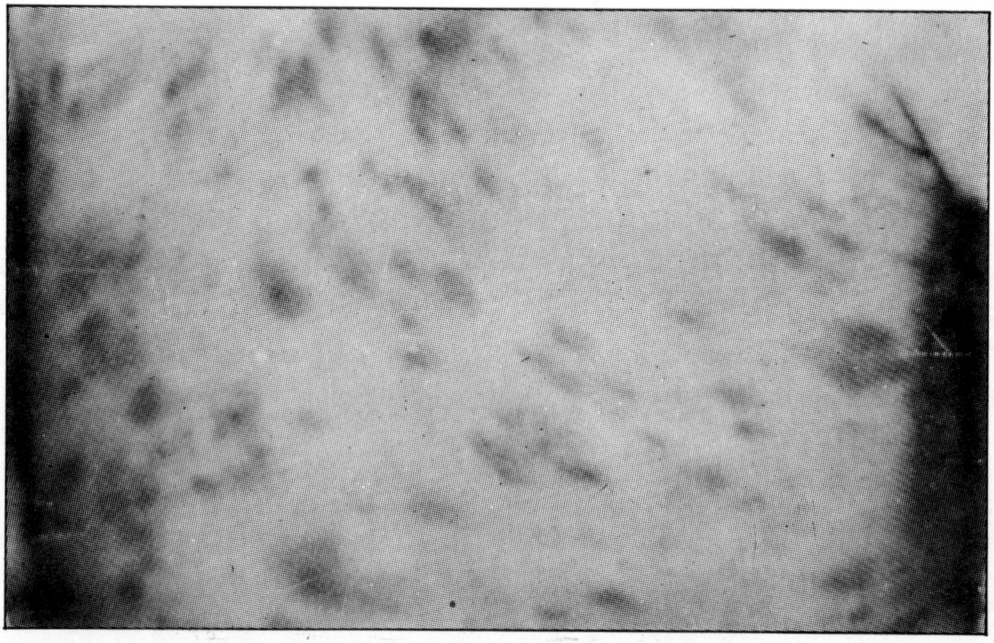

Figure 8.5. Childhood type of urticaria pigmentosa.

In addition, there may also be other symptoms and signs of mastocytosis, such as weakness, weight loss, flushing, headache, hypotension, tachycardia and shock. There may also be abdominal pain, nausea, vomiting, diarrhoea, hepatomegaly, lymphadenopathy, and bony changes in x-rays.

Diagnosis

The condition is diagnosed by a simple bedside test in which when the lesions are stroked firmly, they rapidly produce urticarial wheals. The diagnosis can however be confirmed on skin biopsy.

It is differentiated from other conditions that present with urticaria, nodules and pigmentation.

Treatment

No effective treatment of the condition is yet available. For the relief of the condition preventive measures are however taken so as to control degranulation of mast cells. This includes avoidance of certain drugs, such as analgesics and NSAIDs, exposure to extreme hot or cold environment, and friction or massage of skin.

The patient is given antihistamine for the relief of itching. In this respect administration of serotonin antagonist, such as cyproheptadine, or mast cell stabiliser, such as ketotifen, appears to be quite superior. Cyproheptadine is given at 4 mg three or four times daily orally (children: 2-6 years, 2 mg three times daily; 7-14 years, 4 mg three times daily), and ketotifen is given at 1-2 mg twice daily orally with foods (children: over 3 years, 1 mg twice daily). Other oral anti-allergic drugs given with satisfaction are clemastine, 1 mg (children aged 3-6 years, 0.5 mg; over 6 years, 0.5-1 mg) twice daily at morning and evening, and hydroxyzine hydrochloride, 25 mg at night increasing as necessary to 25 mg three or four times daily (children aged 6 months-6 years, 5-15 mg at night increasing to maximum 50 mg daily in divided doses; over 6 years, 15-25 mg at night increasing to maximum 50-100 mg daily in divided doses).

The treatment is however continued for an extremely prolonged period of time until clinical cure.

LICHEN SIMPLEX CHRONICS

Neurodermatitis is a relatively common condition affecting the neurotic individuals in which, even though there is no evidence of any dermatological disorder, persons feel intense irritation due to varieties of emotional stress. Lichen simplex chronic is just a localised form of that neurodermatitis and develops due to chronic scratching and rubbing of the skin. It may also develop as a complication of dermatitis resulting form the irritants.

Histologically it causes thickening of the epidermis, acanthosis with hyperkeratosis and parakeratosis, oedema, and perivascular infiltration.

Clinical Manifestations

It presents with severely itchy, thickly arranged, flat papules or dry licheniified patches with irregular but usually well-demarcated borders on any part of the body (Fig. 8.6). The lesions however show a predilection the back and sides of the neck, antecubital and popliteal areas, forearm close to wrist, scrotum, ano-genital region, anus, and back of the legs and ankles. Chronic scratching and rubbing cause the integument to be thickened pigmented and infiltrated. The lesions tend to persist for a long time and show an exaggeration on emotional stress. Repeated scratching of the area may lead to the development of secondary bacterial infection.

Diagnosis

Diagnosis of the condition is made on clinical grounds. Biopsy of skin can aid the diagnosis.

It may at times need to be differentiated from atopic dermatitis, lichen planus and seborrhoeic dermatitis.

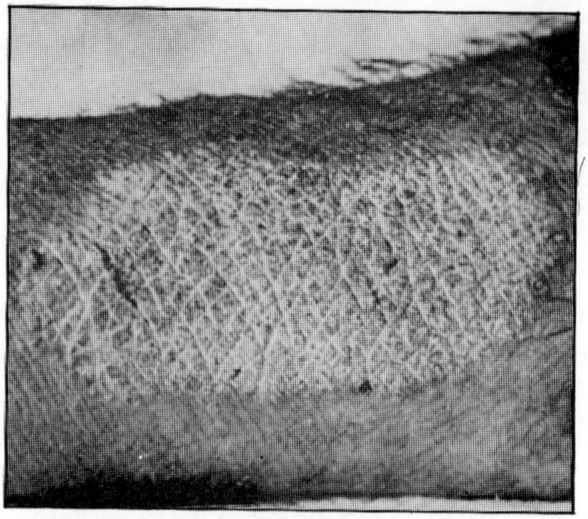

Figure 8.6. Lichen simplex chronicus.

Treatment

The patient is sympathetically counselled and advised to avoid every kind of tension, and to avoid or minimise scratching and rubbing if the skin.

The patient is given local soothing compressions with hypertonic saline or potassium permanganate solution, followed by administration of topical corticosteroids.

The patient may also be given oral anti-allergic drugs, such as hydroxyzine hydrochloride, 25 mg at night increasing as necessary to 25 mg three or four time daily, trimeprazine, 10 mg two or three times daily (maximum: 100 mg a day), or chlorpheniramine, 4 mg every four to six hours, for the relief of itching.

In cases of severe disturbances, the patient may also be given anxiolytic, such as diazepam, 6-30 mg daily in divided doses orally.

Appropriate antibiotic is also given in case of secondary bacterial infection.

Part II
Venereology

CHAPTER 9

About the Genitalia

In men, the most prominent part of external genitalia is the penis, and the scrotum that lies below the base of the penis and contains testicles (Fig. 9.1).

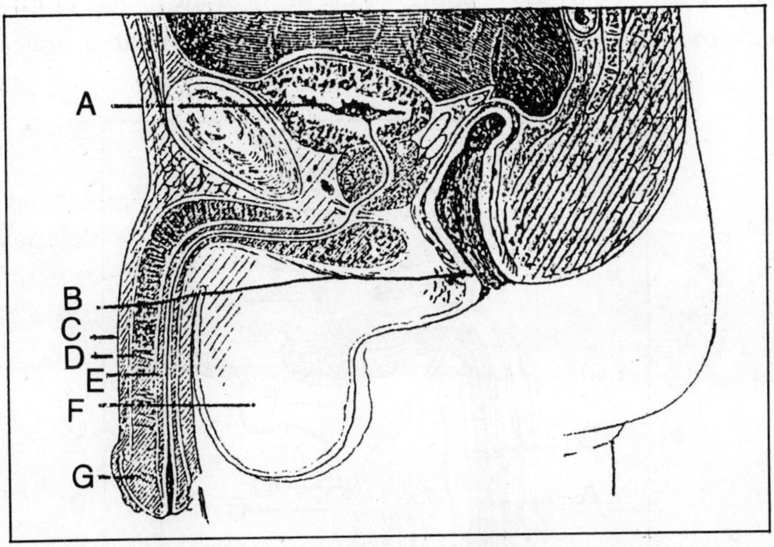

Figure 9.1. Ventral section through a male penis.
A. Bladder; B. Rectum; C. Skin covering the penis; D. Corpus cavernosum;
E. Urethra; F. Scrotum; G. Glans penis,

Penis is composed of two structures: corpus cavernosum, lying more dorsally, and corpus spongiosum, lying more ventrally. The bulk of the forepart of penis consists of two corpus cavernosum lying side by side, and is covered by a fibrous sheath, tunica albuginea, and is covered by the skin. Posteriorly the corpus cavernosum splits into two separate crura penis, which are firmly attached to other side of the inferior pubic ramus and ischium. Distally, the corpus cavernosum ends in a blunt projection.

Corpus spongiosum lies in a groove on the corpus cavernosum and is tunnelled by the urethra along its whole length. Distally the corpus spongiosum is expanded to form the glans penis, the base of which is encircled by a groove, the coronal sulcus. Posteriorly, the corpus spongiosum forms another expansion, called the bulb that lies on the perineal membrane between the crura.

The skin covering the shaft of the penis extends distally from the coronal sulcus to cover the extent of the glans and is called prepuce or foreskin, and is covered by the mucous membrane of the undersurface that is continuous with that lining the urinary meatus, and is attached posteriorly with the glans just below the urinary meatus, called franeum. On each side of the frenum there are Tyson's glands in the sub-preputial sac, which secretes greyish-white smegma.

Urethra is a tunnel that runs along the whole length of the penis from the bladder to the urinary meatus, and is divided into two parts: the membranous and the prostatic urethra. The interior of the urethra is not smooth but shows depression in the mucous membrane caused by the lacunae of Morgagni and by the openings of the ducts of the glands of Littré. These glands are situated in the roof and walls and to the floor of the anterior urethra, and secrete mucus.

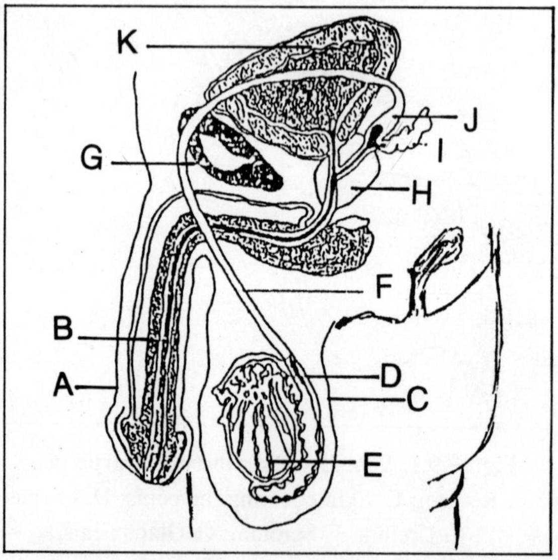

Figure 9.2. Cross-section of male reproductive organs.
A. Penis, B. Urethra, C. Scrotum, D. Epididymis, E. Seminiferous tubules, F. Vas deferens, G. Pubic bone, H. Prostate gland, I. Seminal vesicle, J. Ampulla, K. Bladder.

In man, spermatozoa are conveyed by the vas deferens from the testis to the urethra (Fig. 9.2). It begins from the tail of the epididymis, ascends along the medial side of the epididymis, and joins the other constituents of the spermatic cord at the upper end of the testis. The vas deferens travels through the inguinal rings and descends again and at the base of the bladder the vas of either side come between the seminal vesicle, become dilated forming ampulla and ends by joining the seminal vesicle duct so as to form the ejaculatory duct. Prostate is a chestnut shaped gland, partly glandular and partly muscular, surrounds the neck of the bladder and the beginning of the urethra.

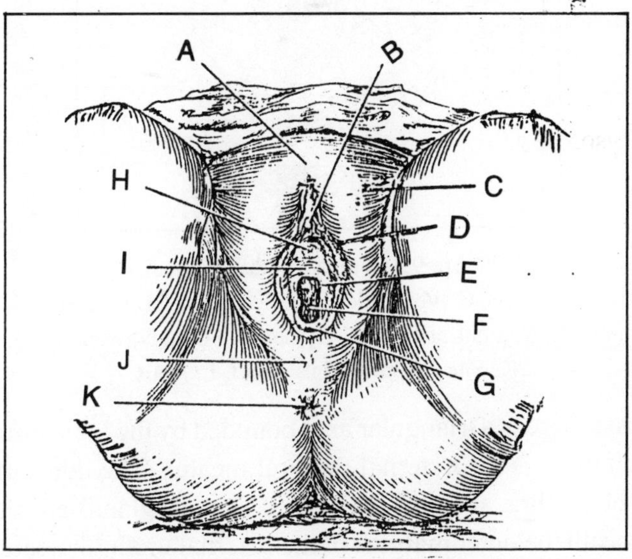

Figure 9.3. External genitalia of adult woman.
A. Mons veneris, B. Clitoris, C. Labia majora, D. Labia minora, E. Hymen, F. Vaginal orifice, G. Fossa navicularis, H. External urethral meatus, I. Vestibule, J. Perineum, K. Anus.

In women, external genitalia (Fig. 9.3) includes the vulva, which is a fossa bounded on either side by the labia majora extending from the mons veneris as crescentic folds and ending to the perineum. There is another mucosal fold on the internal aspects of labia majora, called labia minora, and is situated on either side so as to surround the vulvar fossa. Labia minora unite together posteriorly to form posterior boundary of the vulva, the fourchette. At the vertical confluence of the mucosal linings of both labia majora and labia minoira, it gives rise to an erectile projection, the clitoris, a penis-like sensitive organ and has a minute glans and two small corpora cavernosum.

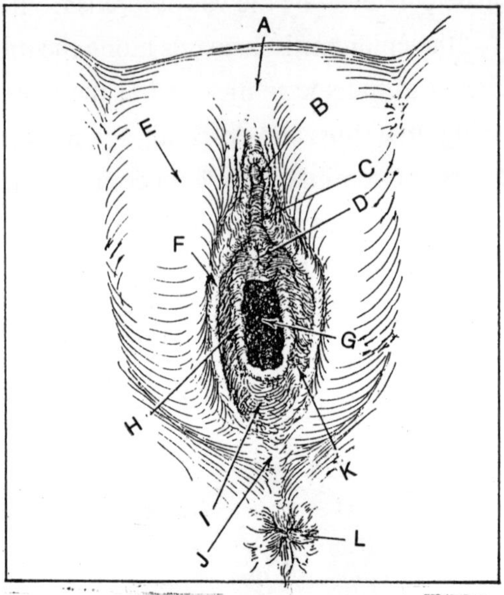

Figure 9.4. Vulva of adult woman.
A. Mons veneris, B. Clitoris, C. Vestibule, D. External urethral meatus, E. Labia majora, F. Labia minora, G. Vaginal orifice, H. Hymen, I. Fossa Navicularis, J. Perineum, K. Site of Bartholin's gland, L. Anus.`

In the vulvar fossa there is a triangular area bounded by the labia minora, called vestibule, in the middle of which there is the external urethral meatus. The ducts of the Skene's tubules open on each side of the urethra, and the small-sized Skene's glands are situated near the lower end of the urethra. Beneath the outer margins of the external urethral meatus there are vestibular glands. Vagina is situated on the posterior part of the vulvar fossa which, in the virgins, may be covered with a thin mucous membrane, called the hymen. Bartholin's glands (Fig. 9.4) are situated deep in the posterior third of the labia majora. The area between the posterior border of the hymen and the fourchette is called fossa navicularis.

Vagina is a dilatable canal that extend from the posterior part of the vulvar fossa to the cervix of the uterus which projects into four fornices: anterior fornix lies in relation to the bladder, posterior fornix to the rectum, and the remaining two fornices lie adjacent to the broad ligament, Fallopian tube and ovaries.

Uterus is a hollow pear-shaped muscular organ. Its upper end is called the fundus, and the lower end, the cervix, which opens into the upper end of the vagina. The Fallopian tube, one on each side of the uterus, conveys the ova from the ovary to the uterus. Its one end opens at the upper part of the uterus, and the other end curls around the ovary and opens into the peritoneal cavity. The ovary, one on each side, lies within the broad ligament of the uterus. Its upper or tubal end has the ovarian fimbria attached to it, and the lower or uterine end is connected with the uterus by a fibrous cord, called the ovarian ligament.

CHAPTER 10

Venereal Diseases

Venereal diseases or venereology or sexually transmitted (STD) is a group of disease that are transmitted in principal through sexual act. Some pathogens are responsible for producing the disorders, which are often contagious and spread from person to person. Whether it is the increasing tolerance and leniency of most modern societies towards sexual relation or whether availability of wide range of effective remedies play any part, there is no doubt that the incidence and prevalence of these diseases are now showing alarming heights in most communities of the world. Economic prosperity, economic depression or deprivation, lack of sexual bond, scarcity of social outlet, increasing women traffic on the street, and several other known and unknown factors, either singularly or conjointly, favour the spread of the infection within the community.

However, as the conditions, excepting congenital syphilis, are acquired through sexual act, often the principal manifestations become apparent on or around genitalia. Scabies, on the other end, though not a true sexually transmitted disease, yet it is usually reckoned as a sexually transmitted disease because its transmission is only possible through intimate bodily contact. Emphasis needs to be made that congenital syphilis is not a sexually transmitted disease but a complement of it, and yet the disease has been included in this chapter for the ease of description. On the other hand, AIDS is principally a blood borne disease but can also occur from sexual relation. The disease has therefore been included here because in recent years far too publicity has been made on its venereal transmission.

The diseases are identified through bacteriological and serological tests, and are effectively treated with potent antimicrobial, antiviral or antifungal agents, as appropriate Wide availability of potent antibiotics has no doubt changed the entire prospects of this group of disorders but still there remains certain amount of taboo, prejudice and shame which, in turn, may cause much complication or hindrance in treating or preventing STD.

On the other hand, emphasis needs to be made that the availability of potent therapeutic agents though have simplified the treatment of this group, STD is not a manifestation of an individual patient alone. As the transmission of the infection depends exclusively to the extent of sexual promiscuity, STDs are rightly reckoned as social or communal diseases which, in turn, require not only adequate medical treatment of the persons seeking medical help or suffering from the ailments but also require a community involvement. The responsibility of the venereologists therefore embraces a group of people that included the source from where the infection has been acquired and to whom the infection has possibly been passed over so that a better care and management of the conditions are possible within the community, including prevention of further transmission of the infection.

Clinical manifestations of the STDs vary widely. Sometimes sign of primary inoculation of the infection may be evident in some cases, while there may not be any trace thereof in others. In some cases the initial lesion may present as development of a sore or urethral discharge in some but in others the presentation may be quite different, to the extent may even remain unrecognisable. However, the characteristic feature that may sometimes be evident may include:

Argyll Robertson pupil is a small irregular pupil that though reacts normally to accommodation but not to light. It is almost exclusively seen in neurosyphilis.

Chancre is a painless localised ulcerative lesion, usually develops on the external genitalia, lips, eyes, denoting the site of inoculation. It is seen in syphilis and in trypanosomiasis.

Charcot's joints is a neurogenic arthropathy producing chronic progressive degeneration of one or more joints, which are relatively painless, with pronounced swelling, and is characterised by the formation of synovial effusion and of osteophytes, subluxation of articular surfaces and hypertrophy of the joint, leading to sensory disturbances. This type of joint is seen in tabes dorsalis, diabetic neuropathy, leprosy, syringomyelia, tumour or injury to the spinal cord or peripheral nerve, and in subacute combined degeneration of spinal cord.

Clutton's joints are asymmetrically distributed painless effusion of large joints with very little impairment o joint function, and are seen to occur in congenital syphilis.

Ducrey's skin test (Ito-Reenstierna reaction) is an intradermal test, given with *Haemophilus ducreyi* and a positive reaction gives rise to an indurated area, measuring 5 mm in diameter that occurs 48 hours after the injection. It is done for diagnosis of chancroid but appears nonspecific because a positive result may indicate a present as well as a past infection.

Frei test is an intradermal test for lymphogranuloma venereum. It is done by heat-inactivated egg-grown antigen. A positive result following 48-72 hours of the injection indicates an inflammatory nodule of more than 6 mm in diameter at the site of injection. It is however a nonspecific diagnostic test and a positive result may indicate that the person had lymphogranuloma venereum at any time in the past, while the test also gives certain cross-reaction.

Gumma (gummata) is soft tumour and consists of firm, sometimes partially hyalinised, irregular central portion, and coagulation necrosis. The tumour may be solitary or multiple, and may develop in the connective tissue, bone and other internal organs. The lesion may be seen in syphilis and in other treponematosis.

Herxheimer reaction (Jarisch-Herxheimer reaction, therapeutic shock) occurs in some cases of syphilis and other treponematosis following commencement of potent therapy. It results from sudden release of endotoxin of treponemas from initiation of potent therapeutic agent. The reaction may appear as localised or generalised form or both. In this reaction a rise of body temperature is usual within 12 hours of commencement of the treatment. The temperature may be slight or may reach up to 104°F (40°C). There may be malaise, headache, rigors, sweating, pain in the limbs, and flushing of the face. Development of sore throat is frequent. The primary chancre or the local lesions may be intensified, and a secondary skin rash may become worse or be apparent for the first time. It is a calculated unavoidable risk but does not cause any alarm, and is harmless. The reaction usually subsides within 12 to 24 hours, and confirms the potency of the therapeutic agent used. This reaction is seen in syphilis and in other treponematosis.

Hutchinson's incisors, a pathognomic sign of congenital syphilis, represented by the presence of oval shaped notch on the anteroposteriorly thickened and gapped permanent incisors, usually upper central.

Moon's molar (mulberry molar) represents hyperplastic molar, generally the first molar, with flat occlused surface (dome-shaped), and is seen in congenital syphilis.

Serological tests for syphilis (STS) include several serological tests, some with non-treponemal antigens, and others with treponemal antigens. The tests done with non-treponemal antigens, such as ***venereal disease research laboratory*** (***VDRL***), ***rapid plasma reagin*** (***RPR***), ***Wassermann reaction*** (***WR***) and ***Kahn test***, are however widely used because they are very easy to perform and least expensive but have the disadvantage of having some cross reaction with others, and of giving biological false results. A combination of tests (e.g. VDRL and WR) can however remove the confusions and hence be more suggestive though, it may be remembered, and they can show similar reaction with other treponemal infections as well. In this respect, serological tests done with treponemal antigens are more specific and indeed conclusive. Of them ***treponema pallidum immobilisation*** (***TPI***) test is more specific but extremely complicated and is relatively costly to perform, while most laboratories are not properly equipped to undertake such a test. ***Reiter protein complement fixation*** (***RPCF***) test, though somewhat less specific and sensitive than TPI, is simple to perform and quite cheap, and can therefore have a place as suitable alternative. ***Fluorescent treponemal antibody*** (***FTA***) test though similar but the modified type of it, ***fluorescent treponemal antibody-absorption*** (***FTA-ABS***) appears quite specific and sensitive for the diagnosis of syphilis. ***Treponema pallidum haemagglutination* (*TPHA*)** test is another similar test. Application of these tests however depends on the merit of the condition. A combination of test is however used for the purpose of cross checking. On the other hand, quite simple test like VDRL or RPR, which in fact is a modified method of VDRL, is used principally for screening purposes.

CHAPTER 11

Sexually Transmitted Disorders

GONORRHOEA

Caused by Gram-negative, often intracellular, diplococcus, *Neisseria gonorrhoeae* (gonococcus), it is principally responsible for producing an acutely contagious urethritis, **gonococcal urethritis**, more popularly known as ***gonorrhoea***. The organism is serologically heterogeneous and exhibits four morphological types of colony. Of them types 1 and 2 possess pili that can attach themselves to epithelial cells, and resist phagocytosis. Some gonococci, on the other hand, secrete protease that can break down surface IgA antibodies. *In vivo*, however, some IgM antibodies of human sera are found to be bactericidal for gonococci. The organism prospers in warm condition, in the mucus-secreting epithelia as in anterior urethra, accessory urethral glands, Bartholin's and Skene's glands, and uterine cervix. It can also invade squamous epithelium of the infantile vagina.

It is a most common infection, almost exclusively transmitted by sexual contact; it may involve vulval and vaginal epithelium (vulvovaginitis) through accidental contamination or by sexual assault in little girls before puberty. Involvement of rectum (proctitis) occurs in passive homosexual males and in females either as an extension of the infection from the genital tract or due to rectal intercourse. The infection may involve oral cavity due to oral coitus. Involvement of eyes occurs due to accidental contamination or, in cases of newborn, from contact of genital tract of the infected mother during the process of birth (ophthalmia neonatorum).

Women appear to be more susceptible to the infection than that is in the males. Although a substantial proportion of female cases may acquire the infection after a single exposure, only about one-fifth of male patients acquire the infection after a single exposure and a great proportion of them take several exposures (up to 4) to acquire the infection. Once urethritis has disappeared most male patients appear non-infectious. The infection can affect persons of any age, more particularly sexually active, and the highest incidence of the condition occurs in the age group of 15-20 years.

The incubation period of the infection is 1 to 5 days but may extend from 1 to 14 days.

Gonococci attack mucous membrane of the genitourinary tract and also other mucus membrane, get themselves attached to the surface epithelial cells and pili, cause suppuration, followed by chronic inflammation, and fibrosis. In males, the anterior urethra is involved first, with purulent, viscid, yellowish exudate, containing fresh and degenerated epithelial cells, extracellular and intracellular gonococci. Meatus appears hyperaemic, oedematous, and inflamed. In females, the labia and the region of Bartholin's and Skene's glands are often appearing red and swollen.

In acute urethritis, there are oedema of the mucosa, infiltration with polymorphonuclear leucocytes, distension of capillaries, extravasation of RBCs, and desquamation of lining mucosal cells. The infection spreads upward causing chronic suppuration followed by fibrosis, often with serious consequences. Bacteraemia and septicaemia may occur. Invasion of bloodstream produces metastatic complications.

Clinical Manifestations

The organisms nowadays do not usually exhibit the virulence as that used to be in the past. Whether a very wide, sometimes even indiscriminate, use of antibiotics for varieties of reasons or the environmental or other factor has any role to play with, the strains of the organism somehow appear less virulent. For this difference in virulence the symptoms of ***gonorrhoea*** now-a-days vary from mild to acute, to the extent some may even remain asymptomatic, more particularly the females.

In males, initially there is discomfort or tingling in the urethra, followed by burning on micturition, slight frequency of micturition, and a thick, creamy and purulent urethral discharge. The urethral meatus may be red and swollen. There may also be slight malaise, and perhaps tender inguinal lymphadenopathy.

Gonococcal balanitis or **gonococcal balanoposthitis** may be associated with the acute condition. If untreated, the infection passes down to the posterior urethra, and the condition then presents with severe dysuria, urgency and frequency in micturition, and passage of turbid urine, containing pus, threads and, sometimes, blood. The condition may later show local extension of the infection to involve the surrounding structures, and causes complications.

Bacteraemia and septicaemia may develop. Invasion of bloodstream may produce metastatic and general complications, such as arthritis, conjunctivitis, haemorrhagic skin rash, gonococcal dermatitis, keratosis blenorrhagica, meningitis and endocarditis. Urinary stricture and permanent sterility are the common complications on the condition in the late stage.

In cases of local extension, it may involve para-urethral sinuses and may penetrate the substance of the glans penis and open near the urethral meatus. Tyson's glands, situated on either side of frenum, may show unilateral or bilateral swelling and may appear as hard, tender bodies on palpation. Involvement to the glands of Litré may give rise to Litritis that causes a gleet and tiny swelling along the line of the urethra. In addition, or alternatively, the infection may cause peri-urethral abscess.

Involvement of the prostate may cause **gonococcal prostatitis**, which may be acute and presents with pyrexia, intense pain on defaecation and even acute retention of urine. The gland appears large, extremely tender and fluctuant, if there is any abscess formation. The symptoms are however less severe when the infection causes subacute prostatitis. Development of chronic prostatitis is nevertheless more common and causes persistent gleet but gross enlargement and marked tenderness of the gland are not so obvious.

The infection may also involve seminal vesicles (**gonococcal vesiculitis**) and gives rise to bloodstained semen.

Involvement of epididymis causes **gonococcal epididymitis**, causing painful inflammation and swelling of the epididymis, but the testis appears to be markedly resistant. Therefore **gonococcal epididymo-orchitis** develops only rarely, and gives rise to extremely painful inflammation and swelling have the both epididymis and testis, with fever.

Gonococcal cystitis may accompany posterior urethritis or prostatitis, and causes frequent desire of micturition with passing of very little urine, in addition.

In females, no less than one-third cases may remain symptomfree. Even when there is any symptom, it is usually less marked in them than that is in males, and often appears confusion due to the existence of several other conditions that involve female genitalia. The patient may however present with vaginal discharge, dysuria, increased frequency of micturition, and backache or pain in the lower abdomen. Patients may also complain of spotting following intercourse. There is enlarged and tender inguinal lymphadenopathy. Oedema and inflammation of the urethral meatus is often much less conspicuous but abscess formation with bulging of Bartholin's and Skene's glands is obvious. Labia appear reddened and oedematous. Gonococci are the most common cause of pelvic inflammatory disease (PID) in young women. In addition, there is acute cervicitis with mucopurulent or purulent cervical discharge and, in some cases, acute cervical erosion.

Local extension of the infection may involve surrounding structures. Bacteraemia and septicaemia may occur. Invasion of bloodstream may produce metastatic and general complications such as iritis, conjunctivitis, gonococcal dermatitis, keratosis blenorrhagica, meningitis, and endocarditis. Infertility is a common sequel of the condition.

In local involvement, there may be **gonococcal bartholinitis**, which may be acute with very painful and tender swelling on one side of the vulva, and the Bartholin's gland appear grossly enlarged and fluctuant. Otherwise, the infection may be chronic in which the glandular swelling may come and go periodically and appears less tender.

In cases of involvement of cervix uteri, the condition frequently causes **gonococcal cervicitis**, with mucopurulent or purulent discharge and, in some, with acute cervical erosion. Spreading of the infection to the Fallopian tube may cause **gonococcal salpingitis** with severe bilateral or unilateral lower abdominal pain, fever, headache, and rigidity and tenderness on the affected side of the lower abdomen, but when the involvement is chronic, it gives rise to episodes of, sometimes colicky, lower abdominal pain during the menstrual periods, which may be irregular and often associated with severe menorrhagia. Development of salpingitis may seal off the tubes, resulting pyosalpinx. The condition may however rarely produce **gonococcal perihepatitis** in women with gonococcal salpingitis, giving rise to severe pain and local tenderness in the upper quadrant of abdomen, accompanied by high fever but without any sign and symptom of toxaemia.

Gonococcal pharyngitis develops from oral coitus. The condition is asymptomatic. Otherwise, it gives rise to sore throat and difficulties in swallowing. The pharynx and tonsillar region appear red and show mucopurulent exudates.

When **gonococcal vulvovaginitis** develops, underwear will show staining. The patient complains of soreness on the vulva or around the anus, dysuria, and frequency of micturition, discomfort on defecation. Vagina appears swollen and inflamed. There is greenish discharge from the vagina and urethra, and redness of perineal region, perhaps with discharge from anus.

Involvement of eye may occur in both sexes when the condition is known as **gonococcal ophthalmia** but **ophthalmia neonatorum** when it occurs in newborn, and may involve either one or both eyes. Conjunctivitis presents with conjunctival congestion and severe irritation. Ophthalmia neonatorum gives rise to redness and oedematous conjunctivae and eyelids, with purulent discharge. In severe cases, keratitis may develop, followed by cornel ulceration, perforation of eyeball and panophthalmia.

Rectal coitus in both sexes can produce **gonococcal proctitis**. The patient then presents with discomfort, soreness, or pain in the anus during defecation, but otherwise the patient may only notice staining on the underwear due to anal discharge.

In a small proportion of cases, gonorrhoea may become systemic and cause dermatitis, arthritis, tenosynovitis, myositis, fascitis, bursitis, and septicaemia (for example, endocarditis, meningitis) in both sexes as complications.

Diagnosis

History of sexual exposure may be a helpful guide. Urine is turbid, and contains pus, threads and, also, blood, in cases of involvement of posterior urethra. Two glasses or three-glass test at the bedside can make a presumptive diagnosis of anterior and posterior urethritis. Urethral discharge may be apparent. The causative organism can be identified from the exudate, but this may be quite tricky and may need repeated examination in female cases. No serological test is however available for the diagnosis of the condition but, in late cases, complement fixation test may be helpful.

The condition is differentiated from bacterial, fungal and chemical urethritis, nonspecific urethritis, trichomoniasis, nonspecific vaginitis, senile vaginitis, nonspecific vulvitis, mycotic vulvovaginitis, cervicitis, non-gonococcal salpingitis, and leucorrhoea.

Cases of vulvovaginitis in young girls are differentiated from threadworm infection, trichomoniasis, foreign in the vagina, and trauma or excessive fornication due to masturbation.

The condition also needs to be differentiated from bacterial infection, chemical irritant and trauma in cases of eye involvement.

In all cases, however, identification of *Neisseria gonorrhoeae* makes the differentiation quite easy.

Treatment

Uncomplicated cases are most effectively treated with single dose of acrosoxacin, 300 mg orally, or spectinomycin, 2 g (4 g in females) by IM injection, both of which have most specific antibacterial activity against *Neisseria gonorrhoeae*. Other drugs which are recommended for the purpose include cefixime, 600 mg as single dose orally, ceftriaxone, 250 mg as single dose by IM injection, ciprofloxacin, 500 mg as single dose orally (not recommended for pregnant women), and streptomycin, 2 g as single dose by IM injection. Alternatively, the treatment may be given with kanamycin, 2 g as single dose by IM injection, co-trimoxazole, containing trimethoprim, 800 mg, and sulphamethoxazole, 4 g, as single dose orally for consecutive 23 days.

Recent increasing emergence of gonococcus resistant to a large number of antibiotics may create enormous problem in the management and control of the condition. This is more so as sensitivity study of the organisms takes much time that one can ever safely afford to spare for the cure of gonococcal infection. In such circumstances it is highly advisable to give more than one potent antibiotic simultaneously and to follow up the cases so that appropriate alternate medication can be given. On the other hand, less responsive cases may need further treatment, while the late conditions may require prolonged therapy.

Acquiring syphilis concurrently with gonorrhoea is not unusual. Emphasis therefore needs to be made that many antibiotics for gonococcal infection can, in fact, mask in incubating syphilis. Selection of antibiotics therefore requires great cautiousness so that the incubating syphilis cannot go underground without being recognised.

Following cure of the condition strict and regular follow up and serological tests for syphilis are required.

CHANCROID

Chancroid (**soft sore, soft chancre, ulcus molle, chancre mon**) is caused by short, slender, aerobic, Gram-negative rod with rounded ends, *Haemophilus ducreyi*, occurring in groups or clumps. Transmission of infection occurs through sexual intercourse, though accidental spread is also possible. Infectivity of the condition persists as long as there is ulcer. Transmission from mother to foetus or during delivery is not however possible.

The condition is usually common in highly promiscuous and in urban poor population. It affects more men than women. There also exists an asymptomatic carrier state.

Its incubation period is usually 3 to 7 or up to 10 days, but the period may also be shortened or delayed.

The organism gains entry through the skin or mucus membrane, and produces ulceration at the site of inoculation. There is superficial necrosis and ulceration consisting disintegrating leucocytes and red cells, beneath which there is granulation tissue with hyperplasia of endothelial cells and mixed inflammatory reaction within and about the vessel wall, and beneath this there is more chronic inflammatory reaction with fibroblastic proliferation and infiltration with mononuclear leucocytes.

Clinical Manifestations

A small vesicle, later changing to painful circular or oval papule or pustule appears at the site of inoculation which may be on the foreskin, frenum of shaft of the penis and, occasionally, inside the urethra in man, and labia, vulva, perineal region and, more rarely, on the cervix of woman. Later, the papule or pustule breaks down to for a soft, non-indurated, painful, irregularly shaped ulcer, often multiple, with ragged undermined edges (Fig. 11.1). The ulcer later spread by extension or through autoinoculation.

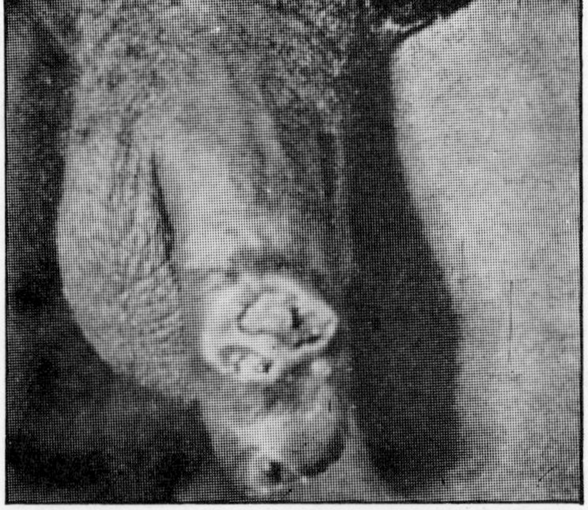

Figure 11.1. Multiple ulcers on shaft of penis in chancroid.

In cases of men, there may be tenderness in the groin. Women cases may have no symptom, or there may be pain on micturition or defecation, rectal bleeding, pain on intercourse or vaginal bleeding.

Ulcers disappear even without treatment usually in about a month but may also continue for up to 12 weeks. In about one-half case painful inguinal lymphadenopathy develops in one or both groins. The lymph nodes finally matted together, and the overlying skin appears red and hot. The lymph nodes may fluctuate, and may lead to suppuration, sinus or large ulcer formation. The condition may be associated with other sexually transmitted diseases.

The condition may however produce gangrene of the external genitalia, haemorrhage, urethral stricture, and phimosis or paraphimosis as complications.

Diagnosis

Diagnosis of the condition is generally based on clinical manifestations. History of suspected sexual exposure may also be available. The causative organism can be isolated from smear and culture of pus for bubo or material from edges of the ulcer. Intradermal test, Ducrey's skin test, may be an aid but carry little diagnostic value because the test becomes positive 1 to 3 weeks after the infection is being acquired, and may remain positive for years.

Is its differentiated from granuloma inguinale where there is no inguinal lymphadenopathy, and it causes relatively painless ulcer with bright beefy-red base, while examination of material collected from edge of the ulcer show Donovan bodies. Chancre of primary syphilis may mimic the condition but the lesion is usually painless with a hard base, and the enlarged lymph nodes are generally painless with a hard base, and the enlarged lymph nodes show no tendency of matting together, while lesion is found teeming with *Treponema pallidum*. The buboes in lymphogranuloma venereum are multilocular, and the condition begins with constitutional symptoms, the causative organism may be isolated and the condition gives a positive complement fixation test and the skin test (Frei test). Herpes genitalis is differentiated for having multiple shallow ulcers, vesicles and erythematous papules, and the enlarged inguinal lymph nodes are not matted together, nor show any tendency for suppuration, while the lesions show recurrences. In septic adenitis there are inflamed skin lesions below the level of the umbilicus, and in septic scabies, signs of scabies are present and the mite or the ova may be detected.

Treatment

The condition is effectively treated with erythromycin, 500 mg three times daily orally for 7 days. Alternatively, the patient may be given sparfloxacin, 400 mg orally on first day followed by 200 mg once daily for further 5-10 days, ciprofloxacin, 500 mg as single dose orally, ceftriaxone, 250 mg as single dose by IM injection, or co-trimoxazole, consisting trimepthoprim, 160 mg, and sulphamethoxazole, 800 mg, twice daily orally for 7 days. Ciprofloxacin is however avoided in pregnant women, while the condition associated with HIV is better given erythromycin and co-trimoxazole, as stated above.

The patient is given analgesic, such as aspirin, 600-900 mg, or codeine, 10-60 mg, as required, every four hours orally, for relief of pain. The buboes may also need aseptic aspiration.

The patient is also given supportive treatment as required.

GRANULOMA INGUINALE

The chronic relapsing disorder of venereal in origin is also known as **Donovanosis** and **ulcerating granuloma of pudenda**. The infection is caused due to Gram-positive coccobacillus, related to Klebsiellae, known as *Calymmatobacterium* (*Donovani*) *granulomatis*. The infection is usually transmitted through sexual contact. Extra-genital infection is uncommon.

It is common in the tropics and sub-tropics, in men than in women, and is prevalent in Hindus than in Muslims.

The incubation period of the infection is 8-80 days.

It produces inflammatory papule that increases in size, ulcerates, and spreads. Histologically, it gives a nonspecific inflammatory picture with granulation tissue crowded with a large number of plasma cells, macrophages, and polymorphonuclear leucocytes. There are large vacuolated macrophages containing intracellular, but may also be extracellular, *Donovan bodies* within the monocytes.

Clinical Manifestations

It begins insidiously with infiltrated papule on the skin or mucous membrane of genitalia or perineal region or, very rarely, on extra-genital site, such as lip. In men, the lesion very commonly occurs on the penis or glans penis but at the labia in women. The lesion enlarges and soon sloughs, leaving a shallow, sharply demarcated ulcer (Fig. 11.2), with a bright beefy-red friable base of granulomatous tissue. The ulcer spreads by continuity. Autoinoculation of the infection may also occur. Of ten there is bad-smelling and bloodstained discharges from the ulcer. Systemic manifestations are however usually absent Despite the extensiveness of the lesion, the condition is least painful, while the women may have no symptom There is however no lymphadenopathy. Systemic manifestations are usually absent, but secondary infection is common. Scar formation and healing may occur. Women cases however frequently remain asymptomatic.

Without treatment the condition may erode genitalia or block the urethra. In addition, the condition produces lymphatic obstruction and elephantiasis due to extensive fibrosis and scarring.

Diagnosis

It is diagnosed clinically, and is confirmed by identification of Donovan bodies in the scrapings from the edge of the lesion and from biopsy. Serological tests are of no help. A history of suspected sexual exposure may be available.

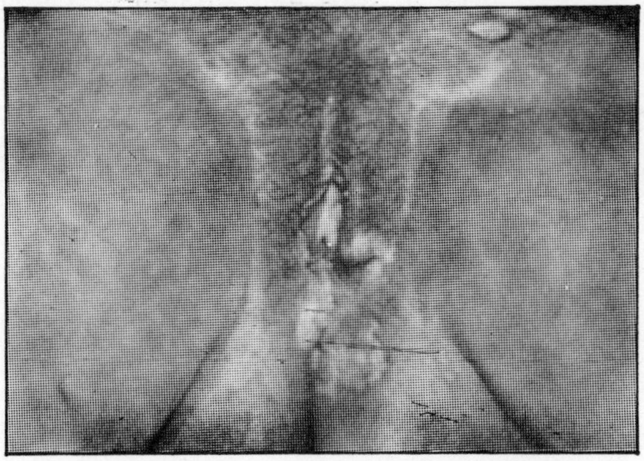

Figure. 11.2. Granuloma inguinale.

The condition is differentiated from condylomata lata of secondary syphilis (*c.f.* flat, moist, raised, round or oval papule, with firm, non-tender lymphadenopathy, and presence of *Treponema pallidum*), primary syphilis (*c.f.* painless, indolent chancre, non-tender regional lymphadenopathy, and presence of Treponema pallidum), chancroid (*c.f.* tender and suppurative inguinal adenitis), lymphogranuloma venereum (*c.f.* enlarged inguinal lymph nodes matted together into a tender, sausage shaped fluctuating mass, with constitutional symptoms, and positive intradermal Frie test and complement fixation test), cutaneous tuberculosis (c.f. indurated nodule or plaque that ulcerate with raised edges and presence of regional lymphadenitis which may finally break down), and from genital tuberculosis (*c.f.* multiple, small indurated ulcers covering the vulva which later change to form serpinginous ulcer with oedematous edge and yellowish base).

Treatment

The patient can effectively be treated with potent antibiotic but that can also mask incubating syphilis. In choosing the drug a conscientious approach is therefore needed to avoid the masking problem. The patient can therefore be ideally treated with streptomycin, 1 g every twelve hours by IM injection for 21 days. Otherwise, the patient may be given tetracycline or erythromycin, 500 mg every six hours orally for, at least, a fortnight. It is however preferable to continue the treatment until clinical cure is achieved.

Surveillance of the patients after recovery for six months is highly desirable.

SYPHILIS

Motile, slender, spiral organism, *Treponema pallidum*, causes it. Sexual coitus is the commonest method of transmission of the infection. Infection also spreads through intimate bodily contact (for example, kissing), through the site of previous or coexisting trauma (such as minor skin or mucosal lesion), blood transfusion and, rarely, from sharing drinking cups or glasses, pipes and other intimate objects contaminated by the infected person. The condition may also occur as occupational hazard amongst the medical and laboratory personnel.

An infected individual may remain contagious for 3 to 5 years since acquiring the infection but becomes less infectious after the second year of infection, and after the expiry of fifth year, the condition is rarely transmissible sexually.

STS (serological tests for syphilis) are negative during the incubation period and may remain so for a varying length of time, though the patient remains contagious during all these time.

Over one-third of early cases of acquired syphilis may perhaps progress spontaneously to complete cure without any treatment.

Its incubation period is 9 to 90 days but usually between 17 and 28 days, means being 21 days.

Untreated infected women, when become pregnant, can transmit the infection through placenta after third or fourth month of pregnancy and can thus infect the foetus, causing *congenital syphilis*. The newborn can also acquire the infection during birth from direct contact with early genital lesion of the mother. Pregnant women may however remain most contagious to the foetus during the first 5 years of acquiring the infection. As times passes the opportunity of transmission of infection to the foetus becomes progressively lessen until late stage of the condition. In infected and untreated mothers, the child may escape the infection, or there is miscarriage usually after 12th to 16th week of gestation, or stillbirth of macerated child. Otherwise, the child may born with syphilis, or may develop signs of syphilis during the first few months of life or even years after.

In its natural course, over one-fourth of early syphilis cases perhaps progress spontaneously to complete cure even without any treatment.

For descriptive purposes acquired syphilis is arbitrarily divided into three stages: primary, secondary and tertiary (late), with a latent phase, though, in practice, one stage commonly overlaps another, for descriptive purposes. The *primary stage* is characterised by the development of lesion at the site of inoculation. *Secondary stage* develops after 1 to 6 months but usually within 6 to 12 weeks from the appearance of primary lesion, and is characterised by generalised lesions. In untreated cases, both the primary and secondary stages usually disappear in 3 to 1[illegible] months. Then there is symptom-free *latent phase*, which may last for 2 years, but rarely less, [illegible] 20 years or more, and is characterised by positive standard STS, negative cerebrospinal fluid (CSF) tests, and complete absence of any clinical evidence of the condition. This is followed by *tertiary* or *late stage*, characterised by gummatous and other destructive lesion.

Following inoculation *Treponema pallidum* spreads rapidly by the lymphatic to the regional lymph nodes and by the bloodstream to all parts of the body. In the lymphatic and perivascul[illegible] lymphatic vessels there infiltration with small lymphocytes, plasma cells, epitheloid cells and giant cells. Later, fibrosis occurs. Proliferation of the intima of the blood vessels develops, leading to obliterative endarteritis, and gives rise to tissue induration, necrosis, and finally replacement of fibrous scar tissue.

In the primary stage, necrosis of the surface of the lesions results to erosion and ulceration. The chancre presents with an intense mononuclear leucocytic infiltration, chiefly of plasma cells with macrophages and lymphocytes.

In the secondary stage, the epithelium covering the papule becomes necrotic and leads to fine scaling.

In the later stage, tissue hypersensitivity may develop and produce widespread necrosis of granulomatous type. Inflammatory lesion may later lead to degenerative changes.

In tertiary lesions, gummas develop containing coagulated necrotic material in the centre, and plump or palisade macrophages and fibroblasts surrounded by large number of mononuclear leucocytes, chiefly plasma cells in the margins. The gummata cause impairment of blood supply and thus lead to considerable tissue destruction. Bone involvement causes osteochondritis and periosteitis. Osteomyelitis may also develop. Gummas may develop in the bone marrow cavity, causing destruction of bony tissue. New bone is then deposited on the surface of the bone, and sclerotic tissue replaces the destroyed one.

In the testes and epididymes, there may be diffuse interstitial inflammation with oedema and infiltration with lymphocytes and plasma cells.

In cardiovascular involvement, it begins as aortitis around the root of the aorta, extending up to the mouth of the great vessels arising from the arch. The tunica intima is raised into patches, causing fine transverse wrinkling of the intervening tissue. It produces saccular, fusiform, and cylindroids types of aneurysm, which begins in the adventitia of the aorta, particularly in the vasa vasorum, and causes obliterating endarteritis, with lymphocytes and plasma cell infiltrates. The lesion further leads to ischaemic injury in the media of the aorta. Aortitis develops in the aortic wall distal to the aortic cusps and spreads horizontally around the rest of the aorta, extending up to the mouth of the great vessels arising from the arch. The tunica intima is raised into patches, causing fine transverse wrinkling of the intervening tissue, and produce valvular insufficiency. There are sclerosis and contracture of the aortic cusps, widening and dilatation of the vessel, and narrowing of the openings of the coronary ostia from inflammatory scarring.

There is also obliterative endarteritis with perivascular infiltration by lymphocytes and plasma cells. In central nervous system (CNS) involvement, there is obliterative endarteritis with a perivascular inflammatory reaction predominantly by plasma cells. There is thickening of meninges with lymphocytic cell infiltration. In cases of general paralysis of insane, parenchymal invasion of the treponema causes loss of cortical neurones with proliferation of microglial and glosses. In tabes dorsalis, there is damage of the sensory nerves in the dorsal roots, which show loss of both axons and myelin, with pallor and trophy in the dorsal columns of the spinal cord.

PRIMARY SYPHILIS

It usually presents with a primary sore, known as **primary chancre**, that develops at the sire of inoculation, usually papers on the external genitalia (Fig. 11.3) or on the adjacent skin surface but may also occur on the cervix, vagina, eyelid, lip, finger, tongue, nipple or at anal orifice from rectal coitus. Primary chancre may also develop extra-genitally on the eyelid, lip (Fig. 11.4), tongue, finger and nipple. The lesion develops as a small macule, changing to papule, which ulcerates into a clear ulcer due to erosion of surface epithelium, following which the lesion heals spontaneously, even without any treatment. The chancre may be indurated or non-indurated, and feel hard or palpation. It is usually single but may also be multiple (Fig. 11.5), especially on the contiguous surfaces. The lesion is painless and indolent. It does not bleed easily but expresses clear, colourless serum on pressure. In some cases the lesion may be trivial and thus, may remain unrecognised. However, of secondary infection occurs, the chancre may be painful and the ulceration may be deep and severe, and along with this, but usually after a few days of appearance of the chancre, the regional lymph nodes become painlessly enlarged, giving rise to a firm and a rubbery feeling.

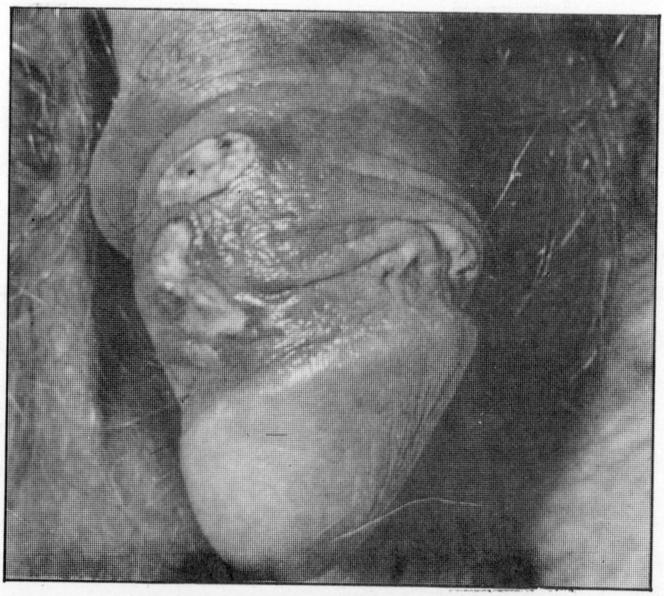

Figure 11.3. Primary chancre on penis.

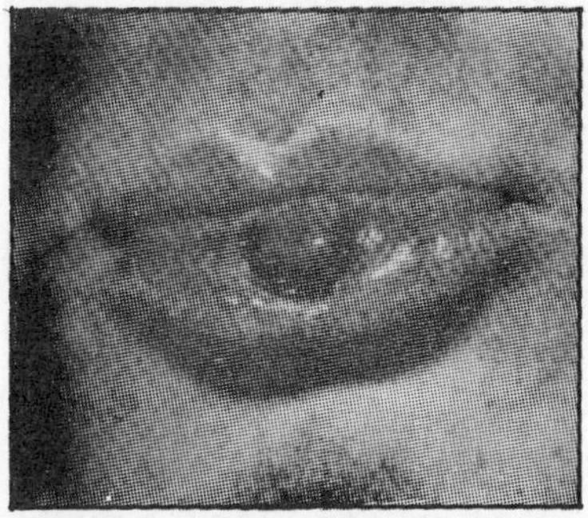

Figure 11.4. Primary chancre on lip.

Primary chancre on the buccal mucosa however appears as a chronic or indurated ulcer, and that on the finger as a typical ulceration, or as a chronic whitlow with minimum pus formation.

Primary chancre is however missed when the infection is acquired from blood transfusion or needle prick.

The chancre may heal spontaneously, but the painless enlargement of the lymph nodes may persist for sometime.

The condition may lead to chronicity, relapses and secondary infection.

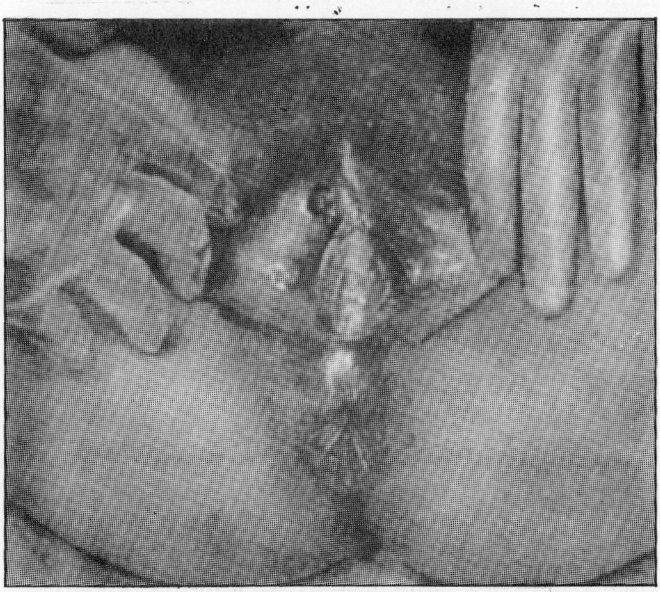

Figure 11.5. Multiple ulcerative chancres on labia.

Diagnosis

Diagnosis of the condition is based on clinical grounds, supported by a history of suspected sexual contact, and is confirmed by identification of the organism by dark-ground microscopy from the clear serum exudate of the base of the lesion. Specimen obtained from puncture of the nearest lymph node can also be used for the identification of the causative organism. This is of special value particularly in those cases where topical antiseptic or antibiotic preparation has been used on the chancre, resulting reduction of the number of organism in the lesion. If no treponema is detected, the test should be repeated emphasising the fact all genital ulcers are syphilitic in origin, until it is not otherwise proved. At this stage STS are however only of limited value and may remain negative for a variable length of time.

It is differentiated from chancroid (c.f. short incubation period, often with multiple sores, and tender and suppurative inguinal lymphadenitis), condylomata accuminata (*c.f.* soft genital warts, pedunculated, with no involvement of regional lymph nodes), granuloma inguinale (*c.f.* shallow, sharply demarcated ulcer with bright beefy-red friable base of granulomatous tissue, and no lymphadenopathy), lymphogranuloma venereum (*c.f.* tender lymphadenitis show tendency of matting together to form sausage-shaped mass), and herpes genitalis or progenitalis (*c.f.* vesiculoulcerative lesions show recurrences, and painful bilateral inguinal lymphadenopathy).

It is differentiated for lymphadenopathy from tuberculous lymphadenitis (*c.f.* affection of inguinal lymph nodes is rare, and causes caseation and liquefaction of the lymph nodes, and formation of 'cold abscess'), and from traumatic sore (*c.f.* history of trauma, and painful adenitis).

The condition may also need to be differentiated for oral lesions from herpes simplex infection, Vincent's infection, agranulocytosis and neoplasms, and from anal fissures and haemorrhoids for anal lesion.

Treatment

Penicillin still remains to be the drug of choice. The patient is therefore effectively treated with benzathine penicillin G, 2.4 million U as single dose (1.2 million U in each buttock), or aqueous procaine penicillin G, 1.2 million U daily, by IM injection for 10 days. In cases of intolerance to penicillin in men and non-pregnant women, treatment may be given with doxycycline, 100 mg twice daily, or tetracycline, 500 mg four times daily, orally for 15 days. Pregnant women and individuals hypersensitive to penicillin are given erythromycin, 500 mg four times daily orally for 15 days, and the pregnant women are advised to bring their babies within first seven days of birth for screening for congenital syphilis.

No additional treatment is required for the local lesion except in cases of secondary infection or delay in healing of the wound. In such cases topical antiseptic my be given for local use.

During commencement of treatment some patients may give rise to Herxheimer reaction (Jarisch-Herxheimer reaction, therapeutic shock). The reaction is usually transient and, no doubt inconvenient but in no way serious. Nor does it call for interruption of treatment. Rather this is an evidence of potency of the therapeutic agent used. Patients must therefore be cautioned of this anticipated reaction prior to commencing the treatment.

After treatment, ideally follow up of the patient is maintained with STS at monthly interva for the first 6 months, then quarterly for a year, and six monthly for another year. Alternativel rapid plasma reagin (RPR) test at 3, 6 and 12 months after the initial treatment can also confirm the cure.

SECONDARY SYPHILIS

This stage is characterised by the development of several lesions such s skin rash, mucous patches, generalised adenitis and condylomata lata but not all cases may show them all. Symptoms in this stage are therefore variable and seldom severe, and appear a few weeks (but may be delayed by 1 to 6 months also) after the appearance of primary chancre. A healing chancre may therefore be seen but many patients, particularly women, may not give any history even or may be fully unaware of that. However, there may be mild constitutional symptoms of malaise, fever, headache, sore throat, hoarseness, and pain of bones and joints. Some patients may also present with acute meningitis.

It may present with widespread skin rash, known as ***syphilide***, mucous patches, condylomata lata and generalised lymphadenopathy, but not all cases do however equally show all these manifestations.

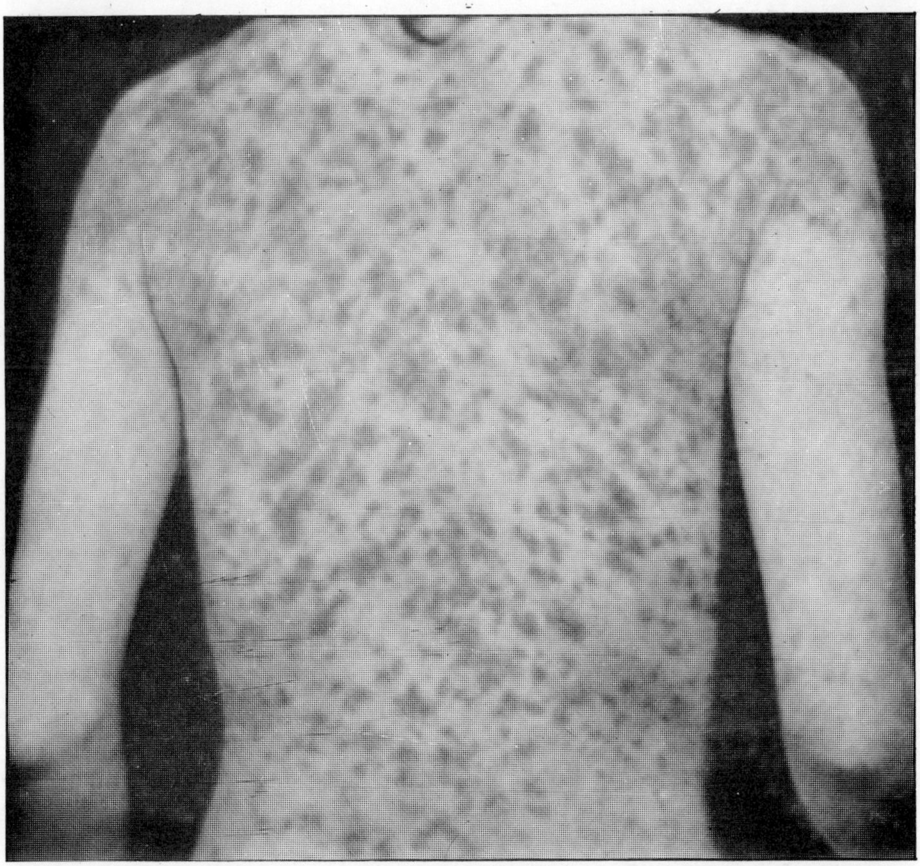

Figure 11.6. Maculopapular syphilide on back.

The condition gives rise to a wide variety of skin rash and the syphilides may assume macular, papular, maculopapular (Fig. 11.6), follicular (Fig. 11.7), psoriasiform, rupial, pustular, ulcerative and priliferative, but often macular or papular. The rashes are non-itching, do not fade on pressure, and are symmetrical in distribution, occurring anywhere in the body, including palms (Fig. 11.8), but mostly on the chest, abdomen, back and arms. Sometimes the skin lesions may be very faint and sparsely distributed, or may appear for the first time or may become intensified due to Jarisch-Herxheimer reaction. The lesions heal after a few weeks, leaving residual pigmentation or depigmentation.

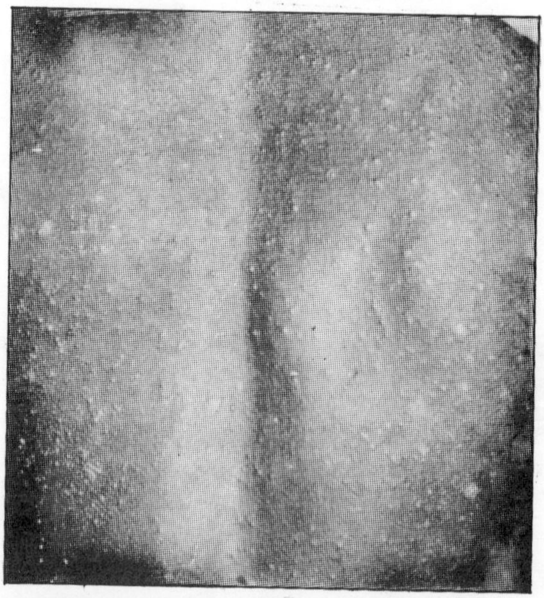

Figure 11.7. Follicular syphilide on back.

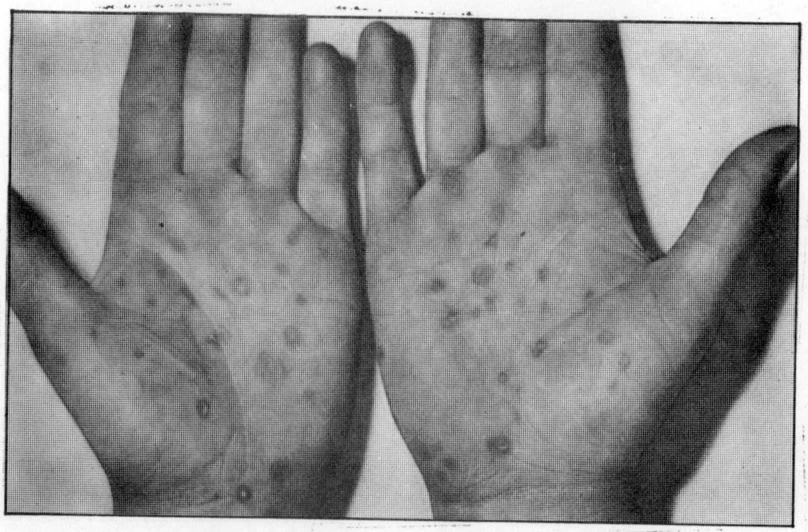

Figure. 11.8. Secondary syphilide on palms.

Mucous patches are however more liable to occur in cases of relapses following treatment but can also develop as a general manifestation. The patches may be seen on any part of the mouth, on the lips, vulva, cervix, glans penis, prepuce, and just inside the anus. The lesions form as white patches, the surface of which is easily eroded to leave superficial erosive lesions. When the mucous patches develop on the larynx, they may cause chronic sore throat or hoarseness of voice. Otherwise, the mucous lesions do not give rise to any symptom, and in absence of secondary infection the lesions are quite painless. The lesions generally persist for weeks, but may also be very transient in some cases.

Another form of lesion, **condylomata lata**, occurs as moist, flat, raised, round or oval papule of varying size. Its colour varies between greyish, reddish-brown, and violet. The lesions may occur on moist areas, usually around the genitalia (Fig. 11.9 and 11.10) and anus but also at other sites such as axillae, groins, beneath the pendulous breasts, between the toes, and at the angle of mouth (Fig. 11.11). These secondary lesions are extremely infectious, and the moist lesions are found teeming with *Treponema pallidum*.

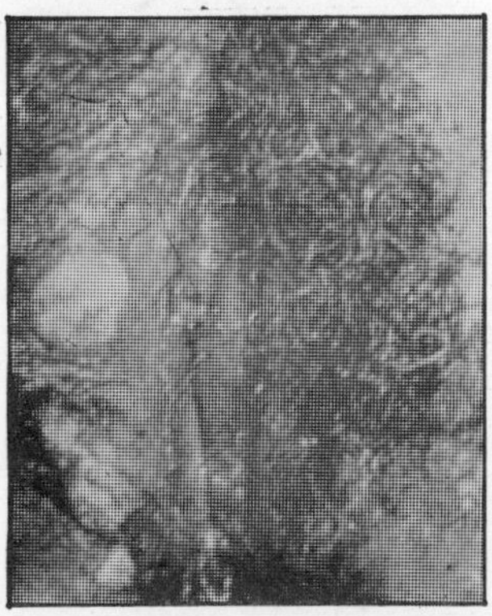

Figure 11.9. Condylomata lata on labia.

Secondary lesions are extremely infectious, and the moist lesions are teemed with *Treponema pallidum*. Generalised firm, non-tender lymphadenitis is also common. The lymph nodes feel rubbery and discrete, and remain palpable for some weeks. Some cases may present with splenomegaly, hepatomegaly and jaundice, and nephritis with albuminuria and a few red cells and casts in urine, and acute uveitis affecting one or both eye (in late stage). There may also be patchy alopecia, onychia or paronychia, persistent headache, depression, cranial nerve palsies, migrating polyarthralgia, painless effusion in the joints and involvement of tendon sheaths, nocturnal bone pain but without any radiological abnormalities, and localised periosteitis. Some cases may also present with loss of body weight.

The condition may lead to relapses or chronicity as complication.

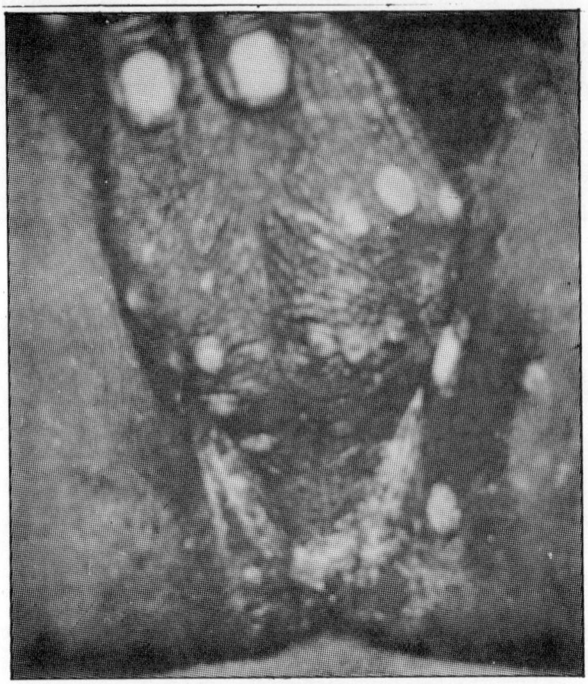

Figure 11.10. Condylomata lata on scrotum and perineum.

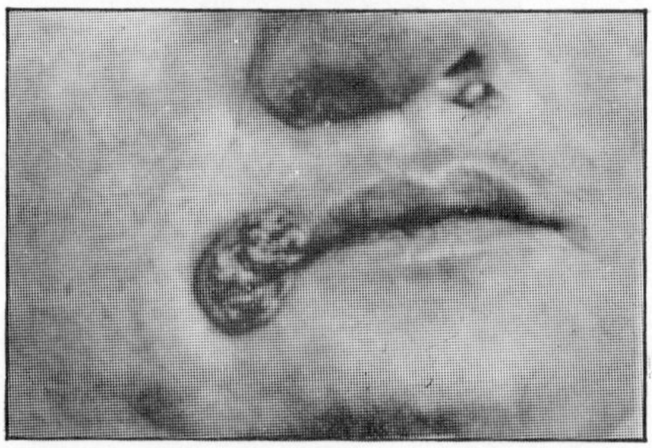

Figure 11.11. Split pea-like condylomata lata at mouth angle.

Diagnosis

Peripheral blood shows leucocytosis with lymphocytosis, and lowered haemoglobin. STS are positive in most cases. Identification of the causative organism by dark-field microscopy is possible from the cutaneous and mucous membrane lesions.

Depending on the presenting features the condition may need to be differentiated from a large number of conditions.

The condition is differentiated for cutaneous rashes from lichen planus which has violaceous, flat-topped or umbilicated, smooth, glistening, slightly raised lesions with puncta or streaks, pruritus and negative STS; from erythema multiforme which shows slightly raised, flat-topped papules or oedematous macules, wheals, vesicles or tense bullae, and the lesions tend to spread to the periphery and fuse together, with itching, burning sensation and soreness; from psoriasis which presents with well-demarcated, symmetrically distributed lesions, covered with greyish-white or silvery-white scales which when removed on pressure leave bleeding point behind; from measles which is a childhood disease, gives rise to rashes that are soft and velvety on touch and fades on pressure and presents with diagnostic Koplik's spots; from rubella which gives rise to fine, pink, slightly raised maculopapular rash, and characteristically shows enlarged suboccipital, posterior cervical and postauricular lymph nodes; from drug eruptions in which a history of exposure to an offending drug is always available and the rash subsides following withdrawal of the drug. The condition is also differentiated from urticaria which causes intense itching and burning sensation and gives rise to the development of wheals with rings of erythema and oedema; from scabies that causes intense itching and shows the presence of burrows and mite or ova of *Sarcoptes scabies*; and from acne vulgaris which has lesions with comedones.

The mucous patches and moist lesions may cause confusion and is differentiated from primary chancre that presents with painless, indurated or non-indurated papule, feels hard on palpation or ulcer which does not bleed easily but expresses clear, colourless serum on pressure; from aphthous ulcer that shows shallow erosion with slightly raised margin, covered with coagulated tissue fluid and surrounded by narrow hyperaemic zone and gives negative STS; from diphtheria which presents with dirty white or greyish-yellow pseudomembrane on the tonsils and pharyngeal wall which when removed leave raw bleeding surface with reformation of membrane, and gives rise to constitutional symptoms; from Vincent's infection that gives rise to pinched-out lesions covered with greyish membrane and the lesion bleeds on slight pressure or irritation and also gives rise to pain on swallowing or talking; from tonsillitis that presents with prodromal symptoms, oedematous and hyperaemic tonsil, sore throat and pain and from agranulocytosis that gives rise to painful mucosal ulcers associated with dysphagia.

For condylomata lata the condition is differentiated from genital warts (condylomata accuminata) that presents with soft, moist, cauliflower-like pedunculated growth, shows no *Treponema pallidum*, and is diagnosed by biopsy; from pemphigus vegetans that presents with fungoid vegetation in which the lesions tend to coalesce to form large patches and shows recurrences and prolonged remissions; from perianal; tags which present with small, small, pedunculated protrusion of skin with no symptom, and neither show *Treponema pallidum*, nor give positive STS; from haemorrhoids in which the prolapse occurs initially during defaecation and the condition is associated with bleeding but later the prolapse may be permanent, and the diagnosis is confirmed by rectal examination; and from molluscum contagiosum that presents with smooth, pink or white, waxy, umbilicated papules and the matter expressed there from shows inclusion bodies.

The lymphadenopathy of the condition is differentiated from tuberculous lymphadenitis that presents with evidence of tuberculosis elsewhere in the body, shows typical histopathological picture and gives a positive tuberculin test; from infectious mononucleosis that gives rise to firm, discrete, elastic, enlarged lymph nodes with constitutional symptoms and shows detectable serum IgM antibodies; from Hodgkin's lymphoma that gives rise to painless, discrete, firm, rubbery, enlarged superficial lymph glands with freely moveable overlying skin, and the lymph node biopsy shows Reed-Strenberg cells; and from lymphatic leukaemia that presents with firm, rubbery, discrete, enlarged superficial lymph nodes, and shows characteristic blood and bone marrow picture.

Treatment

Management of the condition and follow up of the patients are same as those specified under primary syphilis but a larger dose of penicillin is preferred. For example, the patient is given procaine penicillin G, 4.8 million U as single dose or 2.4 u initially followed by one or several IM injections totalling to another 2.4 million U by IM injection. In cases of CNS involvement, the patient is given larger doses of short-acting penicillin, such as aqueous procaine penicillin G, 20 million U daily in two or four divided doses by IV injection for 10 to 20 days.

LATENT SYPHILIS

This is a quiescent stage of the condition in which the patient does not show any clinical evidence of the condition. If not diagnosed earlier, most cases are however identified accidentally on routine serological examinations for other purposes or general medical check ups. Suspected cases are however cautiously tested by standard STS, supplemented by additional test with treponemal antigens and, if found infected, are treated as per treatment schedule mentioned below under tertiary syphilis.

TERTIARY (LATE) SYPHILIS

This stage of tertiary or late syphilis may occur at any time after secondary syphilis, sometimes even after years of symptom-free latency. The stage may however develop much earlier in cases that have been treated inadequately. The characteristic lesion it produces is solitary or multiple gummas. The lesion is large, infiltrative, destructive and indolent, with a tendency to spread at the periphery and to heal at the centre, and is distributed asymmetrically. The lesions do not spare any part of the body and may occur on the skin, mucous membrane, bone or viscera. Solitary skin lesion starts as painless subcutaneous nodule, which becomes enlarged, attached to the overlying skin and eventually ulcerates with punched-out edges, often with yellow slough covering the floor. When it is multiple, it occurs as a group of small painless nodulo-ulcerated lesions (Fig. 11.12), indurated on deep palpation, and tends to form raised, active, area of crusted papules and nodules with a circular or serpiginous outline, and scarring and atrophy in the centre (Fig. 11.13). The ulcers may resolve by deforming atrophic, pigmented scar, Disfigurement may occur from skin lesions on the face. Areas of depigmentation and hyperpigmentation may also be seen elsewhere in the body.

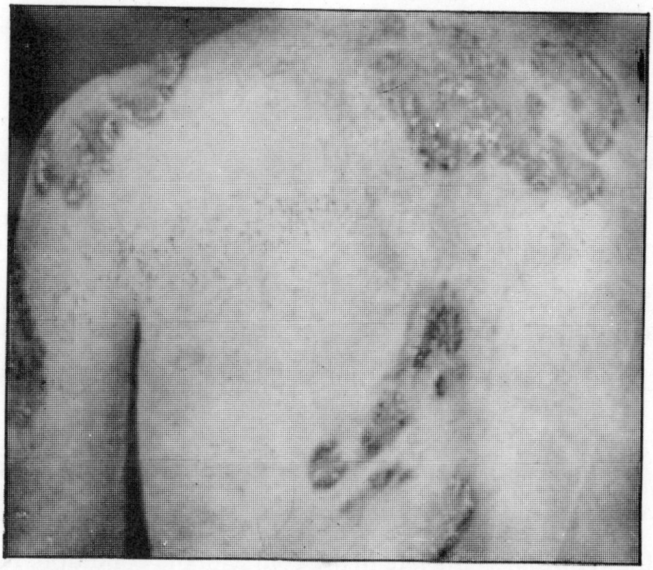

Figure 11.12. Nodulo-ulcerative lesions on back and arm.

Late lesions of mucous membrane appear as painless gummatous ulceration, which result in gross tissue destruction or in scarring and deformity on healing. Well-marked grey or white, thickened patches or leucoplakia may occur within the mouth.

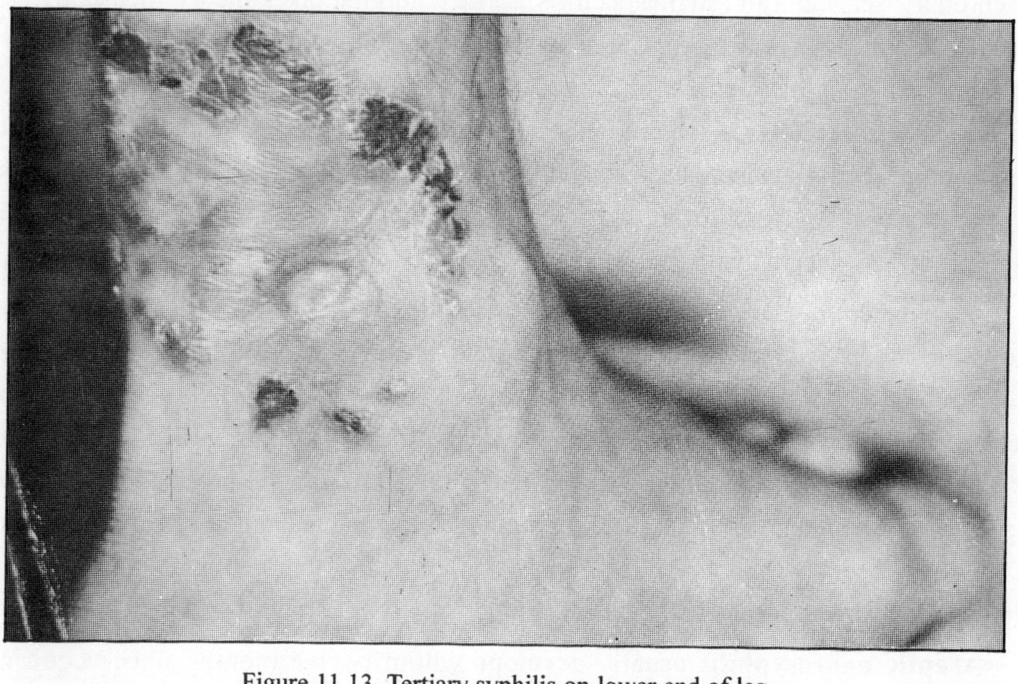

Figure 11.13. Tertiary syphilis on lower end of leg.

Gumma of larynx, trachea and bronchi produce hoarseness, aphonia, laryngeal stenosis, and collapse of the lung lobe.

Involvement of lungs is very rare and may be asymptomatic, or may accompany dyspnoea, haemoptysis, night sweats, and loss of body weight, or may present as pneumonia, bronchiectasis or fibrosis of the lung.

Osseous involvement is more common in men than in women, and usually occurs at the site of trauma. The lesions are distinctive causing periosteitis and osteitis. There may be deep pain, usually worse at night, and soft, rubbery swelling of the joint, tendon, sheath and bursae.

There may be iritis, choroidoretinitis, optic atrophy, corneal ulcer, and gumma of the eye in ocular lesion.

The lesions may involve the salivary glands, oesophagus, stomach, small and large intestine, rectum, liver, pancreas, kidney, bladder and testis.

Cardiovascular syphilis occurs late in the course of the condition. It is often progressive, disabling and life threatening. It is more frequent in males than in females, and the prognosis is considerably worse in heavy manual workers. Initially it begins as aortitis in the ascending aorta and, also, in the coronary arteries, causing exertional dyspnoea, paroxysmal dyspnoea, often nocturnal dyspnoea, and dull substernal aching pain. The condition progresses further to form coronary ischaemia and angina pectoris, aortic regurgitation or aneurysm, usually 10 to 20 years after acquiring the infection. Characteristically syphilis produces aneurysms of the large arteries by damaging the media of the arterial wall, and development of fusiform or saccular aneurysm of the thoracic aorta is common. Aneurysm of small arteries is either seldom or absent. Rarely, embolism and subacute bacterial endocarditis may develop. Complete heart block may also occasionally develop due to gumma of the myocardium. Syphilitic endarteritis of the cerebral vessels produces neurological signs.

Involvement of CNS is a complement of syphilis. This may occur as early s secondary stage of the condition or earlier or as late as in late latency. **Neurosyphilis** therefore develops due to syphilitic endarteritis of the cerebral vessels generally within 20 years or more after acquiring the infection. This involvement produces 4 different clinical entities as asymptomatic neurosyphilis, meningovascular syphilis, general paralysis of insane, and tabes dorsalis. Despite the presence of meningovascular, general paralysis of insane and tabes dorsalis, most patients of CNS involvement present with incomplete or mixed manifestations, notably the combination of general paralysis of insane and tabes dorsalis.

Aseptic neurosyphilis usually develops within twelve months since acquiring the infection, and presents with headache but without any neurological sign. Headache may resolve spontaneously or persists in latent form, with vomiting, neck rigidity, and positive Kernig's sign, or complication may follow within months to many years. Cerebrospinal fluid (CSF) however shows an elevated cell count, increased content of protein, and positive STS.

Meningovascular syphilis is the commonest form of neurosyphilis, and affects a proportion of untreated syphilitic patients. The manifestations generally become apparent from a few months to many years after acquiring the infection. Sometimes the condition may also be predominantly meningeal or vascular in type. In its mixed type the condition gives rise to headache, dizziness, lassitude, vomiting, insomnia, blurred vision, neck rigidity, and positive Kernig's sign. There may also be aphasia, epileptiform seizures, and monoplegia or hemiplegia. The patients show papilloedema, inequality in tendon reflexes and extensor plantar reflexes. Irregularity and unequally of pupils with normal accommodation but sluggish reaction to light (*Argyll Robertson pupil*) is an important feature of the condition. The patient may also develop cranial nerve palsies. Later, there are weakness and paralysis of the muscles, retention of urine, and loss of sphincter control.

Only a small proportion of untreated or inadequate treated syphilitics may finally develop **general paralysis of insane (general paresis, GPI)**, and take 10 to 20 years time to manifest. The condition affects more males than females, usually aged between 35 and 55 years. Initially the condition characteristically presents with mental manifestations as irritability, headache, insomnia, difficulty in concentration, failure of memory, and changes in behaviour. Sometimes hallucinations and delusions may develop. An outburst of mania or melancholia, and euphoria may become prominent. Mental deterioration progresses, and the patient may become bed-ridden and may eventually give rise to nasty bedsores. In somatic involvement, coarse tremors develop and affect the lips, tongue, facial muscles, and hands and whole body. Tremor in the hands because difficulty in writing legibly. Consequently speech becomes slow and tremulous. Epileptiform seizures are often encountered with in this condition. Monoplegia or hemiplegia may develop, and may cause increased deep reflexes and extensor plantar responses. The pupils are irregular and unequal, with loss of light reflexes and, sometimes, with accommodation. Bladder disturbances are frequent, and incontinence of urine and faeces constitute troublesome features, particularly during the late stage. Optic atrophy and loss of deep reflexes and sensory changes may develop in addition in patients who also develop tabes dorsalis.

As with general paralysis of insane, only a proportion of untreated patients may develop **tabes dorsalis**, in which male patients predominate. The condition usually involves the posterior spinal root and the dorsal ganglia. It begins with lightning or stabbing pain down in the legs, particularly calves and heels, and sometimes around the abdomen, occurring as if in paroxysms. In cases of elevation of body temperature for any reason, the pain gets worse. Patients also complain of pricking sensation in the legs. Sometimes there may also be a feeling of tightness around the trunk. Sensory changes occur with loss of superficial sensation, particularly on the face, thorax, inner arms, legs, soles, and perineum. So there is loss of deep sensation. Tendon reflexes are also lost. Loss of sensation may therefore cause perforating ulcers on the soles (Fig.

11.14), particularly on pressure points (Fig. 11.15), which may later extend to extend to the bone or communicate a joint through a sinus. There may also be trophic changes. Testicular sensation is lost, and impairment of sexual function or impotence is common. Patients show unsteadiness of gait and ataxia. The patient cannot stand steadily with eyes closed **(Romberg's sign)**. Paroxysmal painful disorder of function of various viscera as gastric crises, laryngeal crises and peptic ulcer are common. Retention of urine is frequent. Eye involvement causes falling vision, diplopia, Argyll Robertson pupil and, sometimes, optic atrophy and blindness, though a primary degenerative optic atrophy may also develop in some cases. In addition, the patients may develop osteoarthritis and later, *Charcot's joints*, with some pain, effusion and sublaxation and instability of the joint.

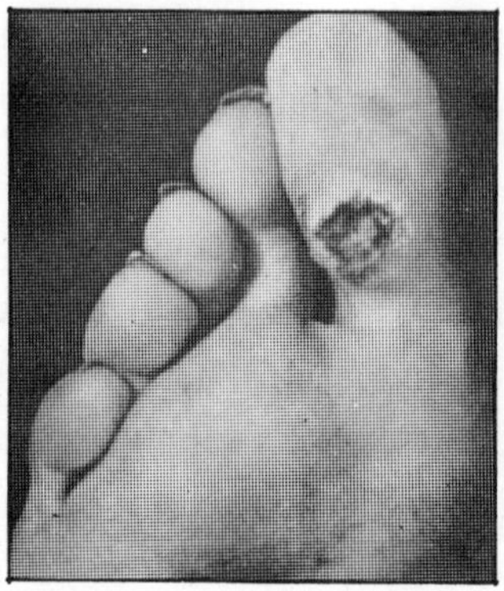

Figure 11.14. Typical perforating ulcer in tabes dorsalis.

Tertiary or late syphilis may lead to cardiac failure, rupture of aneurysm, progressive paresis, and blindness as complications.

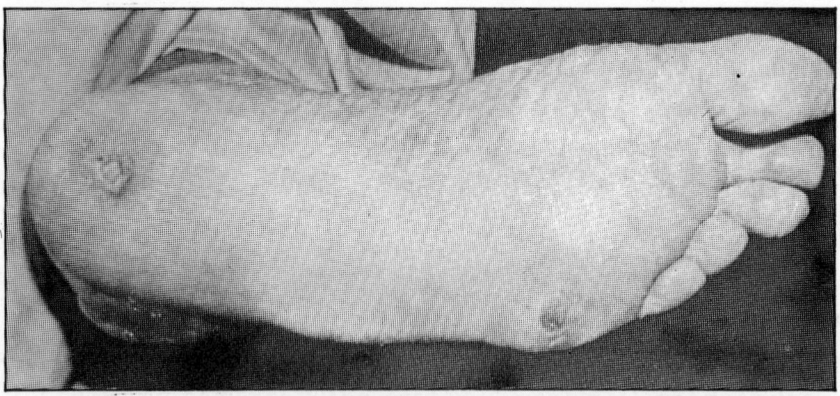

Figure 11.15. Perforated ulcer of tabes dorsalis at pressure points.

Diagnosis

History of infection may not always be recollected. Conventional STS are always positive, some even with non-treponemal antigens. Radiological examination is valuable in bones and joint involvement and, also, in cardiovascular involvement. The latter may also require cardioscopy. In CNS involvement, CSF usually shows increased pressure, and an increase in protein content and lymphocyte count, and gives positive STS. The colloidal gold curve (Lange) is either paretic or leutic in type.

In *syphilitic aortitis* serological tests for syphilis with non-treponemal antigen are positive in 70% cases but tests with treponemal antigens are sensitive indicators. In addition, several other tests, such as x-ray, CT and angiocardigraphy may be needed to confirm the diagnosis.

Depending upon the site of involvement the condition may need to be differentiated from a large number of medical conditions, such as erythema nodosum, psoriasis, keratoderma haemorrhagica, furunculosis, yaws, pyoderma, lupus vulgaris and actinomycosis for cutaneous involvement; from streptococcal infection, diphtheria, Vincent's infection, tuberculosis and agranulocytosis for oral lesions; from chronic osteomyelitis, multiple myeloma, Paget's disease and osteosarcoma for bone involvement; from congenital heart disease, other causes of aortic regurgitation, bronchial carcinoma, tuberculosis, Hodgkin's lymphoma and lymphosarcoma for cardiovascular involvement; from aortitis for aseptic neurosyphilis; from brain tumour, brain abscess, cerebral thrombosis, disseminated sclerosis, epilepsy and tumour of spinal cord for meningovascular syphilis; from psychoneurosis, hysteria, cerebral arteriosclerosis, schizophrenia and frontal lobe tumour for GPI; and from syringomyelia, psoriatic arthritis, peripheral neuritis and disseminated sclerosis for tabes dorsalis.

Treatment

It is treated by benzathine penicillin G, 2.4 million U once weekly by IM injection for 3 to 4 weeks, or aqueous procaine penicillin G, 1.2 million U daily by IM injection for 14 days. In cases of penicillin hypersensitivity, other alternative antibiotics, such as erythromycin or tetracycline, 500 mg every six hours orally, for 21 days with careful follow up.

Treatment for cardiovascular and neurosyphilis though in principle follow the same treatment schedule, the drug is given for a longer period of time, for example, procaine penicillin G, 0.6-1.2 million U daily by IM injection for not less than 21 days. In addition, however, these cases require adequate supportive and symptomatic treatment as situation warrant.

In cases of severe destruction due to gumma, plastic surgery needs to be considered.

In cases of angina pectoris occurred due to cardiovascular syphilis, the patient is given glyceryl trinitrate, 0.8-1 mg sublingually as required, or 0.4-0.8 mg aerosol sprayed under the tongue and kept closed the mouth at onset of attack or prior to exertion, or isosorbide mononitrate, 20-120 mg daily in divided doses orally, and the cases of cardiac failure are treated with digitalis and diuretics as digoxin, 125-250 μg daily in divided doses orally, and spironolactone, 100 mg daily orally increasing if necessary to 400 mg daily. *For general treatment schedule see the respective disease pattern.* Aortic regurgitation and aneurysms will however need surgical corrections.

General paralysis of insane are treated with phenothiazine, chlorpromazine, 25 mg three times daily orally increasing as necessary by 25 mg daily and then to a maintenance at up to 300 mg daily orally, or 25-50 mg as single dose daily by deep IM injection and repeated if necessary every six to eight hours. Cases of tabes dorsalis are given dibenzazepine, carbamazepine, 100 mg once or twice daily orally increasing gradually to control, usually 600-800 mg daily in divided doses, along with vitamin B_{12}, and if the patient is restless, chlorpramazine, 25 mg three times daily orally, may be given. Adrenaline or ephedrine may be given for gastric crises, saline enema followed by chlorobutol suppository for rectal crises, and inhalation of nitrate for laryngeal crises. In Charcot's arthropathy, treatment is given to minimise the strain and every effort is made to reduce the weight carried by the damaged joint.

In cases of neurosyphilis, treatment is judged by the reversal of CSF abnormalities. In this respect lumbar puncture is preferred 6 weeks and 3 months after the treatment, followed by 6-monthly during the first year and then yearly for several years.

Tertiary syphilitic patients are needed to remain under strict surveillance for the rest of their life.

CONGENITAL SYPHILIS

A woman suffering from syphilis but remains untreated can, when becoming pregnant, transmit the infection through the placenta after the third or fourth month of pregnancy and can thus, infect the foetus, causing congenital syphilis. The newborn may also acquire the infection during birth from direct contact with the early genital lesion of the mother. Pregnant women may however remain extremely contagious to the foetus during the first 5 years since acquiring the infection. As the time passes the chance of transmission of the infection to the foetus becomes progressively lessened until the late stage of the condition. However, in infected and untreated mother, the child may escape the infection, or there is miscarriage usually after 12th to 16th week of gestation, or stillbirth of macerated child. Otherwise, the child may born with syphilis, or may develop the signs and symptoms of the condition during the first few months of life or even years after.

In cases of congenital syphilis, the placenta of the mother many be bulky, pale and greasy, with evidence of endarteritis. Skin of the foetus may be macerated or show bullous lesions. Liver is enlarged with pericellular cirrhosis. Isolation of hepatic cells into small nests develops from diffuse fibrosis, along with vascular changes and infiltration with leucocytes. Lungs may show diffuse interstitial fibrosis. There may be diffuse interstitial inflammatory reaction in all organs of the body, including the heart, spleen, kidneys, pancreas, endocrine glands and thymus. Bone involvement results osteochondritis and the junction of the metaphysis and epiphysis with fibroproliferative inflammatory reaction causing considerable damage of epiphyseal cartilage. There are obliterative endarteritis and massive infiltration with perivascular mononuclear cells principally plasma cells. There is also periosteitis on the long bones, with formation of granulation tissue between the cortical bone and the periosteum, with lying down of new bone.

Clinical Manifestations

Early congenital syphilis behaves like acquired secondary syphilis, and the child fails to thrive and presents with characteristic expression of old man's face. In this condition, the child may bear with widespread bullous eruptions on the skin. In other cases, there may be no evidence of syphilis but the child soon, within the first few weeks of life, may develop various types of skin rash, usually macular, papular pr maculopapular. The lesions are distributed all over the body but more so around the mouth and nose, on the napkin areas, palms and soles. There may be condylomata lata, onychia, paronychia, and rhinitis with running bloodstained nasal discharge (**snuffles**). The condition also involves the bone and produces osteochondritis of long bones, accompanied by local tenderness, swelling and pain on movement of the limbs, and periosteitis and osteitis. Sometimes dactylitis may also occur. The child shows characteristic radiating scars (**rhagades**) around the mouth and anus, which are resulted from healing of the early lesions. Ulceration in nasal septum may result flattening of the bridge of the nose. There may also be painless generalised lymphadenopathy, hepatomegaly, splenomegaly, ascites and, occasionally, meningeal irritation with CSF abnormalities.

In **late congenital syphilis**, there may be developmental deformity or nasal bones and maxillae, dome-shaped skull with high forehead, radiating scars (*rhagades*) around the mouth and anus. The permanent incisors, usually upper central, are gapped and show increased anteroposterior thickness, with notched edges (*Hutchinson's teeth*), and the molars, usually first molars are hyperplastic with flat occluded surfaces (*Moon's molar*). In the late stage, there may be condylomata lata, interstitial keratitis, optic nerve atrophy that may perhaps lead to blindness, nerve deafness, periosteitis and gumma. There may also be synovitis, giving rise to asymptomatic painless effusion into both knee joints (*Charcot's joints*). Later, neurosyphilis, usually meningovascular, or cardiovascular syphilis may develop.

It may produce complications as those develop in tertiary (late) stage of acquired syphilis.

Diagnosis

Early congenital syphilis is diagnosed on clinical grounds, aided by identification of *Treponema pallidum* from serum and skin lesions, positive STS and by radiological examinations of long bones.

Late congenital syphilis is diagnosed on clinical grounds, supported by positive STS, and by CSF abnormality in cases of suspected neurosyphilis.

The condition is differentiated from conditions as stated under acquired (venereal) syphilis.

Treatment

The children are treated as those specified under primary and secondary syphilis, and the patient is given aqueous procaine penicillin G, 50,000 U per kg of body-weight by IM injection for 10 days. In cases where CSF abnormalities are detected, the child is given treatment as per schedule outlined under acquired tertiary syphilis.

Follow up the patient is maintained by STS at 3, 6 and 12 months after treatment.

TRICHOMONIASIS

Flagellate protozoon, *Trichomoniasis vaginalis*, causes the condition with vaginitis and vaginal discharge in women, and. urethritis in men. Although the protozoa are harmless vaginal commensal, the terminology however appears misnomer because the organism affects both men and women equally. A nomenclature of *Trichomonas urogenitalis* therefore appears more appropriate and convincing because it is responsible for urogenital involvement in both sexes.

The protozoon is a pear-shaped organism with 3-5 flagella projecting from the broad end and a flagellum forming the border of an undulating membrane, contains a nucleus and cytoplasm, and shows a jerky movement on wet form. The organism however has no cystic form.

Transmission of infection usually occurs through sexual intercourse, though accidental and through contact of infected materials is also possible. It affects both sexes equally. A large proportion of infected individuals may remain symptomfree and thus, can act as carriers and a potential source of infection. Women however appear more susceptible to the infection than men do. A substantial proportion of women acquire the infection from men, while about one-third of men acquire it from women. Only a small proportion of girls born of infected mothers become infected during birth.

The incidence of infection is high in sexually promiscuous people and prostitute, in pregnant women, and in people of poor socio-economic group. The infection is frequently associated with other sexually transmitted diseases.

Its incubation period is 3 to 28 days.

The infection is generally limited to the vulva, vagina, and cervix in women, and urethra, seminal vesicle and prostate in men. The organism is seen in women in the secretions of infected Bartholin's glands. There is spotty reddening and oedema of the mucosa, perhaps with small blister or granuloma. The mucosa and superficial submucosa may be infiltrated by lymphocytes and plasma cells but by polymorphonuclear leucocytes in cases of intense lesions. The inflamed mucosal surface may be covered with seropurulent discharge. In men, it is found in the secretions of the urethra or prostate, and in urine and seminal fluid.

Clinical Manifestations

In women, most cases are asymptomatic, or may just give rise to trivial symptom. In others, its occurrence may be sudden and acute. There may be green or yellow, abundant, frothy vaginal discharge, which may have an unpleasant odour. With it there may be redness and oedema of the vulva and vagina, and burning and itching of the vulva and of the skin of inner thighs. There may be dyspareunia, dysuria, and frequency of micturition. Inguinal lymph nodes may be enlarged and tender.

In untreated women, the symptoms may persist for years, being worsened during or after menses. In most cases the condition causes no complication but in some, it may produce Bartholinitis and cervicitis.

In men, the condition produces **trichomonal urethritis** but may be asymptomatic. Otherwise, there may be slight itching or discomfort inside the penis, slight moisture at the tip of the penis, slight early morning urethral discharge before first micturition, or urine may be little cloudy. In some cases there may be purulent discharge, while in some, there may be pain on urination. In uncircumcised men, the organism may produce mild balanoposthitis with subprepetual discharge, and in circumcised, balanitis.

In men most cases however resolve spontaneously. Otherwise, the condition may produce proctitis. prostatitis, epididymitis, and infertility as complications.

Diagnosis

It is made by identification of the causative organism.

It is differentiated from gonococcal and other forms of urethritis and vaginitis.

Treatment

Management of the condition essentially requires concurrent treatment of both sex partners.

Metronidazole is the drug of choice. It is given orally as 2 g as single dose, or 400-800 mg two times daily. As the drug may have teratogenic effect on foetus, even though there is no conclusive evidence, it is better avoided during pregnancy but, if unavoidable, it may only be given during the second and third trimester. Again, as the drug passes through breast milk, the breast-feeding is interrupted for 24 hours. Other equally effective drugs, which can be given orally in cases where metronidazole is ineffective, are tinidazole, 2 g as single dose orally during or after meal and repeated once if there is no clinical improvement, and synthetic derivative of nitroimidazole, secnidazole, 2 g as single dose orally before meal.

NONSPECIFIC URETHRITIS

Nonspecific urethritis is a most common condition of urethral inflammation and is frequently described under various nomenclatures, such as **non-gonococcal** or **post-gonococcal urethritis**, and **Chlamydial Urethritis**. This wide variation existed for long time as the precise aetiology of the condition is not known. However, it is now evidently proved that *Chlamydia trachomatis* and *Ureaplasma urealyticum* are responsible for producing the condition. *Chlamydia trachomatis* has several serotypes. Of them serotype D to K, particularly D, E and F, transmitted sexually, are responsible of producing more than one-half of cases. The condition may also have an association with trauma and infection with herpes simplex virus.

As the condition is transmitted through sexual intercourse, it is therefore quite common in sexually active individuals.

Its incubation period varies between a few days and a few weeks, but that of chlamydial infection is 7-21 days.

Pathologically there is superficial inflammation limited to the mucosa of the urethra, with outpouring of acute inflammatory cells. The epithelial cells characteristically show inclusion bodies.

Clinical Manifestations

In women, it is often asymptomatic, or sometimes there may be some symptoms due to associated infection with *Trichomonas vaginalis*. There may be mucopurulent urethral secretion, vaginal discharge, mild dysuria for long time a, frequency of micturition, dyspareunia, spotting after sexual intercourse, and pelvic pain. There may also be symptoms of cervicitis and proctitis.

In men, it may be asymptomatic. Otherwise, the patient may present with mucopurulent or purulent urethral discharge, or the discharge may be scanty and watery. The discharge is more marked early in the morning hours. In addition, there may also be dysuria, frequency and urgency of micturition, and pain in the penis, perineum and lower abdomen. Bloodstained urethral discharge, haematuria and strangury may develop but occasionally.

In both sexes symptoms and signs of proctitis and pharyngitis may occur due to rectal and orogenital coitus.

If untreated, symptoms and signs of the condition subside in a considerable number of cases within 4 weeks time but may persist in others. Otherwise, the condition may lead to periurethral abscess, vasculitis, cystitis, epididymitis, prostatitis, and urethral stricture as sequelae in men. In women, the complication may occur as cystitis, salpingitis, endometritis, and Bartholinitis.

In pregnant women, it may rupture the membrane and cause pre-term delivery. In late cases, there may also be infertility or ectopic pregnancy.

In both sexes, Reiter's syndrome may also occur as complication.

Diagnosis

It is made on clinical grounds, supported by urine examination and exclusion of other causes, which simulate the condition. A history of sexual exposure may also be available.

Chlamydia trachomatis can be isolated and identified through specific monoclonal antibodies and fluorescent staining.

It is differentiated from gonococcal urethritis, bacterial urethritis, fungal urethritis and trichomoniasis, and in women from gonorrhoea, trichomoniasis, candidiasis, and senile vaginitis.

Treatment

The condition is treated with oxytetracycline or erythromycin, 500 mg every six hours orally, or doxycycline, 100 mg twice daily orally, for at least 10 days. Ciprofloxcin, 1 g as single dose orally, or sparfloxacin, 400 mg orally on first day followed by 200 mg once daily for further 5-10 days, is also effective. Relapsing or complicating cases my however need continuation of the treatment with oxytetracycline, erythromycin or doxycycline for at least 21 to 28 days.

LYMPHOGRANULOMA VENEREUM

The acute and chronic contagious disorder is (also known as **lymphogranuloma inguinale**, **climatic bubo** and **lymphopathia venerea**) caused by *Chlamydia trachomatis* of serotype L_1 and L_2 or L_3, an obligatory intracellular parasite, closely resembling Gram-negative bacillus. Transmission of infection occurs through sexual contact but accidental infection (for example, inoculation in the eye) may also occur. The condition however appears to be less transmissible than gonococcal infection. A carrier state of the condition exists, and latent disease is frequent in the promiscuous individuals. The disease is widespread in tropical and subtropical areas.

The incubation period is 3-12 days for genital lesion but 10 to 30 days for inguinal bubo.

Lymph nodes are enlarged, usually matted, and show focal areas of softening with abscess cavities and formation of granulation tissue with epitheloid cells, fibroblasts, giant cells and polymorphonuclear leucocytes. Epithelial cells show characteristic inclusion bodies. Lymph nodes may burst, discharging a purulent fluid, and leave chronic ulcer with sinuses. Blocking of the lymphatic may also occur, producing elephantiasis.

Clinical Manifestations

There may be a transient, small papule or herpetiform shallow ulcer on the glans penis or in the urethra in men, and on the vaginal wall or the cervix uteri in women, which heals quickly. Thereafter, the symptoms develop gradually.

In men, it presents with tenderness in the groin, fever, anorexia, headache, and joint pains, with or without constitutional symptoms. The inguinal lymph nodes, frequently unilateral, are enlarged and matted into a tender, sausage-shaped fluctuating mass (Fig. 11.16), with reddened overlying skin. The enlarged lymph nodes or bubo eventually become chronic and indolent, and may shrink and form fibrous mass, or break down to form multiple draining sinuses with extensive scarring. Occasionally, the femoral or other groups of lymph nodes may be affected. In male passive homosexuals, symptoms and signs of proctitis may develop.

Following the initial genital lesions, in women, there may be no symptom or the patient may present with lower abdominal or back pain. Only less than about one-third cases may develop inguinal bubo. Otherwise, the inguinal or perirectal and pelvic lymphatic may be involved. Involvement of perirectal glands (Fig. 11.17) gives rise to proctitis with tenesmus and bloody mucopurulent anal discharge, and difficulty in defecation. Blocking of the genital lymphatic may produce ulceration or oedema.

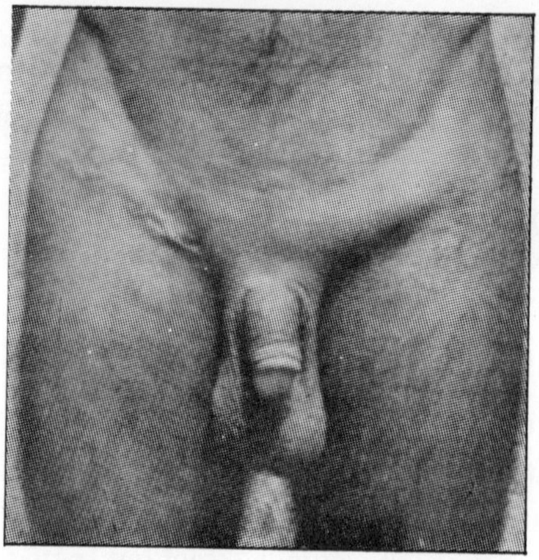

Figure 11.16. **Inguinal bubo** in lymphogranuloma venereum.

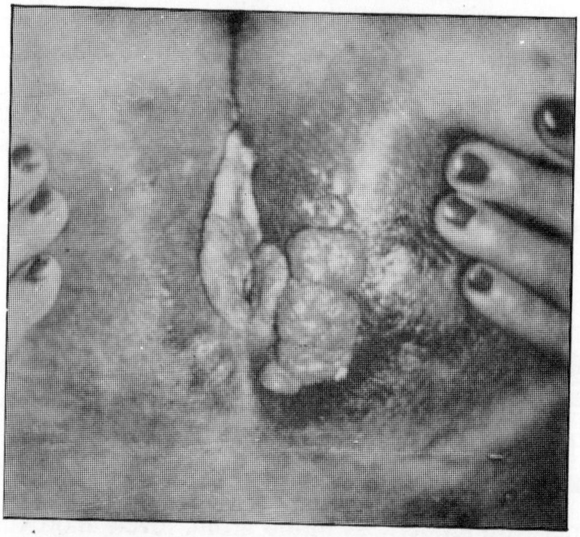

Figure 11.17. Perineal involvement of lymphogranuloma venereum.

Extragenital lesions may involve submaxillary and other glands following oral coitus, and axillary gland usually from accident.

Eyes may also be infected but accidentally.

Two-thirds buboes shrink and form fibrous scars. Remaining one-third ruptures and leave scars.

Individuals suffering from lymphogranuloma venereum also frequently harbour other sexually transmitted diseases.

Chronic infection continues with inflammation and extensive scarring causing rectal stenosis in women and male homosexuals, elephantiasis of penis, scrotum, or vulva (***esthiomene***), rectal stricture, perirectal abscess, rectovesicle or rectovaginal fistula, and fistula-in-ano as complications.

Diagnosis

Diagnosis of the condition is usually made on clinical grounds, often supported by a history of suspected sexual exposure, and is confirmed by laboratory investigations. Isolation and identification of the causative organism is possible. Complement fixation test becomes positive in 2 to 4 weeks after the onset of the illness. A rising antibody titre or a single titre of 1:64 or more is a good evidence of active infection. An intradermal test (Frei test) with heat-inactivated egg-grown antigen is available, which may be positive when read after 48-72 hours, giving rise to an inflammatory nodule of more than 6 mm in diameter. The test is however, nonspecific as a positive result may indicate the existence of the condition or that the individual had had the infection in the past. Similarly, biopsy is of help but nonspecific.

The condition is differentiated from syphilis in which the glandular enlargement is non-tender and STS are positive, and from tuberculous lymphadenitis, which runs a chronic course with non-tender lymphadenopathy, usually affecting the lymph nodes of upper part of the body. Herpes genitalis or progenitalis is differentiated for having multinucleated giant epitheloid cells surrounded by acantholytic balloon cells and in which the causative virus can be isolated. In chancroid the causative organism can be identified and a Ducrey's skin test may be positive, while the condition gives rise to fluctuating inguinal buboes, usually unilocular. Bubonic plague may cause certain confusion in which the causative organism can be identified and, in addition, a history of exposure to the rodents may be available. Hodgkin's lymphoma presents with painless lymphadenopathy and biopsy of lymph node shows a characteristic picture. Infectious mononucleosis and malignant neoplasm produce non-tender lymphadenopathy.

Rectal stricture of the condition may be differentiated from ulcerative colitis, and elephantiasis from filariasis.

Treatment

Treatment is given with tetracycline, 0.5-1 g every six hours orally, or doxycycline, 100 mg twice daily orally, for up to 3 weeks. Sulphadiazine, 1 g three times daily orally for 2-3 weeks, is also effective. Late cases, including cases with abscesses or fistulae, need surgical interference. Reconstructive surgery may also be needed for extensive scarring and elephantiasis.

BALANOPOSTHITIS

It is an inflammatory condition of the glans penis (**balanitis**) and of the prepuce (**posthitis**). Balanitis occurs in circumcised but balanoposthitis in uncircumcised males. In many cases the cause of its development is unknown but it frequently develops due to sexual intercourse and is often found associated with gonorrhoea, Reiter's syndrome, herpes simplex infection, trichomoniasis and candidiasis, and in both primary and secondary syphilis. Diabetes mellitus is another important association of the condition. It may also occur in psoriasis, lichen planus, and seborrhoeic dermatitis. Lack of personal hygiene or presence of tight prepuce may lead subpreputial secretion to become infected and to lead to the development of the condition. It is more common in uncircumcised persons than in circumcised persons. The condition is however extremely rare in circumcised persons.

Pathological changes show superficial inflammation of the glans penis (balanitis) and of the mucosal surface of the prepuce (posthitis) with ulcer formation.

Clinical Manifestations

The condition gives rise to soreness, irritation, and subpreputial discharge. Glans penis is inflamed with ulcerations, and oedema. Phimosis may occur consequently. The inguinal lymph nodes may be enlarged and tender. Phimosis is often an accompaniment of the condition, and may be quite painful. In severe cases there may be severe tissue damage and deformity (**gangrenous balanitis**).

It may cause severe phimosis and gangrene of glans penis as complications.

Diagnosis

The condition is diagnosed on clinical grounds.

It may need to be differentiated from gonococcal infection, and erosive lesions of both primary and secondary syphilis.

Treatment

If the predisposing factor is known, treatment of the cause is usually sufficient for the management of the condition. Otherwise, the glans penis is given saline wash several times a day, and subpreputial irrigation, if phimosis is presents.

In cases of infection, the patient is given co-trimoxazole orally. In cases of candidial infection, following thorough washing of glans penis with soap and water, nystatin cream is applied locally twice daily for 7-10 days.

Circumcision is indicated in persons with recurrent phimosis.

VAGINITIS

It is an inflammatory condition produced by several organisms, most frequent being herpesvirus, *Neisseria gonorrhoeae*, *Candida albicans*, *Corynbacterium vaginale*, *Trichomonas vaginalis*, *Mycoplasma species*, and Entamoeba histolytica. In other instances, when no organism can be detected, the condition often seen to develop due to small, Gram-negative bacillus, *Gardnerelis*. The infection is usually transmitted through sexual intercourse.

Pathological changes however depend on the organisms involved. Thus, there may be superficial mucosal and submucosal inflammation in gonococcal infection. In herpes simplex infection, painful red papules appear in the vagina, which progress to vesicles, then erosion, and finally coalescent ulcer. Mycotic and yeast infections produce white patches on the surface of vagina.

A marked depletion of oestrogen or a failure of end organ response to oestrogen however produces **senile vaginitis (postmenopausal vaginitis, atrophic vaginitis)** in menopausal women but when the common pyogenic organisms invade the tissue. It is however not a sexually transmitted disorder.

General Features

In general, vaginal discharge is the principal manifestation of the condition. Depending upon the organism involved, the discharge may be profuse or scanty, may be milky, yellowish-green or brown in colour, and may be viscid, musty, or there may not any odour. Associated with this there is always inflammation. There may also be discomfort, pain and dysuria. Dyspareunia is however a common accompaniment. Intensity of symptoms is dependable on the organisms involved.

Senile vaginitis is however not a sexually transmitted disorder but a condition of menopausal women. Yet, it has been included here for general descriptive purposes. This condition however presents with purulent vaginal discharge, sometimes blood stained. There is also excoriation and soreness of vulva. The patient complains of dysuria and a feeling of fullness of vagina. There may be pruritus and dyspareunia. Mucous membrane of introitus and vagina appear thin, tender and fragile.

Diagnosis

Diagnosis is comparatively easy on clinical grounds. This is supported by physical examination and proper identification of the causative organisms.

It is differentiated from all other conditions causing vaginal discharge.

Treatment

Treatment of the condition is directed to the involved organisms.

Herpetic cases are treated with acyclovir, 200 mg every four hours (omitting nighttimes dose) orally for 5 days. In addition to, or alternatively, acyclovir, 5% cream, is given for topical application every four hours for 5 days.

Cases developed due to gonococcal infection are treated with appropriate antibiotic, such as spectinomycin, 4 g (2 g in each buttock) by deep IM injection as a single dose, or ceftriaxone, 250 mg as single dose by IM injection. Cases with other bacterial infection are treated with appropriate antibiotics.

Candidial cases are treated with econazole, 150 mg pessary inserted high up in the vagina as single dose at night, nystatin, 100,000-200,000 U pessary or 4-8 g of cream inserted high into the vagina every night for at least 14 nights, or miconazole, 1200 mg vaginal capsule inserted high into the vagina as single dose at night or 2% cream or 200 mg pessaries high intravaginally every night for 2 nights.

Cases due to *Corynbacterium vaginale* are treated with cream or suppository of sulphonamides, applied intravaginally twice daily, or by application of 0.1% hexetidine once daily. In either case the treatment is continued for 2 weeks. Metronidazole is also effective against the organism and can therefore suppress the infection.

Trichomonal cases are treated with metronidazole, 400 mg three times daily orally for 7 days. The infection can also be adequately controlled by nimorazole, 2 g as single dose orally and repeated, if necessary.

Infection with E*ntamoeba histolytic* is treated with metronidazole, 400 mg three times daily orally for 7-10 days. It is however more effective when given with tetracycline, 250 mg every six hour orally.

In cases of coexisting urinary tract infection, the patient may be given nalidixic acid, 1 g daily four times a day for a minimum of 7 days, ciprofloxacin, 250-500 mg twice daily orally, or any other potent antibiotics.

Tuberculin cases are treated as per schedule laid down under pulmonary tuberculosis.

HERPES GENITALIS

Herpes genitalis or **herpes progenitalis** develop due to herpesvirus type 2 (HSV-2) but, occasionally, type 1 (HSV-1) may also be involved in some cases. Infection spreads through sexual exposure. Infants may acquire the infection during birth from contact of the genitalia of the infected mothers. Highest transmission of the condition occurs during the acute stage but the transmissibility is less from contact with asymptomatic carriers.

In cases of infected pregnant women, transplacental spread of the infection occurs and may thus produce congenital malformation of the foetus. Most transmission however occurs when the mothers are asymptomatic. The incidence of infecting the child is quite high when mothers have only one exposure to the infection but the transmissibility decreases considerably when mothers have several episodes of the infection.

Like other HSV infection recurrences in the condition may occur from latent infection in which the virus remained established in the sacral sensory nerve ganglion, become reactivated due to certain infection or drug, and causes recurrences.

Its incubation period is between 3 and 7 days but usually 1-26 days, average being 6-7 days.

Alike other HSV infection, the condition produces lesions, which are marked by acantholytic changes, with formation of intranuclear inclusions. Vesicles appear on mucous membrane as well as on skin surface, which soon change to superficial ulcerations, surrounded by inflammatory infiltrates.

Clinical Manifestations

Initially it gives rise to itching and soreness, followed by development of small patches of erythema on the prepuce, glans penis, and shaft of the penis in males, and on the vulva (Fig. 11.18), labia, clitoris, vagina, cervix, perineum, and thighs in females. Later, groups of vesicle develop which may erode and produce painful ulcers (Fig. 11.19). The lesions are more painful in females than in males, while a substantial proportion of cases may however show no symptom.

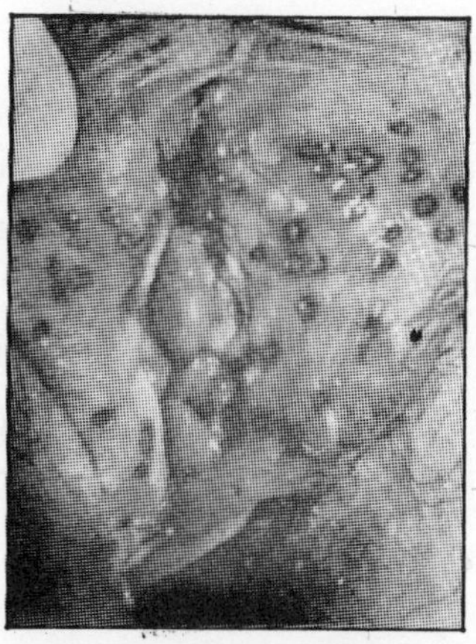

Figure 11.18. Herpetic lesions on vulva.

The patients may also complain of systemic manifestations, such as malaise, anorexia, fever, headache, backache, and genital pain and, in females, leucorrhoea and vaginal bleeding. The patient may experience difficulty in micturition or walking. Inguinal lymph nodes are slightly enlarged and tender.

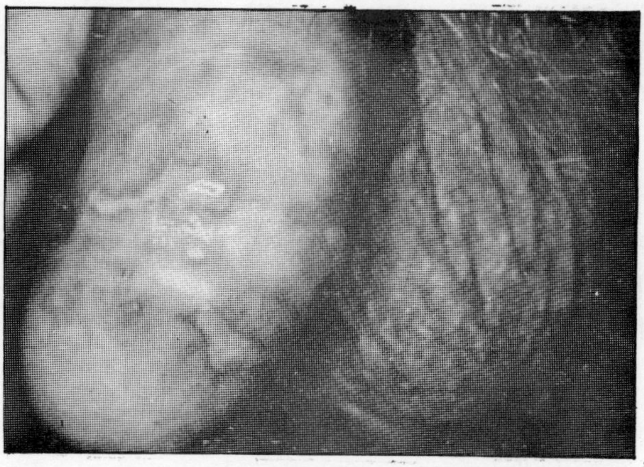

Figure 11.19. Herpetic ulcer on penis.

Lesions may also develop around the anus and in the rectum in homosexual males and from rectal coitus in females. The vesiculoulcerative lesions may coalesce to form large ulcers and may show secondary infection. Sometimes its presentation as a large solitary ulcer on genitalia with satellite lymph nodes may even simulate primary syphilitic chancre.

In young girls, **herpetic vulvovaginitis** may develop due to fornication. The condition then presents with narcotising lesions and ulceration on the external genitalia, giving rise to perhaps soiling or staining of underwear. The lesions are painful, and associated with malaise and fever.

Herpetic ulcers later become crusted and finally heal with scarring. Usually spontaneous remission occurs in many within 1 to 3 weeks but latent infection may also develop.

Most cases may show recurrent episodes in both sexes. In subsequent episodes however the condition produces few lesions, which **are not** so widespread like the primary infection, and complaining of systemic symptoms is less **common**. Pain, numbness or tingling in the buttocks, legs or thighs may precede the outbreak.

Infection during pregnancy may cause abortion, stillbirth or neonatal death.

The condition may produce several complications, such as recurrences, haematogenous spread of infection elsewhere, aseptic meningitis, autonomic nervous system dysfunction, and transverse myelitis.

Diagnosis

The condition is diagnosed clinically, and can be confirmed by tissue culture of the material collected from the base of the ulcers or aspiration of a vesicle. Identification of multinucleated giant epithelial cells surrounded by acantholytic balloon cells in the stained material can make a rapid diagnosis. In primary infection, a rising titre of antibody can be seen in paired sera obtained at 10 to 14 day's interval. Other diagnostic aid is complement fixation test. Tzanck may also be positive.

The condition may cause certain confusion with syphilitic chancre and chancroid but in both cases, ulcers heal too slowly while syphilitic chancre shows positive STS. Chancroid, on the other hand, shows a tendency of the enlarged lymph nodes to be matted.

Treatment

The cases are treated with acyclovir, 200 mg every four hours daily orally (omitting the night-time dose) for 7 days, or inosine pranobex, 4 g daily in divided doses orally for 7 to 14 days.

The patient may be given analgesic, such as lidocaine, 2%, for topical application on the painful lesions for local relief.

GENITAL WARTS

It is a benign condition of epithelial overgrowth and is also known as **condylomata acuminata** and **venereal warts**. It develops due to human papilloma virus (HPV). Although several types of HPV may be involved in its causation, types 6 and 11 are principally found to be responsible for it. It most commonly involves the warm, moist surfaces. It spreads through sexual intercourse and affects genitalia, producing. It also affects perianal area and rectum from rectal intercourse.

As the condition involves the mucocutaneous junctional areas, the condition is also known as **mucocutanmeous warts.**

It affects adult women and uncircumcised men. It is extremely rare in circumcised men. So it is before puberty provided there is no sexual abuse. The condition may however develop before puberty due to sexual assault.

The incubation period of the infection is variable and may range between 1 and 6 months.

It gives rise to solitary, but frequently multiple, pink papillary excrescence, showing tree-like proliferation of stratified squamous epithelium, supported by a fibrous stroma. The lesion produces papillary acanothosis with marked hyperkeratosis in the epidermis, and cellular infiltration in the dermis. There may be vacuolisation of the cells of rete and widening of rete pegs.

Clinical Manifestations

It gives rise to soft, moist, pink, pedunculated or vegetating growth on any mucocutaneous surface, such as about the coronal sulcus (Fig. 11.20), inner surface of the prepuce, urethral meatus and penile surface of the penis in males, and vulva, vagina, perineal surface and, occasionally, cervix in females, and in rectum and perianal region (Fig. 11.21) in both sex. The growth of warts is however greatly accelerated in pregnant women and in those with immunosuppression or maceration of the skin.

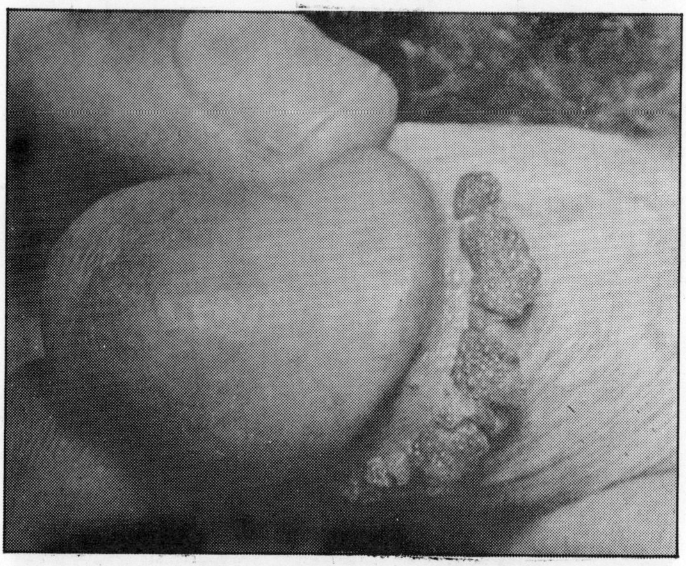

Figure 11.20. Condylomata acuminata on penis.

Very occasionally genital warts may form a large vegetating bunch of cauliflower-like masses resembling condylomata accuminata (Fig. 11.22). The warts may be malodorous, and their colour may be grey, pale yellow or pinkish.

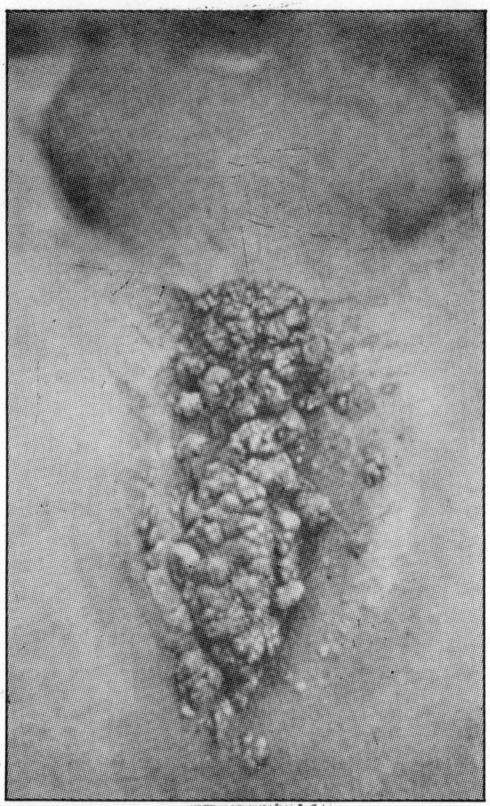

Figure 11.21. Perineal genital warts.

The condition by itself is not precanceroius but in the females, the condition may sometimes coexist with areas of dysplasia and carcinoma.

Figure 11.22. Large cauliflower-like genital warts.

Diagnosis

It is diagnosed clinically, and can be confirmed through biopsy.

It is differentiated from flat-topped condylomata lata of syphilis where the lesion is teemed with *Treponema pallidum*, and gives a positive STS. When the lesion develops on the cervix, that may be confused with cervical carcinoma but Papanicolaou smear can establish the diagnosis.

Treatment

No treatment is however satisfactory. Antiviral-immunopotentiater, inosine pranobex, can however be given as 1 g three times daily orally for 14 to 28 days. In addition, or alternatively, the warts are treated with podophylotoxin, 0.5% solution, which is applied directly on the warts twice daily for 3 days and repeat if necessary after 4 days interval to a maximum of 5 times. Otherwise, local treatment is given with podophylum, 50% in water, tincture benzoin or spirit, and left for 6 hours and then wash away thoroughly with soap and water. The treatment may be repeated on alternate days as required. Podophyline, 20%, mixed with salicylic acid, 25%, can also be applied directly on the warts and cover up with plaster two to three times a week. Otherwise, the growth is removed through electrocauterisation, laser, cryotherapy or surgical excision.

Intractable lesions re treated with interferon alfa injected intralesionlly or by IM injection.

Following treatment the patients and their sex partners are needed to be followed up.

MOLLUSCUM CONTAGIOUS

Poxvirus produces the condition. The condition is transmitted through direct body contact, generally venereal in origin, or indirectly through the use of contaminated materials of the patients. In addition, autoinoculation of the infection may occur.

The infectivity of the virus varies, and in cases of non-venereal origin, children are more frequently affected than the adults are.

It causes acanthosis and parakeratosis with dense melanin pigmentation at the basal cell layer of the epidermis, proliferation and later degeneration of prickle cells, and show eosinophilic inclusion bodies (**molluscum bodies**).

Clinical Manifestations

It presents with multiple, but may also be single, small, smooth, skin-coloured, waxy, almost transparent, raised, umbilicated papules, filled with semi-solid white material. The lesions occur on any part of the body (Fig. 11.23), but usually on the genitalia (Fig. 11.24) or perineal area in venereal origin. The papules are slid and firm, and express cheesy material when squeezed hard. The condition is generally asymptomatic but secondary infection may occur. The lesions may heal spontaneously after some months or years.

It only causes secondary infection as complication.

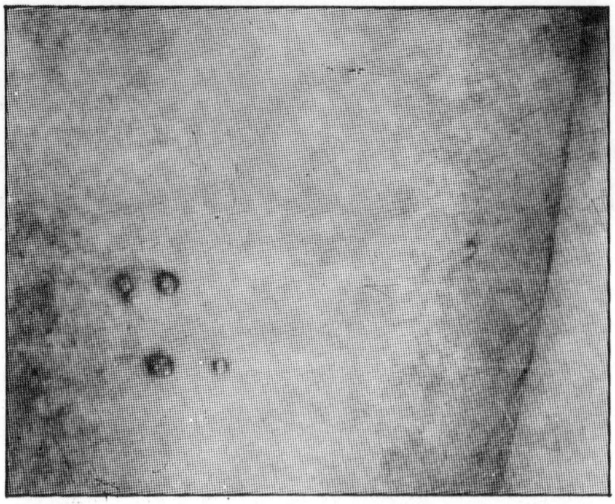

Figure 11.23. Molluscum contagiosum on thigh.

Diagnosis

Materials expressed from the lesion show inclusion bodies (molluscum bodies), which are characteristic of the condition. In addition, suspected history of sexual exposure may be available.

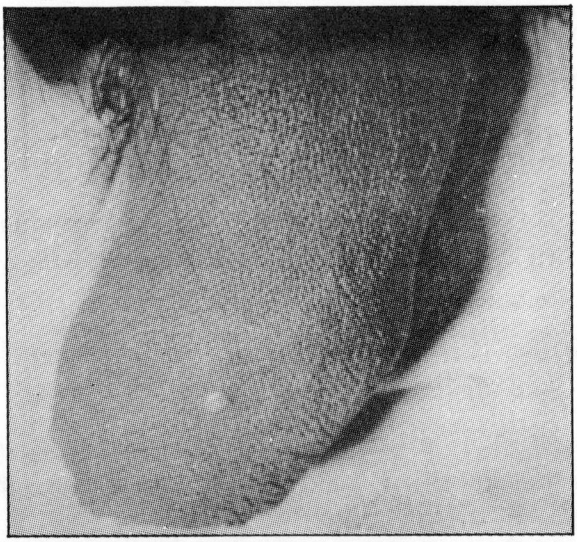

Figure 11.24. Molluscum contagiosum on penis.

The condition may however cause certain confusion with warts, folliculitis and pyogenic granuloma but the characteristic lesions of the condition and presence of molluscum bodies make the differentiation easy.

Treatment

The lesions are treated with cryosurgery or curettage. Squeezing of the lesions very hard between the fingers or forceps, though quite painful is also effective.

Otherwise, the lesions are painted with podophylin, 10%, left for 12-24 hours, and then wash away.

AIDS

AIDS or **acquired immunodeficiency syndrome** is a symptom complex, frequently fatal, and is associated with a defect in cell-mediated immunity, causing persistent unexplained lymphadenopathy, central nervous system manifestations and gastrointestinal manifestations, associated with development of opportunistic infections or certain secondary cancers or both. It develops due to Human immunodeficiency virus (HIV), previously known as human T-cell lymphotroic virus type III (HTLV–III) or lymphadenopathy-associated virus (LAV), previously known as human T-cell lymphotroic virus III (HTLV –III) or lymphadenopathy-associated virus (LAV). The causative virus may have two types. Of them human immunodeficiency virus type 1 (HIV-1) and type 2 (HIV-2) have been identified as the primary cause of the condition. HIV–2 however appears to be less virulent than HIV–I.

As the virus has tropism, especially for helper T lymphocyte, HIV is liable to attach itself with CD4 molecule of the helper lymphocyte and thus to cause damage or destruction of helper T lymphocytes which thus lead to the development of a cellular immunodeficiency disease, making the patients vulnerable to a wide variety of infection. The condition therefore gives rise to unusual susceptibility to certain types of cancer, such as Kaposi's sarcoma, and to a wide variety of serious infections from any organism which otherwise can produce minor illness in normal individuals.

The condition is essentially a blood-borne infection, spreading directly through transfusion of blood and bloods products, and from the use of unsterilised but contaminated surgical appliances, injectable syringes and needles, equipment used for acupuncture, ear pricking, tattooing, etc. Transmission of infection also occurs from intimate sexual contact, more particularly rectal coitus, but only when there is any rupture, abrasion or otherwise contact with the blood stream. Heterosexuals with multiple partners are also found prone of acquiring the infection. Any injury, wound, or even ulcer as seen in syphilis and chancroid can act as a route of inoculation of the causative virus. Infants born of infected mothers may acquire the condition, and transplacental transmission may be reckoned as an important route of transmission of the infection from mother to child. Exposure to any infection acts as predisposing factor to the condition.

In the infected human beings, the virus has been isolated from lymphoid cells, cerebrospinal fluid, saliva, urine, and tears. It has also been detected in the semen of infected males, and from vaginal and cervical secretions and breast milk of infected females.

Transmission of the infection is however complicated due to a complex epidemiology. Firstly, not all persons infected with HIV and showing sero-positivity for antibody to HIV do actually develop the condition. They therefore act as antibody-positive symptomatic carriers

Secondly, it takes a long and variable latent period for conversion from sero-negativity to sero- positivity for antibody to HIV. Because sero-negative blood may well be infectious, these person therefore act as sero-negative asymptomatic carriers. Thirdly, there exist some sero-positiv asymptomatic carriers and some cases, which though give rise to persistent generalise lymphadenopathy but do not show any constitutional symptoms. On the other end, the clinica progress of the condition amongst the females is still not fully documented. While male t female transmission of infection is firmly recognised, the risk of female to male spread is no clear.

On the basis of our present knowledge the risk group of acquiring the infection include homosexual and bisexual males, heterosexuals with multiple partners, intravenous drug abuser haemophilics who need factor VIII concentrates and random recipients of blood transfusion.

The condition can occur at any age but, in cases of transmission of infection throug sexual act, the highest rate of infection occurs in the sexually active age groups.

The incubation period of the condition is yet not known but may be very long, perhap occupying several years. Most cases however develop within 2 months to 5 years time.

Pathological changes are nonspecific. There is however lymphopenia with profoun suppression of cell-mediated immunity, but humoral immunity remains intact, Morphologicall there is marked lymphoid cell depletion in the cortical and paracortical areas of lymph nodes, c marked hyperplasia of lymphoid follicles, paracortex, or sinusoidal histiocytes. Marke hypocellularity is also seen in other lymphoid tissue, such as thymus, spleen, Payer's patche appendix, and bone marrow. Evidence of coexisting opportunistic infections may also be see in every organ.

Depending upon its presentation the condition is however classified into three grour clinically:

Group I includes typical AIDS cases which is always accompanied by opportunisti infections due to any organisms or by neoplasms such as Kaposi's sarcoma, Burkitt's lymphom primary CNS lymphoma and immunoblastic lymphoma.

Group II cases include AIDS–related complex (ARC) but lack the involvement c opportunistic infection and neoplasm. Although the persons suffering from ARC have a goo prognosis they however run the risk of developing AIDS later.

Group III cases include certain manifestations of AIDS, such as lymphadenopathy, asept meningitis and infectious mononucleosis-like manifestations but they cannot be classifie clinically as AIDS or as ARC.

Clinical Manifestations

Many cases may remain asymptomatic but otherwise the manifestations are presente subclinically so as to remain unrecognised. In this stage, perhaps as the virus remains latent reproduces slowly the infected person shows a sero-negativity for antibody to HIV.

Some cases may develop **AIDS-related complex** (*ARC*) with intermittent or continued ever lasting for 3 months or longer. This is associated with fatigue, malaise, night sweats, and eneralised lymphadenopathy. Loss of body weight is a characteristic feature for which it is lso known in some communities as **wasting syndrome**. The patient also complains of chronic iarrhoea. In addition, frequently there may be anaemia, thrombocytopenia, and ypergammaglobulinaemia. Patients suffering from ARC however run a potential risk of eveloping AID later.

On the other end, some patients may present with remittent symptoms and signs, which o not fall as such to be AIDS or ARC (group III).

However, within 2 to 4 weeks after acquiring the infection about half of the cases present ith acute influenza or infectious mononucleosis-like manifestations. The patients complain of ore throat, headache, myalgia, joint pains, malaise, and fever. Development of skin rash is ommon. In addition, there is generalised lymphadenopathy. Some cases may give rise to aseptic eningitis with abrupt onset of headache, stiff neck, and photophobia, showing cerebrospinal uid changes with mononuclear pleocytosis, elevated protein, and slightly depressed glucose. he symptoms are however short-lived, and the patients may remain healthy for years together. ome of these patients as well as persons without any previous signs and symptoms of the ondition may present with persistent generalised lymphadenopathy with or without any onstitutional symptoms.

Patients suffering from AIDS may also present with several other manifestations, which ay develop during the course of the infection or may occur as first presenting manifestation. hese include ill-health, loss of body weight, unexplained fever of long duration, frequent rolonged diarrhoea, dry cough, chest pain, shortness of breath, pneumonia showing diffuse filtration of the lung fields on chest x-ray, idiopathic thrombocytopenic purpura, and focal egmental glomerulonephritis. In addition, or apart from the above mentioned, there are wide nge of neurological manifestations that, along with several others, may include lethargy, rgetfulness, confusion, impaired speech, seizures, peripheral neuropathies, meningitis, ultifocal encephalopathy, brain abscess, cerebral haemorrhage, thrombotic accident, dementia nd psychoses,

Characteristically AIDS cases always show development of opportunistic infection or econdary neoplasm or both. Any kind of organism even though not virulent otherwise, can ause serious opportunistic infections though normal individuals may suffer minor ailments om such involved organisms. The secondary neoplasms, which may accompany the condition, e Kaposi's sarcoma, Burkitt's lymphoma, primary CNS lymphoma, and immunoblastic mphoma. The condition also shows an increased association with dilated (congestive) ardiomyopathy.

AIDS is often fatal and is apt to produce several complications, including severe infections, *pneumocystis carinii* pneumonia, subacute encephalitis, nonbacterial endocarditis, non-Hodgkin's lymphoma, and squamous cell carcinoma of oral cavity and anus.

Toxoplasmic encephalitis however develops commonly as a complication in AIDS.

Diagnosis

In the Diagnosis of the condition clinical manifestations and a careful history are often suggestive. The condition may be suspected in persons who present with vague symptoms, are injectable drug abusers, have received uncontrolled blood transfusions, or have multiple sex partners. Demonstration of cellular immune deficiency and immunofluorescence are helpful. Enzyme-linked immunosorbent assay (ELISA) is a highly sensitive and specific test to detect antibodies to HIV proteins. But false positive result is not infrequent. If such false positive results occur in persons who belong to the risk group or in whom the condition is highly suspected, ELISA is repeated for screening purpose and, if yet positive, further investigations are needed with more sensitive technique of immunoelectrophoretic procedure, western blot. Diagnosis of the condition is firmly established when both ELISA and western blot are positive.

For the presence of lymphadenopathy AIDS may mimic several conditions, and infectious mononucleosis is differentiated for having leucocytosis with absolute lymphocytosis and many atypical T-lymphocyte, and the condition shows positive Paul-Bunnel test and detectable serum IgM antibodies. Hodgkin's lymphoma characteristically shows Reed-Strenberg cells. Non-Hodgkin's lymphoma shows characteristic lymph nodes histological picture, while bone marrow aspirate and trephine biopsy can also establish the diagnosis. In lymphatic leukaemia there is leucocytosis with absolute lymphocytosis, usually of small variety, and bone marrow shows reduced megakaryocytic and an increase in both small and large lymphocytes.

For other presentations AIDS may be differentiated from conditions, which may simulate the condition. For example, malaria is differentiated for having malarial parasites in the blood. Kala-azar is differentiated for having LD bodies in the blood, sternal bone marrow, liver, and spleen. Pneumonia or tuberculosis is differentiated as the causative microorganism thereof can be isolated and identified. Malabsorption syndrome can also cause confusion but intestinal biopsy and the characteristic signs and symptoms of the condition can establish the diagnosis.

Treatment

The basic principle of management of the condition aims to inhibiting the replication of the virus using antiretroviral agents, and treatment and prophylaxis of opportunistic infections. In addition, the patient needs every kind of psychological support.

The condition is treated with antiretroviral therapy, and British HIV Association recommends that the treatment should be instituted before irreversible damage develops in the immune system as judged by the CD4 count above 350 cells/ml. Treatment should also be instituted immediately when the CD4 count falls below 300 cells/ml. Treatment should also be considered when viral loads below 10,000 copies/ml but with falling CD4 counts. The antiretrovirals are available in three groups: nucleoside reverse transcriptase inhibitors (NRTIs), which include zidovudine, stavudine, lamivudine, didamosine, zalcitabine and amprenavir; non-nucleoside reverse transcriptase inhibitors (NNRTIs) that include nevirapine, efavirenz and delavirdine; and protease inhibitors (PIs) such as indinavir, nelfinavir, ritonavir, saquinavir, abacavir and lopinavir. It is recommended that person who has not received antiretroviral therapy yet should be given a combination of two NRTIs with either one PI or one NNRTI.

In the management of the condition it is evident that combination therapy has achieved greater success than monotherapy. The patient is therefore given treatment with thymidine nucleoside analogue, such as zidovudine or nevirapine, stavudine, in combination with a non-thymidine nucleoside analogue, such as didanosine, zalcitabine, or lamivudine, but a combination of stavudine with zalcitabine is contraindicated. Of all these groups, zidovudine, 500-600 mg daily in two or three divided doses, or 1-2 mg/kg every 4 hours by slow IV infusion over an hour period and transfer to oral therapy as soon as possible (children: 3 months-12 years, 360-480 mg/m2 daily orally in three or four divided doses, maximum 200 mg every 6 hours, in combination of other antiretrovirals. It can also be given as monotherapy in HIV-positive pregnant women of over 14 weeks gestation and their newborn infants to prevent maternal-foetal transmission, as 100 mg orally five times daily until beginning of labour, and then 2 mg/kg until cord is clamped, and then to baby 2 mg/kg orally every 6 hours (or 1.5 mg/kg over 30 minutes by IV infusion every 6 hours) starting within 12 hours after birth and continue until 6 weeks old. Stavudine is given as antiviral combination treatment at 30 mg twice daily orally for patients weighing under 60 kg but 40 mg twice daily for patients weighing over 60 kg (children over 3 months, 1 mg/kg twice daily for children weighing under 30 kg, but adult dose for weighing over 30 kg).

Lamivudine, 150 mg (children over 3 months, 4 mg/kg, maximum 300 mg/day) twice daily orally, is used for combination therapy. Zalcitabine, 0.75 mg every 8 hours orally (children, not recommended) is used with antiretrovirals. Abacavir, 300 mg (children aged 3 months-12 years, 8 mg/kg, maximum 600 mg/day) twice daily orally is given along with another antiretrovirals. Didanosine is given along with another antiretrovirals as 250 mg daily orally in one or two divided doses for patients weighing under 60 kg but 400 mg daily in one or two divided doses for patients weighing over 60 kg, to be taken at least 30 minutes before meal followed by sufficient antacid. Corresponding doses for children over 3 months are 240 mg/m2 daily or 180 mg/m2 daily in combination with zidovudine in one or two divided doses.

Combination therapy is also available for HIV infection in a single preparation, for example, capsule containing abacavir, 300 mg, lamivudine, 150 mg, and zidovudine, 300 mg. This preparation is however given following treatment with three components separately for 6-8 weeks and then the patient s transferred to the above-mentioned fixed combination as 1 capsule twice daily orally.

Other potent drugs effective in the treatment of HIV-1 infection along with antiretrovirals is protease inhibitor, such as indinavir, 800 mg (children aged 4-17 years, 500 mg/m^2, maximum 800 mg every 8 hours) every 8 hours orally 1 hour before or 2 hours after food, saquinavir, 1200 mg three times daily within 2 hours after a meal (children aged under 16 years, not recommended), ribonavir, 600 mg twice daily orally preferably with food (children over 2 years, 250 mg/m^2 twice daily increasing at 2-3 day intervals by 50 mg/m^2 twice daily to maintenance 350 mg/m^2 twice daily, maximum 600 mg twice daily, or nelfinavir, 1250 mg twice daily or 750 mg three times daily orally with food (children aged 3-13 years, 25-30 mg/kg three times daily). Ritonavir can also be given as single protease inhibitor regimens, as 300 mg twice daily for 3 days, increase by 100 mg twice daily increments to 600 mg twice daily within 14 days. Other effective protease inhibitor amprenavir, 1200 mg twice daily orally for patients weighing over 50 kg (if used with ritonavir, reduce dose to 600 mg twice daily), but 20 mg/kg twice daily (maximum 2400 mg/day) in patients weighing under 50 kg (children over 4 years, 20 mg/kg twice daily, maximum 2400 mg/day, may be given.

A combination of lopinavir, 399.9 mg, and ritonavir, 99.9 mg, may be given with antiretroviral agents to treat HIV-1 infection. The corresponding dose for children over 2 years is 230 mg/m2 lopinavir and 57.5 mg/m^2 ritonavir twice daily with food (maximum 400 mg lopinavir and 100 mg ritonavir twice daily).

In cytomegalovirus (CMV) disease in AIDS or immunocompromised patients, ganciclovir, 5 mg/kg every 12 hours by IV infusion for 14-21 days is given and maintenance at 6 mg/kg daily by IV infusion for 5 days per week or 5 mg/kg daily for 7 days per week. But the drug is given at 1000 mg three times daily orally or 500 mg six times daily with food following at least 3 week IV therapy, in cases of maintenance treatment of CMV retinitis in AIDS patients but 1000 mg three times daily orally for the prevention of CMV disease in liver or kidney transplant recipients. For CMV retinitis in AIDS patients foscarnet, 60 mg/kg every 8 hours by IV infusion for 2-3 weeks then maintenance, 60 mg/kg daily increased to 90-120 mg if tolerated. Fomivirsen sodium, 165 μg weekly by intravitreal injection for 3 weeks followed by 165 μg every 2 weeks in newly diagnosed cases but 330 μg by intravitreal injection every other week for 2 doses followed by 330 μg every 4 weeks in previously treated cases, is quite effective as second line treatment in CMV retinitis in AIDS patients. Cidofovir, 5 mg/kg by IV infusion over 1 hour once weekly for 2 weeks, maintenance, beginning 2 weeks after completion of induction, 5 mg/kg over 1 hour by IV infusion once every 2 weeks. The treatment regime must include probenecid, 2 g 3 hours before cidofovir infusion followed by 1 g at 2 hours and 1 g at 8 hours after the end of cidofovir infusion, and sodium chloride, 0.9%, 1 litre over 1 hour by IV infusion immediately before cidofovir infusion and if tolerated 1 litre over 1-3 hours during or immediately after cidofovir infusion.

Patients with persistent neutropenia in advanced HIV infection are treated with filgrastim, 100,000 u/kg daily by SC injection, increased as necessary until absolute neutrophil count normal (maximum 400,000 u/kg/day). Molgramostim, 60,000 u/kg by SC injection daily for 5 days and then adjusted to maintain desirable absolute neutrophil and WBC count, may also be given as an adjunct in cases of neutropenia in patients treated with ganciclovir in AIDS-related cytomegalovirus retinitis.

Patients who have developed *pneumocystis* carinii pneumonia are treated with co-trimoxazole comprising trimethoprim, 160-240 mg, and sulphamethoxazole, 400-600 mg, four times daily orally or by IV injection for 21 days, or with pentamidine, 4 mg/ kg once daily by IV injection, for 21 days. Patients intolerant to co-trimoxazole are treated with antiprotozoal, atovaquone, 750 mg three times daily orally (children, not recommended) with food for 21 days.

For other opportunistic infections, treatment is given according to the organism involved.

Children with symptomatic HIV infection presenting with recurrent bacterial infection can be treated prophylactically with 5% solution of human normal immunoglobulin, 400-800 mg/kg, by IV infusion and then 200 mg/kg every 3 weeks.

Because HIV specifically targets the CD4 cells, this acts as a potential indicator of immunodeficiency. As the number of it increases (normal value is about 1,000 cells per litre) so is the improvement of the patients can be ensured. Similarly as the number decreases it indicates of advancing stage of the condition.

Index

R

S

INDEX

INDEX

INDEX